Dictionary of
MARKETING
TERMS

IRVING J. SHAPIRO
Professor Emeritus, Monmouth College

Fourth Edition
1981

LITTLEFIELD, ADAMS & COMPANY

Library of Congress Cataloging in Publication Data

Shapiro, Irving J
   Dictionary of marketing terms.

   (Littlefield, Adams quality paperback series; 363)
   First-3d ed. published under title: Marketing terms.
   1. Marketing—Dictionaries. I. Title.
HF5412.S52   1980   658.8'003'21   80-24998
ISBN 0-8226-0363-2

Printed in the United States of America

Preface to the Fourth Edition

The ever-widening discipline of marketing has taken a number of turns since the third edition of this "dictionary" was published. The expanded, third edition received generous reviews from the JOURNAL OF MARKETING, SALES & MARKETING MANAGEMENT MAGAZINE, CHOICE, and other publications. The response from the market was again most gratifying. My thanks to all of you for your encouragement, most particularly to the many of you who saw the teaching possibilities inherent in the book and used it so in marketing courses at all levels, including the graduate level where many students enter MBA programs from disciplines where business courses are unknown. Perhaps, without my intending it, this book has approached becoming (as one user wrote) a "marketing text in dictionary form."

The suggestions and comments that have come to me from all over the world have been enlightening and stimulating. So much so that I have been inspired to increase the compass to over 5,000 entries, enlarging the content of every area. Commentary has again been increased where that was pertinent. I have given special attention to the numerous requests for more terms from the behavioral sciences and from marketing research. While accommodating these, I have emphasized the managerial aspects of decision-making techniques, leaving the technical details to the specialized textbooks. The result has been not only the inclusion of a large number of terms new to this edition, but also the rewriting of many from the third edition to reflect new thinking and developments and to facilitate cross-referencing.

I owe new debts for their interest to A. B. Blankenship of Bowling Green University, and once more, to William S. Penn, Jr., of San Jose State University.

As before, all responsibility for errors is mine alone.

I invite your comments, suggestions, and criticisms. Please send them to me at P.O. Box 199, West Long Branch, NJ 07764.

Irving J. Shapiro

Preface to the Third Edition

This book developed gradually from repeated requests by students to explain terms they had encountered in their reading. It was apparent that they all could well use explanations of the special marketing terminology largely taken for granted by authors of articles and books in the field. The first "book" contained about 180 terms. It was followed quickly by a supplement of another 100.

Encouraged by student response and by suggestions from my colleagues, I continued to expand the book until the edition just prior to this had over 1,000 entries. Thanks to kind notices in SALES MANAGEMENT, ADVERTISING AGE, MARKETING INFORMATION GUIDE, JOURNAL OF MARKETING, and other publications, reaction from the business world was immediate. Orders came from virtually all of the United States and from many foreign countries. Feedback was entirely positive and constructive, many readers offering valuable comments which I have already acknowledged with gratitude.

I discovered that a number of former students were using the book in their jobs and that many still in college were reading the book for, as one explained, "exposure to ideas in marketing that I did not know existed." The most important benefit of this book to both student and practitioner alike may be just this.

Inspired by an expression of confidence in the form of an assisting sum by the Monmouth College Faculty Grant-in-Aid-for-Creativity Committee and many letters requesting that the "dictionary" be expanded, I enlarged the scope of the book so that this edition contains nearly 3,000 entries, representing the special language of over thirty areas within the marketing discipline. Commentary has been increased where that could be useful.

My debt is to so many people who have been generous with their ideas and assistance that I cannot name them all here. They know that I know who they are. I wish particularly to acknowledge the especially generous contribution of time and talent made by Professor William S. Penn, Jr., of San Jose State College and Marketing Abstracts Editor for the JOURNAL OF MARKETING. Mr. Charles H. Martin of OMARK INDUSTRIES, Mr. Marvin V. Schylling of SYLVANIA ELECTRIC PRODUCTS, Mr. Herb L. Mitchell of H. L. MITCHELL & ASSOCIATES, Mr. Joe M. Turner of CIBA PHARMACEUTICAL COMPANY, Dr. Alfred E. Seidel of Switzerland, and Dr. Bertil Neuman of Sweden also helped in ways above and beyond anything expected. My special appreciation is expressed to Professor Harry B. Roggenburg, Chairman of the University College Department of Marketing, Rutgers University, for his support at a crucial juncture in this venture.

All responsibility for errors is mine alone.

I hope users will send me comments and suggestions. They will be received most gratefully. Please address them to me at Monmouth College, West Long Branch, New Jersey 07764.

Irving J. Shapiro

Key to Cross-indexing System

A term shown in all CAPITAL LETTERS within the text provided for another term is treated in its regular alphabetical position. Numbers are alphabetized in the positions that would be theirs if they were in word form.

AAA Abbreviation for: American Academy of Advertising, the professional organization of practitioners and teachers of ADVERTISING interested in furthering advertising education.

AAAA Abbreviation for: American Association of Advertising Agencies, the national association of ADVERTISING AGENCIES.

AAF Abbreviation for: American Advertising Federation, a federation of associations of ADVERTISERS, ADVERTISING AGENCIES, MEDIA, advertising clubs, and allied companies, the major objective of which is to make ADVERTISING more effective for business and more useful to the public. Formed by the consolidation of the AFA and the Advertising Association of the West. Media associations are affiliate members.

ABANDONMENT OF MARK Abandonment of a MARK is considered prima facie if the mark has not been used for two consecutive years; when its use has been discontinued with intent not to resume; or when any course of conduct of the registrant, including acts of omission as well as commission, cause the mark to lose its significance as an indication of origin.

ABC Abbreviation for: Audit Bureau of Circulations, a non-profit, cooperative organization sponsored by over 4,000 publishers, ADVERTISING AGENCIES, and advertisers to validate the circulation claims of magazines and newspapers. About three-fourths of all print media are covered. It has reported this data objectively since its inception in 1914.

ABC ANALYSIS Same as: ABC INVENTORY MANAGEMENT

ABC DATA BANK More accurately titled "ABC Newspaper Audience Research Data Bank," it provides audience data by key DEMOGRAPHICS based upon "yesterday readership" for all daily and Sunday ABC member NEWSPAPERS within a given MARKET that have 10% or more circulation-to-household COVERAGE. The geographic base is the SMSA, but other areas may be available. There are strict measures to insure proper data-gathering techniques. The data may be arranged by the computer to meet individual decision-making needs.

ABC INVENTORY-CONTROL SYSTEM Same as: ABC INVENTORY MANAGEMENT

ABC INVENTORY MANAGEMENT In PURCHASING, the practice of dividing inventories into A, B, and C categories based on relative high or low usage and/or high or low costs. This arrangement makes EOQ analysis more efficient by providing for selective inventory control.

A, B, C etc. RATES See: CLASS RATE (2)

"A" BOARD A large, outdoor, two-sided sign shaped as the letter A, enabling it to stand on its own. Its sides are usually made of two or more swinging parts so that the wind cannot tip it over.

ABOVE THE MARKET STRATEGY Same as: MARKET-PLUS PRICING

ABP Abbreviation for: American Business Press, an organization of industrial, professional, and trade papers. Makes annual awards for editorial achievement to encourage continued striving for excellence in this medium. Formed by the merger of the Associated Business Publications and the National Business Publications groups.

ABSENCE OF DEMAND A situation within a MARKET in which a significant segment of the market finds no possibilities of benefits from a PRODUCT and is, therefore, entirely uninterested in the product.

ABSOLUTE ADDRESS   (1) The actual, interpretable location in storage of a specific datum which the ADP equipment can recognize. (2) The designation of a particular storage area in a computer. See: ADDRESS

ABSOLUTE FREQUENCY   In MARKETING RESEARCH, the number of data elements in a given defined category. See: DISPERSION (2)

ABSOLUTE SALE   A transaction in which no qualifications to completion are imposed by buyer or seller. See: CONDITIONAL SALE

ABSOLUTE THRESHOLD   The minimum level at which an individual can detect a specific STIMULUS. This level tends to increase with constant stimulation, so that a degree of accommodation occurs which requires that the stimulus be ever stronger if it is to be detected. ADVERTISERS may change CAMPAIGNS to avoid the AUDIENCE'S "getting used" to the ADVERTISEMENTS. See: DIFFERENTIAL THRESHOLD

ABSORPTION OF FREIGHT   See: FREIGHT ABSORPTION

ACB   Abbreviation for: The Advertising Checking Bureau, Inc., an organization which offers its over 1,600 clients a COOPERATIVE ADVERTISING checking service to audit the advertisements and to calculate the amounts due advertisers, a TEAR SHEET service on new advertisements, position reports analyzing the page, and advertisement numbers, linage, and cost of space by newspaper for each BRAND covered. It includes all of the 1,471 principal RETAIL MARKETS in the United States. The firm provides a number of research tabulations developed from its services rendered and special activities.

ACCELERATION PRINCIPLE   A postulation in economics that society's stock of CAPITAL will be increased only when total income is growing. A requisite to maintaining business investment is that consumption must continue to increase. After a time, as an arithmetic model will show, a recession would set in if the rate of sales growth declines below a given point.

ACCENT   The emphasis given a FASHION to enhance its particular underlying STYLE. For example, Egyptian accent.

ACCEPTANCE SAMPLING   The use of a specific pattern of statistical SAMPLING as part of the inspection activity of a manufacturing firm; designed to determine the acceptance or rejection of particular lots of materials or products. See: DECISION RULE

ACCESSORIES   In RETAILING, those items which coordinate with a basic article of wearing apparel and make it more attractive, and hence more attractive the complete appearance of the wearer. Usually applied to women's wear. Includes such articles as gloves, handbags, hosiery, jewelry, and scarves.

ACCESSORY EQUIPMENT   Major units of processing equipment of a general nature, useful in a variety of plants. Usually of a type to facilitate plant operations rather than to determine the product. See: INSTALLATIONS

ACCESS TIME   In ADP, the time lapse between the moment information is called for from storage and the moment delivery of the information is completed, called the read time. Also, the time lapse between the moment information is ready for storage and the moment storage is completed, called the write time.

ACCOMMODATION AREA   In RETAILING, an area devoted to giving auxiliary services to customers, such as wrapping, approving checks, validating parking cost receipts, and other sales-supporting but non-selling activities. Same as: ACCOMMODATION DESK, SERVICE AREA

ACCOMMODATION DESK   Essentially the same as: ACCOMMODATION AREA

ACCORDION FOLD   A way of folding an ADVERTISING piece so that the panels fold alternately inward and outward.

ACCORDION THEORY   An attempt to explain RETAILING development by pointing to a seeming historical tendency for retail business to become dominated in an alternating pattern by general-line, wide ASSORTMENT retailers followed by specialized, narrow-line retailers. Because there are no valid historical statistics on merchandise assortments, this theory cannot be proved conclusively. Nevertheless, many students of retailing history claim to have discerned this pattern.

ACCOUNT   (1) In the field of ADVERTISING, a client of an ADVERTISING AGENCY or a firm placing advertising directly with MEDIA. (2) Generally in MARKETING, a CUSTOMER. See: KEY ACCOUNT, NATIONAL ACCOUNT (3) In the practice of accounting, a device for storing and accumulating financial information about a particular part or detail of the operations of a business.

ACCOUNT EXECUTIVE   That person in an ADVERTISING AGENCY who is responsible for the planning and preparation of advertising for one or more clients. He is the primary liason man between the advertiser and the agency. Same as: ACCOUNT SUPERVISOR, CONTACT MAN

ACCOUNTING MACHINE   See: TABULATOR

ACCOUNT OPENER   The gift offered by a bank or savings and loan association to a depositor opening a new account or adding a specified minimum amount to an existing account. See: DIRECT PREMIUM

ACCOUNT SUPERVISOR   Same as: ACCOUNT EXECUTIVE

ACCREDITED LIST   A list of persons to whom a PUBLIC WAREHOUSEMAN may make issue of merchandise stored without the specific authority in each instance by the owner of the merchandise.

ACCUMULATION   (1) Same as: ASSEMBLY (2) Buying of contracts on a COMMODITY EXCHANGE by traders who expect to hold the contracts for a fairly extended period.

ACCURACY   See: STANDARD ERROR OF ESTIMATE

ACCURACY IN SAMPLING   Same as: SAMPLING ACCURACY

ACHIEVEMENT MOTIVATION   See: THEORY OF ACHIEVEMENT MOTIVATION

ACHIEVEMENT NEED   One of the TRIO OF NEEDS. The drive for personal accomplishment as an end in itself. Individuals in whom this is high tend to exhibit confidence, enjoyment of risk-taking, willingness to do research. See: EGOISTIC NEEDS, PSYCHOGRAPHICS, SOCIAL NEEDS

ACI   Abbreviation for: Automatic Car Identification, a system using optical light to receive, translate, and store freight car movement data from color-coded bars on the sides of passing freight cars. Can scan cars passing at speeds up to 80 miles per hour. Data can be called for and utilized by a computer to report car movements. Has resulted in much greater freight car utilization. See: COMPASS, TPC, TRAIN, UMLER

ACM   (1) Abbreviation for: ANDEAN COMMON MARKET (2) Abbreviation for: Association of Computing Machinery, an organization of about 32,000 professionals in the computing sciences, founded in 1947 to advance the professional stature of its members. It publishes a number of special interest journals, and since 1973 has been a member of the other computer-related societies that formed the Institute for Certification of Computer Professionals, a coordinating body for certifying the professional qualifications of practitioners in the information process- ing disciplines.

ACME   Acronym for: Association of Consulting Management Engineers, with membership consisting of highly selected professional consulting firms engaged in the public practice of management counsel. Its main purpose is to further universally the highest standards of professional performance. It issues a variety of books and studies, and engages in numerous educational and informational activities.

ACME DECISIONS As referred to by professional sales trainers, the planning decisions about aim, content, method, execution and evaluation of a sales training program.

ACQUIRED NEEDS Same as: SECONDARY NEEDS

ACQUISITION (1) The process by which the whole or a part of a company becomes a part of another company. (2) Purchase by a firm of required items or materials.

ACREAGE ALLOTMENT A program developed by the Federal Government to establish and maintain levels of production of certain agricultural commodities that the MARKET could absorb at prices considered fair to producers. A variety of plans have followed one another, including limits on acreage planting, subsidies for not planting, and price supports or government purchases of surplus crops. See: CCC (2)

ACROSS THE BOARD A designation for a BROADCAST PROGRAM scheduled for the same time period on consecutive days of the week, usually Monday through Friday.

ACTION PLANNING PLANNING activity directed especially toward organizational goals through emphasizing the improvement of internal communication, cooperation, and motivation. See: STRATEGIC PLANNING

ACTUALS Commodities available in the SPOT MARKET, on hand and ready for shipment, storage, or manufacture. See: SPOT DEAL

ACTUAL SELF CONCEPT Same as: SELF CONCEPT

ACTUAL TIME In ADP, refers to the specific time in which the process or event is taking place on which the computing system is to have a resulting influence.

ADAPTATION The process by which one becomes so accustomed to a STIMULUS that one's reaction to it is dulled. See: ABSOLUTE THRESHOLD

ADAPTIVE PLANNING AND CONTROL SEQUENCE Same as: APACS

ADAPTIVE PRODUCT A variant of another offering of the same firm, designed to broaden the firm's MARKET SHARE. See: EMULATIVE PRODUCT, MULTIPLE BRAND ENTRIES

ADDED GRAVY The sales which result from items needed to provide satisfaction from another item, such as the sheets and other bedding required to outfit a king-size mattress. Also, the result of ADDED SELLING.

ADDED SELLING The attempt to sell additional products and/or services to a customer who has just made a purchase. A valid aspect of SALESMANSHIP.

ADDITIONAL MARKUPS In the RETAIL accounting method, increases that raise the prices of merchandise above ORIGINAL RETAIL. See: MARKUP CANCELLATIONS

ADD-ONS In RETAILING, the additional purchases added to the account of a charge account CUSTOMER before the previous balance in the account has been fully paid. See: REVOLVING ACCOUNT

ADD-ON SELLING Same as: ADDED SELLING

ADDRESS (1) In ADP, a name, number, or other symbol which identifies a location, register, or device where information is stored. (2) The portion of an instruction which determines the operation. (3) To place a datum in the memory or to recall a datum from the memory. See: ABSOLUTE ADDRESS, ARITHMETIC ADDRESS, EFFECTIVE ADDRESS, IMMEDIATE ADDRESS

ADI   Abbreviation for: American Documentation Institute, now known as American Society for Information Science.

AD INSERT   Same as: INSERT (5)

ADJACENCY   A program immediately preceding or following a specific BROADCAST time period or program.

ADJACENT PROGRAM   Same as: ADJACENCY

ADJUSTMENT   (1) The satisfying of a CUSTOMER'S claim that a shipment was not as ordered or that the price was incorrectly charged, by an agreeable financial settlement.   (2) The correction of errors involving wrong recording of invoices or wrong dating of purchases bought on open account.

ADMINISTERED PRICES   As defined by a Senate committee, these were held to be "prices which are administratively set, administratively maintained, and are insensitive to changes in their market." This view does not admit the competitive aspects of all sorts of variables in determining the MARKET acceptability of goods besides price. Stress should be placed on total market behavior with respect to a product or service.

ADMINISTERED VERTICAL MARKETING SYSTEM   Any vertically aligned group of FIRMS , not necessarily VERTICALLY INTEGRATED, which works as a unit to reduce the costs inherent in MERCHANDISING a LINE or CLASSIFICATION of goods. Care must be taken to avoid conflict with the ROBINSON-PATMAN ACT. See: CONTRACTUAL VERTICAL MARKETING SYSTEM, CORPORATE VERTICAL MARKETING SYSTEM

ADMINISTRATIVE MANAGEMENT SOCIETY   Same as: AMS

ADOPTION CURVE   Same as: ADOPTION CYCLE

ADOPTION CYCLE   See: INNOVATION DIFFUSION

ADOPTION PROCESS   The mental activity which occurs from the time an individual first becomes aware of an innovation until he accepts it; usually in the instance of real things, buying them. See: AIDCAS PROCESS, DIFFUSION PROCESS

ADP   Abbreviation for: AUTOMATIC DATA PROCESSING

AD VALOREM DUTIES   Taxes on imports determined as a specified percent of the money price of the goods, applied by a formula defined by the law.

ADVANCE DATING   An arrangement in which the seller sets a specific date in the future when the terms become applicable. Same as: SEASON DATING
   Example: For an order placed on January 10 and shipped on January 25, 1/10, n/30 as of June 1, the payment dates in full or less discount are calculated from June 1.

ADVANCED PROCESSED GOODS   A classification used by the CONFERENCE BOARD when reporting on manufacturing CAPACITY. The goods include furniture, electrical and nonelectrical machinery, transportation equipment instruments, food, tobacco, apparel, printing and publishing, chemicals, and leather. See: PRIMARY PROCESSED GOODS

ADVANCE PREMIUM   A PREMIUM given to a new customer by a home-service route firm in the expectation that it will be earned by later purchases.

ADVERTISEMENT   The message of an ADVERTISER. See: ADVERTISING MEDIUM, COMMERCIAL, SPOT

ADVERTISER   Anyone who engages to pay for ADVERTISING.

ADVERTISING   A non-personal, paid message of commercial significance about a product, service, or company made to a MARKET by an identified SPONSOR. It is the aspect of the selling function which can pave the way for the SALESMAN'S activity. It has recently become common to include messages promoting ideas and causes. Contrary to popular belief, advertising can cause people to act only in a manner to which they were predisposed. Advertising _can_ cause the realization and recognition of WANTS not previously known to the market, and it can lead directly to the sale where personal contacts are not involved.

ADVERTISING AGENCY   A specialist organization which prepares COPY and LAYOUT, studies MARKETS, selects MEDIA, works on advertising STRATEGY and campaigns, and performs the physical production aspects of the advertisement in preparation of the medium's requirements. See: A LA CARTE AGENCY, BOUTIQUE, IN-HOUSE AGENCY, MODULAR SERVICE AGENCY

ADVERTISING AGENCY COMMISSION   See: 15 & 2

ADVERTISING AGENCY RECOGNITION   The qualifying of an ADVERTISING AGENCY, according to the criteria established by a MEDIUM, to gain approval to receive commissions on ADVERTISEMENTS placed with the medium by the agency. Such criteria usually involve credit worthiness, professional expertise, and clients ready to advertise using that agency. See: 15 & 2

ADVERTISING ALLOWANCE   A discount or price reduction made by wholesalers or manufacturers in return for the promotion of a product or service. See: ROBINSON-PATMAN ACT

ADVERTISING APPEAL   An APPEAL presented through an ADVERTISING MEDIUM.

ADVERTISING BUDGET DETERMINATION   See: ASSESSMENT METHOD, TASK METHOD

ADVERTISING CAMPAIGN   A coordinated ADVERTISING effort over a certain period of time in carefully selected MEDIA with a specific objective, such as by a bank to announce a new savings plan, or by a manufacturer to persuade the MARKET of the superiority of his product's benefits so that his MARKET SHARE will rise. See: CAMPAIGN PLAN

ADVERTISING CHECKING BUREAU, INC, THE   Same as: ACB

ADVERTISING COUNCIL   The joint body of the AAAA and the ANA and MEDIA. Through this unit, public service projects are developed and presented to advertisers for their support.

ADVERTISING FEDERATION OF AMERICA   Same as: AFA

ADVERTISING MANAGER   See: MARKETING SERVICES DIRECTOR

ADVERTISING MEDIUM   The class of vehicle by means of which the advertiser's message is carried to its AUDIENCE. Commonly considered to be advertising media are: NEWSPAPERS, BILLBOARDS, CAR-CARDS, MAGAZINES, RADIO, POINT-OF-PURCHASE DISPLAYS, TELEVISION, DIRECT MAIL, ADVERTISING SPECIALTIES, HOUSE ORGANS, AND TRADE SHOWS. This list is intended to be illustrative rather than inclusive. Advertising media are often classified into (1) print media, (2) broadcast media, and (3) position media.

ADVERTISING NETWORK   A group of ADVERTISING AGENCIES, non-competing and independently owned, who agree to exchange ideas and services in the interests of their clients.

ADVERTISING NOVELTY   A small, interesting, sometimes personally useful item with the name and the advertising message of the issuing company printed on it. Same as: ADVERTISING SPECIALTY

ADVERTISING QUADRANGLE   A concept advanced by some ADVERTISING theorists which views advertising from the communications side as having four elements: the sender or advertiser, the message or the advertisement, the receiver or PROSPECT, and the MEDIUM; and from the MARKETING side as having four elements: the product, the prospect, the SPONSOR, and the CHANNEL OF DISTRIBUTION.

ADVERTISING REGISTER   One of the directories of NATIONAL ADVERTISERS or ADVERTISING AGENCIES that are published on a regular basis.

ADVERTISING RESEARCH FOUNDATION   Same as: ARF

ADVERTISING REVIEW BOARD   An organization of ADVERTISERS, ADVERTISING AGENCIES, and MEDIA to which an advertisement claimed to be misleading or untruthful may be referred. Although the Board has no legal powers, it can through publicity make known its adverse decision. The possibility of this publicity is expected to act as a real deterent to the type of advertising which does not give proper information on which CONSUMERS can base their decisions in the market. Same as: ARB

ADVERTISING-SHOULD-BE-MANAGED THEME   See: DAGMAR

ADVERTISING SPECIALTY   Same as: ADVERTISING NOVELTY

ADVERTISING SPECIALTY DISTRIBUTOR   A firm handling SPECIALTIES on a WHOLE-SALE basis. May sometimes have expanded to include INCENTIVE items.

ADVERTISING STAGE   See: SPIRAL

ADVERTISING SUBSTANTIATION   The documentation ADVERTISERS must be able to supply to the FTC in support of their claims made in their ADVERTISING, and must also be able to show that this formed the base on which the advertising was constructed. See: CORRECTIVE ADVERTISING, TRUTH-IN-ADVERTISING ACT

ADVERTISING THEME   A central thought of an ADVERTISING CAMPAIGN conveyed to the AUDIENCE in a way to prove the superiority of the benefits of the product or service or idea offered. May be applied to a single ADVERTISEMENT.

ADVERTISING TYPOGRAPHER   A typographer who specializes in type-setting only, does not print, and who can provide work superior to that which a publication can usually do in its composing room. Often do work only for advertisers. Most of the NATIONAL ADVERTISING which appears in print media is type-composed by such firms.

ADVERTORIAL   An ADVERTISEMENT laid out to look like news copy. A deceptive practice if not properly identified. See: READING NOTICE

AEDS   Abbreviation for: Association for Educational Data Systems, a private, non-profit educational organization founded in 1962 to provide a forum for the exchange of ideas and information about the relationship of modern data systems and computer technology to education. It publishes quarterly a Journal, a Bulletin, and a Monitor, and runs various Conferences and Conventions.

AEROSPACE INDUSTRIES ASSOCIATION OF AMERICA, INC.   Same as: AIA

AFA   Abbreviation for: Advertising Federation of America, a federation of member divisions representing different advertising activities. See: AAF

AFFECTIONAL DRIVES   PSYCHOGENIC DRIVES characterized by the need to form and maintain warm, harmonious, and emotionally satisfying relations with others. See: EGO-BOLSTERING DRIVES, EGO-DEFENSIVE DRIVES

AFFIDAVIT   The sworn statement made by a BROADCAST station that a COMMERCIAL appeared as stated on the invoice rendered. Verified by the LOG.

AFFILIATE   An independent BROADCAST station that agrees to carry programs provided by a NETWORK.

AFFILIATED STORE   (1) A RETAIL STORE that is part of a VOLUNTARY CHAIN or a FRANCHISE. (2) A retail store operated under a name other than that of the controlling store.

AFFILIATED WHOLESALER   A WHOLESALER acting as initiator of a VOLUNTARY CHAIN.

AFFILIATION NEED   One of the TRIO OF NEEDS. In individuals where such needs are high, there tends to be a strong social dependency on others. See: REFERENCE GROUPS, SOCIAL NEEDS

AFFIXED MERCHANDISE   In POP ADVERTISING, used to denote products attached to a display in some permanent way so that the display remains intact.

AFLOATS   Commodities loaded on vessels and on route to destination.

"A" FRAME   Same as: "A" BOARD

AFRO-MALAGASY ECONOMIC UNION   An African mutual market group comprising Cameroon, Central African Republic, Chad, Congo, Dahomey, Gabon, Ivory Coast, Mali Republic, Mauritania, Niger, Senegal, Togo, Upper Volta.

AFTER-MARKET   The potential sales associated with the requirements of owners after they have bought a piece of equipment, e.g., repair and replacement parts.

AFTERMATH MARKET   Same as: AFTER-MARKET

AFTER-SALES SERVICE   Same as: AFTERSERVICE

AFTERSERVICE   The activity which comes after the delivery of an item to a CUSTOMER. Usually involves instruction in use, set-up, repair, and such other factors designed to insure satisfaction in use.

AFTRA   Abbreviation for: American Federation of Television and Radio Artists, a union involved in television and radio activities.

AGATE LINE   A unit of measurement of print media advertising space one-fourteenth of an inch deep and one column wide, whatever the actual width of the column.

AGENCY COMMISSION   See: 15 & 2

AGENCY NETWORK   ADVERTISING AGENCIES individually affiliate to act as local offices in major cities to provide local services for other members of that network. There exists a number of different such networks.

AGENCY OF RECORD   When an ADVERTISER employs a number of ADVERTISING AGEN-CIES, he may designate one of them to coordinate the total activity. The one so designated is the "agency of record."

AGENCY RECOGNITION   An action by a unit of an ADVERTISING MEDIUM signi-fying acceptance under its terms of the qualifications of an organi-zation purporting to be an ADVERTISING AGENCY entitling that organiza-tion to receive the AGENCY COMMISSION for business placed.

AGENCY STRUCTURE   The various business units which perform the entire range of MARKETING FUNCTIONS, and their interrelationships through CHANNELS OF DISTRIBUTION. See: CONCENTRATION, DISPERSION

AGENT MIDDLEMAN   Same as: FUNCTIONAL MIDDLEMAN

AGGREGATED SHIPMENT   A number of individual shipments from different shippers to one consignee that are consolidated and treated as a single unit shipment. See: FREIGHT FORWARDER

AGGRESSION   A way of coping with FRUSTRATION by engaging in an extreme behavior pattern. The CONSUMER boycott of certain foods to protest high prices is an example. See: AUTISM, IDENTIFICATION, PROJECTION, RATIONALIZATION, REGRESSION, REPRESSION

AGGRESSIVE PHILOSOPHY   A philosophy of competitive behavior under which a firm chooses to try to increase MARKET SHARE by engaging in vigorous com-petition, employing all the legal and ethical TACTICS at its command.

See: NEUTRAL PHILOSOPHY, PASSIVE PHILOSOPHY

AGREE AND COUNTERATTACK TECHNIQUE   Same as: YES, BUT TECHNIQUE

AGREEING AND NEUTRALIZING TECHNIQUE   Same as: YES, BUT TECHNIQUE

AGRIBUSINESS   All activities directed to the production and distribution of farm products and supplies. Involves operations on the FARM, processing, TRANSPORTATION, and in general the MARKETING of farm commodities.

AGRICULTURAL COOPERATIVE   An organization formed by a number of small farmers to enable them to achieve some of the competitive advantages of larger scale MARKETING.

AGRICULTURAL MARKETING RESEARCH INSTITUTE   Same as: AMRI

AGRICULTURAL PUBLISHERS ASSOCIATION   Same as: APA

AGRICULTURAL RESEARCH SERVICE   See: AMRI

AGRICULTURAL STATISTICS AND COMMODITY YEARBOOK   See: CENSUS OF AGRICULTURE

AIA   (1) Abbreviation for: Association of Industrial Advertisers, the professional organization of MARKETING and ADVERTISING executives in the INDUSTRIAL GOODS field. Name changed recently to: Business and Professional Advertisers Association. (2) Abbreviation for: The Aerospace Industries Association of America, Inc., the national trade association of companies in the United States engaged in the research, development and manufacturing of aerospace systems. Its major objectives are to provide cooperative studies on major problems affecting both the industry and society; to enhance the state of the art and science associated with the industry; to effect and maintain operating channels of communication between the industry and the government; to foster independent research and development; and to keep the general public informed about the industry's goals and accomplishments. Membership totals approximately 100.

AIC   Abbreviation for: American Institute of Cooperation, a national educational organization whose membership includes nearly all FARM COOPERATIVES in the United States.

AIDA PROCESS   An explanation of how PROSPECTS buy. It is thought that they go through a series of mental states: Attention, or focusing on the salesman and permitting him to begin his presentation; Interest, or wishing to hear more; Desire, or a strong urge to acquire the salesman's offering; and Action, or placing the order. While tension theories seem to have become more popular, this is still a very useful way for a salesman to plan his sales talk or for a copywriter to construct his advertisement. See: AIDCAS PROCESS

AIDCAS PROCESS   An expansion of the AIDA PROCESS to include: Conviction, or the conclusion that the salesman's offering provides benefits as good or better than those of any other offering which may be available; and Satisfaction, or enjoyment of the purchase in the belief that the right decision was made and the anticipated benefits have actually been had.

AIDED-RECALL METHOD   A device used in testing memory of advertisements. The RESPONDENT is given a clue that may assist in recalling BRAND name.

AIDS   Acronym for: American Institute for Decision Sciences, a professional organization dedicated to the development and application of quantitative and behavioral methods in all areas. Through meetings and its journal it provides a forum for the exchange of ideas and experiences among academicians and practitioners.

AIO   Abbreviation for: attitudes, interests, and opinions profiles. Sometimes used in the same meaning as PSYCHOGRAPHICS.

AIO INVENTORY   See: AIO

AIO PROFILE   See: AIO

AIR BRUSH   A commercial art method of painting by using a fine spray to create tonal variations, and to retouch photographs.   See: ARTIST'S MEDIUM

AIRPORT OPERATORS COUNCIL INTERNATIONAL, THE   Same as: AOCI

AIR TAXI CHARTER OPERATOR   See: NATC

AIR TAXI SERVICE AGREEMENT   A mutual arrangement for reservations and ticketing between NATC members and major airlines.

AISLE JUMPER   An overhead wire reaching across aisles in a store on which flags or pennants may be draped, or signs or banners may be hung. See: POP ADVERTISING

A LA CARTE AGENCY   An ADVERTISING AGENCY which offers services in parts as needed on a negotiated basis.   Same as: MODULAR SERVICE AGENCY   See: BOUTIQUE (2)

ALGORITHM   A systematized procedure for solving a quantitative problem. Most often involves a mathematical model.

ALL-BANDING   Wiring a CATV system to carry all 12 channels of the conventional television set, or more as required by government regulation. Not all systems have the same capacity, but a capacity of 50 or more channels is becoming common.

ALL-COMMODITY RATES   Same as: FAK

ALLIED PRODUCTS   Especially as used in RETAILING, products associated with one another in the same use category. See: COMPLEMENTARY GOODS

ALLOCATION   (1) Essentially the same as BREAKING BULK, but where it is considered that breaking bulk is a WHOLESALE level activity, then allocation applies to the successive changes in ownership and to geographical dispersion, so that a homogeneous supply becomes contained in smaller and smaller and more numerous lots.   (2) The assignment of frequency and power made by the FCC to a BROADCAST station.

ALLOCATION RIGHTS   AUTHORITY granted managers in the area of PURCHASING to implement procurement STRATEGIES. See: CRITERIA RIGHTS, EVALUATION RIGHTS, POLICY RIGHTS, SAMPLING RIGHTS, STRATEGY RIGHTS

ALLOTMENT   In OUTDOOR ADVERTISING, the unit of sale comprising a SHOWING in a certain MARKET. May be one or more POSTERS depending on the size of the market and its traffic pattern.

ALLOWANCE   A grant made by a manufacturer to a WHOLESALER or by a wholesaler to a RETAILER for rendering services usually linked to some form of ADVERTISING or other PROMOTION. May be accomplished by a reduction in the purchase price on a percent basis. See: ROBINSON-PATMAN ACT

ALL-PURPOSE REVOLVING ACCOUNT   In RETAILING, a charge account for which the agreement with the CUSTOMER provides that no service charge will be imposed if the account is paid in full within a specified time after statement has been rendered. If the account is not paid in full, the agreement provides the amount of and the mechanism for imposing a service charge. Details of operation and imposition of service or finance charges are governed by the TRUTH-IN-LENDING ACT. Same as: REVOLVING CHARGE ACCOUNT

ALPHA ERROR   Same as: TYPE I ERROR

ALTERNATE SPONSORSHIP   A sharing of program time by two SPONSORS, with one dominant one week, the other dominant the next week. See: FULL-PROGRAM SPONSOR, PARTICIPATING PROGRAM

ALTERNATIVE HYPOTHESIS A HYPOTHESIS that differs from the NULL HYPOTHESIS in that it proposes a PARAMETER for the UNIVERSE other than the PARAMETER stated in the null hypothesis if any is there stated.

ALTRUISTIC DISPLAY (1) A display which includes products of advertisers other than the ones who pay for the display. (2) A store-wide event featuring seasonal products which includes the advertiser's product but not specifically name it.

AM Abbreviation for: Amplitude Modulation. Indicates that the SIGNAL alters the amplitude (height) of the waves, which travel along the earth's surface little affected by obstacles or the earth's curvature. Used in a majority of RADIO BROADCASTS. They are reflected back to earth at night by the HEAVISIDE LAYER. Television pictures are transmitted by means of these waves. See: FM

AMA (1) Abbreviation for: American Marketing Association, a professional organization of MARKETING teachers, executives, and research practitioners, devoted to bettering the state of the discipline. It publishes the foremost publication in the field, the Journal of Marketing, the Journal of Marketing Research, numerous books, and a twice-monthly newspaper. It sponsors an International Congress in the Spring and an Educator's Conference in the Fall. It issues a detailed and categorized roster of members numbering in 1979 about 20,000. (2) Abbreviation for: Automobile Manufacturers Association, a trade association of domestic makers of motor vehicles, about ten firms. Founded in 1913, its main objectives are research in all areas of vehicle safety and pollution, liason with government agencies, and compilation and dissemination of INDUSTRY data. (3) Abbreviation for: American Management Associations, a not-for-profit educational membership organization for all types of management development. Conducts many courses, some of which are home-study. Produces programmed instruction courses for company training programs. The largest publisher of management books in the world, the organization also produces letters and special reports, and runs meetings to provide an additional forum for expression and exchange of ideas.

AMC Abbreviation for: American Movers Conference, an organization serving movers with current information regarding ICC rules and regulations, interpretation of court decisions, and trends in ethical practices.

AMERICAN ASSOCIATION OF ADVERTISING AGENCIES Same as: AAAA

AMERICAN ACADEMY OF ADVERTISING Same as: AAA

AMERICAN ADVERTISING FEDERATION Same as: AAF

AMERICAN BUSINESS PRESS, INC Same as: ABP

AMERICAN COTTON MANUFACTURERS ASSOCIATION See: ATMI

AMERICAN FEDERATION OF TELEVISION AND RADIO ARTISTS Same as: AFTRA

AMERICAN INSTITUTE FOR DECISION SCIENCES Same as: AIDS

AMERICAN INSTITUTE OF COOPERATION Same as: AIC

AMERICAN MANAGEMENT ASSOCIATIONS Same as: AMA (3)

AMERICAN MARITIME ASSOCIATION Formed in 1961, this association is open to any firm owning or operating American-flag vessels. Its major purposes are to promote the interests of the American-flag maritime industry, to take appropriate supportive or opposing action regarding legislation, to compile and disseminate information about all segments of the maritime industry whether domestic or foreign, and to assist in labor relations with American Maritime unions.

AMERICAN MARKETING ASSOCIATION Same as: AMA (1)

AMERICAN MOVERS CONFERENCE Same as: AMC

AMERICAN NEWSPAPER PUBLISHERS ASSOCIATION   Same as: ANPA

AMERICAN PLYWOOD ASSOCIATION   An organization of softwood plywood manufacturers formed to research and promote uses for the various types of
plywood, now numbering over 300. The association has been able to establish STANDARDS for the industry which it protects through its Division
for Product Approval. Members stamp the DFPA registered symbol and data
on the back of each panel to provide full information for users.

AMERICAN PRODUCTION & INVENTORY CONTROL SOCIETY, INC   Same as: APICS

AMERICAN RAILWAY CAR INSTITUTE   Same as: ARCI

AMERICAN RESEARCH BUREAU   Same as: ARB

AMERICAN SHORT LINE RAILROAD ASSOCIATION, THE   An association of about 200
Class I and Class II line-haul, switching, and terminal companies, the
major objectives of which are to provide cooperative action in consideration and solving of problems of management and POLICY affecting the operation or welfare of short-line RAILROADS, and to promote Federal legislation of benefit and resist the enactment of legislation that would be
detrimental to the railroad INDUSTRY.

AMERICAN SOCIETY FOR TESTING AND MATERIALS   Same as: ASTM

AMERICAN SOCIETY OF COMPOSERS, AUTHORS, AND PUBLISHERS   Same as: ASCAP

AMERICAN SOCIETY OF TRAFFIC AND TRANSPORTATION   Same as: ASTT

AMERICAN STANDARD CODE FOR INFORMATION INTERCHANGE   Same as: ASCII

AMERICAN STANDARDS ASSOCIATION   A federation of many trade associations,
professional societies, and more than 2,000 company members, the main
functions of which are: 1) to provide systematic means for the development of American STANDARDS, 2) to promote the development and use of standards in the United States, 3) to coordinate activities of STANDARDIZA-
TION in the United States, 4) to serve as a clearing house for information on American and foreign standards, 5) to approve standards as
American Standards provided they are accepted by a consensus of all national groups concerned in a major way with their provisions, and 6) to represent American interests in international standards work. Same as: ASA

AMERICAN TEXTILE MANUFACTURERS INSTITUTE   Same as: ATMI

AMERICAN TRANSIT ASSOCIATION   Same as: ATA

AMERICAN TRUCKING ASSOCIATIONS   See: ATA

AMERICAN WAREHOUSEMEN'S ASSOCIATION   Same as: AWA

AMERICAN WATERWAYS OPERATORS   Same as: AWO

AMPLIFICATION AND DETAILS   A section of verbal COPY in an ADVERTISEMENT
which augments and extends, often in considerable length, the idea
presented by the HEADLINE. Usually follows the SUBHEADLINE if one is
used.

AMPLITUDE MODULATION   Same as: AM

AMRI   Abbreviation for: The Agricultural Marketing Research Institute,
created in 1972 concurrently with a major reorganization of the Agricultural Research Service. It conducts research to find ways of delivering farm products to CONSUMERS at minimum cost. It is mainly concerned with the technological and operational problems of improving the
facilities, equipment, instruments, and techniques used to handle,
process, package, store, transport, and market agricultural products.

AMS   Abbreviation for: Administrative Management Society, an organization
of over 13,000 members in 150 chapters throughout the free world, all of
whom are professionals in administrative management, consultants, educa-

tors teaching the administrative management process, or persons in marketing primarily responsible for duties other than direct CUSTOMER contact.
It publishes a variety of periodicals, maintains an information center,
and runs seminars and conferences. It was founded in 1919 as the National Office Management Association and changed its name to reflect modern
practices which make the office the center of all of a firm's information
flows.

AMTRAK   Same as: Railpax   See: NATIONAL RAILWAY PASSENGER CORPORATION

ANA   Abbreviation for: Association of National Advertisers, a national
organization of advertisers, with the majority of members being
larger manufacturers.

ANALOG DATA   In ADP, data in the form of continuously variable quantities,
e.g., averages, or the amounts of rainfall in small units of volume.
See: DIGITAL DATA

ANALYSIS OF VARIANCE   See: VARIANCE ANALYSIS

ANALYTICAL MODEL   A MODEL used for a problem-solving situation. May be
MATHEMATICAL MODEL or PROSE MODEL.

ANALYTICAL STUDY   A design for statistical observations to provide a basis
for dealing with the factors causal to a situation. This type of study,
dealing with a process, produces information which can only be regarded
as a SAMPLE from that process, which could continue indefinitely without
its conditions changing. A complete set of such observations is called
an infinite population. See: ENUMERATIVE STUDY

ANAMORPHIC LENS   A single lens mounted in front of a normal camera lens,
that reduces COPY in one direction only, each such lens by a specified
percent. A certain amount of optical distortion is inevitable. Used to
make the ADVERTISEMENT fit into the column measurement of a PRINT MEDIUM.
Same as: Shrink Lens See: FLEXING SYSTEM

ANCHOR   An enduring reference used by CONSUMERS to evaluate communications. It is often a "rule-of-thumb" such as: Price is a good indicator
of quality. The ADVERTISER who is aware of any anchors used by the TARGET
MARKET can enhance positive reactions and avoid negative reactions.

ANCILLARY CUSTOMER SERVICES   Optional services offered to CUSTOMERS to enhance the NON-PRICE COMPETITION activities of a seller. They are always
of a nonessential nature.

ANCOM   Acronym for: ANDEAN COMMON MARKET

ANDEAN COMMON MARKET   A regional subgroup within LAFTA, organized in 1969
to foster domestic business and to increase the flow of science and technology, mainly through the purchase of a majority interest in foreign
investments by private groups or the governments. The countries in this
group are Bolivia, Chile, Columbia, Ecuador, Peru, and Venezuela. The
economic policies proposed by this group are subject to considerable discussion because they may deter the outside investment usually considered
necessary to fuel the economies of developing nations. Indications of
change are in evidence. Same as: ACM, ANCOM, ANDEAN GROUP

ANDEAN GROUP   Same as: ANDEAN COMMON MARKET

ANGLED POSTER   A POSTER situated so that it can normally be viewed by
traffic moving in one direction only. To be so classified, a poster
must have one end six feet or more farther back from the traffic flow
than the other end. See: FLASH APPROACH, PARALLEL POSTER

ANNOUNCEMENT   Same as: COMMERCIAL

ANNUAL SURVEY OF MANUFACTURERS   See: CENSUS OF MANUFACTURERS

ANOVA   Acronym for: ANALYSIS OF VARIANCE

ANPA   Abbreviation for: American Newspaper Publishers Association, the
major trade association of daily and Sunday newspaper publishers.

ANSWERING TIME   In data communications, the elapsed time between the input
of the signal and the response to the signal. See: CONNECT TIME, TIME
SLICE

ANTHROPOLOGIST   A social scientist who views man in relation to the
CULTURE into which he was born or in which he grew up. Would view the
United States as a pluralistic society made up of a host of subcultures.
See: ANTHROPOLOGY

ANTHROPOLOGY   The behavioral science which studies the development of man
and his customs. The marketer can use information from this discipline
to avoid errors in the use of symbols, the themes of a culture, and the
encroachment on taboos. See: ANTHROPOLOGIST

ANTICIPATION DISCOUNT An extra amount in addition to the CASH DISCOUNT
allowed if the bill is paid before the expiration of the cash discount
period. Usually the extra amount is calculated on the basis of an
annual rate of percent agreed upon in advance, just as in the instance
of an interest rate. Either the total bill amount or the net amount
after cash discount may be specified as the base for an anticipation
discount.

ANTICIPATORY GROUP   A REFERENCE GROUP to which an individual aspires
membership.

ANTICIPATORY SOCIALIZATION   Refers to implicit, often unconscious learning
for roles which will be assumed sometime in the future. See: SOCIALIZA-
TION

ANTI-MERGER ACT   See: CELLER-KEFAUVER ANTI-MERGER ACT

ANTI-TRUST LAWS   See: CELLER-KEFAUVER ANTI-MERGER ACT, CLAYTON ACT,
FEDERAL TRADE COMMISSION ACT, SHERMAN ACT, WHEELER-LEA ACT

AOCI   Abbreviation for: The Airport Operators Council International, an
organization founded in 1948 as a cooperative, non-profit trade association the main objective of which is to serve the public interest by
promoting sound policies dealing with financing, construction, management, operations, and development of airports. Its membership includes
only those governmental bodies that own and/or operate public airports
throughout the world. Member airports now enplane about 60% of the total
passengers enplaned at world airports. The association publishes various
handbooks and a weekly newsletter.

AOG   Abbreviation for: arrival of goods dating. Same as: ROG

AOPL   Abbreviation for: Association of Oil Pipelines, its name changed in
1960 from the Committee for Pipe Line Companies established in 1948.
Deeply involved in legislation and education activities related to liquid
pipelines, its about 80 members transport over 95% of all crude oil and
petroleum products moved by pipeline in the United States.

APA   Abbreviation for: Agricultural Publishers Association, an association
of farm magazine and farm newspaper publishers.

APACS   Abbreviation for: Adaptive Planning and Control Sequence, the
result of a Marketing Science Institute study that resulted in an analytical framework of eight steps for reaching promotional decisions.

APATHETIC SHOPPERS   One of a four-way, sociological classification of
CONSUMERS, the others being ECONOMIC SHOPPERS, ETHICAL SHOPPERS, and
PERSONALIZING SHOPPERS. The apathetic shopper has little interest in
making comparisons. He is willing to patronize the most convenient store.

APICS   Abbreviation for: American Production & Inventory Control Society,
the professional society of leaders in production and inventory manage-

ment. Its main objectives are to promote the advancement of profession-alism in the study and application of scientific methods to production and inventory management problems, to encourage research and education for improvement of production and inventory management, to disseminate information through publications and meetings, and to assist the academic profession in the development and improvement of education programs and courses in production and inventory management. It makes a number of awards as research grants and for recognition each year.

APPEAL   Direction of a sales effort toward a MOTIVE, designed to activate that motive, and to stir a potential buyer toward the goal of purchase of the product, or acceptance of an idea.

APPLAUSE MAIL   Letters of a laudatory nature received by ADVERTISERS, or by BROADCAST stations. Equivalent to fan mail addressed to individuals.

APPLIED RESEARCH   Any investigation the major purpose of which is to pro-vide information that can help managers improve their decision-making. See: MARKETING RESEARCH

APPORTIONING   Same as: BREAKING BULK

APPROACH   (1) In OUTDOOR ADVERTISING, the distance on the line of travel between the point where the POSTER first becomes comprehendible to the point where the COPY ceases to be readable. Approach is often classi-fied as: long, medium, short, and FLASH. (2) The type of APPEAL used in an ADVERTISING MESSAGE. (3) The theme of an ADVERTISING CAMPAIGN.

APPROACH-APPROACH CONFLICT   One of a three-way classification of conflict which may cause decision delays and which may require MOTIVATION to resolve, this one has two or more desirable goals in competition. See: APPROACH-AVOIDANCE CONFLICT, AVOIDANCE-AVOIDANCE CONFLICT

APPROACH-AVOIDANCE CONFLICT   One of a three-way classification of conflict which may cause decision delays and which may require MOTIVATION to resolve, this one involves a goal that can be obtained only at a cost. See: APPROACH-APPROACH CONFLICT, AVOIDANCE-AVOIDANCE CONFLICT

APPROVAL SALE   In RETAILING, a sale to a CUSTOMER in which the customer has unlimited returns privileges. See: ABSOLUTE SALE

APRON   (1) An open area in a STORE in which displays are arranged, either on free-standing fixtures, or built entirely of merchandise from the floor up. (2) See: APRON SYSTEM (3) Hard surfaced areas adjacent to buildings, loading docks, wharfs, and gasoline pump islands. (4) In OUTDOOR ADVER-TISING, the lattice or other decorative finish just below the bottom of the display area of an outdoor unit.

APRON SYSTEM   A receiving mechanism in which a separate slip is filled out for each individual shipment and the original copy of the slip (apron) is attached to the vendor's invoice for that shipment. The apron carries the signatures of the different persons who price and otherwise ready the merchandise for sale. Used commonly in large retail establishments.

APRON TRACK   Railroad track along the APRON of a pier designed for the direct transfer of CARGO between car and ship.

A.Q.   Abbreviation for: any quantity. Used in the TRAFFIC field.

ARB   (1) Abbreviation for: American Research Bureau, a television rating service using both the viewer DIARY METHOD and an electronic recording and tabulating system called ARBITRON. (2) Abbreviation for: Advertising Review Board.

ARBITRAGE   Simultaneous purchase and sale of the same commodity or secur-ity in the SPOT MARKET in order to profit from price differentials on the various exchanges.

ARBITRARY MARK   A dictionary word used as a TRADEMARK which effects no connotation about the PRODUCT it is to identify, for example, Dial soap.

ARBITRON   A system for obtaining instantaneous television program ratings by means of electronic devices placed in homes and wired to a central tabulating area. See: ARB

ARCH   A POP display designed to go from one gondola to another, over and above the aisle.

ARCI   Abbreviation for: American Railway Car Institute, founded in 1915 as a trade association of railroad car and components manufacturers, concentrates on engineering and design, MARKET FORECASTING, and statistics. It is the only agency that compiles statistics relative to orders, deliveries, and backlogs of new freight cars. It works closely with the AAR.

ARC OF FASHION   A description of the course through time of a FASHION. It is said to begin with early acceptors who will pay high prices for new concepts. As popularity for the STYLE increases, these are followed by early followers, general acceptors, and decline laggards in that order and as price decreases as mass merchandisers enter the supply pattern. See: INNOVATION DIFFUSION

AREA OF DOMINANT INFLUENCE   Same as: ADI

AREA SAMPLE. Used in MARKETING RESEARCH, it is a SAMPLE of persons derived by marking the study UNIVERSE off into grids and then selecting a number of grids at random. An attempt is made to interview all the people or consuming units in the selected grids. There is a reasonable statistical probability that the selected grids represent a cross-section of the area.

AREA STRUCTURE   Natural resource specialization based on the expected marketing returns on them, leading to a particular location for each institution in the AGENCY STRUCTURE. See: PRIMARY TRADING AREA, SECONDARY TRADING AREA, ZONE OF INDIFFERENCE

ARF   Abbreviation for: Advertising Research Foundation, a non-profit organization of advertisers, agencies, and colleges devoted to the promotion of research in advertising effectiveness.

ARITHMETIC ADDRESS   A specific location in an ADP unit that is used for the results of computations. See: ADDRESS

ARITHMETIC MEAN   See: AVERAGE (1)

ARMORPLY   Plywood or lumber coated with a metal veneer.

ARQ   In ADP, abbreviation for: Automatic Request for Repetition, a system employing an error-detecting code and so conceived that any false signal initiates a request for the repetition of the transmission of the CHARACTER incorrectly received or being in error.

ARRAY   (1) An arrangement of values ordered by magnitude. (2) A group of numbers arranged in sequence from lowest to highest or from highest to lowest. See: MEDIAN

ARS   Abbreviation for: Agricultural Research Service. See: AMRI

ARTIFICIAL OBSOLESCENCE. The decline in market acceptance of one product brought about by change in that product or a new model of the product introduced to supersede the old one on the logic that it is better to lose sales of a product to a new one of one's own firm than to that of a competitor. See: PLANNED OBSOLESCENCE

ARTIST'S MEDIUM   The materials that an artist uses to produce his work. May be air brush, crayon, ink pen, oil paint, pastel stick, pencil, wash, photography, etc.

ASA. Abbreviation for: American Standards Association.

ASCAP   Abbreviation for: American Society of Composers, Authors, and Publishers, an organization that protects the COPYRIGHTS of its members and
collects royalties in their behalf.

ASCII   Abbreviation for: American Standard Code for Information Interchange, developed by the American Standards Association as an effort to
overcome problems arising from lack of code STANDARDIZATION among the
business communications and data processing industries.

ASIS   Acronym for: American Society for Information Science, at one time
known as American Documentation Institute.

AS IS   Denotes an article of merchandise sold without recourse of any sort.
The buyer accepts the full risk of any hidden or apparent complication.

ASM   Abbreviation for: Association of Systems Management, an organization
devoted since its founding in 1947 to enhancing professional skills in
all areas of systems endeavors. It publishes the monthly "Journal of
Systems Management," features a variety of specialized educational
programs through its 135 chapters, and issues a number of reports of
current interest.

ASPIRATION   Goals people set for themselves and subjectively strive to
achieve. Directly connected with MOTIVATION, they may wax and wane, be
of long or short duration, and are subject to change as reality becomes
more apparent.

ASPIRATION GROUP   A group in which an individual desires membership. May
be in the interest of some type of status-seeking or emulation. See:
REFERENCE GROUP

ASSEMBLER   A MERCHANT MIDDLEMAN whose economic justification lies in his
performance of the activity of ASSEMBLY.

ASSEMBLY   (1) The process of bringing together the produce of a number of
farmers into a unit of economical shipping size. (2) The process of
bringing together the products of a number of manufacturers so that a
limited number of each item may be available to the user, e.g., as in
WHOLESALING.

ASSEMBLY SERVICE   An arrangement with a CARRIER in which the carrier
consolidates shipments from a number of CONSIGNORS to a single CONSIGNEE.
See: DISTRIBUTION SERVICE

ASSESSMENT METHOD   A method of arriving at an ADVERTISING BUDGET by summing
a specific, arbitrary amount of money for each unit sold. Convenient to
use, it is nevertheless arbitrary and does not consider the actual need
to reach objectives. May be applied as well to the development of the
budget for the total MARKETING MIX. See: PERCENTAGE OF LAST YEAR'S SALES
METHOD, PERCENTAGE OF NEXT YEAR'S SALES METHOD, PLUNGE METHOD, TASK
METHOD

ASSIMILATION-CONTRAST THEORY   Suggests that CONSUMERS will reject an
ADVERTISEMENT that requires an extreme change in ATTITUDE. Such a
message is likely to be seen as more extreme than it actually is, further
reinforcing the rejection action.

ASSOCIATED BUSINESS PUBLICATIONS GROUP   See: ABP

ASSOCIATION FOR COMPUTING MACHINERY   Same as: ACM

ASSOCIATION FOR EDUCATIONAL DATA SYSTEMS   Same as: AEDS

ASSOCIATION FOR SYSTEMS MANAGEMENT   Same as: ASM

ASSOCIATION OF CONSULTING MANAGEMENT ENGINEERS   Same as: ACME

ASSOCIATION OF COTTON TEXTILE MERCHANTS OF NEW YORK   See: ATMI

ASSOCIATION OF INDUSTRIAL ADVERTISERS   Same as: AIA

ASSOCIATION OF INTERSTATE COMMERCE COMMISSION PRACTITIONERS   An organization of attorneys and others who have been admitted to practice before the ICC. The Association is devoted to the proper administration of the Interstate Commerce Act and related Acts, to fostering educational opportunities, and to maintaining high standards of professional conduct. It holds annual meetings on pertinent topics and publishes a comprehensive journal. One of its latest activities is a program of transportation law seminars.

ASSOCIATION OF NATIONAL ADVERTISERS   Same as: ANA

ASSOCIATION OF OIL PIPE LINES   Same as: AOPL

ASSORTING   The second phase of the sorting process, the first phase of which is STANDARDIZATION and GRADING. Assorting occurs in two stages. The first is BREAKING BULK of EOQ shipments into smaller quantities. The second is assembling these into ASSORTMENTS and quantities desired by CUSTOMERS.

ASSORTMENT   (1) Indicates various forms of the same general type of product. See: VARIETY (2) As to an individual CONSUMER, it is the particular combination of goods and services recognized by him as necessary to maintain or improve his standard of living.

ASSORTMENT DISPLAY   The complete ASSORTMENT that a STORE carries is presented for the shoppers' viewing. The display is called open assortment display if the shoppers can handle the merchandise, a closed assortment display if the merchandise is in a locked case requiring personal assistance from a SALES CLERK. If groups of related merchandise are shown in a special arrangement, the display is often called a setting display.

ASSORTMENT PLAN   The range of merchandise of one type established to meet the requirements of customers by a determination of inventory levels. See: BASIC STOCK, MODEL STOCK

ASSUMPTIVE CLOSE   In SALESMANSHIP, a CLOSE accomplished without the buyer's verbal agreement. This becomes presumed when the buyer does not protest the SALESPERSON'S beginning to write the order, or to wrap the item.

ASTM   Abbreviation for: American Society for Testing and Materials, an organization cooperating with over 200 societies and trade associations to establish voluntary standards for use in the best interest of every segment of our society. This is accomplished by providing an authoritative forum, unbiased and free of control by any special interest, yet responsive to the specific needs of each. Since its inauguration in 1898 it has regularly and consistently updated its standards. Presently it publishes for sale a very large number of specifications, technical reports, transcripts of symposia, the annual proceedings, and other data.

ASTT   Abbreviation for: The American Society of Traffic and Transportation, Inc., a professional group organized in 1946 as the culmination of a period of study and research by The Associated Traffic Clubs of America in 1927. The objectives of the Society are: to establish standards of knowledge, technical training, experience, conduct and ethics, and to encourage the attainment of high standards of education and technical training requisite to the proper performance of the various functions of traffic, transportation and physical distribution management, by composing and publishing syllabi for study and assistance to organizations offering applicable courses of study, and by conducting examinations for membership in the Society.

ASYMMETRICAL BALANCE   Same as: INFORMAL BALANCE

ATA   (1) Abbreviation for: American Trucking Associations, Inc., an
organization of associations of truckers which publishes a weekly
newspaper of motor freight carrier topics to keep the industry informed
and instructed. It runs educational workshops and engages in various
activities designed to raise the level of competence within the industry
to its greatest potential. (2) Abbreviation for: American Transit Association, the professional association of transit operating organizations,
such as companies, regional authorities, and communities which operate
U.S. urban transit systems. Distinguish the latter from TAA.

ATA FOUNDATION   The public information, education and research organization for supplier support of the trucking industry. It publishes a
series of reports on the industry sponsored by various companies with
significant interest in the trucking industry.

ATMI   Abbreviation for: American Textile Manufacturers Institute, Inc.,
the national trade association for the man-made fibres, cotton, and silk
segments of the American textile industry. Its programs range widely,
covering orderly control of imports, statistics, trading rules, and
actions before government bodies. It merged in 1949 with the American
Cotton Manufacturers Association and Cotton Textile Institute, in 1958
with the National Federation of Textiles, in 1964 with the Association
of Cotton Textile Merchants of New York, and in 1965 with the National
Association of Finishers of Textile Fabrics. It is highly regarded in
government circles where it has assisted in the formulation of legislation favorable to both consumers and industry. It issues weekly, monthly and quarterly publications covering timely topics.

AT-THE-MARKET PRICES   In the RETAIL field, those prices which are generally the same for all stores in an area. See: MARKET-MINUS PRICES,
MARKET-PLUS PRICES, PRICE LEADERSHIP

ATTITUDE   Most commonly thought of as a disposition to act. Social psy-
chologists consider it a variable by which differences in response among
individuals may be explained. In his attempts at persuasion, a marketer
may try to confirm or to change existing attitudes, or to create new
attitudes. Changing and creating CONSUMER'S attitudes are difficult and
complex activities. See: BELIEF, OPINION

ATTRIBUTE   In statistics, the term used to describe the CHARACTERISTICS of
an ELEMENTARY UNIT. For example, an elementary unit may be a salesperson, the characteristic may be effectiveness, the attributes may be:
under QUOTA, just meeting quota, or over quota.

ATTRITION RATE   See and same as: DECAY RATE, EROSION RATE

AUCTION COMPANY   A FUNCTIONAL MIDDLEMAN characterized by its importance
in the marketing of leaf tobacco. Service to a PRINCIPAL is intermittent.
May perform the acts of sorting, grading, arranging, cataloging, displaying, and publicizing in preparation for the bidding process which it will
conduct. Same as: AUCTION RECEIVER

AUCTION RECEIVER   Same as: AUCTION COMPANY

AUDIENCE   (1) Total number of people who may be exposed to an advertising
message delivered by a MEDIUM or combination of media. See: REACH (2)
See: THEORY OF ROLE ENACTMENT

AUDIENCE ACCUMULATION   Same as: CUME

AUDIENCE COMPOSITION   Same as: AUDIENCE PROFILE

AUDIENCE DUPLICATION   The number of the same listeners or viewers REACHED
by two or more programs of the same SPONSOR.

AUDIENCE FLOW   The gain or loss in AUDIENCE from one program to another,
or from a variety of other causes. See: HOLD-OVER AUDIENCE

AUDIENCE PROFILE   A DEMOGRAPHIC description of the people exposed to an advertising medium or vehicle.

AUDIENCE RATING   The percent of all listeners in the MARKET that a particular RADIO station gets at a given time. See: AUDIENCE SHARE, RATING POINT

AUDIENCE SHARE   The number of listeners a RADIO station has at any time compared to the total potential listening AUDIENCE. See: AUDIENCE RATING, RATING POINT, TOTAL AUDIENCE

AUDIENCE TURNOVER   The ratio between the CUMULATIVE AUDIENCE and the average audience for a BROADCAST program.

AUDIMETER   A device patented by the A.C. Nielson Company, attached to home receivers to record the periods of set operation and station tuning. Data from this service provides the information from which the Nielson Radio Index is derived. See: MECHANICAL RECORDER METHOD

AUDIO   (1) Frequencies which can be heard by the human ear, usually between 15 and 20,000 cycles per second. (2) The sound portion of television.

AUDIT BUREAU OF CIRCULATIONS   Same as: ABC

AUDITED SALES   The net figures for sales of a particular period. In the RETAIL field these figures are usually computed daily, because close internal watch on sales trends is vital.

AUDITING DEPARTMENT   A unit of organization in a FIRM'S structure which has the responsibility for verifying the propriety of financial transactions. i.e., correct calculation, proper authorization and recording, supervision of inventory taking, etc. In the RETAIL field the auditing of sales and returns transactions usually is continuous on a daily basis.

AUTHORITY   The power to act or to command the actions of others. While technically it is a delegated right, actually the right is conferred by the persons who are being told what to do. Authority carries with it a commensurate responsibility.

AUTHORIZATION TEST   In ADP, a validation check performed to determine whether an initiating source is authorized to start that type of transaction. The check is usually made against a list of prescribed numbers. See: COMPLETENESS TEST

AUTHORIZED DEALER   A RETAILER accepted by a manufacturer to be permitted to sell a particular item or group of items under a plan of EXCLUSIVE DISTRIBUTION or SELECTIVE DISTRIBUTION. This arrangement may be similar to FRANCHISING, and in fact such DEALERS are said to have a "franchise to sell the manufacturer's products."

AUTISM   A way of coping with FRUSTRATION by fantasizing the gratification of one's unfilled needs and wants. It is an imaginary attainment of goals. See: AGGRESSION, IDENTIFICATION, PROJECTION, RATIONALIZATION, REGRESSION, REPRESSION

AUTISTIC THINKING   Same as: AUTISM

AUTOCORRELATION   The internal relationship among the elements of a stationary TIME SERIES.

AUTO DEALERS TRAFFIC SAFETY COUNCIL   See: HIGHWAY USERS FEDERATION FOR SAFETY AND MOBILITY

AUTOMATIC BASEMENT   The downstairs or otherwise separated section of a RETAIL STORE to which goods are relegated with decrease in price after the lapse of a specific time period, and in which the prices continue to be reduced at specified intervals until sold, or, after a certain period of time, given to charitable purposes. The best known RETAILER operating such a unit is the William Filene & Sons DEPARTMENT STORE in Boston.

AUTOMATIC CAR IDENTIFICATION   Same as: ACI

AUTOMATIC DATA PROCESSING   The accumulation, sorting, tabulating or otherwise processing data by using a system of electronic machines so constructed as to reduce to a minimum the requirement for human intervention.
Although Electronic Data Processing Systems are technically one of the
possible components of Automatic Data Processing Systems, which include
assorted other electrical machines such as punch card accounting
machines, the two terms are for practical purposes now generally used
synonymously.   Same as: ADP   See: COMPUTER

AUTOMATIC DOWNSTAIRS STORE   Same as: AUTOMATIC BASEMENT

AUTOMATIC GROUP   A REFERENCE GROUP in which an individual belongs because
of sex, education, race, or etc.   See: ANTICIPATORY GROUP, NEGATIVE
REFERENCE GROUP, PARTICIPATION GROUP

AUTOMATIC MARKDOWN   A reduction in price taken by a retailer according to
a predetermined time schedule.   See: AUTOMATIC BASEMENT

AUTOMATIC MARKDOWN BASEMENT   Same as: AUTOMATIC BASEMENT

AUTOMATIC MERCHANDISING   Same as: AUTOMATIC SELLING

AUTOMATIC REORDER   An order for STAPLE GOODS issued on a basis for reaching an established minimum inventory quantity.   The reorder quantity is
predetermined.   See: EOQ

AUTOMATIC REQUEST FOR REPETITION   Same as: ARQ

AUTOMATIC SELLING   The retail sale of goods or services through machines
operated by the CONSUMER using currency or some form of charge card or
other authorization device.   Includes VENDING.   A few attempts, some
successful some not, have been made to establish completely automatic
stores.   Effort is being directed toward the popularization of automatic gasoline stations.

AUTOMATION SYSTEM   A computer-monitored production or work cycle.   Has the
potential for greatly increasing PRODUCTIVITY.   Will have highly significant impact on the purchasing activity within the firm because of its
great capacity for handling and keeping track of the flow of details.

AUTOMOBILE INFORMATION DISCLOSURE ACT   Requires manufacturers to put on
new passenger cars of all types a tag showing the suggested retail price
of the car, the price of each extra piece of equipment, and the cost of
transport to the dealer.

AUTOMOBILE MANUFACTURERS ASSOCIATION   Same as: AMA

AUTONOMOUS INVESTMENT   Investment motivated primarily by technological
innovations in product and/or processes.   See: INDUCED INVESTMENT

AUTO-TRAIN   A system of moving car and passengers by rail, housed separately.   Developed in the United States by Auto-Train, Inc. as an offshoot
of a study made for the Office of High Speed Ground Transportation of
the DOT, it has since December 6, 1971, been operating between Virginia
and Florida by agreement with the Seaboard Coast Line and the Richmond,
Fredricksburg, and Potomac Railroad.   The cars' passengers ride in sleep-
ers or well-appointed coaches.   The concept has been well received.
Countries in Europe have run this service successfully, as have Canada
and Australia.   Tied in with AMTRAK. Additional routes are in the
proposal stage

AVAILABILITY   (1) A time period in BROADCAST ADVERTISING offered to a
SPONSOR.   (2) In OUTDOOR ADVERTISING, units such as SHOWINGS or PAINTED
BULLETINS which a PLANT OPERATOR has open for contract.

AVAILS   Sometimes used in the ADVERTISING field as a short form for
AVAILABILITIES.

AVERAGE   Usually used interchangeably with Arithmetic Mean, which is found by summing a group of numbers and dividing by the number of items. It is important to know the data from which the average is derived before concluding anything from it. Example: one group of RESPONDENTS may rank a product 50% as 100, 50% as 0. Average, 50. Another group may all rank the product at 50. Average also 50, but interpretation very different. (2) Any of the several MEASURES OF CENTRAL TENDENCY.

AVERAGE COST   Total cost divided by the related quantity. See: AVERAGE FIXED COST, AVERAGE REVENUE, AVERAGE VARIABLE COST

AVERAGE DEMURRAGE AGREEMENT   An arrangement between a shipper and a CARRIER whereby the shipper is charged for the time units are held for loading or unloading beyond a certain period, and credited for the time units are released within a certain period. The net DEMURRAGE is usually assessed at the end of each month.

AVERAGE FIXED COST   FIXED COST divided by related quantity. See: AVERAGE COST

AVERAGE QUARTER HOUR PERSONS   The number of persons estimated to have listened at home or away to a station for a minimum of five minutes within a given quarter hour.

AVERAGE REVENUE   Total revenue divided by related quantity. Same as: DEMAND See: AVERAGE REVENUE LINE

AVERAGE REVENUE LINE   Same as: DEMAND CURVE

AVERAGE VARIABLE COST   VARIABLE COST divided by related quantity. See: AVERAGE COST

AVOIDANCE-AVOIDANCE CONFLICT   One of a three-way classification of conflict which may cause decision delays and which may require MOTIVATION to resolve, this one involves a choice between two or more undesirable alternatives. See: APPROACH-APPROACH CONFLICT, APPROACH-AVOIDANCE CONFLICT

A/W   Abbreviation for: actual weight. Used in the TRAFFIC field.

A.W.   Abbreviation for: all water. Used in the TRAFFIC field.

AWA   Abbreviation for: American Warehousemen's Association, the only national trade association for the public merchandise WAREHOUSING industry. Founded in 1891 it is today one of the oldest national trade associations in existence. It publishes a variety of managerial aids to members. Its major objectives are: to promote the general business interests of firms in the industry, to promote high ethical standards, to collect and offer pertinent information, and to conduct efficiency research. It has over 560 member locations in about 200 cities in the U.S.

AWARENESS   (1) In MARKETING RESEARCH, refers to what RESPONDENTS know or do not know about the object of the investigation. (2) The amount of information respondents possess about the PRODUCT in all of its ramifications. See: PERCEPTION

AWO   Abbreviation for: American Waterways Operators, Inc., the national, non-profit trade association of the BARGE and towing INDUSTRY. Since its inception in 1944 the Association has tried to focus in unified action the strength of its members to seek to influence the various agencies of the government having responsibilities that affect the industry. The association publishes a number of books, bulletins, and letters dealing with the current state of the industry.

BACK CARD   An ADVERTISING message on a card attached to the back of a MERCHANDISER, projecting above the merchandiser to present the message at eye level.

BACK-DOOR SELLING   A situation in which a SALESPERSON deliberately bypasses the Purchasing Department and makes a call on personnel in the department which he believes can use his product. Most firms try to discourage this and some have strict rules that all selling must begin with the Purchasing Department. See: KBI

BACK-HAUL ALLOWANCE A reduction in price given to CUSTOMERS making their own pickups at the seller's WAREHOUSE. Such allowances made by a seller using a uniform ZONE PRICING system could have been questioned under a 1973 FTC statement regarding the availability to customers of an option of buying at a true f.o.b. shipping point price. However, on March 28, 1975, the FTC issued the following announcement: "Some unfortunate confusion has arisen as a result of the Commission's use of the term 'true f.o.b. shipping point price.' In fact, no question of unlawful discrimination would arise so long as the f.o.b. price is (1) uniform and (2) available to all customers on a nondiscriminatory basis. No legal requirement exists that the alternative f.o.b. price be of any particular amount or computed in any particular way."

BACK-HAULING The process of moving goods from a WAREHOUSE to a CUSTOMER who is situated between the warehouse and the plant. While it is not practicable to eliminate this entirely because of time limitation on supplying dealers, an effort should be made to locate warehouses where this condition is reduced to a minimum. See: CROSS-HAULING

BACKHAUL TRAFFIC The service an otherwise PRIVATE CARRIER may be permitted to perform as a COMMON CARRIER on the return trip from delivering a shipment to a CUSTOMER. Until March 24, 1978, (the TOTO Purchasing and Supply Co., Inc. case) such service was barred by the ICC under all circumstances. Subsequent to this date private carriers may apply for permission which will be granted if the customary requirements governing common carriers are met.

BACKING ACTIVITIES Those activities in a RETAIL STORE which do not involve direct interaction with CUSTOMERS. When these activities can be done during periods of low customer load by the same persons who do the CLERKING ACTIVITIES, the store is said to be intrinsically backed. When the store is so large that specialized employees must be hired to handle the backing so that it is no longer a free good, the store is said to be extrinsically backed. A common manifestation of this distinction is in the tendency of sales per employee to decline as a store opens BRANCHES.

BACKING UP Denotes the printing of one side of a sheet after the other side has been printed.

BACKLIGHTING A full-color ADVERTISEMENT printed on a translucent sheet rather than on paper stock so that special lighting behind the sheet turns it into a dramatic color slide. Sometimes placed on a bus top.

BACK LOG The total unfilled orders of a firm or INDUSTRY on hand at any one time. The size of the back log is often considered an indicator of the health of the business or industry. Unfilled orders sometimes are used as an ECONOMIC INDICATOR.

BACK ORDER A customer's order which is being held pending the supplier's ability to ship.

BACK-TO-BACK (1) A situation in broadcasting in which two COMMERCIALS follow one another without intervening editorial or entertainment matter. A direct sequence of the two or more. There is a decided tendency to place an ever larger number of commercials back-to-back. (2) Also applied to two programs which follow one another. See: CLUTTER, TRIPLE-SPOTTING

BACK-UP INVENTORY Same as: BUFFER INVENTORY

BACK-UP MERCHANDISE Goods held in reserve at some storage point removed from access to customers but available to personnel for restocking purposes. See: FLOOR STOCK

BACK-UP STOCK   In RETAILING, the amount of merchandise available in WARE-HOUSE or in-store stockroom reasonably close to the selling floor. Important to RUNNERS that this be properly managed.

BACKWARD VERTICAL INTEGRATION   See: VERTICAL INTEGRATION

BAGMAN   The earliest true SALESPERSON, selling from bags of samples at the time of the Industrial Revolution in England, late 18th C. Same as: Manchester Man

BAIT ADVERTISING   An unethical and frequently illegal practice sometimes used by RETAILERS in which a product is advertised at an extremely low price, but when a customer wants to buy the item, the SALES CLERK refuses to sell it, using every persuasive power at his command to disparage it and to switch the customer to a higher-priced item. Often called: Bait-and-Switch Tactics.

BALANCED SCALE   In MARKETING RESEARCH, a query which provides an equal number of favorable and unfavorable category choices. See: SCALES, SCAL-ING

BALANCED SELLING   The action of selling all items in a vendor's LINE in proportion to the sales potential within a given area, or to the profit associated with the items.

BALANCED STOCK   A planned inventory which makes available to customers in proportion to the demand all the merchandise they want in all price ranges.

BALANCED TENANCY   A condition in RETAILING in which an area's type and number of STORES exactly correspond to the mix proper to meet the wants of that area's population. Applied also in a narrower sense to the mix of stores in a large SHOPPING CENTER.

BALANCE OF AREA   The total population of a specific SUBURBAN area found by subtracting the central city's population from the SMSA totals. Same as: Metropolitan Ring

BALANCE OF PAYMENTS   The difference between the flow of money into and the flow of money out of a country. See: BALANCE OF TRADE

BALANCE-OF-STORES RECORD   The central record of a PERPETUAL INVENTORY SYSTEM. Same as: Stock Record, Stores Ledger

BALANCE OF TRADE   The difference between the monetary values of a country's imports and exports. See: BALANCE OF PAYMENTS

BALANCE SHEET EQUATION   See: EQUITY

BALLPARK PRICING   A method of arriving at a price for a PRODUCT by consid-ering the average price level for similar products, selecting a price in this range, and generally working backwards to determine the feasibility of producing at the cost constraint disclosed.

BALOP   Trade shortword for an opaque projector used in television, or the art work prepared for such use.

BANDED PREMIUM   An item offered with another item as a form of factory package. The item is attached to the PACKAGE by a band of paper, tape, or plastic film. Same as: ON-PACK PREMIUM,PACKAGE BAND

BANDWAGON EFFECT   People are buying a product because others are buying it. DEMAND is increased by the desire to conform or to be fashionable. The slope of the DEMAND CURVE may be positive if this effect continues through a situation of rising price of the product. See: LAW OF DEMAND

BANGTAIL   A remittance envelope with merchandise offers printed on the reverse side. Frequently used by high volume mailers such as oil companies and credit-card companies which find it profitable to engage in DIRECT MARKETING of unrelated merchandise. Usually supplied free by the merchandise SYNDICATORS.

BANNER   Any eye-catching device made of paper, cloth, or plastic designed to be hung from its top. Usually rectangular or triangular, it may be taped to a window or wall, or strung overhead or between poles. Most often carries an advertising message, but may be attention-getting only. See: POP ADVERTISING

BANTAM STORE   A small, supermarket type store established to serve the convenience wants of its area. Sales of this type store run about $150,000 annually. They usually stay open odd hours, some all 24 hours. Same as: VEST-POCKET SUPERMARKET

BAR CHART   A pictorial graph in which the bars of varying length are used to show the relative amounts of the variables or characteristics of interest. See: HISTOGRAM, LINE CHART, PICTOGRAM, PIE CHART

BARGAIN SQUARES   Tables arranged in units of four to form squares on which merchandise is offered at reduced prices as a regular practice.

BARGE   A roomy boat, usually flat-bottomed, used chiefly on inland waterways. Essentially the same as LIGHTER. See: DUMB BARGE, LASH

BARNACLE BRAND   A competitive BRAND which enters and attaches itself to the MARKET in the latter stages of the PRODUCT LIFE CYCLE. Brought about by the characteristic of **MONOPOLISTIC COMPETITION** to breed its own competition.

BAROMETRIC PRICE LEADER   The company that generally interprets best the current economic situation in an INDUSTRY and is, therefore, followed in the setting of prices for the industry.

BARRIER   Any person whose job it is in a firm to control the interview time available to a PURCHASING AGENT, personnel manager, or the like, on a general basis. SALESPEOPLE often need to use special skills in order to be allowed to pass "barriers" such as secretaries or receptionists.

BARTER   (1) The process of effecting transactions by the direct exchange of one good or service for another good or service in an agreed-upon ratio. Presently used quite frequently among countries. (2) In BROAD-CASTING, the giving of merchandise by firms to stations in exchange for air time. The merchandise is to be used for prizes. The advertiser usually deals through a barter broker, not directly with the station. Some stations will not so trade.

BARTER BROKER   See: BARTER (2)

BARTER SYNDICATION   A way for a BROADCAST MEDIUM to obtain programming with no outlay of cash. An advertiser creates a program through a syndicator and places the program with a station. The program contains a number of COMMERCIALS for the advertiser with the remaining positions open for the station to sell. In effect, the advertiser is giving the station a program in exchange for his amount of commercial time over that station; hence the BARTER in the term.

BASEMENT STORE   Originally in the basement of a DEPARTMENT STORE, to which bargain merchandise was consigned, the concept has grown to mean any part of the store which specializes in merchandise priced to go easy on the average CONSUMER'S budget. Sometimes called budget stores or budget departments. See: AUTOMATIC BASEMENT

BASE PERIOD   A specific year or time interval used as a reference point for business and economic data. Where an interval of several years is used, the data for those years are averaged and the resulting numbers are adopted as representing 100 in the computation of INDEX NUMBERS. The base period is sometimes erroneously referred to as a "normal" period, which practice can be extremely misleading.

BASIC (1) Abbreviation for: Beginner's All-Purpose Symbolic Instruction Code, a computer language that is one of the easiest programming languages to learn, although not the most powerful for many applications. (2) In RETAILING, a FASHION that has become a constant. (3) A FASHION that persists over long periods of time, perhaps even generations, such as some STYLES of sweaters.

BASIC BUS The contract arrangement in which an ADVERTISER using TRANSIT ADVERTISING has every CAR CARD inside the vehicle. See: TOTAL BUS

BASIC ECONOMIC UTILITIES See: UTILITY

BASIC NETWORK The minimum grouping of stations for which an advertiser must contract in order to use the facilities of a radio or television NETWORK. There is an increasing trend toward ignoring the "basic network" and allowing the advertiser to pick as he chooses. See: KEY STATION

BASIC RATE Same as: ONE-TIME RATE

BASIC STATION A station which an ADVERTISER must include if he wishes to use the NETWORK.

BASIC STOCK Usually applied for STAPLE ITEMS, it is the ASSORTMENT PLAN of items to be kept continuously on hand for a period usually of at least one year. BRAND identification generally is of considerable significance. Much more specific as to name, size, style number, color, etc., than a MODEL STOCK. Includes a list of items to be carried in stock, reorder points, and reorder quantities. Non-staple items can become BASIC while, for FASHION or FAD reasons, they enjoy intensified customer demand.

BASIC STOCK METHOD One of the four primary methods used by RETAILERS for STOCK PLANNING. Most useful where STOCKTURN is less than six times per year, it supplies the beginning-of-the-month (BOM) stock necessary to meet planned sales and end the month with a BASIC STOCK inventory. Using RETAIL prices for convenience, the formula becomes: BOM stock level = planned sales for month + average stock - average monthly sales.

BASIC WEIGHT Refers to the weight of a REAM of paper when cut to the standard size of that class of paper. These sizes are: 17" x 22" for writing papers, 25" x 38" for book papers, and 20" x 26" for cover stock.

BASING POINT The shipping point from which freight is charged to a CUSTOMER regardless of where the shipment actually originates. See: BASING POINT PRICING, PRICE EQUALIZATION

BASING-POINT PRICING A system of PRICING in which the price to the BUYER is the price of the product plus freight from a specified point, regardless of the buyer's or the seller's location. As a rule, this practice is considered illegal when more than one seller is involved, the basing point is common to all, and prices are uniform. See: ZONE PRICING

BASIS Used in trading in commodities to denote the difference between the cash price (SPOT MARKET) and the futures price (FUTURES MARKET) of the RAW MATERIAL involved in a HEDGE. Unusually large changes in the basis may lead to possible large gains or losses which hedging normally almost entirely eliminates.

BASIS GRADES For each commodity traded on a FUTURES contract, the most generally demanded grades for actual delivery against the contract. These are practically defined by the COMMODITY EXCHANGE and are the grades for which prices are quoted. Variations from these grades are usually permitted for delivery at fixed premiums or discounts for defined superior or inferior grades. See: CONTRACT GRADES

BATCH A group of similar documents handled as input in an ADP system during the same RUN.

BATCH CONTROLS   In ADP, techniques for insuring the completeness and the accuracy of BATCHES during movement through the system's processing points. Generally includes counts of items, control totals, and HASH TOTALS.

BATTLEGROUND MAP   Used sometimes to describe a map maintained by a RETAIL-ER to show the locations of the FLAGSHIP STORE, BRANCH STORES, and competitive units within the retailer's TRADING AREA.

BATTLE OF THE BRANDS   Descriptive of the vying between NATIONAL BRANDS and PRIVATE BRANDS to achieve acceptance in the MARKET. Normally, similar or substitutable goods are involved.

BAYESIAN DECISION ANALYSIS   See: FORMAL DECISION ANALYSIS

BBB   Abbreviation for: BETTER BUSINESS BUREAU

BCU   In TELEVISION, abbreviation for: big close-up. See: CU, ECU

BEAR   One who believes prices are likely to decline. See: BULL

BEARER   Same as: DEAD METAL

BEHAVIOR   Refers to the physical acts the subjects of MARKETING RESEARCH have done or are doing, such as their buying habits. MARKETERS are interested in the "why" of behavior and much time, effort, and money are expended in trying to discover the basic causes. See: MOTIVATION

BEHAVIOR THEORIES   See: THEORY OF ACHIEVEMENT MOTIVATION, THEORY OF COG-NITIVE DISSONANCE, THEORY OF ROLE ENACTMENT, THEORY OF SOCIAL CHARACTER

BELIEFS   Very basic ideas about the central values of life, such as moral-ity, to which a person adheres generally out of pure faith or intuition. See: ATTITUDE

BELLY CARGO   The air freight transported in the belly of a passenger plane. See: BELLY FREIGHT

BELLY FREIGHT   The designation given to air freight handled in some type of CONTAINER, on a secured pallet load, or as special-handling large-sized items.

BELLY-TO-BELLY SELLING   Describes the type of selling which takes place when the SALESPERSON personally confronts the PROSPECT or CUSTOMER. Same as: NOSE-TO-NOSE SELLING See: SALESMANSHIP

BELOW-THE-MARKET STRATEGY   Pricing by a RETAILER according to a plan of offering merchandise below usual levels. See: DISCOUNT HOUSE

BENDAY   A method by means of which an engraver applies shaded tints in a choice of various patterns made up of lines or dots to sections of art work that otherwise would be printed only as a solid color or white.

BENEFITS / FEATURES APPROACH TO SELLING   See: FEATURES/BENEFITS APPROACH TO SELLING

BENEFIT SEGMENTATION   One of a four-way classification of the STRATEGIES of SEGMENTATION, this considers the benefits the MARKET derives from PRODUCTS. NEED analysis may be of help. The other three are: PRODUCT USAGE SEGMENTATION, STATE-OF-BEING SEGMENTATION, and STATE-OF-MIND SEG-MENTATION.

BEST TIME AVAILABLE   Same as: ROS

BETA ERROR   Same as: TYPE II ERROR

BETTER BUSINESS BUREAU   A non-profit organization, sometimes called the "Three Bees," whose objectives are to promote ethical business practices in advertising, selling, investments, and fund raising.

b.f.   Abbreviation for: BOLDFACE TYPE

BIAS   In research, anything which prevents the right answer from appearing, or which alters the answer in some way, e.g., an unconscious emphasis by a researcher asking a question of a RESPONDENT.

BID BUYING   The initiation of the procedures which result in BIDDING by prospective sources of supply.

BIDDING   The activity of making an offer of price and other details as solicited by a prospective BUYER who wishes to, or is required by law to, get competitive offers before placing an order. Same as: COMPETITIVE BIDDING   See: BID BUYING

BID PEDDLING   Taking the lowest bid around to potential suppliers to find who will take the contract for even less. In a recent case involving bid clearances through an association, which was ruled to have discouraged competition and promoted price fixing, the California Supreme Court called bid peddling "Open price competition in its purest form." Any buyer who practices this should expect eventual reluctance by suppliers to bid, perhaps even to the point of being left only with the poorest sources.

BIG TICKET MERCHANDISE   In RETAILING, items that are of large price size, and usually large physical size as well.

BIG TICKET SELLING   Same as: MEGASELLING

BILATERAL MONOPOLY   A structure of the MARKET such that MONOPOLY exists on the selling side and MONOPSONY exists on the buying side. See: COUNTERVAILING POWER

BILLBOARD   (1) Same as: POSTER   See: OUTDOOR ADVERTISING   (2) In TELEVISION, consists of the statement, "This portion of the program is brought to you by (name of advertiser), (SLOGAN)." Depending upon the station's policy and the amount of advertising used, the advertiser may get this statement without additional cost to him.

BILL OF LADING   Same as: B/L

BILL OF MATERIALS   A list of every item and its quantity used in a firm's product. The Purchasing Department receives a copy after the manufacturing schedule has been set by production planning, and with items not in stock noted. Effectively used mainly where manufacture is to order rather than to stock. See: REQUISITION

BIMODAL   See: MODE

BIN   (1) A holder for merchandise displayed in bulk. Can be made of a variety of materials, such as wood, wire, heavy paperboard, etc. See: DUMP BIN, JUMBLE BASKET   (2) A materials compartment in a STORAGE area.

BINARY NUMBER   One number in the binary number system, which uses 2 as its base and only the digits zero and one. Modern computers have the ability to translate inputs of numbers, letters, or special symbols into 0-1 combinations of a complex type which can later be retrieved as outputs of the data in desired form.

BIOGENIC NEEDS   Same as: PRIMARY NEEDS

BIPOLAR ADJECTIVES   The pair of adjectives that define the opposite ends of the variations in an ATTITUDE. See: SEMANTIC DIFFERENTIAL SCALE

BIRD DOG   An individual used by a SALESPERSON to point to PROSPECTS. usually someone in a position to know as quickly as anyone about a prospect's requirements. The salesperson has some arrangement agreed about the reward for good information. Not as common as in the past because in many lines of business it is considered unethical to give out pertinent information.

BIRDIEBACK   Same as PIGGYBACK except that planes are used rather than trains. See: FISHYBACK

BIRTH RATE   Defined by the Bureau of the Census as the total number of births during a specified period of time per 1,000 persons in the population. See: CRUDE BIRTHRATE

BIT   A single CHARACTER in a BINARY NUMBER. Modern computers can store millions of memory bits. One must bear in mind that these enter the computer's memory as inputs gathered and fed in by the user of the computer, a painstaking and laborious process. No computer comes with these self-contained, only with the capability of accepting and retaining a certain large number of them for use as directed by the computer's user. Derived from the words binary number and digit.

BIT RATE   In ADP, the speed at which BITS are transmitted, usually expressed in bits-per-second.

B/L   Abbreviation for: Bill of Lading, a document issued by a carrier to a shipper as a receipt and a contract governing the transportation and delivery of goods. If made negotiable, the original carries title to the goods. Distinguish from: WAYBILL

BLACK BOX   Any generally mysterious instrument used in the decision-making process, such as an executive's mind. The business world is constantly probing such units in an attempt to discover the laws or principles which make them effective.

BLACK LIGHT   Ultra-violet lighting that causes phosphorescent paints to glow.

BLANK DUMMY   A full-size, practical mock-up model of a display, without lettering or art.

BLANKET BRAND   Same as: FAMILY BRAND

BLANKET ORDER   A buying agreement to acquire a certain proportion of requirements for repetitive items from one supplier during a given time, usually one year. The terms negotiated will hold for the period. Same as: OPEN-END ORDER, YEARLY ORDER   See: SYSTEMS CONTRACTING

BLANKET PRICING AGREEMENT   A PURCHASING agreement whereby the buyer's orders for anticipated time-period requirements are placed in advance, the seller agreeing to make shipments as wanted at the contract price throughout the contract's duration. See: BLANKET ORDER, INCREMENTAL PRICING AGREEMENT

BLANKET RATE   A common transportation rate covering a large geographic area. Same as: Group Rate

BLANKING   A white paper border surrounding the area of a POSTER devoted to copy. Sets off the poster design within the poster molding.

BLEED   (1) Extending an illustration to one or more edges of a printed page, leaving no margin. Designated as one-, two-, three-, and four-side bleed. (2) Running the design on a POSTER PANEL right to the molding without any BLANKING at top or sides. (3) Unwanted wandering of camera image into wrong areas.

BLIND AD   A WANT AD in which only the job is listed and the identity of the employer is concealed by using a box number for replies, either at the newspaper or at the post office. See: OPEN AD

BLIND BIDDING   A practice in the motion-picture INDUSTRY in which theaters must bid competitively for films that are not yet completed. May be in opposition to our ANTI-TRUST LAWS. See: BLOCK BIDDING, PRODUCT SPLITTING

BLIND CHECK   A system for checking quantities of incoming goods by having the receiving clerk fill in the number received on a form which then goes to the accounting department for comparison with the invoice.

BLIND ITEMS. Mainly unusual items which can carry a higher-than-normal

MARGIN because of special and only occasional appeal to customers who are more interested in filling their requirements than they are in price.

BLIND PRODUCTS   Same as: BLIND ITEMS

BLISTER PACK   A way of packaging in which a preformed hollow of plastic holds merchandise to a card. Used mainly for relatively small items. Same as: Bubble Card

BLOCK   (1) A wood or other material base on which a PLATE is mounted to make it the same height as the type used. (2) In BROADCAST MEDIA, the same period from day to day, or a group of consecutive time periods.

BLOCK BIDDING   A practice in the motion-picture INDUSTRY in which theaters must take films of little popularity in order to get hits. Suspect under our ANTI-TRUST LAWS. See: BLIND BIDDING, PRODUCT SPLITTING

BLOCK BOOKING   A practice in the film distribution INDUSTRY whereby theaters are forced to accept less popular films in order to get more popular or hit films. A 1951 CONSENT ORDER banned this practice. See: FULL-LINE FORCING

BLOCK PROGRAMMING   An attempt by a TV station to hold an AUDIENCE during an entire evening by starting out with a top show and following it with similar type programs.

BLOW-UP   A greatly enlarged reproduction of printed matter, a drawing, or a photograph.

BLUE SKY   Term often applied to designs or thinking that is so extreme that the boundaries of possibility seem to have been exceeded.

BLUR   Same as: ZIP PAN

BMI   Abbreviation for: Broadcast Music, Inc., an organization the major function of which is to provide music to radio and television shows at minimum royalty fees.

BOARDS   A colloquial umbrella term which includes POSTERS and PAINTED BULLETINS.

BODY COPY   The main portions of verbal matter in an advertisement, as distinct from HEADLINES, SUBHEADLINES, etc.

BODY TYPE   The kind of type ordinarily used for reading matter, as distinguished from DISPLAY type which is used for HEADLINES.

B of A   Abbreviation for: Bureau of Advertising, American Newspaper Publishers Association. Its major purpose is to promote the use of daily NEWSPAPERS as ADVERTISING MEDIA.

BOGUS WORK   The work done as required by some union contracts in which compositors reset advertisements for which the publication has received MATS or PLATES. The reset material is not used for printing.

BOILER PLATE   Pages in STEREOTYPE, sometimes including news and advertisements, supplied to small weeklies by news syndicates to help cut the cost of composition. Same as: PATENT INSIDES

BOLDFACE TYPE   A type FACE which prints so that it stands out prominently. Generally has thicker lines than that usually found in the body of copy. In contrast to: LIGHTFACE TYPE

BOLT   A roll of cloth. A usual unit in which cloth is sold, it consists of a stated number of yards of a given width. The number of yards is fairly standard for cloth of a particular type.

BOM   Abbreviation for: beginning-of-the-month. See: BASIC STOCK METHOD

BOM INVENTORY   Inventory counted at the beginning of the month. See: BASIC STOCK METHOD, EOM INVENTORY

BONA FIDE   A Latin phrase meaning "in or with good faith."

BONDED WAREHOUSE   A warehouse under bond to the U. S. Treasury Department, permitted to store goods on which a tax must be paid before they can be sold. See: PUBLIC WAREHOUSE

BOOKING   (1) Orders for merchandise accepted on hand as at a given time. See: BACKLOG (2) The act of taking (accepting) an order for goods to be shipped.

BOOK INVENTORY   When a PERPETUAL INVENTORY SYSTEM is in use, the amount of a particular item which should be on hand according to the record at a certain time. The amount by which the actual count is less than the book inventory is called the shortage; the amount by which the actual count is more is called the overage.

BOOKLET   A LEAFLET expanded to several pages. It allows for much more extensive treatment of a product or institution story than the leaflet, and is usually bound in some way. May be made very impressive. See: BROCHURE

BOOMERANG TECHNIQUE   A SALESMANSHIP technique used in dealing with OBJECTIONS. The SALESPERSON uses the PROSPECT'S statements of reasons for not buying as the basis of the very reason for buying. Also called: Conversion Process

BOOSTER   A colloquialism for a professional shoplifter.

BORAX GOODS   Shoddy merchandise made so poorly that price appeal may be the determining factor inducing purchase.

BORDER   A line or elaborate design that surrounds an ADVERTISEMENT. Sometimes verbal material such as the firm's name or SLOGAN is repeated.

BOTTLE COLLAR   A cardboard display designed to fit around the neck of a bottle and to carry an advertising message.

BOTTLE GLORIFIER   A display designed to fit on a bottle, or to serve as a background for a bottle with a cutout area or recess to hold the bottle in place.

BOTTLE TOPPER   Essentially the same as: BOTTLE COLLAR

BOTTOM MANAGEMENT   Essentially equivalent to the sum of the supervisory positions in the lower ECHELONS of the firm. See: MIDDLE MANAGEMENT, TOP MANAGEMENT

BOTTOM-UP APPROACH   Same as: ASSORTMENT PLAN See: BALANCED STOCK

BOTTOM UP TECHNIQUE   A budgeting technique in RETAILING in which the budgeter starts with an estimate of the spending required to supply each CLASSIFICATION, finally arriving at a total for the department, and ultimately for the FIRM. See: OPEN-TO-BUY, TOP DOWN TECHNIQUE

BOUNCE-BACK   An additional offer sent with a SELF-LIQUIDATOR. Sometimes several related items are offered. May be effective for increasing total sales.

BOUTIQUE   (1) A small shop, whether independent or a special area within a larger store. Recently used to designate one rather specialized in some way, such as high fashion or mod. (2) A relatively new development in the ADVERTISING field, it is a small, independent ADVERTISING AGENCY which specializes in only one aspect of advertising, such as MEDIA purchasing, usually on a fee basis.

BOX   A printed message, or a portion thereof, set off from the rest of the COPY by a BORDER.

BOX STORE   Same as: WAREHOUSE STORE

BOX-TOP OFFER   An offer of a PREMIUM which requires the return of the package top or a portion of it as proof of purchase.

BPA   Abbreviation for: Business Publications Audit of Circulations, an auditing organization for business publications primarily concerned with CONTROLLED CIRCULATION.

BPAA   Abbreviation for: Business and Professional Advertisers Association, formerly the Association of Industrial Advertisers. See: AIA (1)

BPI   Abbreviation for: BUYING-POWER INDEX

BPQ   Abbreviation for: BUYING-POWER QUOTA

BPX   Abbreviation for: BUS PACKAGE EXPRESS

BRANCH HOUSE   Same as: MANUFACTURER'S SALES BRANCH

BRANCH OFFICE   See: MANUFACTURER'S SALES BRANCH, MANUFACTURER'S SALES OFFICE

BRANCH STORE   An arm of a CENTRAL BUSINESS DISTRICT store extended into another area of the MARKET.

BRAND   A word, mark, symbol, device, or a combination of these used to identify some product or service. See: BARNACLE BRAND, FAMILY BRAND, FIGHTING BRAND, INDIVIDUAL BRAND, NATIONAL BRAND, PRIVATE BRAND, PRODUCT TRADEMARK

BRAND CONSCIOUSNESS   The degree of AWARENESS that CONSUMERS or INDUSTRIAL USERS have of a particular BRAND. See: BRAND IMAGE, BRAND INSISTENCE, BRAND LOYALTY

BRAND EXTENSION   A competitive TACTIC which involves applying a market-accepted BRAND to other company products provided doing so will not confuse existing CUSTOMERS or tend to lessen the original image of PRODUCT or BRAND. Often most effective in conjunction with other tactics. See: BLANKET BRAND

BRAND IMAGE   How people in the MARKET perceive the identifying marks of the product, rather than the characteristics of the product itself. Thus, the BRAND may convey an impression of economy, status, high value, etc. Recognizing this aspect, many marketers engage in considerable study before deciding on a name for a product which they intend to use as a brand. See: SYMBOL   Compare with: PRODUCT IMAGE

BRAND INSISTENCE   BRAND LOYALTY at the extreme. The user will accept no substitute. See: SPECIALTY GOOD

BRAND LABEL   A simple LABEL which tells little more than the BRAND NAME of the product, the maker, and such other minimum information required by law.

BRAND LOYALTY   The faithfulness displayed by a user toward a BRAND, measured by relative length of time or regularity of the item's use. It is known that much switching occurs. A considerable amount of research is devoted to finding the reasons for and the volume of the switches. See: BRAND SWITCHING, BRAND INSISTENCE

BRAND MANAGER   Essentially the same as: PRODUCT MANAGER

BRAND NAME   Often used when referring to words, numbers, or initials used as a TRADEMARK of a product. Usually means the vocalizable portion of a trademark.

BRAND NAMES FOUNDATION   A non-profit association of persons interested in promoting awareness of BRANDS in buying.

BRAND RATING INDEX   Same as: BRI

BRAND SWITCHING   The decision of a user to select from among the available products or services of like type, one different from that which he bought the last time. See: BRAND LOYALTY

BREAD-AND-BUTTER ASSORTMENTS   Same as: NEVER-OUT LIST

BREADTH OF ASSORTMENT   Same as: WIDTH OF ASSORTMENT

BREADTH OF LINE   The extent of the VARIETY and/or ASSORTMENT of items produced or bought for resale. The range among manufacturers and MIDDLE-MEN extends from a few items to many thousands. See: LINE

BREAK   A quick, extensive decline in the price of a commodity. See: BULGE

BREAK-DOWN APPROACH   A way of allocating the ADVERTISING budget to LINES of offerings. It begins with a sum total budget; this is divided by the one in charge of PROMOTION in conference with the various persons responsible for the lines. See: BUILD-UP APPROACH

BREAK-EVEN ANALYSIS   The activity which usually results in a BREAK-EVEN CHART. If calculated in units, the BREAK-EVEN POINT is found by dividing total FIXED COST by the excess of price over AVERAGE VARIABLE COST.

BREAK-EVEN CHART   A projection, based on FIXED COSTS and VARIABLE COST elements, of the unit volumes required at various selected selling prices for the firm just to cover all of the costs associated with a PRODUCT. Often includes, also, the relative profit or loss position for the selling prices at various selected unit volumes.

BREAK-EVEN POINT   The volume level at which a firm's revenue exactly covers total FIXED and VARIABLE COSTS, given a specific price situation. The volume at which the FIRM has neither profit nor loss.

BREAKING BULK   (1) The physical act of dividing a large, homogeneous lot into small lots. (2) Unloading and distributing all or a portion of the contents of a freight vehicle. See: ASSORTING

BRI   Abbreviation for: Brand Rating Index, an organization which has conducted since 1962 annual surveys with CONSUMERS in their own homes covering their purchases of hundreds of specific products and BRANDS, their MEDIA exposure, and their DEMOGRAPHICS. Its reports to its many clients classify the product usage by heavy, moderate, and light users; teenage boys and girls; switching and loyal users; and consumer motivations. In general, the reports are constructed to show the percent difference between the level in the total population and the level for that particular group or factor shown. Its services are constantly being expanded as the data collection grows.

BRIDAL REGISTRY   In RETAILING, a system which provides for the listing of the bride-to-be's selection of china, linens, and other patterns, and maintains a record of what has already been purchased as gifts so that duplication can be avoided. The STORE favored with the specific choices usually becomes the source of the bulk of the bridal gifts.

BRIDGE   In BROADCAST MEDIA, the transition from one scene to another by means of sound effects, music, or various VISUALS.

BROADCAST   Program transmission by means of waves which travel through the air or ground, such as in radio and television. (2) The sending of letters, bulletins, and the like, to all DEALERS at the same time.

BROADCAST DISTRIBUTION   Same as: INTENSIVE DISTRIBUTION

BROADCAST MUSIC INC   Same as: BMI

BROAD-LINE STRATEGY   The offering by a business of a large number of variations of a product. See: LIMITED-LINE STRATEGY

BROAD MARKET   A situation in a MARKET in which there are included a large numer of segments of widely differing characteristics. May also refer to a market of great geographical size. See: NARROW MARKET

BROADSIDE   A giant FOLDER, often used as a SELF-MAILER.

BROCHURE   An elaborate or impressive BOOKLET.

BROKEN LOT   A quantity of goods offered for sale which is smaller than that normally considered a unit of sale. See: JOB LOT

BROKER   A FUNCTIONAL MIDDLEMAN whose distinguishing features are: his services to a PRINCIPAL are intermittent, he has limited authority to make terms, and he finances his principal only under unusual circumstances. He may represent either the buyer or the seller. Sometimes called: MERCHANDISE BROKER   Infrequently misapplied to a MERCHANT.

BROKERAGE   A charge, sometimes in the form of a commission, made by a FUNCTIONAL MIDDLEMAN for bringing buyer and seller together. Usually applied to the side for whom the middleman is working, sometimes both buyer and seller pay.

BROKERAGE FEE Same as: BROKERAGE

BROOD HEN AND CHICK METHOD   A system of treating BRANCH STORES in RETAILING from a centrally controlled organization policy, much as CHAINS are operated, but with firmer controls on MERCHANDISING and general store operations.

BROOD HEN CONCEPT   The RETAIL buyer at the parent store keeps in close touch with the BRANCHES, receives requests for merchandise and acts on them at his discretion. Merchandise comes to the parent store from sources; after processing it is sent to the branches.

BROWN GOODS   Household appliances having the characteristics of furniture, particularly as to finish, e.g., television sets, stereos, etc.

BTA   Abbreviation for: Best Times Available. Same as: ROS

BUBBLE CARD   Same as: BLISTER PACK

BUDGET   Any projection or plan of receipts and expenditures over a given period of time. See: CASH BUDGET, MERCHANDISE BUDGET, SALES BUDGET

BUDGET-BOOK SALE   The customer contracts for a certain amount to be paid back on a regular basis with a small carrying charge. The customer is given a book containing coupons in various denominations aggregating the contracted amount. These coupons can then be used as cash in any department in the store.

BUDGET DEPARTMENT   See: BASEMENT STORE

BUDGET EFFECT   An attribute possessed by a commodity which makes it possible to cause a transfer of a CONSUMER'S patronage to the source offering it because the consumer is convinced he can in so doing buy more with the same income. See: TRANSFER EFFECT

BUDGET STORE   See: BASEMENT STORE

BUFFER INVENTORY   An amount of stock kept on hand to avoid, or at least minimize, the risk of running out due to delivery failure, unanticipated supplier problems, and other contingencies. Same as: Back-Up Inventory

BUILD-UP APPROACH   A way of allocating the ADVERTISING budget to LINES of offerings. It begins with requests for advertising budgets from those responsible for the lines. These are adjusted as necessary by the one in charge of PROMOTION and then combined to produce a total. See: BREAK-DOWN APPROACH

BULGE   A quick advance in the price of a commodity. See: BREAK

BULK BREAKING   Same as: BREAKING BULK

BULK CHECKING   A way of verifying the receipt of goods by comparing the carton markings with the packing list or invoice. When items are shipped in standard-quantity packages and the source is reliable, it is usually not worth the time to open each package for complete verification of the contents.

BULK DISCOUNT   A schedule of payment for ADVERTISING set by a publisher, in which the charge per unit of space or time decreases as the total units accumulate to specified amounts. See: FLAT RATE, FREQUENCY DISCOUNT

BULK DISTRIBUTION AUDIT   See: CCAB

BULK FREIGHT   Same as: BULK GOODS

BULK GOODS   Items which are sold and delivered in loose form, such as coal, gravel, grain. They generally have the common quality of flowability, so that they may be loaded and unloaded by either gravity or blower devices. Sometimes applied to any large shipment of one item.

BULKING   Essentially the same as ASSEMBLY and the opposite of BREAKING BULK.

BULK PACKAGING AND CONTAINERIZATION INSTITUTE   Same as: The Containerization Institute

BULK PLANT   A secondary storage facility which receives product from a refinery or TERMINAL and delivers principally by bulk wagon to customers in its area. It may be operated on a salary, commission or jobber basis.

BULL   One who believes prices are likely to rise. See: BEAR

BULLDOG EDITION   That edition of a morning newspaper that is printed on the preceding evening and sent to out-of-town readers on night trains or planes.

BUNDLE OF BENEFITS CONCEPT   The idea that CONSUMERS or INDUSTRIAL USERS do not buy things as such, but rather buy the benefits that those things are expected to provide. Without the expected benefits the things would be meaningless and lack the power to attract those who would own them. See: SALESMANSHIP

BUNDLE OF SERVICES CONCEPT   An argument favoring leasing rather than owning of equipment in the INDUSTRIAL GOODS MARKET based on the consideration that the purchase of a machine can be thought of as the purchase of the number of yearly services that the machine is expected to last. The costs thus calculated can be compared with the yearly cost of the lease on a present value basis.

BUREAU FOR INTERNATIONAL REGISTRATION OF TRADEMARKS   See: MADRID CONVENTION

BUREAU OF ADVERTISING   Same as: B of A

BURIED OFFER   Same as: HIDDEN OFFER

BURIED POSITION   That position on a publication page in which the advertisement is surrounded by other advertisements or is a bottom corner inside of a page with advertisements at top and side. A generally poor position for an advertisement.

BUSHELING   Applied to the alteration of garments after purchasing by a customer. The term is gradually fading out of use.

BUSINESS AND PROFESSIONAL ADVERTISERS ASSOCIATION   Same as: BPAA

BUSINESS CONSUMER   A misnomer except in the economic sense of one engaged in CONSUMPTION. See: CONSUMER

BUSINESS CYCLE   Changes which take place in business conditions with some rhythm over a period of time. Usually, the phases of the cycle are identified as depression, when GNP is low and unemployment is high, also called trough; recovery, the start of betterment in the BUSINESS INDICATORS, also called upturn, revival, expansion; prosperity, when production is approach-

ing capacity and enployment full; <u>peak</u>, at which DEMAND outruns SUPPLY
and INFLATION accelerates; <u>crisis</u>, the beginning of a downturn in production which unchecked leads to <u>decline</u>, which if also unchecked goes down
to depression. Much has been learned over the past forty years about
man aging the economy, but no precise formula has been developed. The
many theories put forward to explain the cycle have all proved lacking
in one way or another.

BUSINESS CYCLE DEVELOPMENTS   A monthly publication of the Bureau of the
Census. It contains many indicators of business activity used in FORE-
CASTING, graphed on BUSINESS CYCLE timing as a background. See:
BUSINESS INDICATOR

BUSINESS DEVELOPMENT   (1) Most frequently, same as: RECIPROCITY. (2) Sometimes used to indicate the activity at the top echelons of a firm which
aims to seek out and extend the use of its products into other industries.

BUSINESS ETHIC   A moral practice that puts personal gain foremost among
other values. See: SOCIAL ETHIC

BUSINESS FILMS   See: SPONSORED FILMS

BUSINESS GIFT   A gift to a customer or other business friend as an expression of appreciation. Unless the gift is of nominal value, a serious
question may arise as to the propriety of accepting it, or even of offering it. See: COMMERCIAL BRIBERY

BUSINESS INDICATOR   A series of data related to a particular aspect of business activity, such as sensitive commodity prices, that gives insight into
general economic and business conditions. Indicators are usually classified as LEADING INDICATORS if they usually reach their PEAKS or TROUGHS
before those in aggregate economic activity as measured by the ROUGHLY
COINCIDENT INDICATORS, which move up or down almost together with aggregate economic activity; and LAGGING INDICATORS, which usually reach turning points after aggregate economic activity has turned. These are all
determined by the NBER. See: BUSINESS CYCLE

BUSINESS PUBLICATIONS AUDIT OF CIRCULATIONS   Same as: BPA

BUSINESS STATISTICS   Published biennially by the Department of Commerce, it
provides an historical record of the data series that appear monthly in
the SURVEY OF CURRENT BUSINESS.

BUSORAMA   TRANSIT ADVERTISING illuminated panels carried on top of buses
and backlighted with fluorescent tubes. They run the length way of the
bus.

BUS PACKAGE EXPRESS   A formalized service for sending small packages via
scheduled buses. Many buses have a considerable amount of unused baggage
space which can be devoted to this. Delivery is quick over the medium
distance. Same as: BPX

BUY-AND-SELL TRANSPORT   An activity in which a firm operating trucks as
furtherance of its business, uses those trucks to transport goods to
others as a way of filling the truck and obtaining revenue for the return
trip, or operating a system whereby the truckload is bought and resold to
others. This activity is not permitted under present law. The ICC has
recently confirmed this interpretation in a case where three paving firms
were transporting asphalt from major oil companies to users. It was held
that they were engaging in for-hire transport in interstate commerce
without appropriate ICC authority. See: PRIMARY BUSINESS TEST

BUY-BACK   In international trade, an agreement by which the seller of
goods agrees to accept as partial or full payment items made by or from
the goods originally sold. See: COMPENSATION DEAL, COUNTERPURCHASE

BUYER   (1) In a DEPARTMENT STORE, the key person who is really a department head responsible in his department for buying, selling, pricing,

and controlling his lines of goods, as well as managing his area and his personnel. (2) In an individual firm, usually equivalent to purchasing agent, although an assistant may be so designated for a specific material or class of materials. (3) In a multi-unit RETAILING business, a person responsible for buying certain goods for resale. Separated from the SELLING function.

BUYER'S CALL   Same as: CALL SALE

BUYER'S MARKET   A condition of the MARKET in which BUYERS are able to bargain and to be selective because there is an over-abundance of goods available in relation to DEMAND. See: SELLER'S MARKET

BUYER'S SURPLUS   The difference between what a buyer pays for an item and the amount more he would be willing to pay for it. A broader term than CONSUMER'S SURPLUS because it includes INDUSTRIAL USERS.

BUYER'S WHEEL   A circular device usually made of cardboard, designed to give quick profit calculations based on cost and selling price. The revolving part of the device acts as a type of slide rule. Being small enough to carry in a pocket, it is a valuable aid in the MARKET.

BUYING   (1) A MARKETING FUNCTION devoted to the efficient acquisition of the materials and services needed for the operation of a business. Includes the determination of the suitability of goods, the proper price, an adequate source, and economic order and inventory quantities. Assists in the creation of POSSESSION UTILITY. (2) Although the CONSUMER usually does not analyze as painstakingly as the INDUSTRIAL USER, he always has a reason valid to him for making his decision, e.g., to reach a goal, solve a problem, or otherwise achieve some personal satisfaction.

BUYING BY DESCRIPTION   Purchase from a verbal and/or visual picture of the product. May be from the catalog of the seller or from a set of specification developed by the BUYER. To use this method satisfactorily, the buyer must have full confidence in the seller's business honesty.

BUYING BY INSPECTION   Purchase after examination of the actual products to be bought.

BUYING BY SAMPLE   Purchase after examination of a representative piece or portion of the good. Applicable where the product is reasonably uniform because of standardized GRADING or manufacture.

BUYING CALENDAR   A chronological plan of a BUYER'S activities for a particular season of a given number of months. Provides for anticipation of special selling events, especially in RETAILING.

BUYING COMMITTEE   A group of persons given the authority to accept or reject new items proposed for addition to stock, and to review the record of items being handled to decide the fate of those items for the FIRM. Common in firms such as SUPERMARKETS where exposure space is critical and CUSTOMER acceptance changeable.

BUYING DIRECT   Acquisition of merchandise or materials from the producer rather than from a MIDDLEMAN. Because there are many factors involved in final satisfaction from a purchase, this TRADE CHANNEL is not necessarily the most desirable one. See: DIRECT CHANNEL

BUYING DISTRIBUTION   A concept related to CHANNELS OF DISTRIBUTION which emphasizes that the price paid (profit margins built into the price structure) to gain channel support must reflect not only the MARKETING job expected of the channel, but also the competitive environment in which the channel operates.

BUYING ERROR   Especially in RETAILING, the failure to match purchases with DEMAND, necessitating a MARKDOWN in order to move the merchandise. See: PRICING ERROR, SELLING ERROR

BUYING INFLUENCE   See: MULTIPLE BUYING INFLUENCE

BUYING OFF THE PEG   An older term in RETAILING that denoted merchandise bought to be taken away with the buyer. Essentially the same as: TAKE TRANSACTION

BUYING POWER   (1) The ability of a CONSUMER to acquire goods and services. See: DISPOSABLE INCOME   (2) The capacity of a FIRM to purchase in large quantities and thereby obtain concession in price, deliveries, packaging, and other marketing-related advantages. See: MARKET POWER

BUYING-POWER INDEX   A relative measure of the effective buying power of a segment of the MARKET, published annually by Sales & Marketing Management magazine. It provides an approximate value of the ability of an area to purchase CONSUMER GOODS. For example, if area A has a BPI of .012, its market potential is double that of area B which has a BPI of .006. Most applicable to mass products sold at popular prices. Other products need more discriminating factors, the farther they are from the MASS MARKET. See: SURVEY OF BUYING POWER

BUYING-POWER QUOTA   Same as: BUYING-POWER INDEX

BYTE   Indicates consecutive BITS in a measurable pattern. Such a sequence may be operated upon by the computer as a unit of data.

CAAAA   See: NAMA

CAAB   Abbreviation for: Canadian Advertising Advisory Board, a non-profit organization representing all phases of the ADVERTISING industry in Canada. Its main objectives are to develop, promote, and encourage adherence to approved national advertising standards and practices, including the "Canadian Code of Advertising Standards;" to develop appropriate educational and training programs in the hope of improving advertising effectiveness; to sponsor and support research in advertising; to improve public awareness of the contributions of advertising to Canada's economic and social well-being; and in general to serve the common interests of the Canadian advertising industry.

CAB   Abbreviation for: Civil Aeronautics Board, the federal agency vested with the responsibility for regulating air commerce and air carriers in the United States.

CABLECASTING   A term sometimes applied to the programming originated by the CATV operator other than the signals picked up by the system.

CACM   Abbreviation for: CENTRAL AMERICAN COMMON MARKET

CALL PURCHASE   A purchase of a commodity of a specified quality under a contract providing for the seller to choose a day in the future on which the price in the contract will be fixed on the basis of a stipulated number of POINTS above or below the price of a designated FUTURE on that chosen day. Same as: Seller's Call See: CALL SALE

CALL REPORT   A SALESPERSON'S report to a supervisor of calls made to PROSPECTS OR CUSTOMERS during a given time or in a specific MARKET. A recent study indicates that although over half of the sales managers responding used call reports and were reasonably well satisfied that they were receiving useful data, the indicated areas of importance were very diverse. Inspired by data collecting methods some consider superior to call reports, which now take between 10 and 20 hours of a salesperson's time per week to complete, a considerable amount of debate is emerging as to the reality of the values to be derived from the call report in comparison to benefits from other uses of salespersons' time and from better morale.

CALL SALE   A sale of a commodity of specified quality under a contract providing for the buyer to choose a day in the future on which the price in the contract will be fixed on the basis of a stipulated number of POINTS above or below the price of a designated FUTURE on that chosen day. Same as: Buyer's Call See: CALL PURCHASE

CALL SYSTEM   A method used in RETAILING areas where the SALESPERSON's compensation is based at least in some measure on the amount of business he completes. Each salesperson is given an equal chance to wait on PROSPECTS or CUSTOMERS. Very frequently used for major appliances, furniture, cars.

CAMERALISM   Same as: KAMERALISM

CAMERA READY   COPY that is prepared so that without further processing it can be used to create plates needed for OFFSET printing. Abbreviated: CR

CAM FOUNDATION   Abbreviation for: Communication Advertising and Marketing Education Foundation, Limited, an organization established in England to provide for that country a unified examining body setting standards of vocational education in the entire range of its title and to encourage the offering of courses and other facilities for improving the professional knowledge of its individual members. It was incorporated in 1969 as an educational charity, an amalgamation of the already existing educational operations of a number of well-known associations. Since 1975 it has offered various diplomas achieved by examination in defined areas.

CAMPAIGN   Same as: ADVERTISING CAMPAIGN

CAMPAIGN PLAN   A series of mailings of a variety of pieces over a period of weeks, all designed to arouse interest in a coming event, such as the opening of a new facility or the introduction of an innovation. This type of plan ends with a final mailing presenting the announcement for which interest and curiosity have been built. Plans of this sort must be of duration not so long as to create boredom, since that would negate the intent of creating suspense. Sometimes called, as applicable, a "Teaser Campaign." See: DIRECT MAIL ADVERTISING

CANADIAN ADVERTISING AND SALES ASSOCIATION   Same as: CASA

CANADIAN ADVERTISING ADVISORY BOARD   Same as: CAAB

CANADIAN BUSINESS PRESS   Same as: CBP

CANADIAN CIRCULATIONS AUDIT BOARD   Same as: CCAB

CANADIAN DAILY NEWSPAPER PUBLISHERS ASSOCIATION   Same as: CDNPA

CANADIAN INDUSTRIAL TRAFFIC LEAGUE   Same as: CITL

CANALIZATION   In SELLING, the building by a SALESPERSON or ADVERTISER on some association, fear, or bit of information possessed by a PROSPECT or CUSTOMER and thereby bringing about a dramatic behavior change.

C & C   Abbreviation for: Coal and coke. Used in the TRAFFIC field.

C & F   Abbreviation for: cost and freight. Part of TERMS OF SALE, this indicates that the seller will pay freight charges to a destination, but not insurance. See: CIF

CANNED PRESENTATION   A sales talk to be memorized and rehearsed for presentation word for word exactly as written. Especially useful where many PROSPECTS must be approached under similar circumstances, such as house-to-house selling. See: VARIABLE PRESENTATION

CANNED SALES PRESENTATION   Same as: CANNED PRESENTATION

CANNED SALES TALK   Same as: CANNED PRESENTATION

CANNIBALIZING A MARKET   What happens when a new form of a product, instead of producing new business from MARKET SEGMENTS not before reached, eats into the volume already enjoyed from the existing product, so that no sales increase occurs. This did occur with Maxwell House Instant Coffee when Maxim Instant was introduced, until steps were taken to correct it.

CANONICAL CORRELATION ANALYSIS   A multivariate technique not yet used extensively in MARKETING RESEARCH, it can determine the relationships among a number of DEPENDENT VARIABLES and a number of INDEPENDENT VARIABLES treated as sets. Its use can free the investigator from having to pick a single criterion variable from two or more possible criterion variables, or arbitrarily weighting the set of criterion variables in order to fit the problem into the standard format of MULTIPLE CORRELA- TION analysis. PARAMETRIC or NONPARAMETRIC.

CANVASSING   Same as: COLD CANVASSING

CAPABILITY SURVEY   Used in PURCHASING to denote an inspection of a pros- pective VENDOR'S entire operation to answer key questions regarding engi- neering ability, level of quality control, amount of equipment, capacity to manage and finance, and any other area considered important to the choice of the source of supply. Generally involves a visit by the pur- chasing officer or team to the vendor's plant.

CAPACITY   Generally, the productive potential of a FIRM, INDUSTRY, or economy. See: CAPACITY UTILIZATION RATE, FULL-CAPACITY OUTPUT, PREFERRED OPERATING RATE

CAPACITY UTILIZATION RATE   Ratio of actual output to FULL-CAPACITY OUTPUT of a FIRM, INDUSTRY, or economy. Essentially, the proportion of CAPACITY in actual use.

CAPITAL   (1) Produced goods withheld from CONSUMPTION for purposes of fur- ther PRODUCTION. (2) The owner's equity in a business. (3) The owner's investment in a business. (4) All economic goods in existence at a certain time which produce INCOME in a society.

CAPITAL GOODS   All types of GOODS of relatively long life used to produce other products. Includes manufacturing plants, INSTALLATIONS, and ACCESSORY EQUIPMENT. Same as: CAPITAL-INVESTMENT GOODS See: CAPITAL

CAPITAL INTENSIVE INDUSTRY   An INDUSTRY in which the requirement of plant and equipment is large in relation to the requirement for labor input. Petroleum refining, chemicals, and paper making are such industries. See: LABOR INTENSIVE INDUSTRY

CAPITAL-INVESTMENT GOODS   Same as: CAPITAL GOODS See: CAPITAL

CAPS   Short form for: capital letters, or UPPERCASE letters in contrast to LOWERCASE letters.

CAPTION   (1) Explanatory words accompanying an illustration. (2) The head- ing of a page, section, or chapter. See: LEGEND

CAPTIVE ITEMS   Those products made by the firm, or by a firm which is vertically integrated.

CAPTIVE MARKET   The customers for a PRODUCT or service who have but one source of supply, there being no reasonable alternatives. Because this may be considered a MONOPOLY situation, government agencies are sometimes given regulatory powers as, for example, with respect to public utili- ties. The term is often applied to shops located in airports, hotels, railroad stations, college centers, and the like, where anyone who requires an available item would find it impractical to seek to compare alternate sources of supply.

CAPTIVE ROTARY   A set of OUTDOOR ADVERTISING locations used mainly for one advertiser with several different products to expose to the MARKET.

CAR ALLOWANCE PLAN   See: RUNZHEIMER PLAN

CAR CARD   A large card on which an advertising message is displayed in sub- way trains, buses and commuter trains. See: TRANSIT ADVERTISING

CARD FIELD   A set of card columns of a standard card used in ADP. The same set of columns (same field) is usually used on successive cards to store similar data. The cards supply the input data for whatever calculations or manipulations the machines are directed to perform within the scope of their capabilities.

CARGO   Product in the process of being moved by a TRANSPORTATION facility.

CARGO & MAIL CONFERENCE   See: NATC

CARGO BUYER   A purchaser who takes delivery in full shipload quantities.

CARGO DISTRIBUTOR   Same as: TERMINAL OPERATOR

CARGO FLIGHT   An aircraft flight exclusively to move freight. See: COMBINATION FLIGHT

CARGO MEASUREMENT   See: CARGO TONNAGE

CARGO TONNAGE   In the United States CARGO may be charged for by weight using either the ton of 2,000 pounds or the British long ton of 2,240 pounds. In countries using the metric system the weight ton is 2,204.62 pounds. Or, measurement may be used, considering a ton equal to 40 cubic feet (in some instances a larger number). Most ocean freight is taken at weight or measurement (W/M) at ship's option.

CARGO WEIGHT   See: CARGO TONNAGE

CARIBBEAN COMMUNITY   See: CARIFTA

CARIBBEAN FREE TRADE ASSOCIATION   See: CARIFTA

CARICOM   See: CARIFTA

CARIFTA   Abbreviation for: Caribbean Free Trade Association formed in 1968 by Jamaica, Montserrat, Trinidad and Tobago to promote and expand trade within the region. In 1972 the Association became the Caribbean Community with the objectives of establishing a common market among the members, expanding and integrating members' economic activities, and achieving greater economic independence in dealing with nations outside the group. Now called the Caribbean Common Market, abbreviated CARICOM, and includes Barbados, Guyana, Jamaica, Trinidad-Tobago.

CARLOAD   (1) The quantity or weight of freight required to qualify for the carload rate. (2) A freight car loaded to its carrying capacity. See: TRUCKLOAD

CARLOADINGS   The number of railroad freight cars loaded in a period. Frequently used as a measure of business activity.

CAR-LOT WHOLESALER   A MERCHANT MIDDLEMAN whose main function is to accept carload shipments of fruits and vegetables and then to divide the shipments into smaller lots for sale to JOBBERS and to CHAIN STORE buyers.

CARNET   A document issued by the International Road Transport Union of Geneva, Switzerland, and made available in the United States through the EIA, the carnet permits freight shipments to cross international boundaries without customs inspections at intermediate points. The issuing agent guarantees customs duties, penalties, fees and other charges will be paid at destination, and that the shipment is what it claims to be. Developed in 1949 by the United Nations Economic Commission to help restore commerce in Europe, it is designed primarily for trucking operations. The carnet is sold only to CARRIERS, never to shippers.

CARRIAGE TRADE   An expression carried over from times gone by, it refers to a class of wealthy CUSTOMERS who expect and get special services for which they seem willing to pay.

CARRIER   A general designation for a FIRM the business of which at least in part is to transport goods from one place to another. See: ASSEMBLY SERVICE, CARROUSEL TRUCK, COMMON CARRIER, CONSIGNEE, CONSIGNOR, CONTRACT CARRIER, PRIVATE CARRIER

CARROUSEL TRUCK   A concept of truck loading using shipment cages any one

of which the driver can bring at will to the tail gate. In the developmental stage still, but the many advantages are prompting a concentrated
effort toward solving mechanical problems and designing conversion kits
to equip existing trucks.

CARRY-OUT   Same as: TAKE-WITH TRANSACTION

CARRY-OVER   Same as: HOLD-OVER AUDIENCE

CARRYOVER EFFECTS   In general the influence that is exerted on the sales
of future periods by a MARKETING expenditure today. There is evidence
enough to support a conclusion that an expenditure such as for a short
ADVERTISING CAMPAIGN may have a continuing effect indefinitely. The
strength of the effect is dependent on so many uncontrollable variables
that it is presently not predictable. Much effort is being expended
continually in an attempt to develop a good model. See: HOLDOVER EFFECT,
DELAYED RESPONSE EFFECT

CARTAGE   Generally applied to the charge made for hauling freight by motor
vehicle (except train) over land. Usually medium to long distance. See:
DRAYAGE

CARTEL   The most organized phase of OLIGOPOLY. Pricing, MARKET SHARES,
and output levels are determined centrally. An American marketer may not
legally enter into a cartel in the domestic market because of our anti-
trust legislation, but he is exempt as to such activity in the international markets.

CART WRAP   A printed advertising message made of paper, designed to go
around shopping carts. By the nature of user habits, this type of device
is quite perishable.

CASA   Abbreviation for: Canadian Advertising and Sales Association, an
association of clubs working for sound advertising and selling in Canada.

CASE DIVIDER   A strip of material arranged to fit in display cases or food
freezers in STORES, which besides helping the RETAILER to organize his
display, carries an ADVERTISING message to the CUSTOMER.

CASE STRIP   Same as: SHELF STRIP

CASE WRAP AROUND. An elaborate SALES PROMOTION piece something like a long
BANNER, designed to go around a case of merchandise used as the base of
a special display.

CASH-AND-CARRY WHOLESALER   A WHOLESALER exhibiting the following features:
CUSTOMERS call to pick up the merchandise, cash is required with the purchase, SALESPERSONS are not widely used to call on PROSPECTS.

CASH BUDGET   A projection of the cash requirements a firm will have to
meet in each of successive time periods. Will indicate at what points
the firm will need to borrow, because a cash budget reflects buying and
selling forecasts. See: PURCHASE BUDGET, SALES BUDGET

CASH COMMODITY   Same as: SPOT COMMODITY

CASH DISCOUNT   An allowance given by a seller to a buyer provided the invoice is paid within the time limits specified in the TERMS OF SALE. Its
original purpose was to induce quicker payment of the invoice. In RETAIL-
ING, where competition forces low MARGINS, firms often find the cash discount is the difference between net profit or loss, so cannot afford not
to take it.

CASH FLOW   The change in cash position during a given period resulting
from cash receipts and disbursements for that period. In general, it is
equivalent to net profit plus all non-cash charges such as depreciation.

CASH MARKET   That part of the MARKET for a commodity in which orders are
accepted for delivery at once. See: FUTURES MARKET

CASH ON DELIVERY   Same as: COD

CASH REGISTER DISPLAY   A small MERCHANDISER designed to mount on the cash
register and to hold small items subject to frequent IMPULSE BUYING, such
as cigarettes and transparent tape.

CASH-REGISTER-TAPE REDEMPTION PLAN   Same as: TAPE PLAN

CASH-SEND   Same as: SEND-TRANSACTION

CASH-TAKE   Same as: TAKE-TRANSACTION

CASH WITH ORDER   Same as: CWO

CASTING OFF   Estimating the amount of space COPY will occupy when set in
type of a given size. Often results in a determination of how many words
can be used, or the size of type required for a given space. See: COPY
FITTING

CATALOG   A buying guide intended for long use, which so completely describes
the merchandise it presents that a person can make ordering decisions
directly from it. Some catalogs contain several hundred pages. When
large, their cost dictates that an attempt be made to restrict their placement in the hands of PROSPECTS to whom the probability of a sale is good,
or with established CUSTOMERS.

CATALOG RETAILING   Offering PRODUCTS or services to CONSUMERS in a CATALOG
from which orders are placed to be delivered using an appropriate transportation mode. May be essentially the same as MAIL-ORDER, or may employ
a CATALOG SHOWROOM.

CATALOG SHOWROOM   A RETAILER operating from a warehouse to which customers
come prepared to purchase and take away items which they have already selected from the retailer's CATALOG. Items on display are not available
to customers, but are brought from the warehouse section which is often
two-thirds of the outlet's space. It rarely deals in anything other than
appliances, jewelry and other hard goods. A low cost operation rivaling
the DISCOUNT HOUSE as it was originally conceived, it has been adopted by
discount chains and such large retailers as Dayton-Hudson Corp., Grand
Union Co., and May Department Stores as a means toward expansion through
a relatively new institution with proven advantages. See: INVITATION
POINT THEORY

CATALOG WAREHOUSE   Same as: CATALOG SHOWROOM

CATEGORICAL METHOD.   A procedure for evaluation of sources of supply whereby the BUYER keeps a record of all VENDORS and their products according
to a list of factors to which performance grades are assigned as more experience with the suppliers is gained. Its major advantages are simplic-
ity and low cost. Its major disadvantages are reliance on memory and
subjective judgment, and the possible routinization of the process, which
could lead to lack of critical consideration. See: COST-RATIO METHOD,
WEIGHTED-POINT METHOD

CATEGORY WIDTH   Applied to the number of choices an individual will consider when making PRODUCT decisions. The broader the category width,
the more risk the individual is evidently willing to accept that in the
SEARCH for a good choice, a bad one will be made instead.

CATV   Abbreviation for: Community Antenna Television System, a method whereby the SIGNAL received by an advantageously placed antenna can relay programs to subscribers through a cable. Provision is made to originate
programs and commercials through the facility. In 1972 the U.S. Supreme
Court upheld an FCC rule requiring cable television systems with at least
3,500 subscribers to originate programming. A cable system can provide
dozens of channels. Proved desirable in may areas even where the reception
of free television programs is good.

CAUSAL RESEARCH   Sometimes used to mean the same as CONCLUSIVE RESEARCH when the study is to determine the relationships among variables. See: MARKETING RESEARCH

CAUSAL STUDIES   Same as: CONCLUSIVE STUDIES or CONCLUSIVE RESEARCH

CAVEAT EMPTOR   The Latin phrase which means "let the buyer beware." It denotes the philosophy that the buyer had better take care what he is getting because once the sale is made, the buyer will have no recourse. See: CAVEAT VENDITOR

CAVEAT VENDITOR   The Latin phrase which means "let the seller beware." See: CAVEAT EMPTOR, PRIVITY OF CONTRACT RULE

CB   Abbreviation for: CHAIN BREAK

CBD   (1) Abbreviation used by the trucking industry to refer to: CENTRAL BUSINESS DISTRICT   (2) Cash Before Delivery TERMS OF SALE. See: C.W.O.

CBP   Abbreviation for: Canadian Business Press, the association of specialized NEWSPAPERS and MAGAZINES. Its major purpose is to educate the relevant MARKETS to the benefits obtainable through INDUSTRIAL and TRADE ADVERTISING.

CCAB   Abbreviation for: CANADIAN CIRCULATIONS AUDIT BOARD, INC., an independent, non-profit organization established to provide verified information about the publications of its member companies. Any company publishing, advertising, or operating in Canada may join. The CCAB Board consists of 11 ADVERTISER representatives, 4 from agencies, and 9 from MEDIA, giving the advertisers dominance. Among its services are: monitoring the integrity of a publication's recipient qualification standards, distribution of a newsletter called "Circulate:," a "Unit Audit" which verifies the exact number of units, plants, or establishments a publication covers and the number of copies distributed to these units, a "Selected Distribution Audit" which verifies the number of a publication that is delivered to households rather than individuals, a "Bulk Distribution Audit" which verifies bulk distributions such as to a hotel or school, a "Product Postcard Audit" and a "Trade Show Audit" which counts and describes visitors by occupation, geographic origin, and industry.

CCC   (1) Abbreviation for: Contract Carrier Conference, an association of CONTRACT CARRIERS, a minority segment of the trucking industry, which intervenes for the membership before Congress, the ICC, and the courts. It has been effective in getting equitable rulings in cases before all authoritative bodies. (2) Abbreviation for: Commodity Credit Corporation, a United States agency formed in 1933 under a permanent Federal charter as a wholly owned corporation. A major function of the CCC is to support prices of agricultural commodities through purchases, payments, non-recourse loans, and other operations.

CCP   See: Institute for Certification of Computer Professionals in ACM (2)

CCTV   Abbreviation for: Closed-Circuit Television

CDNPA   Abbreviation for: Canadian Daily Newspaper Publishers Association. This organization has since 1968 sponsored and published a series of studies dealing with the effectiveness of specific ADVERTISING CAMPAIGNS in Newspapers in Canada. Using an interesting research design, one of the measurements, the percent of all adults likely to switch to an advertised BRAND, indicates that in some instances an advertising campaign can lessen the probability. Some studies done in test markets in the U.S. corroborate this possible negative effect. Explanations advanced for this include unbelievable claims and promises which were not keepable. More work is in process in this area to try to pin down the specific factors which give rise to this phenomenon.

CEEFAX   A phonetic rendering of "see facts," the British Broadcasting Corporation (BBC) has given its "newspaper on the air," which permits subscribers by means of a decoding device attached to an ordinary television set to select from a number of particular areas of news. The viewer may take whatever time necessary and then switch to other news or regular programming.   See: ORACLE

CELLER-KEFAUVER ANTI-MERGER ACT   This amendment to the CLAYTON ACT passed in 1950 closed a loophole by prohibiting the acquisition of any part of the assets of a competing company, as well as its stock, where the effect "may be substantially to lessen competition or to tend to create a monopoly" and added the following specific: "in any line of commerce in any section of the country."   See: FEDERAL TRADE COMMISSION ACT, ROBINSON-PATMAN ACT, SHERMAN ACT

CEM   Abbreviation for: COMBINATION EXPORT MANAGER.   Same as: EMC

CENSUS   (1) A complete enumeration of a statistical POPULATION.   See: SAMPLE (2) The process of measuring the population for the data of interest to the one making the study.

CENSUS OF AGRICULTURE   Contains detailed data by state and county about, among others, number of farms, value of products, acreage, type of products, and employment.   Authorized to be taken by the Bureau of the Census every five years in those years ending in "4" and "9."   Current data is available in the Agricultural Statistics and Commodity Yearbook and in the irregularly issued bulletins of the Department of Agriculture.

CENSUS OF BUSINESS   Compilation of detailed statistics on RETAIL, WHOLESALE, and SERVICE trades according to about 150 business groups.   Data include sales volume, expenses, storage facilities, and the like for counties, cities, and SMSAs.   Does not cover the professions nor the insurance and real estate firms.   Authorized to be taken every five years in the years ending in "2" and "7."   More current information on some of the series is contained in the publications "Monthly Retail Trade," "Monthly Selected Services Receipts," and "Monthly Wholesale Trade."   Collected by the Bureau of the Census of the Department of Commerce.

CENSUS OF GOVERNMENT   Presents information about state and local governments such as size of payroll, number of employees, operating revenues and costs, and amount of indebtedness.   Authorized to be taken every five years in the years ending in "2" and "7."   Because of the time lag involved in compiling the data, this census may not be current enough for some purposes.

CENSUS OF HOUSING   Taken in conjunction with the CENSUS OF POPULATION and in the same years, it provides details on type of structure, rent, facilities, equipment, and other items of interest for planners.   For large METROPOLITAN areas detailed statistics are compiled by city block. More current information is available in the frequent "Current Housing Reports."   Collected by the Bureau of the Census of the Department of Commerce.

CENSUS OF MANUFACTURERS   Contains detailed INDUSTRY and geographic statistics in about 450 classes regarding number of ESTABLISHMENTS, VALUE ADDED BY MANUFACTURE, employment, wages, inventories, sales by customer class, and utilities consumption.   Taken in the same years as the CENSUS OF BUSINESS.   Annual data is contained in the "Annual Survey of Manufacturers" and monthly and annual production figures for some commodities are found in "Current Industrial Reports."   Collected by the Bureau of the Census of the Department of Commerce.

CENSUS OF MINERAL INDUSTRIES   Compiles information similar to the CENSUS OF MANUFACTURERS but just for the mining INDUSTRY.   Covers about 50 mineral industries.   Taken in the same years as the Census of Manufacturers.   Collected by the Bureau of the Census of the Department of Commerce.   Annual data may be found in the "Minerals Yearbook," which is

published by the Bureau of Mines of the Interior Department. Because
the latter is a product classification while the former is an industrial
classification, the two are not entirely comparable.

CENSUS OF POPULATION   A count of the population by geographic region, with
detailed DEMOGRAPHIC characteristics some of which are determined by the
need of business to have certain information. Some specific computer runs
may be had on a fee basis. Taken every ten years in the years ending with
"0." More current data is available in the annual "Current Population
Reports." Collected by the Bureau of the Census of the Department of
Commerce.

CENSUS OF TRANSPORTATION   Data cover passenger travel, the transportation
of commodities by the various transport modes, and truck and bus inventory
and use. Taken in the same years as the CENSUS OF BUSINESS and by the
same Bureau.

CENTER SPREAD   (1) See: DOUBLE TRUCK   (2) In OUTDOOR ADVERTISING, two
adjacent PANELS on which the COPY has been coordinated.

CENTRAL AMERICAN COMMON MARKET   Organized in 1960, it includes Costa Rica,
El Salvador, Guatemala, Honduras, Nicaragua. It follows generally the
same aims as the EEC. Same as: CACM

CENTRAL AREA AGRICULTURAL ADVERTISING ASSOCIATION   See: NAMA

CENTRAL BUSINESS DISTRICT   Characteristics: convergence of local and intercity transportation facilities; sale of SHOPPING GOODS predominates; substantial numbers of SPECIALTY SHOPS but usually on tne edges of the area;
numerous CONVENIENCE GOODS stores to accomodate the downtown employment
of a large number of people. Same as: CBD

CENTRAL BUYING   An arrangement within a FIRM whereby the acquisition of
whatever the firm requires is the responsibility of one organization
division. Frequently this one division is subdivided into highly
specialized units each responsible for acquiring but one type of product
under defined conditions. See: BLANKET ORDER, SYSTEMS CONTRACTING

CENTRAL CITY   See: METROPOLITAN AREA

CENTRAL LIMIT THEOREM   States that if SIMPLE RANDOM SAMPLES of a large size
are drawn from a UNIVERSE with a given MEAN and VARIANCE, the sample mean
will be approximately normally distributed. The sample PARAMETERS will
become more and more accurate as the sample size becomes larger.

CENTRAL MARKETS   See: PRIMARY CENTRAL MARKET, SECONDARY CENTRAL MARKET

CENTRAL-PERIPHERAL PATTERN   One of the significant location determinants,
it refers to an activity which originates at some central point and becomes extended through a surrounding area to a boundary. This pattern is
typical of the RETAIL STORE which serves a neighborhood, the New York
Produce Market serving as a central clearance point to move produce to a
large surrounding area through many types of MIDDLEMEN, etc. Other factors such as costs, land contours, and the like, also affect location
decisions. See: FLOW PATTERN

CENTRAL PROCESSING UNIT   Same as: CPU

CENTS-OFF COUPON   See: COUPONING

CEO   Generally accepted abbreviation for: Chief Executive Officer

CERTIFICATION MARK   Applies to a MARK used upon or in connection with the
products or services of one or more persons other than the owner of the
mark to certify regional or other origin, material, mode of manufacture,
quality, accuracy or other characteristics of such goods or services, or
that the work or labor on the goods and/or services was performed by the
members of a union or other organization. May be registered in the
U.S. Patent Office.

CERTIFIED PURCHASING MANAGER   See: NAPM

CETERIS PARIBUS. Latin for: other things being equal.

CFTC   Abbreviation for: Commodity Futures Trading Commission, a Federal
agency endowed in 1974 with broad powers to regulate the commodity
futures activity within the United States. The CFTC replaced the more
limited regulatory powers exercised previously by the Department of
Agriculture through the Commodity Exchange Authority.

CHAIN BREAK   An I.D. in which the station uses two seconds of the time in
order to identify itself.

CHAIN DISCOUNT   A series of discounts taken on a base reduced by each preceding discount, e.g., a chain discount of 40%, 5%, & 5% is the same as
one discount of 45.85% taken on the LIST PRICE.

CHAIN PROSPECTING   A technique of PROSPECTING in which a SALESPERSON seeks
the names of one or more PROSPECTS from each one approached. Same as:
Endless Chain Method

CHAIN STORE   One of a system of two or more stores of similar type which
are centrally owned and managed. In U.S. Census definition four or more
such stores are needed to constitute a chain. See: RETAILER

CHAIN STORE LAW   A name for the ROBINSON-PATMAN ACT derived from its
original intention to protect small businesses from the price competition
the large CHAINS were able to bring to bear because of the much lower
costs they incurred through price concessions achieved by large quantity
buying.

CHAIR EASEL   A vertical display held in place by a chair-like projection
in front. It is dependent upon the weight of the merchandise for
stability.

CHANNEL CONTROL   The use of interorganization management to achieve effective coordination among the members of the CHANNEL OF DISTRIBUTION so as
to result in the most efficient allocation of resources among the channel
members. Much research still needs to be done before a body of information may emerge which will permit the accomplishment of the indicated
goal. Some types of channel activity, such as geographical restrictions
on dealers, are already illegal. Many other areas involving management
tools and incentive plans can benefit from closer attention and analysis.

CHANNEL CAPTAIN   The firm acting in leadership of a TRADE CHANNEL which has
become a single, integrated system. This is not yet common in the market-
place. The position is earned by leadership ability and MARKET POWER,
rather than by appointment by anyone. See: CHANNEL LEADER

CHANNEL FIT   The degree to which a new PRODUCT can be distributed through
a CHANNEL OF DISTRIBUTION currently in use by the maker of the new product.

CHANNEL LEADER   A CHANNEL member which because of its position or economic
power can stipulate MARKETING policies to other channel members, in effect
exercising control over some or all of their decisions and activities.
See: CHANNEL CAPTAIN

CHANNEL OF DISTRIBUTION   The course taken by the title to goods as it moves
from producer to CONSUMER through MIDDLEMEN. For some products the channel has been so shortened that the producer acts himself as a middleman,
selling directly to a user. Same as: TRADE CHANNEL

CHARACTER   (1) In print, an individual letter, figure, or other unit of
type. (2) See: CREDIT

CHARACTERISTICS OF INNOVATIONS   The DIFFUSION RATE is a function of the
degree to which the new PRODUCT'S potential MARKET perceives its RELATIVE
ADVANTAGE, TRIALABILITY, OBSERVABILITY, COMPATIBILITY, AND COMPLEXITY.
See also: PERCEPTION

CHARGING THE TOP OF THE RATE CARD   An expression used in the ADVERTISING field to denote the ability to attract new ADVERTISERS to a MEDIUM at the ONE-TIME RATE because of a DEMAND which exceeds the capacity of the medium to accommodate.

CHARGING WHAT THE TRAFFIC WILL BEAR   A colloquial expression used to denote that the seller is asking the highest price he believes the MARKET will pay. Usually applied to a seller in a local situation where he is thought to have a buyer group which has few choices of supply sources.

CHASE   The steel frame in which type is locked up for the LETTERPRESS printing process.

CHASER FLASHER   An electrical device that produces rapid sequential lighting.

CHEATING   The act of falsifying their interviews by interviewers who are paid to conduct interviews with specified RESPONDENTS, but actually do not conduct them. A form of NONSAMPLING ERROR. See: NONRESPONSE ERROR, SAMPLING ERROR

CHECK PAYMENT ORDERING SYSTEM   A specialized purchasing system applicable to small orders in which a blank, pre-signed check is sent in duplicate with the purchase order. The seller fills in the amount and returns the duplicate of the check. Partial shipments are not permitted. The check is usually limited to a small amount, perhaps $25, and a time limit of 30, 60, or 90 days is specified on the check. This system offers the possibility of savings by reducing the paper work associated with accounts payable.

CHECK QUESTION   In SALESMANSHIP, a specially phrased question designed to elicit an answer from a PROSPECT which will provide a clue as to the progress being made toward the decision to buy. See: TRIAL CLOSE

CHERRY PICKING   (1) The practice of selecting only certain items from a manufacturer's LINES. (2) The practice of visiting only certain selected PROSPECTS or CUSTOMERS in a TERRITORY.

CHINA EGGS   Those who appear to be good PROSPECTS but who do not become CUSTOMERS.

CHINESE MIRROR   A specially coated mirror that is reflective when front lighted and transparent when back lighted. Used in certain applications at TRADE SHOW exhibits.

CHINESE WALLS   Intangible, POLICY barriers which define areas where RETAIL SALESPEOPLE cannot accompany CUSTOMERS who wish to buy items in those other areas. Not present just as a matter of course in all RETAIL STORES.

CHI-SQUARE TEST   A method of statistical inference used frequently to test for GOODNESS-OF-FIT of data to a curve, or the NULL HYPOTHESIS that there is no significant difference between the observed and the expected frequencies of observations. Tables are available which give values designated by the symbol X^2 above which the null hypothesis would be rejected at desired CONFIDENCE LEVELS. This test can accommodate an entire pattern of expected and actual frequencies. The data to be tabulated must be associated with a PROBABILITY SAMPLE, must be DISCRETE and mutually exclusive as well as independent, and the sampled and target POPULATIONS must be the same. Also, each expected frequency must be at least five and the sample size at least 50. A good book on statistics should be consulted for the calculations involved and for refinements in the use of the test. NONPARAMETRIC. See: KOLMOGOROV-SMIRNOV TEST, POISSON PROBABILITY DISTRIBUTION

CHROMA   In color, the dimension of intensity. HUE and VALUE are the other two dimensions.

CHROMA KEY   A device permitting an image to be placed on another image on the television screen; for example, a tiny person may be made to appear dancing on a giant's shoulder.

CIA   Abbreviation for: Cash In Advance. TERMS OF SALE essentially equivalent to CBD terms. See: C.W.O.

CIC-MHE   Abbreviation for: College-Industry Committee on Material Handling Education. See: MHI

CIF   Abbreviation for: cost, insurance, freight. Part of TERMS OF SALE, this indicates that the seller will pay all charges involved in getting goods to a destination. See: C & F

CIFI&E   Abbreviation for: Cost, Insurance, Freight, Interest, and Exchange. Applicable to TRANSPORTATION terms of sale.

CIGARETTE ADVERTISING ACT   Same as: PUBLIC HEALTH CIGARETTE SMOKING ACT

CIPEC   Used to refer in a body to the major copper-producing countries: Chile, Peru, Zambia, the Congo.

CIRCULAR   Regular or small sheets of paper printed on one or both sides intended for delivery by mail or by hand.

CIRCULATION   (1) The number of copies of a publication distributed. May be counted as paid and unpaid. See: CONTROLLED CIRCULATION   (2) Used loosely to refer to the number of homes regularly tuned to a certain BROADCAST station.   (3) The number of persons who have an opportunity to observe a TRANSIT ADVERTISING display during a stated period. Reported by rider, measured by the fare box; and by exposure. A rider is one person riding an inside-display-carrying vehicle for one trip. Exposures equal the total number of persons exposed to displays on the outside of the vehicle.

CIRCULATION RATE BASE   The CIRCULATION that a MAGAZINE guarantees as a minimum. Should the circulation drop below this consistently, the publisher will make pro rata refund.

CIRCULATION WASTE   Same as: WASTE CIRCULATION

CITL   Abbreviation for: The Canadian Industrial Traffic League, an organization of over 1,100 traffic management personnel from over 500 Canadian industrial and commercial firms. It has for more than fifty years served the nation-wide interests of Canadian shippers and receivers. It keeps members current with a weekly news bulletin, various meetings, and a number of published studies.

CITY ZONE   The area in which a NEWSPAPER circulates that is judged to be characteristic of the city as contrasted with the suburbs or rural areas.

CIVIL AERONAUTICS BOARD   Same as: CAB

c.l.   Abbreviation for "carload." Denotes shipping rates for a minimum quantity or weight of a good to qualify for the lowest railroad tariffs. See: l.c.l.

CLASSIC   Same as: BASIC (3)

CLASSIFICATION   As applied to merchandise, this term indicates all the items of a given kind without further breakdown as to price, color, etc., all reasonably substitutable for one another as perceived by a RETAIL CUSTOMER.

CLASSIFICATION CONTROL   Same as: OPEN-TO-BUY control

CLASSIFICATION MERCHANDISING   Emphasis on small, homogeneous classes of merchandise as the most desirable units for control purposes. The major distinction between classifications and departments is that the former are units of selling responsibility whereas the latter are units of buying responsibility.

CLASSIFICATION OF CONSUMER GOODS   See: CONVENIENCE GOODS, SHOPPING GOODS, SPECIALTY GOODS

CLASSIFIED ADVERTISING   One of the two broad divisions of ADVERTISING in
NEWSPAPERS and some MAGAZINES. It appears in special columns on pages
where the advertising is assembled by product or service. Usually the
selection of type FACES and sizes is very limited, as is the freedom of
LAYOUT. The other broad division is DISPLAY ADVERTISING. See:
CLASSIFIED DISPLAY ADVERTISING

CLASSIFIED DISPLAY ADVERTISING   Some NEWSPAPERS offer special sections
devoted to only one product or service, e.g., Real Estate, in which the
LAYOUT and the elements of the advertisement are virtually unlimited, as
in other parts of the paper. Advertising in these sections combines the
freedom of DISPLAY ADVERTISING with the grouping advantages of
CLASSIFIED ADVERTISING.

CLASS MAGAZINE   Used in a general way to describe a PUBLICATION directed
to and which reaches selected groups of high-income readers. In contrast
to: MASS MAGAZINE

CLASS I RAILROAD   One which has annual gross revenues of $50 million or
more. In the United States the around 56 such railroads operate 96% of
the total railroad mileage, handle more than 99% of the ton-miles of
rail freight traffic, and earn about 99% of the operating revenues of all
line-haul railroads.

CLASS RATE   (1) a special TRANSPORTATION rate for certain classes of commodities. Usually expressed as a percent of the BASE RATE. See: COMMODITY
RATE   (2) A charge made for television time according to the desirability
of the time period. The most costly are designated A rates, the next B,
and so on. The time classifications vary from station to station because
each sets its own according to the conditions peculiar to the total environment in which each station exists.

CLASS II TIME   Same as: NON-PREEMPTIBLE

CLAYTON ACT   This Act, passed in 1914, amended and made specific certain
aspects of the SHERMAN ACT. Outlawed were discrimination in prices, exclusive and tying contracts, intercorporate stockholdings, and interlock-
ing directorates, but only where their effect "may be to substantially
lessen competition or tend to create a monopoly." Means of enforcement
were strengthened. See: CELLER-KEFAUVER ANTI-MERGER ACT, FEDERAL TRADE
COMMISSION ACT, ROBINSON-PATMAN ACT, SHERMAN ACT, WHEELER-LEA ACT

CLC   Abbreviation for: Census Laboratory and Clearinghouse, an organization
established by a grant from The National Science Foundation jointly to the
Center for Research Libraries and National Data Use and Access Laboratories
to provide a service whereby a user can write to determine whether the Census can be applied to his research problem, how to overcome technical barriers to application, and how much he can expect the application to cost.

CLEAN   Describes a display program involving the RETAILER in no complicated paper work, no special handling or pricing, and otherwise requiring
a minimum of effort.

CLEANING IN TRANSIT   A privilege granted by a CARRIER whereby a shipment
such as an agricultural product may be stopped at a certain point for
cleaning and then resume its journey with minimal, if any, increase in
charges.

CLEAR-CHANNEL STATION   A RADIO station authorized to use power up to
50,000 watts, which gives it great range. There are relatively few such
stations, which have an exclusive frequency during evening hours. See:
LOCAL STATION, REGIONAL STATION

CLERKING ACTIVITIES   Those activities in a RETAIL STORE which involve
direct contact with customers. See: BACKING ACTIVITIES

CLIMATES   See: UNCONTROLLABLE VARIABLES

CLOSE or CLOSING   (1) In sales, a successful asking-for-the-order resulting in the PROSPECT'S agreement to buy the product or service offered.
See: ASSUMPTIVE CLOSE, TRIAL CLOSE   (2) In ADVERTISING, that section of the
COPY which contains the idea of interest to the advertiser. Sometimes called: urge line.

CLOSED ASSORTMENT   An ASSORTMENT in which the structure of PRODUCTS required
by the CONSUMER is present and complete. See: OPEN ASSORTMENT

CLOSED ASSORTMENT DISPLAY   See: ASSORTMENT DISPLAY, CLOSED DISPLAY

CLOSED-CIRCUIT SYSTEM   A MARKETING system which provides for FEEDBACK only
from within the system. No provision is made for inputs from the environment or the economy. This may work rather well for a firm, but usually
on a lagged basis, information coming back slowly. See: LINEAR SYSTEM,
OPEN-CIRCUIT SYSTEM

CLOSED DISPLAY   Merchandise is placed in cases under or behind glass,
often kept locked so that a SALES CLERK is necessary to assist a customer
in examining the item. See: OPEN DISPLAY

CLOSED-DOOR MEMBERSHIP STORE   A RETAIL ESTABLISHMENT which requires its
customers to qualify on the basis of some employment designation, such
as government employee. Usually a DISCOUNT HOUSE type of operation,
membership generally requires the payment of an initial or annual fee
or both.

CLOSED-END QUESTION   The type of question which elicits a direct response
from RESPONDENTS. Uses a STRUCTURED QUESTIONNAIRE.

CLOSED SALES TERRITORY   A geographically-defined area in which a producer
will permit only one MIDDLEMAN to handle certain goods. See: EXCLUSIVE
DISTRIBUTION

CLOSED STOCK   Sets of items sold with the understanding that replacements
of individual pieces will probably not be possible. See: OPEN STOCK

CLOSE-OUT   An offer to sell at reduced prices a selection of items the FIRM
has decided to discontinue for reasons of slow sale, incomplete ASSORTMENT,
error in judging DEMAND, space priorities and/or the like.

CLOSE RATE   One factor used in evaluating SALESPEOPLE. It is the salesperson's number of successful CLOSINGS divided by that salesperson's
number of sales calls.

CLOSING   The step in the AIDCAS PROCESS in which the SALESPERSON actually
gets the order. See: TRIAL CLOSE

CLOSING CLUE   A verbal statement, or a physical action such as a facial
expression, that suggests a BUYER may be ready to place an order. SALES-
PEOPLE are constantly on the alert for such signals. See: TRIAL CLOSE

CLOSING DATE   The last day on which an ADVERTISEMENT must be delivered to
a MEDIUM if it is to appear in a specific issue or program. See: ISSUE
DATE, ON-SALE DATE

CLOSURE   The fulfilling of an individual's need for a complete picture
formed from organizing PERCEPTIONS so as to achieve this. If STIMULI are
incomplete, the missing pieces are subconsciously or consciously filled
in. See: GROUPING

CLUBBING OFFER   An arrangement whereby subscriptions to two or more different publications are offered at a lower, combination price. A consideration for an advertiser in judging the composition of the CIRCULATIONS of
the publications.

CLUCKING HENS   New or unusual concerns for a RETAIL STORE'S top management
which demand time and attention.

CLUSTER   A group of small SPECIALTY STORES located without overall planning
in a high-density residential area.

CLUSTERING   A heavy CLUTTER situation, especially in BROADCAST MEDIA. If the NETWORKS continue the limitation on nonprogram time and the number of program interruptions, competitive pressures may result in an increase in clustering.

CLUSTER MARKETING   Featuring a group of related PRODUCTS in various ADVERTIS- ING MEDIA as one unit of a number of items suitable for interchangeable use for a specific purpose. The effect is to POSITION them to a particular TARGET MARKET.

CLUSTER SAMPLE   A RANDOM or PROBABILITY SAMPLE that uses groups of people rather than individuals as the RESPONDENT unit. See: CLUSTER SAMPLING

CLUSTER SAMPLING   A method of developing a PROBABILITY SAMPLE by randomly selecting the elements in groups rather than individually. Used where it would be unusually difficult or expensive to get a listing of the entire POPULATION from which to derive the sample. When all the elements in the selected groups are included in the sample, the process is called single- stage; when there is further selection within the groups, it is called multi-stage. See: CLUSTER SAMPLE

CLUTTER   Several COMMERCIALS in BROADCAST MEDIA, or ADVERTISEMENTS in PRINT MEDIA, following one another without intervening program time or EDITORIAL MATTER. Some media will not accept PIGGYBACKS, and otherwise regulate the amount of clutter. Preceding and succeeding advertisements are of great interest to advertisers in all MEDIA. See: PRODUCT PROTECTION

CLUTTER POSITION   An advertisement placed within a series of other adver- tisements, whether in PRINT or BROADCAST MEDIA. Sometimes the first and last of the series are excluded from this designation. See: CLUTTER

CMEA   Abbreviation for: Council for Mutual Economic Assistance, the economic partners of the Soviet Union: Bulgaria, Cuba, Czechoslovakia, Hungary, German Democratic Republic, Mongolia, Poland, Romania, U.S.S.R., Vietnam. Yugoslavia has the status of "observer," not full membership. See: CT

CMO   Abbreviation for: Chief Marketing Officer. The person in this position may officially have one of a wide variety of titles.

COARSE-SCREEN HALFTONE   See: HALFTONE

COBOL   Abbreviation for: Common Business Oriented Language, a computer LANGUAGE by which business data processing procedures may be precisely described in standard form. Mainly uses regular letters and words as the means of communication to direct the computer's operations.

C.O.D.   Abbreviation for: cash-on-delivery terms. Sometimes said to stand for: collect-on-delivery. Used in a situation where the buyer does not qualify for CREDIT terms, yet there is every reason to believe that he will pay for the goods when brought to him by a carrier. See: C.W.O.

CODE PRICE   The price which results when the TRADE DISCOUNT is deducted from the LIST PRICE.

CODING   A technical procedure by means of which data collected, usually on a QUESTIONNAIRE, are placed into one of a group of exhaustive classes that have been either predetermined or determined by the researcher on the basis of the types of responses received. See: EDITING, TABULATION

COEFFICIENT OF CORRELATION   A measure of the relationship between two or more variables, e.g., the degree of response of sales to the number of SALESPERSONS in the field. Designated by the symbol r. A value below 0.6 usually denotes negligible association among the variables studied while a value of 0.9 or more represents excellent CORRELATION. Useful to discover with which of a series of variables one variable has the closest association. PARAMETRIC.

COEFFICIENT OF DETERMINATION   A measure of the proportion of VARIANCE in the DEPENDENT VARIABLE that is associated with the INDEPENDENT VARIABLE. Designated by the symbol r^2. PARAMETRIC.

COEFFICIENT OF ELASTICITY   See: PRICE ELASTICITY OF DEMAND

COEFFICIENT OF INCOME SENSITIVITY   Indicates the average percent that the sales of a product have varied over a period of years relative to a 1% change in PERSONAL DISPOSABLE INCOME. In general it shows by how much a 1% change in spendable money may be expected to change the sales of a product.

COEFFICIENT OF MULTIPLE CORRELATION   See: MULTIPLE CORRELATION

COEFFICIENT OF VARIATION   This is a relative measure of DISPERSION, not expressed in the units measured as is the STANDARD DEVIATION. It is a ratio between two numbers and thus is useful in comparing the dispersion of groups of measurements that would otherwise not be comparable.

COFC   Abbreviation for: Container-On-Flatcar Service. See: CONTAINERIZA-TION, PIGGYBACK

COG   Abbreviation for: customer's own goods. Often used to identify the ownership of items left with a RETAIL STORE for some type of required work such as repair or alteration. Same as: COM

COGNITION   How an individual perceives his environment and the ATTITUDES he holds toward it. Often used to mean the same as PERCEPTION.

COGNITIVE CONSONANCE   The psychologically satisfying state that occurs when all of a person's bits of self-knowledge regarding a particular behavior pattern indicate that the correct action is being taken. See: COGNITIVE DISSONANCE, COGNITIVE JUDGMENT

COGNITIVE DISSONANCE   A type of perceptual bias which causes feelings of regret after an important purchase has been made as alternative oppor-tunities that were considered seem to compare more favorably. The normal course is that the buyer will tend to resolve the tension by finding more advantages in support of his action and downgrading the advantages of the rejected alternatives. If anticipated by the marketer, the first decision can be reinforced and the buyer be made a more enthusiastic supporter of the product, although there is some evidence that this may happen anyway as the tension-resolving process goes on. However, it will take longer without positive action by the seller, who can benefit if he acts to in-clude reinforcing evidence in all his advertisements.

COGNITIVE JUDGMENT   As applied to a buyer of goods or services, the result of his PERCEPTIONS, or communications received from others. See: CONATIVE JUDGMENT, NORMATIVE JUDGMENT, VALUE JUDGMENT

COGS   An acronym for: Consumer Goods System, a computer-based system em-ploying a group of IBM programs to assist in the management of invent-ories. Its application within the MIS include allocations and FORE-CASTING.

COHORTS   Applied in DEMOGRAPHICS to the various age groups that make up the total population.

COINCIDENTAL SURVEY   Some method of checking the AUDIENCE of a BROADCAST program while it is on the air. Most often conducted by telephone. See: TELEPHONE COINCIDENTAL METHOD

COINCIDENT INDICATOR   Same as: ROUGHLY COINCIDENT INDICATOR

COINED WORD   An original combination of letters and/or syllables forming a word, as opposed to words found in the dictionary. Used quite extensive-ly for TRADEMARKS. Examples: Kodel, Zerex.

COLA   Acronym for: Cost of Living Adjustment, a remuneration feature of many employment contracts.

COLD CALL   Paying a visit to a PROSPECT without first making an appointment. Usually more time consuming than warranted, although indicated in
certain circumstances, such as when it is thought that this may be the
only way to get an appointment for a future date.

COLD CANVASSING   Finding LEADS by going from house-to-house or office-to-
office in a systematic manner without previous notice to the people
called upon. Sometimes used to mean the same as COLD CALL.

COLD-STORAGE WAREHOUSE   A PUBLIC WAREHOUSE equipped to keep goods refrigerated, or if need be, at 0°F or below for frozen items.

COLD TYPE   Same as: PHOTOCOMPOSITION, although this usage is incorrect.
See: IMPACT COMPOSITION

COLGATE DOCTRINE   A Supreme Court decision later incorporated into the
ROBINSON-PATMAN ACT, which recognized the right of a seller to select his
own dealers according to his own criteria and judgment, as well as to announce in advance the circumstances under which he would refuse to sell to
others. See: REFUSAL-TO-DEAL

COLLATERAL MATERIALS   Items of an ADVERTISING nature, such as CATALOGS
specification sheets, and the like, not exposed to an AUDIENCE through
the usual ADVERTISING MEDIA. They are often included in the listing of
media as specific, separate types.

COLLECTIVE MARK   A TRADEMARK or SERVICE MARK used by members of a cooperative, an association, or other collective group or organization. Marks
used to indicate membership in a union, an association or other organization may be registered as COLLECTIVE MEMBERSHIP MARKS.

COLLECTIVE MEMBERSHIP MARK   See: COLLECTIVE MARK

COLLEGE INDUSTRY COMMITTEE ON MATERIAL HANDLING EDUCATION   See: MHI

COLLUSION   An illegal agreement among FIRMS to fix prices, define PRODUCTS,
set MARKET SHARES, or otherwise act in concert in an attempt to avoid the
restrictions of the ANTI-TRUST LAWS.

COLOR   The effect of color on the moods and ATTITUDES of people in respect
to merchandise or STORES is being increasingly recognized and reflected
in packaging and interior decorating. It is reflected where feasible in
the coloring of the product itself. Considerable research has been reported on the effects of individual colors and combinations of colors.
See: CHROMA, HUE, VALUE

COLORABLE IMITATION   Any MARK which so resembles a registered mark as to
be likely to cause confusion or mistake or to deceive purchasers.

COLOR LINE CONVERSION   An innovation in the reproduction for NEWSPAPER
ADVERTISING of original continuous-tone art. The process is similar to
HALFTONE, except that the PLATE is made by shooting through a patterned
screen so that the light is broken into a series of lines instead of dots.
A variety of patterns is available. Using a coarser screen than possible
with halftone, yet giving pleasing graphics on the rough newsprint, it
makes possible effects not suitable before. It is claimed to effect
up to a 50% saving in newspaper color work.

COLOR PROCESS PRINTING   See: FOUR-COLOR PROCESS

COLUMN-INCH   A unit of measurement in a print MEDIUM of more or less regular issue, one deep and one column wide, whatever the actual width of the
column. See: AGATE LINE

COM   (1) Abbreviation for: customer's own merchandise. Same as: COG
(2) Abbreviation for: Computer Output Microfilm or Microimaging

COMBINATION EXPORT MANAGER   Same as: CEM

COMBINATION FLIGHT   An aircraft flight including CARGO and passengers on the
same plane. See: CARGO FLIGHT

COMBINATION HOUSE   A MERCHANT MIDDLEMAN who acts as a WHOLESALER in the INDUSTRIAL MARKET as well as in the RETAIL and institutional markets. See: INDUSTRIAL DISTRIBUTOR

COMBINATION PLATE   A HALFTONE and a LINE PLATE in one engraving.

COMBINATION RATE   (1) A special space rate granted in connection with two or more periodicals owned by the same publisher. Usually, the same space and COPY must be used in each. (2) A favorable TIME RATE from two or more associated stations in one geographic area when all those stations are used together.

COMBINATION SALE   An item of merchandise together with a PREMIUM offered at a combination price. Sometimes the premium part of the offer is SELF-LIQUIDATING.

COMECON   Abbreviation for: Council for Mutual Assistance, a regional grouping of the following Eastern European nations: Czechoslovakia, East Germany, Hungary, Poland, Romania, and the USSR. Cuba is included in the group even though geographically separated. Finland is an associate member. Members work out strategies on an individual basis rather than more commonly as in the EEC.

COMMAND   In ADP, a signal or set of signals to a machine such as a computer to start, stop, or continue an operation it is equipped to perform.

COMMAND HEADLINE   A HEADLINE which directly urges the reader to use or buy the product.

COMMERCIAL   The advertiser's message presented on a BROADCAST MEDIUM.

COMMERCIAL ADVERTISING   Same as: PROMOTIONAL ADVERTISING

COMMERCIAL BRIBERY   The illegal practice of giving or promising a gift or favor in order to influence a person in a position of trust in a commercial transaction. Because any gratuity can be presumed to have had, or may have in the future, such influence, many firms forbid personnel to accept anything other than nominal gifts. Some go so far as to forbid gift-taking of any type in any amount of monetary value.

COMMERCIAL FARM   U.S. Census definition limits this to FARMS from which more than half of the total family income is derived, or from which annual product sales amount to $1,200 or more.

COMMERCIALIZATION   The stage a product is in when after testing and changing as found necessary, it is ready for introduction to the MARKET with full promotion. Introduction may be gradual, region by region. Introduction to national markets all at the same time requires large commitment to production facilities, advertising, personal selling and much more.

COMMERCIAL PROTECTION   Same as: PRODUCT PROTECTION, SEPARATION

COMMERCIAL TRAVELER   What a field SALESPERSON was called during the late 1800's. The name still persists in some INDUSTRIES.

COMMERCIAL ZONE   An area within which motor transportation is exempt from Federal legislation. Varies with areas, but normally has some limit beyond the borders of a city. Does not apply to traffic from outside the zone, or to points beyond the zone.

COMMISSARY STORE   A usually small-scale RETAIL STORE which sells primarily to the employees of the company or governmental unit which owns it.

COMMISSION AGENT   A FUNCTIONAL MIDDLEMAN who accepts shipments of goods, mainly perishables, to sell for a PRINCIPAL. Usually has authority to set price. Service to the principal is intermittent. Same as: COMMISSION HOUSE, COMMISSION MERCHANT

COMMISSION BULK AGENT. Same as: COMMISSION BULK PLANT OPERATOR

COMMISSION BULK PLANT OPERATOR A marketer of gasoline and/or heating oils who sells, stores, transports, assembles; who may engage in RETAILING or WHOLESALING operations, and who uses his supplier's BRAND NAME and receives a commission as payment for these functions. Same as: COMMISSION BULK AGENT, COMMISSION DISTRIBUTOR, COMMISSION RESELLER, COMMISSION WHOLESALE MARKETER, CONSIGNEE, CONSIGNMENT DISTRIBUTOR

COMMISSION DISTRIBUTOR   Same as: COMMISSION BULK PLANT OPERATOR

COMMISSION HOUSE   Same as: COMMISSION AGENT

COMMISSION MERCHANT   Same as: COMMISSION AGENT

COMMISSION OPERATED STATION   Same as: CONSIGNMENT SERVICE STATION

COMMISSION RESELLER   Same as: COMMISSION BULK PLANT OPERATOR

COMMISSION WHOLESALE MARKETER   Same as: COMMISSION BULK PLANT OPERATOR

COMMITTEE BUYING   Action by a group of persons set up in a FIRM to investigate and decide upon the PRODUCTS to be handled and the sources of supply for those products. Very frequently found in RETAILING, especially in CHAIN organizations. See: BUYING COMMITTEE

COMMITTEE FOR PIPE LINE COMPANIES   See: AOPL

COMMODITY APPROACH   An approach to the study of MARKETING characterized by the following of a product through all the ramifications of its movements from producer to users. See: FUNCTIONAL APPROACH, INSTITUTIONAL APPROACH

COMMODITY CREDIT CORPORATION   Same as: CCC (2)

COMMODITY EXCHANGE   (1) An organization or association of individuals which provides a place for trading in an item such as wheat under uniform rules and with facilities for gathering and disseminating information. (2) Frequently used to designate just the facilities provided.

COMMODITY EXCHANGE AUTHORITY   The Federal government's regulatory agency which supervises all domestically produced agricultural commodities traded on organized exchanges, except hides. Imported commodities are not involved. Its powers have been transferred to the CFTC.

COMMODITY FUTURES TRADING COMMISSION   See: CFTC

COMMODITY RATE   A special TRANSPORTATION rate approved for certain goods. Such rates tend to be lower and less based on distance than CLASS RATES.

COMMON BUSINESS ORIENTED LANGUAGE   Same as: COBOL

COMMON CARRIER   A TRANSPORTATION FIRM whose franchise to operate requires that it serve all who wish to use its services. Rules governing its operation are made by the ICC.

COMMON MARKET   Same as: EUROPEAN ECONOMIC COMMUNITY

COMMUNICATION, ADVERTISING, AND MARKETING EDUCATION FOUNDATION, LIMITED
Same as: CAM FOUNDATION

COMMUNITY ANTENNA TELEVISION SYSTEM   Same as: CATV

COMMUTER AIR CARRIER CONFERENCE   See: NATC

COMP   A short-form reference to: COMPREHENSIVE

COMPANY MAGAZINE   Same as: HOUSE ORGAN

COMPANY NEWSPAPER   Same as: HOUSE ORGAN

COMPANY-OPERATED SERVICE STATION   Same as: SALARY-OPERATED SERVICE STATION

COMPARATIVE ADVANTAGE   The considerations in international economics that each country will specialize in the producing and marketing of those goods in which it is most efficient. Unless artificial barriers are erected, it will export these and import those products in which it is least

efficient. The same concept can be applied to regions within a country.
See: THEORY OF COMPARATIVE ADVANTAGE

COMPARATIVE ADVERTISING   Same as: COMPARISON ADVERTISING

COMPARATIVE MARKETING   An approach to the study of international MARKETING
which delineates the similarities and the differences among the systems
used in various countries to anticipate DEMAND and to sell PRODUCTS.

COMPARE-A-PRICE   Same as: UNIT PRICING (2)

COMPARISON   A technique in ADVERTISING which attempts to show how the product is similar to something else, so as to imbue the product with the
desired aura. See: CONTRAST

COMPARISON ADVERTISING   The process of constructing ADVERTISEMENTS which
directly compare the ADVERTISER'S PRODUCT or BRAND on one or more specific
characteristics with at least one competing brand that is named or made
clearly recognizable. Not to be confused with the technique of COMPARISON.

COMPARISON DEPARTMENT   The sometimes title of a RETAIL STORE unit charged
with determining how the store's quality, service, styles, prices, and
other merchandise attributes compare with those of competitors.

COMPARISON SHOPPER   An employee of a RETAILER who is responsible for reporting assigned competitor's MERCHANDISING activities.

COMPARISON SHOPPING   In RETAILING, the practice of seeking information about
competitor's activities regarding PROMOTION, price, merchandise, store
arrangement, etc. There are independent businesses that can be employed
to do this, or a retailer may use one of his own employees as a COMPARI-
SON SHOPPER.

COMPASS   Acronym for: Complete Operating Movement Processing and
Service System, initiated by the Burlington Northern Railroad, in which
a computer receives, edits and stores car and train information that is
reported by each location as the events occur. The information is processed for immediate availability on demand by yard and traffic offices
throughout the system, as well as car distributors, to which it gives sum-
marized reports of all types of cars by location. See: ACI, TPC, TRAIN,
UMLER

COMPATIBILITY   (1) The degree to which a CONSUMER recognizes that a new
PRODUCT is consistent with his current requirements, ATTITUDES, and SELF-
IMAGE. (2) With respect to the DIFFUSION RATE, how consistent the INNO-
VATION is with existing behavior patterns and value systems of the poten-
tial MARKET. See: CHARACTERISTICS OF INNOVATIONS.

COMPENSATION   (1) A personal defense mechanism used unconsciously to overcome feelings of inadequacy, inferiority, or frustrated MOTIVE. Important to the seller because some people compensate by buying flashy or
expensive things. See: COGNITIVE DISSONANCE   (2) Remuneration in money
or benefits for work assigned. See: DRAW   (3) A CT transaction involving
PRODUCTS related to the technology or goods delivered by the Western
exporter. They are usually longer-term than COUNTERPURCHASES, have longer
time lag for the reciprocal deliveries, and are usually far larger in
dollar values.

COMPENSATION DEAL   In international trade, a transaction involving payment
in goods and cash. See: BUY-BACK, COUNTERPURCHASE

COMPETITIVE BIDDING   Same as: BIDDING

COMPETITIVE DIFFERENTIAL   The ways in which a firm differs from competing
firms which makes for greater or less acceptance of the firm by the
MARKET.

COMPETITIVE STAGE   The advertising stage a PRODUCT reaches, as advanced by
a certain classification, when its general usefulness as one of a type of

product is widely recognized, but its individual superiority over similar BRANDS needs to be established by the advertiser. Advertisements in this stage usually stress the product's differential. See: SPIRAL

COMPLEMENTARY GOODS. Items related in use so that an increase in the quantity demanded by the MARKET of one results in or accompanies an increase in the quantity demanded of the other, assuming prices remain the same. The CROSS-ELASTICITY value, if algebraically negative, is usually considered evidence that two goods or services are complementary, provided no change in the REAL INCOME of the buyer has occurred. Zero cross-elasticity might be accepted as a criterion of independence. See: SUBSTITUTIONAL GOODS

COMPLETELY RANDOMIZED DESIGN An EXPERIMENTAL DESIGN in which the desired treatments are assigned to the test units in a RANDOM fashion.

COMPLETELY RANDOMIZED LAYOUT Same as: COMPLETELY RANDOMIZED DESIGN, CRL

COMPLETENESS TEST In ADP, a type of validation check to determine that all the necessary data FIELDS are present in a transaction. See: AUTHORIZATION CHECK

COMPLETE OPERATING MOVEMENT PROCESSING AND SERVICE SYSTEM Same as: COMPASS

COMPLEXITY (1) A measure of the relative difficulty a new PRODUCT is to understand, use, and/or comprehend. (2) With respect to the DIFFUSION RATE, how difficult an INNOVATION is perceived to be to understand and to use. See: CHARACTERISTICS OF INNOVATION

COMPONENT PARTS Same as: PARTS

COMPOSITION (1) The activity of assembling type and PLATES in preparation for printing. (2) Often used to mean the same as LAYOUT.

COMPREHENSIVE A LAYOUT prepared to resemble the finished advertisement as closely as possible, but in which the COPY is not written out.

CONATIVE JUDGMENT As applied to a buyer of goods or services, his decision to take a certain action, to try a product or service. See: COGNITIVE JUDGMENT, NORMATIVE JUDGMENT, VALUE JUDGMENT

CONCEALED DISCOUNT A situation in which price-fixed and non-price-fixed items are listed on the same PURCHASE ORDER at a common discount, which is then reflected in the invoice. Care must be taken not to run afoul of the price discrimination provisions of the ROBINSON-PATMAN ACT.

CONCENTRATION The degree to which a small number of firms in an INDUSTRY account for a large proportion of the economic activity of that industry. Frequently used as one factor for determining the existence of MONOPOLY elements in the industry. Because it has been the basis for ANTI-TRUST activity, major firms in an industry try to avoid excessive concentration. See: MARKET STRUCTURE

CONCENTRIC DIVERSIFICATION Expansion in similar MARKETS, the activity confined to existing structures inside the company.

CONCESSION See: LEASED DEPARTMENT

CONCLUSIVE RESEARCH An organized study or investigation to produce evidence on which management may make a DECISION. Before this may be done, it is frequently necessary to do EXPLORATORY RESEARCH. Because of the confidential nature of conclusive research, much of it is not publicly reported. It may well be the most common type of MARKETING RESEARCH undertaken. See: PERFORMANCE RESEARCH

CONCURRENCE Duplication of the structure resulting from the joining of MARKETING elements. This may be horizontal, as in the instance of associations in the same INDUSTRY on both the RETAIL and the WHOLESALE levels; or it may be vertical, as in the instance of CHANNELS OF DISTRIBUTION of competing firms in the same field.

CONDENSED TYPE   Any type style with narrower-than-usual CHARACTERS, thus permitting more characters to the line. See: EXTENDED TYPE

CONDITIONAL PROBABILITY   The measured chance of occurrence that is assigned to event A when it is known that event B has occurred; or that would be assigned to event A if it were known that event B had occurred.

CONDITIONAL SALE   A contract for the sale of an item in which title does not pass to the buyer until payment is completed as required by the contract. Possession and risk of loss are assumed by the buyer.

CONFIDENCE   See: DEGREE OF CONFIDENCE

CONFIDENCE INTERVAL   The RANGE within which a POPULATION MEAN or a POPULATION total is located with a known level of probability. See: DEGREE OF CONFIDENCE, t, Z

CONFOUNDED VARIABLE   In MARKETING RESEARCH, an INDEPENDENT VARIABLE of an extraneous sort whose influence on the DEPENDENT VARIABLE is associated with the true explanatory variable in such a way as to make necessary special techniques to separate the extraneous influence. Examples of confounded variables are: seasonal variations, competitive changes, and changes in CONSUMER'S TASTES.

CONFUSION OF GOODS   The intermingling of the goods of two or more different owners where once so mixed the goods are difficult or even impossible again to separate. See: POOLING

CONGLOMERATE INTEGRATION   Acquisition of one company by another in an unrelated business and not necessarily in the same, or on the same level of, the CHANNEL OF DISTRIBUTION. See: HORIZONTAL INTEGRATION

CONGLOMERATE MARKET COMPETITION   Refers to the sale of the same product by different types of DEALERS and DISTRIBUTORS. The result of the trend toward SCRAMBLE MERCHANDISING, which has had the effect of multiplying CHANNELS OF DISTRIBUTION.

CONGRUENT INNOVATION   One of a four-way classification of new PRODUCTS as to degrees of newness, this type is of a concept accepted by the society and just about the same as an already existing product. For all practical considerations, it is not actually an innovation because it brings about no change in established consumption patterns. The other three are: CONTINUOUS, DISCONTINUOUS, AND DYNAMICALLY CONTINUOUS. Proposed by Thomas S. Robertson.

CONGRUENT PRODUCTION DIVERSIFICATION   Additional products or lines of products are added to a firm's offerings based on the firm's technological skills and/or physical plant. A POLICY which may be dictated by the firm's financial position or structure. Same as: PRODUCTION-ORIENTED DIVERSIFICATION.

CONJOINT ANALYSIS   A methodology for representing the structure of CONSUMER preferences, and predicting consumers' behavior towards new stimuli. Introduced relatively recently, it is still in the process of developing its applications and potentials.

CONMANSHIP   The art of persuading people to part with their purchasing power for something which will not provide benefits, or even for nothing. It is the opposite of SALESMANSHIP

CONNECT TIME   In ADP, the elapsed time while using a remote terminal in a time-sharing system. See: ANSWERING TIME, TIME SLICE

CONRAIL   Created by Federal law as a private, for-profit corporation to take over portions of six bankrupt railroads. Primarily a freight railroad, it operates only in the Northeast, Midwest, and two provinces of Canada. It provides operating personnel and maintenance services for certain commuter lines under contract to local commuter authorities. Money received from the Federal Government is mainly treated as a loan. See AMTRAK.

CONSCIOUS PARALLEL ACTION   Same as: CONSCIOUS PARALLELISM

CONSCIOUS PARALLELISM   Firms doing the same thing in the MARKET, especially as to price. As court decisions now stand, this may well be judged a form of tacit collusion, and thus be illegal even without formal evidence.
See: PRICE LEADERSHIP

CONSENT ORDER   An action taken by a government agency prohibiting a respondent from doing what the agency considers improper. When agreed to by the respondent, it becomes binding. Such an agreement is for settlement purposes only and does not constitute an admission by the respondent that he has violated the law. Numerous such orders are currently being issued by the FTC to effect respondent's refraining from restraints of trade, deceptive sales practices, misleading advertising, etc. Because it carries the force of law, penalties of up to $10,000 may be imposed for each violation.

CONSERVATIVE PHILOSOPHY   Same as: NEUTRAL PHILOSOPHY

CONSERVATIVE RULE OF INVENTORY VALUATION   See: INVENTORY VALUATION

CONSIGNED LIMIT   The maximum dollar amount of the CONSIGNMENT which a DEALER may carry under the CONSIGNMENT TERMS.

CONSIGNEE   (1) The holder of goods under CONSIGNMENT TERMS. See: CONSIGNOR
(2) The one to whom a shipment of goods is addressed.

CONSIGNMENT   (1) A stock of merchandise advanced to a DEALER and located at his place of business, but with title remaining in the source of supply.
(2) A shipment of goods to a CONSIGNEE.

CONSIGNMENT BUYING   See: STOCKLESS PURCHASING

CONSIGNMENT DISTRIBUTOR   In the petroleum industry, same as: COMMISSION BULK PLANT OPERATOR

CONSIGNMENT SERVICE STATION   A service station owned or leased by an oil company, operated by a manager who sells gasoline under the company's BRAND NAME and who receives a commission on sales. Same as: COMMISSION OPERATED STATION

CONSIGNMENT TERMS   Similar to MEMORANDUM TERMS except that title remains with the vendor until the merchandise is sold by the RETAILER.

CONSIGNOR   (1) The holder of title to goods shipped under CONSIGNMENT TERMS.
See: CONSIGNEE   (2) The originator of a shipment of goods.

CONSOLE   In ADP, that part of the computer which is designed to give manual control over the computer. The console provides the means of correcting errors, revising the contents of the memory storage, instructing the computer as to operations, and otherwise monitoring the computer's circuits, registers, and counters.

CONSOLIDATED BUYING   Same as: CENTRAL BUYING

CONSOLIDATED CAR   A carload of merchandise made up by a number of shippers, sent to one location and moving at carload rates. See: FREIGHT FORWARDER, POOL CAR

CONSOLIDATED METROPOLITAN AREA   A large METROPOLITAN complex comprising a metropolitan area of a million people or more, together with other contiguous metropolitan areas the population of each of which is at least 75% urban and meets certain minimum criteria of integration with the central metropolitan area. See: SMSA

CONSOLIDATOR   A transportation activity service agency limited by ICC rules to matching trailerloads tendered to it, shipping them as a single shipment at a volume rail rate. It performs a valuable service by reducing freight costs to the shipper. It must not arrange for BREAKING BULK or for distribution, which would push it into FREIGHT FORWARDER STATUS and a different set of regulations.

CONSPICUOUS CONSUMPTION   The purchase and use of goods and services primarily to raise one's prestige rather than to satisfy material needs.

CONSTANT DOLLARS.   A statistical series expressed in dollars from which the effect of INFLATION has been removed with respect to a BASE YEAR or group of years in the past.   All the dollars in the series are thus constant and comparable, and may be subjected to relative measurement.

CONSTANT RETURNS TO SCALE   See: RETURNS TO SCALE

CONSTRAINT   Anything in the environment or the objectives of an investigation or action which limits its extent, scope, or area.   See: PAYOFF, PROBLEM, MARKETING RESEARCH

CONSTRUCTIVE DISTRIBUTION   Designing CHANNELS OF DISTRIBUTION offering facilities and services necessary to insure satisfied CUSTOMERS.

CONSTRUCT VALIDITY   An attribute of an ATTITUDE measure that involves the degree to which a given attitude is consistent with the total mix of a person's attitudes or personality dimensions.   See: CONTENT VALIDITY, PREDICTIVE VALIDITY, VALIDITY

CONSUMABLE SUPPLIES   Same as: OPERATING SUPPLIES

CONSUMER   (1) A person who purchases for personal or household use.   (2) Anyone who uses up the UTILITIES embodied in goods or services.   In MARKETING, one must consider the MOTIVES and habits inferred in (1), and at the same time take into account the influence of (2).   Industrial and institutional purchasers should be called users.

CONSUMER ANALYSIS   The study of the CONSUMER using appropriate MARKETING RESEARCH techniques to establish as many psychological, sociological and DEMOGRAPHIC understandings as possible considering available time and resources.

CONSUMER BEHAVIOR   The manifestations of the decision processes and the SEARCH activities involved in acquiring and using goods and services.   The entire range of activities in which CONSUMERS engage when in the the search process.   It is now a special field of MARKETING RESEARCH.

CONSUMER CREDIT PROTECTION ACT   A Federal law passed in 1968 to stop abusive practices in the field of consumer credit and collections.   Same as: TRUTH-IN-LENDING ACT.   See: EQUIVALENT RATE OF SIMPLE INTEREST FORMULA

CONSUMER DEAL   A price reduction to a CONSUMER usually offered in one of the following ways: sale of multiple units at a special price for the package, a cents-off COUPON, one package for 1¢ with the purchase of a given number, one unit of new product with one unit of an old product at less than the sum of the two.   See: DEAL

CONSUMER GOODS   (1) Goods bought for personal or household satisfactions. (2) Goods used directly in satisfying human wants.   See: CONSUMER

CONSUMER GOODS SYSTEM   Same as: COGS

CONSUMERISM   An increasingly prominent activity by CONSUMERS and government to take the necessary measures to protect the general public from misrepresentation, poorly made goods, bad service, and obscure warranties. It is forcing business to assume a real responsibility for its product.

CONSUMER JURY   A method of PRETESTING products or advertisements by getting the reactions of potential purchasers or users.   See: PANEL

CONSUMER-PERCEIVED RISKS   In making PRODUCT decisions, the CONSUMER usually considers these uncertainties: 1) functional risk (perhaps the product will not do what it is said to be able to do); 2) physical risk (could it do injury to the physical self of someone?); 3) financial risk (product may not be worth its cost); 4) social risk (could it cause embarrassment?); 5) psychological risk (danger of bruised ego).

CONSUMER PRICE INDEX   Same as: CPI

CONSUMER PRODUCT SAFETY ACT   Same as: CPSA

CONSUMER PRODUCT SAFETY COMMISSION   See: CPSA

CONSUMER RESEARCH   A subclass of MARKETING RESEARCH, it is concerned with the investigation to discover, the assembly, and the analysis of data which may make more predictable the behavior of the CONSUMER in the MARKET.

CONSUMER RIGHTS   Originally stated by President John F. Kennedy and subsequently reflected in much legislation, they are: the right to safety, the right to be informed, the right to choose, the right to be heard. See: CONSUMERISM

CONSUMERS' COOPERATIVE   A voluntary association of CONSUMERS, organized to fulfill some of their needs for goods and services. A credit union is an example of this type of organization. See: ROCHDALE PLAN

CONSUMER SEARCH   See: SEARCH

CONSUMER SOCIALIZATION   The process by which children acquire knowledge, ATTITUDES, and skills pertinent to their effective functioning as CONSUMERS. See: SOCIALIZATION

CONSUMER SOVEREIGNTY   The concept that the CONSUMER is supreme in the MARKET, a concept that has relevance in relation to the degree of access the consumer has to choice in the market; not only the right to reject inferior goods, but the right to choose among a sufficient range of products so that matching may reasonably occur between the characteristics of the product and the demand specifications of a certain consumer.

CONSUMER'S RISK   Used sometimes in PURCHASING to denote the probability of accepting a sample of a lot which is actually defective.

CONSUMER'S SURPLUS   The difference between the UTILITY a buyer of a product or service gets and the utility he pays for. This "bargain" comes about through the pricing process for a DIFFERENTIATED PRODUCT. The seller must ultimately set upon the level of price that will provide him with the volume he wants. Thus the price will give the last PROSPECT an amount of utility exactly equal to the price charged. Prospects who would pay more than this, who see more utility in the product than those for whom it has a weaker appeal, are provided with unpaid-for utility.

CONSUMMATORY PURPOSE   The purpose of a message is accomplished at the moment of its consumption when received. See: INSTRUMENTAL PURPOSE

CONSUMPTION   The destruction of the UTILITIES embodied in GOODS and services.

CONSUMPTION FUNCTION   The relation of personal expenditures to income at different levels of income. See: PROPENSITY TO CONSUME

CONTACT MAN   Same as: ACCOUNT EXECUTIVE

CONTAINERIZATION   Design and use of filled rather-small-van size to trailer-size containers which may be moved interchangeably among various types of carriers without BREAKING BULK. At present there is a move toward standardiztion of container sizes. In order to facilitate intermodal transportation, some TERMINALS and wharfs are providing or planning spaces especially for each of the two most used sizes, 20-foot and 40-foot. The 20-foot size is especially adapted to the LASH concept, the 40-foot size can be accomodated readily on containerships. Recently, a service has been made available to exporters of smaller shipments that offers the same advantages as filled containers.

CONTAINERIZATION INSTITUTE   The only organization in the field of CONTAINERIZATION and bulk PACKAGING (its name originally was Bulk Packaging and Containerization Institute), it acts as industry spokesman, publishes a news bulletin, and acts as liason with industry committees and government agencies.

CONTAINER PREMIUM A product PACKAGE which serves as a reusable container or other household item such as a carafe. All or part of the cost over that of a common package may be added to the price to make the promotion self-liquidating at least to some degree.

CONTENT ANALYSIS Used in the social sciences to examine communications messages by a systematic technique involving categorizing the messages according to predetermined rules and then treating them statistically. It has been used for such diverse purposes as testing the effectiveness of ADVERTISING SUBSTANTIATION and proving the authorship of the "Federalist Papers."

CONTENT VALIDITY An attribute of a QUESTIONNAIRE which relates the relevance of the items in the questionnaire to the total ATTITUDE being SCALED. See: CONSTRUCT VALIDITY, PREDICTIVE VALIDITY, VALIDITY

CONTEST A competition based on skill in which prizes are offered. Care must be taken that this not be interpretable as a lottery, which might be illegal according to the laws of the several states. See: SWEEPSTAKES

CONTINUITY (1) Repetition of the same basic THEME, LAYOUT, or format in ADVERTISING. (2) Repeated use of the same MEDIA. (3) Script for TELEVISION, RADIO, or film production. (4) The period of time over which a steady advertising effort is sustained.

CONTINUITY PROGRAM The offering by a RETAILER of a number of related PREMIUMS at regular intervals over a period of time. Generally SELF-LIQUIDATING. May be items of cookware at the rate of one a week, or an assortment of various size pictures, etc.

CONTINUITY-STRIP COPY Same as: NARRATIVE COPY, but with greater emphasis on the pictorial elements to heighten interest and convey the impression.

CONTINUOUS DATA These are gathered whenever the elements of a POPULATION or SAMPLE are measured. They may be whole or fractional numbers. See: DISCRETE DATA

CONTINUOUS INNOVATION (1) A modification of an existing PRODUCT rather than an entirely new concept. Effects little change in established buying patterns. (2) One of a four-way classification of new products as to degrees of newness, this type usually involves some alteration of a product but causes little disruption in established buying patterns. The others are: CONGRUENT, DISCONTINUOUS, and DYNAMICALLY CONTINUOUS. Proposed by Thomas S. Robertson.

CONTINUOUS PLAN A series of regular mailings to a fixed LIST. May be in the nature of a certain sort of material sent at regular intervals, e.g., a HOUSE ORGAN, or a group of miscellaneous materials sent on a more or less regular schedule. Particularly useful for an advertiser who has a definite group of customers or PROSPECTS before whom he needs to keep his name and product or service, and whose offerings are in reasonably constant or recurring demand. Most of the effect of this plan is to develop a favorable attitude toward the seller, thereby indirectly assisting the sales department. Determining a way of measuring the IMPACT of this plan is often a difficult problem. See: DIRECT MAIL ADVERTISING

CONTINUOUS TONE Illustration shading accomplished by a method other than the use of the HALFTONE dot.

CONTRACT ACCOUNT A RETAILER'S customer with whom there is an agreement that stipulates periodic payments on the basis of a fixed percent of the amount owing as shown by a statement sent regularly.

CONTRACT CARRIER A transportation company serving on an individual contract basis. Some states require that these be licensed.

CONTRACT CARRIER CONFERENCE Same as: CCC

CONTRACT GRADES   Those grades of a commodity which have been officially approved by a COMMODITY EXCHANGE as deliverable in settlement of a futures contract. See: BASIS GRADES

CONTRACTUAL INTEGRATION   INTEGRATION by agreement, leaving all ESTABLISH- MENTS separately owned. Examples: FRANCHISING, VOLUNTARY CHAIN.

CONTRACTUAL VERTICAL MARKETING SYSTEM   Operates as does a VOLUNTARY CHAIN, except that individual ESTABLISHMENTS retain their own identities. See: ADMINISTERED VERTICAL MARKETING SYSTEM, CORPORATE VERTICAL MARKETING SYSTEM See also: CONTRACTUAL INTEGRATION

CONTRACT YEAR   In ADVERTISING, a SPACE CONTRACT running for one year from the first insertion under the contract.

CONTRAST   A technique in ADVERTISING which attempts to emphasize how two products differ from one another in a way that is commercially beneficial to the advertiser's product. See: COMPARISON

CONTRIBUTION PRICING   Setting a price below STANDARD COST but above VARI- ABLE COSTS. Even one dollar above variable costs adds to what is avail- able to pay for FIXED COSTS. See: MARGINAL COST, MARGINAL REVENUE

CONTRIBUTION-TO-OVERHEAD PRICING   Same as: CTO PRICING

CONTROL CHARACTER   A CHARACTER in ADP whose occurance in a certain context initiates, modifies, or stops a CONTROL OPERATION, e.g., a character to control print line spacing.

CONTROL GROUP   The group of individuals associated with a TEST GROUP in a MARKETING RESEARCH activity but who are not exposed to the variable being studied. The existence of a control group makes possible the assessment of the effectiveness of the studied variable by providing the sum results of all other influencing factors with which to compare.

CONTROLLABLE EXPENSES   Those business expenses which in many instances can be reduced without seriously affecting the operation as a whole, at least in the near term. See: VARIABLE COSTS

CONTROLLED BRAND   Same as: CONTROLLED LABEL

CONTROLLED CIRCULATION   The CIRCULATION of specialized publications deliv- ered free to individuals selected by some relevant criteria. There is a trend toward calling it "QUALIFIED CIRCULATION." To meet BPA standards, the publication must be issued quarterly or oftener, and must contain no less than 25% editorial matter.

CONTROLLED LABEL   Same as: PRIVATE LABEL, but sometimes applied particular- ly to the BRAND owned by a WHOLESALER, and sometimes to that of a whole- saler who runs a VOLUNTARY CHAIN. There appears to be a trend toward using the name of the company itself as a controlled label for a LINE of merchandise.

CONTROLLED SHOPPING CENTER   Same as: PLANNED SHOPPING CENTER

CONVENIENCE FOOD STORE   A usually smaller than SUPERMARKET size STORE devoted to quick service of a limited ASSORTMENT of fast-moving food and general household items.

CONVENIENCE GOOD   The type of item which the CONSUMER usually desires to purchase with a minimum of effort at the most convenient and accessible place. While products may be so classified on a broad base, a specific item may be classified only if the ATTITUDE of the consumer toward the item is known. See: SHOPPING GOOD, SPECIALTY GOOD

CONVENIENCE SAMPLE   Data collected from the most readily available elements of an appropriate POPULATION. No known way of measuring the degree of accuracy of the sample can be applied to a sample chosen this way. See: JUDGMENT SAMPLE, PROBABILITY SAMPLE

CONVENIENCE STORE   Same as: BANTAM STORE

CONVERGENT MARKETING   A way of organizing the MARKETING activity within
the firm so that all the same resources are used to sell all the products made. Has the possible advantage of ECONOMIES OF SCALE. See:
DIVERGENT MARKETING

CONVERSION   The process in an ADP system of changing information from one
form of representation to another, e.g., from the LANGUAGE of one type of
machine to that of another type, or from punched cards to magnetic tape
to the printed page. See: CONVERTER

CONVERSIONAL MARKETING   Those activities designed to deal with NEGATIVE
DEMAND so as to develop the MARKET'S thinking about and reaction to the
PRODUCT up to a positive level sufficient to absorb a reasonable quantity
of the available SUPPLY.

CONVERSION PROCESS   Same as: BOOMERANG TECHNIQUE

CONVERTER   (1) A MERCHANT MIDDLEMAN in the textile industry who incidental
to the usual WHOLESALE functions performed as a SERVICE WHOLESALER, fin-
ishes, dyes, prints, etc. the cloth to make it more salable. His manufacturing activities are so small compared to his other functions that he is
regarded as a WHOLESALE MIDLLEMAN.   (2) In ADP, a machine capable of performing the CONVERSION process. EDITING facilities are sometimes included to assist the user.

COOPERATIVE   See: AGRICULTURAL COOPERATIVE, CONSUMERS' COOPERATIVE, CO-
OPERATIVE CHAIN, COOPERATIVE ELEVATOR, FEDERATED ASSOCIATION, PRODUCERS'
COOPERATIVE

COOPERATIVE ADVERTISING (1)A way of attempting to induce local advertising
by a MIDDLEMAN of a manufacturer's product, in which the manufacturer
offers to pay some portion (most commonly 50%) or all of the cost of the
middleman's advertisements in local MEDIA. The contract usually specifies that any advertisement must have the prior approval of the manufacturer. Frequently used also by WHOLESALERS, especially to promote a
PRIVATE BRAND. (2) The PROMOTION carried out jointly by firms in an INDUSTRY
through a TRADE ASSOCIATION.   (3) A joint venture in ADVERTISING by two
or more firms.

COOPERATIVE CHAIN   An organization in which a group of RETAILERS become the
stockholders of a WHOLESALE company established to serve themselves. See:
VOLUNTARY CHAIN

COOPERATIVE ELEVATOR   A grain ELEVATOR controlled by the farmers who have
united to establish it to serve themselves.

COOPERATIVE MAILING   The inclusion of several messages from different advertisers in the same envelope in a mass mailing from a LIST. Addressing,
postage and cover costs are shared. Same as: GROUP MAILING

COORDINATES   See: ENSEMBLE DISPLAY

COPY   In a broad sense, all verbal and visual elements which are included in
a finished ADVERTISEMENT. Used more narrowly to designate the verbal elements only. The latter is probably more common.

COPY APPROACH   The method of opening the text of an advertisement. It may
be factual, imaginative, or human interest.

COPY BOX   Same as: BOX

COPY CASTING   Same as: COPY FITTING

COPY FITTING   Similar in purpose to CASTING-OFF but more precise in its
use of mathematical computations which include provisions for white space
and LEADING.

COPY OUTLINE   Same as: COPY PLATFORM

COPY PLAN   Same as: COPY PLATFORM

COPY PLATFORM   The statement of the basic idea for an ADVERTISING CAMPAIGN, and any instructions as to the order of significance of the various selling points and elements of any advertisement.

COPY POLICY   Same as: COPY PLATFORM

COPYRIGHT   Legal protection granted an author or artist against the reproduction and sale of an original work without express consent. Until 1977 the grant was for 28 years and could be renewed for another 28 years. Now the period of grant is for the originator's lifetime plus 50 years.

COPY SLANT   The particular way in which a selling point is presented in an ADVERTISEMENT. Each individual AUDIENCE segment should have its own matching copy slant.

COPY TESTING   Research done to evaluate proposed ADVERTISING APPEALS as to clarity and impact.

COPYTHINKING   All of the activities, including gathering of data, research, and investigation, required to give the COPYWRITER a clear understanding of the goals sought and the means to reach those goals, before he begins to write the COPY.

COPYWRITER   A person who writes ADVERTISEMENTS.

CORPORATE ADVERTISING   Same as: INSTITUTIONAL ADVERTISING

CORPORATE PURPOSE   A refinement of the MARKETING CONCEPT which provides a base for corporate planning at the highest echelons. It involves a thorough analysis of how a firm may justify the right to exist. It specifies how the firm's products or services will fill the NEEDS that exist within an industrial or social economy, how the firm may be a good citizen, how it may interact with shareholders and employees, and any other matters pertinent to the firm's place in its broad environment. If properly done, this document will provide the guide for POLICY direction for the selection of products, fixed investment, and public relations. To remain effective, it must be monitored constantly to reflect changing influences.

CORPORATE RELATIONS   Another way of referring to RECIPROCITY.

CORPORATE VERTICAL MARKETING SYSTEM   VERTICAL INTEGRATION applied to RETAILING. See: ADMINISTERED VERTICAL MARKETING SYSTEM, CONTRACTUAL VERTICAL MARKETING SYSTEM

CORRECTIVE ADVERTISING   Under present law the FTC may require an ADVERTISER who has been found to have placed deceptive ADVERTISING to devote an amount of space or time in future advertisements with disclosure of the previous deception. This penalty is to attempt to counteract the residual effect of the past deception. It can be an expensive penalty.

CORRELATION   The measurement of the degree to which changes in the DEPENDENT VARIABLE are associated with changes in the INDEPENDENT VARIABLE. Care should be taken not to interpret a high degree of movement of one variable in the same or opposite direction as another, associated variable as a fact of causation. PARAMETRIC. See: CORRELATION COEFFICIENT, MULTIPLE CORRELATION

CORRELATION COEFFICIENT   Same as: COEFFICIENT OF CORRELATION

COSPONSORING   Two or more SPONSORS sharing the cost of a single BROADCAST program. See: ALTERNATE SPONSORSHIP, PARTICIPATING PROGRAM, SPOT

COST ANALYSIS   See: PERFORMANCE ANALYSIS

COST CODE   A method of indicating item cost information on price tickets so that only initiated personnel can interpret it. A common method is through the use of letters from an easily remembered word or expression, with nonrepeating letters corresponding to numerals. Example:

```
A I D   T H E   F O L K      S
1 2 3   4 5 6   7 8 9 0    Repeat
```

COST COMPLEMENT   Same as: COST MULTIPLIER

COST MULTIPLIER   In RETAILING, the average relationship of cost of goods to the actual retail value of the goods handled in an accounting period. Same as: Cost Complement, Cost Percent

COST OF CREDIT   What it costs in addition to cash price for the privilege of buying something with a promise to pay in the future. Found by subtracting from the total of all values given and promised, the cash price of the item plus applicable sales tax.

COST OF LIVING ADJUSTMENT   Same as COLA

COST-ORIENTED PRICING   A way of arriving at a selling price by taking the invoice cost of an item and adding a certain percentage to it. Essentially the same as: COST-PLUS PRICING. See: DEMAND-ORIENTED PRICING

COST OR MARKET   A way of assigning money value to a physical inventory. Each item is valued at cost or market price prevailing, whichever is the lower. Considered a conservative approach. See: FIFO, LIFO

COST PER CALL   The cost incurred on the average for a SALESPERSON to make one call to a CUSTOMER or PROSPECT, based on all the expenses associated with the sales activity. It is estimated to be over $95 and increasing.

COST PERCENT   Same as: COST MULTIPLIER

COST PER INQUIRY   When DIRECT MAIL ADVERTISING is used for the purpose of developing leads for SALESPERSONS to follow up, this is often a tentative measure of selling expense and a base for estimating the probable final cost of a sale. Example: if a mailing costs $5,000 and the mailing produces 500 inquiry replies, then the cost per inquiry is $10. See: COST PER SALE

COST PER SALE   (1) In DIRECT MAIL ADVERTISING, the cost of making one sale as calculated with reference to the cost of the mailing. Example: if the cost of a mailing is $5,000 and if as a result of the mailing 10 sales are made, then the cost per sale is $500. See: COST PER INQUIRY (2) In the usual personal selling situation, the cost of obtaining an order based on all expenses associated with the sales activity. See: COST PER CALL

COST PER THOUSAND   Same as: CPM

COST-PLUS PRICING   Setting the price of an item by adding to its cost a certain percent of its cost, or sometimes a certain dollar amount. See: PRICING

COST-PRICE JUDGMENT   When a BUYER feels he knows the approximate cost of an item, he may react to the price on the basis of whether or not he feels the MARK-UP to be reasonable. Regardless of what he might have to pay for the same satisfactions from another source, he will resent the price if he considers the cost-price relationship too great. See: FAIR PRICE REFERENCE REACTION, PRICE-AURA EFFECT, REVERSE-ORDER PERCEPTION

COST-RATIO METHOD   A procedure for evaluating sources of supply whereby all identifiable purchasing and receiving costs are related to the value of the shipments. The result is a Quality-Cost Ratio found by dividing for any one supplier the associated costs by the total value of purchases. Its major disadvantage lies in the difficulty of arriving at accurate cost data. Perhaps the best procedure is one which combines this one with the CATEGORICAL METHOD and the WEIGHTED-POINT METHOD.

COST TRADE-OFF   Spending more on one aspect of MARKETING in order to reduce the cost of another aspect even more. An overall increase in efficiency may result. See: TOTAL COST APPROACH

COTTON TEXTILE INSTITUTE   See: ATMI

COUNCIL FOR MUTUAL ASSISTANCE   Same as: COMECON

COUNCIL FOR MUTUAL ECONOMIC ASSISTANCE   Same as CMEA

COUNCIL OF THE AMERICAS   A business association of over 200 companies, representing about 85% of United States private investment in Latin America, organized to monitor, advise, and create liason with the economic climate in Latin America as it develops.

COUNT AND RECOUNT   A procedure used to determine the results of a sale: count the merchandise, run the sale, then recount the merchandise. The quantitative effectiveness of the sale is determined by simple arithmetic.

COUNTER AD PLAN   The requirement that an ADVERTISER found to have run misleading advertisements place a percent of the amount of space in the same MEDIA as advertisements correcting the misleading ones. The FTC is urging this practice on the FCC, but is itself involved in several instances on its own. Much controversy can be seen regarding the efficacy of this policy in limiting or eliminating false or misleading advertising. It is too soon to make an evaluation, although to summer of 1972 the FTC had been successful in obtaining a number of consent orders and some corrective advertising had been placed.

COUNTERADVERTISING   The ADVERTISING done by groups in the public interest to persuade against the use of PRODUCTS the groups deem harmful. The FTC seems to consider this activity quite benignly.

COUNTER CARD   POP material equipped with an easel on the back, intended for standing on a counter or near a product on a shelf.

COUNTER-CYCLICAL ADVERTISING   Planning the ADVERTISING PROGRAM so that the bulk of ADVERTISEMENTS are run during periods when sales do not normally occur, and little is run during normally large-volume periods.

COUNTERPURCHASE   (1) A CT transaction in which the Eastern deliveries of goods are ordinarily non-resultant products, that is, they are not derived from or related to the Western technology or goods in the transaction. See: FTO (2) In international trade, an agreement involving two contracts: one by which the seller agrees to deliver a PRODUCT for cash at a set price, the other by which the original seller agrees to buy goods from the buyer for a duplicate or fixed percent amount of the original sale. See: BUY-BACK, COMPENSATION DEAL

COUNTERTRADE   Same as: CT

COUNTERVAILING DUTY   An import duty by one country designed to offset an export subsidy by another country.

COUNTERVAILING POWER   The balancing of one economic group having MARKET POWER with another group having about the same market power, as with oligoposonistic buyers and oligopolistic sellers in the same MARKET.

COUNTRY CLUB BILLING   Sometimes used to describe the practice of enclosing all sales checks for the month with the monthly statement.

COUNTRY ELEVATOR   An ELEVATOR established in a LOCAL MARKET.

COUNTY AND CITY DATA BOOK   Published biennially by the Bureau of the Census, this contains by city and county statistics gathered from the various CENSUSES.

COUNTY BUSINESS PATTERNS   An annual publication issued jointly by the Department of Commerce and the Department of Health, Education, and Welfare (now split into the Department of Health and the Department of Human Services). Its analysis of business within counties by number, type, employment, and payroll provides data frequently useful in industrial MARKET POTENTIAL decisions.

COUPON A certificate that carries an offer of a cash reduction in the price of an item in a RETAIL STORE. Provides a reward to the store for the service of handling. See: COUPONING, CROSS-COUPONING

COUPONING A way of offering CONSUMERS a special, temporary price reduction on an item without actually changing the regular market price. A COUPON good for a specified cents off on the purchase of a product is mailed to the consumer, placed in the PACKAGE of another product, or published in advertisements in PRINT MEDIA. Its promotional value is determined by its ability to induce consumers to purchase the product. This, in turn, is dependent upon the correctness of judgment which established the cents off.

COUPON PAD Essentially the same as: TAKE-ONES, but usually attached to a card which can be hung on a wall or stood on a counter.

COUPON PLAN Continuous offering of a variety of PREMIUMS for COUPONS, LABELS, or other tokens from merchandise.

COURT OF ARBITRATION An organ of the ICC, it provides a means of settling disputes between parties to international contracts. Under the rules established and agreed to by contract clause, the Court has since 1924 handled an ever-increasing number of cases, many involving governments.

COVARIANCE The measure of the expected degree of association between two sets of variables. Frequently the subject of MARKETING RESEARCH to determine the subset of interdependent PRODUCTS that will maximize expected return at a given risk or will minimize expected risk for a given return.

COVER The FIRST COVER of a publication is the front cover. The SECOND COVER is the inside of the front cover. The THIRD COVER is the inside of the back cover. The FOURTH COVER is the outside of the back cover. Cover positions usually are charged for at extra rates because they are considered PREFERRED POSITIONS.

COVERAGE (1) The number of HOUSEHOLDS or individuals who are exposed to a specific advertising medium in a given area. (2) The sum of the total circulations of all the different MEDIA used. See: REACH

COVERAGE AREA The geographic area in which a station's signal can be received satisfactorily. See: COVERAGE MAP

COVERAGE MAP A map showing the prime area of a MEDIUM'S REACH within a MARKET. In TRANSIT ADVERTISING it usually includes street patterns and transit system routes.

COWCATCHER In BROADCAST MEDIA, a brief announcement preceding a program and featuring another product of the advertiser. See: HITCHHIKE

CPI Abbreviation for: Consumer Price Index, a relative measure issued by the U.S. Government, which shows the trend of prices of CONSUMER GOODS, including food, clothing, shelter, recreational items; of services, including professional fees, repair costs, transportation and utilities costs; and of sales, excise, and real estate taxes. It takes into account more than 80% of aggregate private expenditures. A weakness of this index is that its "market basket" is defined in accordance with the average expenditures of moderate income city dwellers, both single and married, and thus may not adequately reflect the prices paid by nor the expenditure patterns of other population groups. In process of revision to reflect the new base of an updated survey of expenditures made in 1972-3, with plans for more frequent surveys, and the inclusion of more and different items in its "market basket."

CPM (1) Abbreviation for: cost per thousand. Must be specified as referring to readers, viewers, CIRCULATION, etc. Used in comparing the costs of alternative vehicles of advertising. (2) Abbreviation for: Critical Path Method, essentially the same as CPS.

C.P.M.   See: NAPM

CPS   Abbreviation for: Critical Path Scheduling, a planning technique using a diagram that shows which jobs must be completed before other jobs can be started, and the times expected. See: PERT

CPSA   Abbreviation for: Consumer Product Safety Act which became law in 1972. It provides for a Consumer Product Safety Commission to administer it. Under this law manufacturers must notify the Commission within 24 hours of discovering that they have produced and sold something that represents "a substantial product hazard." A recall procedure must be instituted to correct the defect. See: PRODUCT LIABILITY

CPU   Abbreviation for: Central Processing Unit, that part of a computer that manages the information flows to and from the machine so as to control the sequence of operations and do the required calculations.

CR   Abbreviation for: CAMERA READY

CRAWL   The list of credits usually shown after a television show. These appear to be on a scroll which moves at some pace determined by the station. It most frequently moves vertically, but can be made to move horizontally.

CREATIVE SELLING   Employing that type of SALESMANSHIP which creates demand. It proves the benefits of an offering to those who have never bought that item from that salesperson before. See: SERVICE SELLING

CREDIT   The attribute of a buyer which enables him to gain immediate possession of a product or service on his promise to pay at some determinable later date. See: THREE Cs OF CREDIT

CREEPIE-PEEPIE   A hand-held TV camera, such is often used in the reporting of sports events.

CRISIS   See: BUSINESS CYCLE

CRITERIA RIGHTS   In PURCHASING, the AUTHORITY granted managers to set performance standards for their subordinates. See: ALLOCATION RIGHTS, EVALUATION RIGHTS, POLICY RIGHTS, SAMPLING RIGHTS, STRATEGY RIGHTS

CRITERION VARIABLE   Same as: DEPENDENT VARIABLE

CRITICAL PATH ANALYSIS   Same as: CPS

CRITICAL PATH SCHEDULING   Same as: CPS

CRITICAL VALUE OF t   See: t DISTRIBUTION

CRL   Abbreviation for: Completely Randomized Layout, same as COMPLETELY RANDOMIZED DESIGN

CROP   Trimming the edges of an illustration PLATE or removing pieces to change proportions or removing unwanted sections.

CROSS-COUPONING   A COUPON given with one item, which carries the price reduction offer for another item. May involve more than one seller. See: COUPONING, PUNCH-CARD COUPON

CROSS ELASTICITY OF DEMAND   Defines the extent to which a percent change in the price of one product affects the sale of another. Where the ratio is high (a small change in the price of Product A results in a large change in the sales of Product B), the products involved may be construed to be in the same MARKET. Where the ratio is low, the possibility of substitution is so remote that the products must be regarded as being in separate markets. This concept has been used by the courts is some anti-trust actions. See: COMPLEMENTARY GOODS, SUBSTITUTIONAL GOODS

CROSS HAULING   Transporting goods from one point to another while goods of the same nature are being transported in the opposite direction. See: BACK-HAULING

CROSS PLUGS   In ALTERNATE SPONSORSHIP, the substitution of one minute of
COMMERCIAL time from one sponsor's program for that of his partner's,
thus maintaining weekly exposure for both.

CROSS-RUFF PROMOTION   An ADVERTISEMENT or PROMOTIONAL PROGRAM involving
cents-off deals, COUPONING, product sampling, and PREMIUMS, in which two
or more companies join to link BRANDS. Companies engaging in this
activity usually deal directly with one another and each continues to
promote its own brands.

CROSS-SELLING   Indicates that a SALES CLERK is permitted to work in more
than one department in a RETAIL STORE. A customer may thus be helped by
one clerk for all of his purchases.

CROW'S FEET   Metal brackets which fit into pole slots at right angles to
each other, forming feet for a POP POLE DISPLAY.

CRT   Abbreviation for: Cathode Ray Tube, important for display of information for direct reading either before or after input into a data processing or word processing system.

CRUDE BIRTH RATE   The BIRTH RATE on an annual basis.

CT   Abbreviation for: Countertrade, a transaction in which a seller (a
Western nation exporter) provides a buyer (an Eastern nation usually in
the Communist bloc) with deliveries of goods and/or services, at the same
time agreeing to accept goods from the buyer equal to an agreed-upon
percent of the original sales contract value. See: BARTER, COMPENSATION,
COUNTERPURCHASE

CTC   Abbreviation for: Central Traffic Control. Used in the TRAFFIC field.

CTO PRICING   Contribution to Overhead Pricing. Setting price at some point
greater than the amount of VARIABLE COST associated with producing or
distributing a particular PRODUCT or service. See: OVERHEAD

CU   In TELEVISION, abbreviation for: close-up, a camera focused to show a
desired display, object, or feature at close range. See: BCU, ECU

CUBED OUT   Refers to a transport vehicle's filling its available space before reaching its allowable maximum weight for a load.

CULTURAL ANTHROPOLOGY   See: ANTHROPOLOGY

CULTURE   As applied to a society, the design for living and adaptation to
the environment specific for that society. It is the social heritage of
man in that society. It includes the art, morals, customs, taboos, laws,
beliefs, and knowledge evolved by man in that society.

CUME   Abbreviation for: cumulative audience. It is the number of unduplicated people reached by a given schedule over a given time period.

CUMULATIVE AUDIENCE   Same as: CUME

CUMULATIVE DISCOUNT   Same as: PATRONAGE DISCOUNT

CUMULATIVE MARK-ON PERCENT   The difference between the delivered cost of
goods and the cumulative original selling prices, divided by the cumulative selling prices.

CUMULATIVE REACH   Same as: CUME, although sometimes used to designate the
total number of HOUSEHOLDS reached by a MEDIUM during a certain time.

CURIOSITY HEADLINE   A headline designed to invite the reader to want to
read further into the ADVERTISEMENT because his curiosity has been aroused.

CURRENT HOUSING REPORTS   See: CENSUS OF HOUSING

CURRENT INDUSTRIAL REPORTS   See: CENSUS OF MANUFACTURERS

CURRENT POPULATION REPORTS   See: CENSUS OF POPULATION

CURVE OF DISTINCTIVENESS   See: PERISHABLE DISTINCTIVENESS

CUSHION   An amount of inventory added to a basic amount to provide for unanticipated increases in demand, unforeseen delays in delivery, one buyer's
purchasing an unusually large quantity, and other unpredictable factors.
Used mainly in RETAILING. See: SAFETY STOCK

CUSTOMARY PRICE   The price of certain goods has become fixed not by deliberate action on the seller's part, but as a result of having prevailed on
the MARKET for so long a time that customers have developed a habit of relating that price to that product. Changes in price of such items may
sometimes be effected by changing the package quantity at the usual price.

CUSTOMER   Someone who has bought a certain product or service from a source.
Most often thought of as being a repeater. A customer may be a PROSPECT
for a product or service he has never before bought from that source.

CUSTOMER DECAY RATE   Same as: DECAY RATE

CUSTOMER FRANCHISE   A loyal product following by a group of CUSTOMERS.
The product's producer can count on repeat sales barring some unusual
event in the MARKET.

CUSTOMER HOLDOVER EFFECT   A CARRYOVER EFFECT evidenced by the continuing
as CUSTOMERS into many subsequent periods of new customers made by a MAR-
KETING expenditure in the present period. See: CUSTOMER RETENTION RATE,
DECAY RATE

CUSTOMER MARKET   An inclusive term that encompasses the buyers of a FIRM'S
offerings in any or all of its MARKETS, e.g., CONSUMER, INDUSTRIAL,
institutional or governmental, and usually includes all MIDDLEMEN.

CUSTOMER MARKET FOCUS   POLICY creation by a FIRM in recognition that buyers
can accept or reject the firm's offerings. See: CONSUMER SOVEREIGNTY,
MARKET CONCEPT

CUSTOMER PROFILE   A DEMOGRAPHIC description of the people who buy a BRAND.
Will probably include their purchasing patterns.

CUSTOMER RETENTION RATE   The converse of the DECAY RATE.

CUSTOMER SERVICE LEVEL   The measure of the efficiency of service to CUSTOM-
ERS, using a time base considered ideal as the 100% level and comparing it
with average times for accomplishing various services to arrive at a percent
of the ideal level.

CUSTOMS BROKER   A licensed individual or firm engaged in handling for a
fee all the necessary steps, procedures, and papers to obtain clearance
of goods through customs. May be applicable to import or export business,
domestic or foreign.

CUSTOM SELLING   A form of CREATIVE SELLING in which at least part of a
PRODUCT or service is designed especially for a particular PROSPECT, for
example, new cabinetry for a household kitchen.

CUT   (1) The engraving used to reproduce a printed illustration. (2) To
delete portions of COPY or program material. (3) An abrupt stop in a
BROADCAST program. (4) An instant switch from one television picture
to another without fading. See: OPTICALS

CUT-CASE DISPLAY   A shipping carton so designed that when cut as indicated
on it a shelf tray is formed which shows the names of the variety and
producer. Commonly used in SUPERMARKETS as provided by the makers of
canned soups.

CUT-IN   An instance in which a BROADCAST medium substitutes in one station
a COMMERCIAL different from the one used in the NETWORK.

CUT LINE   Same as: CAPTION

CUT OUTS   Same as: EMBELLISHMENTS

C.W.O. Abbreviation for: cash-with-order terms. Used in a situation where
    there is danger that the buyer may refuse to accept and pay for a C.O.D.
    shipment and the buyer does not qualify for CREDIT terms.

CYBERNETICS   The science of control systems in which internal feedback de-
    termines the activity within the system. Many complex activities are
    constructed today using this principle. A simple but good example is a
    refrigerator in which the feedback to the compressor switch from the ther-
    mostat starts or stops it according to the temperature inside the refriger-
    ator. The inside temperature is adjustable by the operator by resetting
    the thermostat.

CYCLE BILLING   A method of distributing the statement sending effort over
    the month. Used when first-of-the-month or any same-date sending of
    statements imposes an unnecessary burden on the system. Under this method
    the entire customer group is divided into managable units and customers
    in each unit are sent statements on their same day each month.

CYCLE OF FASHION   Same as: FASHION CYCLE

CYCLICAL FLUCTUATION   See: TIME SERIES

DAGMAR   An acronym for: Defining Advertising Goals, Measuring Advertising
    Results, a controversial concept advanced in 1961 by the Association of
    National Advertisers in a paper authored by Russell Colley. The philos-
    ophy of this concept is that ADVERTISING SHOULD BE MANAGED to attain clear-
    ly stated communication goals so that success and failure can be measured.
    Much has been written pro and con about the DAGMAR concept.

D&TPTC   Abbreviation for: Drug and Toilet Preparation Traffic Conference,
    an organization whose about 130 members ship the preponderance of the
    volume of the INDUSTRY in tonnage and sales dollars. Its objective is
    to protect the TRANSPORTATION interests of its members. To this end it
    holds meetings and distributes a weekly informational bulletin.

DAILY EFFECTIVE CIRCULATION   In OUTDOOR ADVERTISING, the number of persons
    who may be expected to observe a message. Usually measured as one-half
    of all persons passing the display in cars and trucks plus one-quarter of
    total mass-transit passengers.

DATA PROCESSING MANAGEMENT ASSOCIATION   Same as: DPMA

DATING   The practice of extending credit for a longer period than regular
    by calculating the credit period from a date later than the one on which
    the invoice was issued. See: TERMS OF SALE

DAY-GLO   Name of inks and paints that fluoresce in sunlight or BLACKLIGHT.

DAY PARTS   The way in which a BROADCAST MEDIUM divides its on-the-air time.
    Most frequently it is: morning, afternoon, early evening, night, and late
    night. See: DRIVE TIME, FRINGE TIME, PRIME TIME

d.b.a. Abbreviation for: doing business as. Commonly used when the TRADE
    NAME of the business differs from the name of the individual who owns it.

DC   Abbreviation for: Distribution Code, an 11-digit all numeric code, using
    6 digits to identify the manufacturer and 5 to identify the specific item
    of that manufacturer. See: NAW, UPC

DCA   Abbreviation for: Distribution Cost Analysis, an accounting system
    for determining the profit contribution of the firm's individual PRODUCTS.
    Takes into account CHANNELS OF DISTRIBUTION, geographic variables, handling
    peculiarities and other differences among the product cost factors. See:
    TOTAL COST APPROACH

DCI   Abbreviation for: Distribution Codes, Inc. See: NAW

DEAD CORNER   Any location in a RETAIL shopping area which is either vacant or is used for non-retailing purposes so that it adversely affects the drawing power of the area for retailing purposes, or tends to halt the flow of shopper traffic between two retailing areas.

DEADHEADING   Returning empty vehicles and their crews after completing a shipment.   See: PRIVATE CARRIER

DEADLINE   Same as: CLOSING DATE

DEAD MATTER   MATTER which is of no further use.   See: LIVE MATTER

DEAD METAL   Portions of a metal engraving which do not print but are needed to support the engraving during ELECTROTYPING.   Same as: BEARERS

DEAD SPACE   Water carrier space engaged but not used by a shipper.   (2) Any available but unoccupied space on a carrier.

DEAD STOCK   Items in inventory for which there is no demand.   See: STICKERS

DEADWEIGHT TONNAGE   The total number of GROSS TONS of CARGO, stores and fuel that a vessel can transport.   It is calculated by subtracting from the number of tons of water displaced by a ship when submerged to the load water line the number of tons of water displaced by the ship empty.

DEAL   An inducement offered to a MERCHANT MIDDLEMAN to buy a special quantity of a product at one time.   May involve a quantity free of the same goods or an assortment of items to be bought as a unit with a better-than-usual MARGIN.   See: CONSUMER DEAL

DEALER   (1) A MERCHANT MIDDLEMAN who buys goods for resale to CONSUMERS. (2) INDUSTRY practice sometimes makes this term synonymous with INDUSTRIAL DISTRIBUTOR, although most often applied to a RETAILER.   See: AUTHORIZED DEALER

DEALER COOPERATIVE ADVERTISING   Same as: COOPERATIVE ADVERTISING

DEALER INCENTIVE   A POP display incorporating as one of its parts a desirable unit for the DEALER to take home.

DEALER PREMIUM   See: LOADER

DEALER'S PRIVILEGE   A card or similar display piece which carries an advertisement on one side and provides for the RETAILER'S message on the other.

DEALER TIE-IN   Participation by a DEALER in a NATIONAL ADVERTISER'S promotional program,   It may be in a variety of ways, such as in the use of POP materials, COOPERATIVE ADVERTISING, CONTESTS, etc.

DEAL-PACK   An item of merchandise with a PREMIUM attached.   WHOLESALERS and RETAILERS expect some compensation for handling these because regular merchandise must be withdrawn during the promotion period.

DEBUGGING   (1) The process of correcting planning or engineering errors. (2) In ADP, the process of determining the correctness of a computer routine and fixing any errors found in it.   (3) The detection and correction of malfunctions in the computer itself.

DECAY RATE   The proportion of CUSTOMERS lost in a year.   Has much to do with the BRAND SWITCHING propensity of the MARKET.   Indicates the amount of weakening of the effects of prior marketing efforts.   Recognition of this factor explains the need for continued marketing effort just to maintain current share.   See: CARRYOVER EFFECTS

DECENTRALIZATION   Assignment of responsibilities and AUTHORITY involving decision-making functions to an organization unit lower in the firm's hierarchy by a higher unit.

DECEPTIVE PACKAGING   The use of PACKAGES that because of size or shape may create the impression that they contain more of the PRODUCT than is actually

there, or that the product is larger than it actually is. See: FAIR PACK-
AGING AND LABELING ACT

DECILE. Found in the same general manner as the MEDIAN, except that deciles
divide the ARRAY into ten tenths.

DECISION. A determination of a course of action relevant to a PROBLEM, or
the reduction of a question to an actionable answer. See: PROBLEM
SOLVING

DECISION ANALYSIS   See: FORMAL DECISION ANALYSIS

DECISION CRITERION   Same as: DECISION RULE

DECISION FEEDBACK SYSTEM. Same as: ARQ

DECISION-MAKING UNIT. Same as: DMU

DECISION RULE   A statement of the conditions which if found as the result
of a MARKETING RESEARCH study or other valid test would mandate a particular course of action in the firm. Examples: "If at least 40% of the
potential MARKET for a new PRODUCT are found to react positively toward
it, go ahead with its introduction." "Test every twentieth unit of a
shipment of parts. If less than 5% of this SAMPLE are defective, accept
the entire shipment."

DECISION TREE. See: MARKOV CHAIN

DECK. A set of ADP cards punched with specific data.

DECK PANELS   In OUTDOOR ADVERTISING, PANELS erected one above another.

DECLINE. See: BUSINESS CYCLE

DECLINE LAGGARDS   Same as: LAGGARDS   See: ARC OF FASHION, INNOVATION
DIFFUSION

DECLINING DISTINCTIVENESS. See: PERISHABLE DICTINCTIVENESS

DECREASING RETURNS TO SCALE   See: RETURNS TO SCALE

DEDUCTION   A system of reasoning that results in the application of a
general PRINCIPLE to a particular situation. See: INDUCTION

DEFERRED DISCOUNT. Same as: PATRONAGE DISCOUNT

DEFLATION. A condition of the economy characterized by continually declining prices. See: INFLATION

DEGREE OF ACCURACY   See: STANDARD ERROR OF ESTIMATE

DEGREE OF CONFIDENCE. The percent of CONFIDENCE INTERVALS that would include the MEAN of the POPULATION if many such intervals based on independent SAMPLE means were computed.

DEGREES OF FREEDOM   (1) Equal to SAMPLE size minus one when the t distribution is used to estimate the MEAN of the POPULATION or to test its
assumed value. There is a unique distribution of t associated with each
degrees of freedom. There are no such separate distributions associated
with Z. (2) If observed data are arranged for analysis in columns and
rows, as they are in a CHI-SQUARE TEST, the degrees of freedom are equal
to the number of rows minus one times the number of columns minus one.

DELAYED RESPONSE EFFECT. A CARRYOVER EFFECT evidenced by the lags which
occur between the time a MARKETING expenditure is made and the time purchase induced thereby occurs. See: EXECUTION DELAY, NOTING DELAY,
PURCHASE DELAY, RECORDING DELAY

DELIVERABLE GRADES. Same as: CONTRACT GRADES

DELIVERED PRICE. The price which includes transportation charges to the
buyer's ESTABLISHMENT.

DELIVERY PERIOD   Same as: LEAD TIME

DELPHI TECHNIQUE   A method of MARKETING RESEARCH which may be used to resolve problems involving estimates that can be useful only if made by experts. A group of persons considered competent are asked individually by personal interview or mail questionnaire to express their judgments. After compilation, the results are given to the participants, who may revise their estimates. At no time do the participants meet together. The process may be repeated a number of times. Usually a consensus is reached which can then be used as a basis for decision-making.

DELTA NU ALPHA   Same as: DNA

DEM   Abbreviation for: DEMURRAGE

DEMAND   The quantity of product a MARKET will absorb at a given time under conditions of specified price, income, promotional activity, and environmental factors. See: DEMAND CURVE, ELASTICITY OF DEMAND

DEMAND ANALYSIS   The attempt to determine why the DEMAND a firm may have has come into being. The MARKET success of any firm rests on its ability to adapt its resources to the market behavior of potential buyers. See: EXTERNAL STIMULI, INDIVIDUAL CHANGE STIMULI, INTERNAL STIMULI, SELLER ACTIVITY STIMULI

DEMAND-BACKWARD PRICING   Same as: MARKET-MINUS PRICING

DEMAND CREATION   A series of activities essentially the same as: SALES PROMOTION

DEMAND CURVE   The plot of the schedule which shows for all possible prices within the relevant range the quantity of goods the MARKET will absorb, considering the factors prevailing at any one time.

DEMAND ELASTICITY   Same as: ELASTICITY OF DEMAND

DEMAND EXPANSIBILITY   Same as: EXPANSIBILITY OF DEMAND

DEMAND-ORIENTED PRICING   A way of setting price that takes into account the nature and quality of MARKET DEMAND for the offering. See: COST-ORIENTED PRICING

DEMAND SENSITIVITY   The relative rapidity of movement of an item in a RETAIL STORE. A part of the concepts of TURNOVER and ROI.

DEMAND STIMULATION   Same as: DEMAND CREATION

DEMARKETING   The process of attempting to diminish the apparent DEMAND for a PRODUCT to the level that the firm can accommodate. There are a number of economic reasons which may prompt this POLICY in preference to one of expanding to fill the demand.

DEMOGRAPHICS   The statistics of an area's population, or a MARKET, with distinguishing characteristics such as age, sex, income, education, marital status, occupation, etc. delineated. Includes all VITAL STATISTICS. See: PSYCHOGRAPHICS

DEMOGRAPHIC SEGMENTATION   See: SEGMENTATION

DEMONSTRATION   Same as: SALES DEMONSTRATION

DEMONSTRATOR   Usually an employee of a manufacturer, but may be an employee of a STORE, who becomes expert and spends all of his time showing how a particular product works or can be used.

DEMONSTRATOR DISPLAY   A POP unit which shows the functioning of the PRODUCT displayed.

DEMURRAGE   An additional charge made by a COMMON CARRIER when one of his units is held by the consignee beyond the allowed free time.

DENYING METHOD   Same as: DIRECT DENIAL TECHNIQUE

DEPARTMENTIZED SPECIALTY STORE   A SPECIALTY SHOP in essence, which has become large and in which the various types of merchandise carried are accounted for separately for profit knowledge and general managerial
decision making.

DEPARTMENTS   (1) Large stands designed to assist in the MERCHANDISING of the
ASSORTMENT or VARIETY of a PRODUCT LINE.   See: POP ADVERTISING   (2) See:
DEPARTMENT STORE

DEPARTMENT STORE   The RETAIL institution that probably offers the largest
VARIETY of goods under one roof to customers who are invited to the establishment to make their selections.   Highly departmentized for sales and
accounting purposes.   By Census of Business standards it must have at
least 25 employees and its merchandise must include apparel, appliances,
furniture, home furnishings and dry goods. Combined sales of SOFT GOODS
and apparel must be at least 20% of total sales.

DEPENDENCY RATIO   In an economy, the ratio between workers and pensioners.

DEPENDENT VARIABLE   In a cause-and-effect system, the outcome which is produced by the effects of certain factors called INDEPENDENT VARIABLES.   For
example, if the sales of a retail department vary with the amount of floor
space devoted to it, then floor space is the independent or "input" variable and sales is the dependent or "response" variable.

DEPOSIT SALE   Same as: LAY-AWAY SALE

DEPRECIATION   The loss in value of an asset due to the passage of time or
the making of a number of units of product.   See: OBSOLESCENCE

DEPRESSION   See: BUSINESS CYCLE

DEPTH INTERVIEW   A research interview in which the RESPONDENT is encouraged
to speak freely and in full about a particular subject.   The interview is
conducted without the use of a structured questionnaire.   See: FOCUSED
GROUP INTERVIEW

DEPTH OF ASSORTMENT   Refers to the number of variations available within a
class or product LINE, for example, the number of different colors of
cannister sets or the number of different sizes of a model of garment.
See: WIDTH OF ASSORTMENT

DEPTH OF COLUMN   Same as: DEPTH OF SPACE

DEPTH OF SPACE   The dimension of advertising space measured from top to
bottom, usually in reference to a column.   It may be stated in AGATE LINES,
PICAS, COLUMN INCHES.   Same as: DEPTH OF COLUMN

DERIVED DEMAND   A very significant characteristic of the MARKET for INDUS-
TRIAL GOODS which severely affects manufacturers of INSTALLATIONS.   Denotes
a demand for one product which arises from the demand for another product.
Explains that the industrial market fluctuates with the demand for final
products.

DESCRIPTIVE APPROACH   Same as: INSTITUTIONAL APPROACH

DESCRIPTIVE BILLING   The monthly bill is produced by a computer into which
has been entered the detail of each purchase and credit.   The CUSTOMER'S
statement shows the previous balance, the amount of each purchase, an identification of each purchase, total purchases and credits, service charges,
amount currently due, the due date, and the minimum amount payable on the
account.

DESCRIPTIVE LABELING   Labeling goods by characteristic, but without reference to recognized standards or grades.   See: LABEL

DESCRIPTIVE MODEL   Typically used as an aid to conceptualization.   May be a
PROSE MODEL or a LOGICAL FLOW MODEL.   See: MODEL

DESCRIPTIVE RESEARCH   Sometimes used to mean essentially the same as HYPOTHE-
SIS TESTING when the HYPOTHESIS relates to a STATE OF THE UNIVERSE. See:
MARKETING RESEARCH

DESCRIPTIVE THEORY   That type of THEORY which explains the structure and
functioning of institutions and the relationships among MARKETING variables.
Marketing models have been developed of CONSUMER, DISTRIBUTOR, and competitive behavior, among others. Some firms have built computer models
of their MARKETS. Forms a base for PREDICTIVE THEORY and NORMATIVE THEORY.

DESIGN   (1) The completely planned sequence of activities for a MARKETING
RESEARCH project. (2) A specific set of activities designed to validate
answers or solutions to PROBLEMS.

DESIGNATED MARKET AREA   Same as: DMA

DESIRE   A WANT activated.

DESIRE-SET   The entire bundle of benefits a prospective user of a product
would like to derive from it at the same time because he perceives them
as related. Most buyers must eventually compromise among all the elements
comprising the desire-set, which is defined for any individual by the
CULTURE to which he belongs.

DESK JOBBER   A MERCHANT WHOLESALER operating out of an office or showroom
who in the course of business rarely takes physical possession of the
goods he sells. The CUSTOMER is sent the goods directly from the producer
who bills the desk jobber. The desk jobber in turn bills his customer.
Same as: DROP SHIPPER

DETAILER   Found mainly in the food INDUSTRY, this manufacturer's employee
checks inventories and reports out-of-stock items to store managers,
suggests and organizes shelf arrangements, stocks shelves, recommends
STORE displays and sets them up where applicable, makes adjustments for
damaged stock, presents new items, and builds goodwill. Currently a controversial figure in view of activities claimed to create inflationary
pressures. See: DETAIL MAN

DETAILING   The activity of the DETAILER. See: DETAIL MAN

DETAIL MAN   A special kind of MISSIONARY SALESMAN used in the drug business
to call on doctors, dentists, pharmacists, and nurses; also drug wholesalers and retailers. He leaves professional samples and explains possible
uses for new products.

DETERMINING DIMENSIONS   Same as: DETERMINING FACTORS

DETERMINING FACTORS   Those PROSPECT characteristics which are specific to the
buying decision. Useful in constructing a MARKET GRID and selecting the
STRATEGIES that follow. See: QUALIFYING FACTORS

DETERMINISTIC MODEL   A model in which all the factors taken into account
are assumed to be exact. Chance plays no role. See: HEURISTIC MODEL

df. Abbreviation for: DEGREES OF FREEDOM

DEVELOPMENTAL MARKETING   Those activities designed to deal with a MARKET
condition of LATENT DEMAND.

DIARY METHOD   In measuring the size of the AUDIENCE for a BROADCAST MEDIUM,
this method employs a notebook kept next to the set in which members of a
family can record the stations and programs they attend. While there is
always the possibility of invalid entry, the advantages of this method
are that all broadcast hours are covered, all members of the family are
included, and additional information about the audience can be elicited.
Tabulation is done by the research firm after the diaries have been returned to it on a regular schedule. Often used in another context to determine product BRAND preferences. See: MECHANICAL RECORDER METHOD,
TELEPHONE COINCIDENTAL METHOD, PERSONAL INTERVIEW METHOD

DIBA   Abbreviation for: Domestic and International Business Administration, a part of the U.S. Department of Commerce. Besides a wide variety of statistical and advisory publications on domestic business, it analyzes and recommends POLICY on U.S. trade with Communist countries, and encourages and assists U.S. firms to enter export, providing pertinent data on specific foreign countries. See: CT

DICHOTOMOUS QUESTION   See: FIXED-ALTERNATIVE QUESTION

DIFFERENTIAL   (1) Same as: DIFFERENTIAL ADVANTAGE (2) In commodity trading, the premiums paid for the grades better than the basic grade, and the discounts allowed for grades lower than the basic grade, according to the rules and definitions of the COMMODITY EXCHANGE on which the trades are executed.

DIFFERENTIAL ADVANTAGE   An element in the reputation or resources of a firm, or some particular aspect of a product, that can emphasized to create a special value in the minds of PROSPECTS. See: MONOPOLISTIC COMPETITION

DIFFERENTIAL THRESHOLD   The smallest difference that an individual can detect between two STIMULI. Also called the: just noticeable difference, or j.n.d. See: ABSOLUTE THRESHOLD, WEBER'S LAW

DIFFERENTIATED MARKETING   The developing of a unique MARKETING MIX for each TARGET MARKET on which the firm has fixed.

DIFFUSION INDEX   An indicator which permits comparison of the proportion of BUSINESS INDICATORS that predict a rise or a decline of economic activity at a given time with those of previous times in the hope of being able to establish a valid TREND.

DIFFUSION OF INNOVATION   Same as: INNOVATION DIFFUSION

DIFFUSION PROCESS   The way a new idea reflected in real product or service, or abstract, spreads from its source of origin to its ultimate users or adopters. See: ADOPTION PROCESS

DIFFUSION RATE   The speed with which the DIFFUSION PROCESS progresses. See: CHARACTERISTICS OF INNOVATIONS

DIGIT   In ADP, a sign or symbol used to convey a specific piece of data.

DIGITAL DATA   In ADP, data in the form of a code consisting of a sequence of discrete elements, e.g., CHARACTERS representing discrete pieces of information. See: ANALOG DATA

DIMINISHING MARGINAL UTILITY   See: LAW OF DIMINISHING MARGINAL UTILITY

DIMINISHING RETURNS   See: LAW OF DIMINISHING RETURNS

DIORAMA   A three-dimensional, elaborate display in color, usually scenic and illuminated. Frequently employs motion to emphasize some of its elements.

DIRECT-ACTION ADVERTISING   ADVERTISING the goal of which is to get the AUDIENCE to act right away. This may be MAIL-ORDER asking for money for the product, or advertising for leads in which PROSPECTS are encouraged to write for information. Some type of affirmative action is called for. See: INDIRECT-ACTION ADVERTISING

DIRECT ADVERTISING   Any form of ADVERTISING issued directly by the advertiser to specific PROSPECTS.

DIRECT BUYING   The process of purchasing directly from the producer. MIDDLEMEN of all types are not part of the process. See: DIRECT CHANNEL

DIRECT CHANNEL   A CHANNEL OF DISTRIBUTION characterized by the absence of MIDDLEMEN. The maker sells directly to the user. See: INDIRECT CHANNEL, SEMI-DIRECT CHANNEL

DIRECT COSTING   A way of applying costs to products so that only the VARI-
ABLE COSTS associated with a product are allocated to that product, while
the FIXED COSTS are charged off as expenses applied to the period in
which they are incurred and are not reflected in inventories. Under this
method fixed costs affect net income more quickly than in the FULL COST-
ING method because none of the fixed costs linger in inventory valuations.
See: DIRECT COSTS

DIRECT COSTS   Those costs which can be clearly traced and charged to a
product. See: INDIRECT COSTS

DIRECT DENIAL TECHNIQUE   A SALESMANSHIP technique used in dealing with
OBJECTIONS. Involves the SALESPERSON'S contradiction of a statement the
PROSPECT has made. Although dangerous in that it may lead to argument,
it is indicated where the prospect's statement maligns the integrity of
the seller, or shows an erroneous understanding of the seller's POLICIES.
Also called: Denying Method

DIRECT DISTRIBUTION   Selling by a manufacturer to INDUSTRIAL USERS through
his own SALESPERSONS, SALES BRANCHES or OFFICES, and/or WAREHOUSES. Sometimes used to apply to the CONSUMER level. See: DIRECT CHANNEL, INDIRECT
DISTRIBUTION

DIRECTED-RESPONSE QUESTION   See: FREE RESPONSE QUESTION

DIRECT EXPENSES   Business expenses that can readily be assigned to units
of the firm that are constituted as EXPENSE CENTERS.

DIRECT IMPRESSION COMPOSITION   Same as: IMPACT COMPOSITION

DIRECT MAIL ADVERTISING   That ADVERTISING which asks for the order to be
sent by mail. Delivery of the order is by mail. Also the MEDIUM which
delivers the advertising message by mail. Provides greatest control of
direction to a MARKET, flexibility of materials and processes, timeliness
of scheduling, and personalization. Its biggest problem is getting the
recipient's attention. A part of DIRECT ADVERTISING. See: MAIL ORDER

DIRECT MAIL ADVERTISING ASSOCIATION   Same as: DMAA

DIRECT MARKETING   (1) Essentially the same in effect as RETAIL MAIL-ORDER,
it is broader in scope in that the ADVERTISING message may be delivered
by a variety of MEDIA rather than through the mail or a subordinate
section of a LOCAL ADVERTISEMENT. (2) More recently becoming applied to
the activity of selling to CONSUMERS or INDUSTRIAL USERS without the use
of MIDDLEMEN. See: DIRECT CHANNEL

DIRECTORIES OF VENDORS   Among the many available, perhaps the best known
and most used in the industrial field are Conover-Mast Purchasing Directory, MacRae's Blue Book, Thomas' Register of American Manufacturers, and
the Yellow Pages. Specialized lists are available from many trade associations.

DIRECT PREMIUM   An item given free with a purchase at the time of the purchase. The simplest type of premium-giving.

DIRECT PROMISE HEADLINE   A HEADLINE which makes a clear promise to the
reader of a benefit to be had from the product's use.

DIRECT RESPONSE ADVERTISING   Essentially the same as DIRECT MAIL ADVERTIS-
ING except that the message may be delivered by any MEDIUM such as
TELEVISION or RADIO as well as the postal system.

DIRECT RETAILING   The sale of merchandise to CONSUMERS without intervening MIDDLEMEN.

DIRECT SELLING   Same as: DIRECT MARKETING

DIRECT SELLING HOUSE   A firm in the SPECIALTY ADVERTISING field that creates

its own products and sells them directly to ADVERTISERS through its own
sales force. See: ADVERTISING NOVELTIES, SPECIALTY DISTRIBUTOR

DISC   Abbreviation for: Domestic International Sales Corporation, a
type of corporation permitted by Congress, effective in 1972, which may
be only the selling arm for export sales of United States manufacturers.
An indefinite deferral of U.S. taxes is granted on 50% of a DISC's income,
provided that 95% of its receipts and assets are export-related. The net
effect on domestic firms and foreign government cannot yet be assessed,
but it is generally recognized as a protectionist measure designed to promote U.S. exports. Current developments seem to be toward minimizing this
form. See: GMP

DISCONTINUOUS INNOVATION   One of a four-way classification of new PRODUCTS
as to degrees of newness, this type involves the creation of previously
unknown products and the establishment of new usage patterns based on an
idea or behavior pattern that did not exist before. The other three are:
CONGRUENT, CONTINUOUS, DYNAMICALLY CONTINUOUS. Proposed by Thomas S.
Robertson.

DISCOUNT   A reduction from a price which may be stated, usual, or expected
See: ANTICIPATION DISCOUNT, BULK DISCOUNT, CASH DISCOUNT, CUMULATIVE DIS-
COUNT, FREQUENCY DISCOUNT, PATRONAGE DISCOUNT, QUANTITY DISCOUNT, VOLUME
DISCOUNT

DISCOUNT HOUSE   A RETAIL ESTABLISHMENT characterized mainly by its sale of
a large selection of well-known BRANDS of merchandise at less than LIST
PRICES. The distinction between the discount house and the DEPARTMENT
STORE is becoming obscure as each adopts concepts from the other.

DISCOUNT LOADING   An internal bookkeeping computation in RETAILING which
places all inventory and purchase figures on a comparable basis by re-
calculating all invoice prices to reflect an assumed desirable cash discount percent. If a buyer is unable to obtain that size discount from
a supplier, the merchandise is costed in as though he had been successful.
The resultant higher cost base figure usually results in setting higher
retail prices on the merchandise.

DISCOUNT STORE   Same as: DISCOUNT HOUSE

DISCREPANCY OF ASSORTMENT   The difference between the extent of choice among
items that are relatively interchangeable expected by a buyer and the
choice actually available from a given source. See: DISCREPANCY OF
QUANTITY, DISCREPANCY OF VARIETY

DISCREPANCY OF QUANTITY   The difference between the quantity a seller must
buy at one time from a producer and the quantity a buyer wishes to buy
at one time from the seller. See: BREAKING BULK, DISCREPANCY OF ASSORT-
MENT, DISCREPANCY OF VARIETY

DISCREPANCY OF VARIETY   The difference between the number of distinct types
of items that a buyer would like a given source to have available and the
number actually available. See: DISCREPANCY OF ASSORTMENT, DISCREPANCY
OF QUANTITY

DISCRETE DATA   These are gathered whenever the elements of a POPULATION or
SAMPLE are counted. They can be only whole numbers. See: CONTINUOUS
DATA

DISCRETIONARY BUYING POWER   Same as: DISCRETIONARY INCOME

DISCRETIONARY COSTS   Those costs not dependent on the level of output, but
vary directly with the quality of the service and are above a certain minimum to keep the ESTABLISHMENT open at zero output. Examples: utilities,
maintenance, advertising, accounting service. See: FIXED COSTS, VARIABLE
COSTS

DISCRETIONARY INCOME · That part of a CONSUMER'S income which he has the choice of spending or saving. Usually considered to be that portion above an amount required for essentials. Same as: DISCRETIONARY PURCHASING POWER, DISCRETIONARY SPENDING POWER

DISCRETIONARY PURCHASING POWER   Same as: DISCRETIONARY INCOME

DISCRETIONARY SPENDING POWER   Same as: DISCRETIONARY INCOME

DISCRIMINANT ANALYSIS   This provides a method of treating data which is on qualitative SCALES whereby groups may be separated or segmented on the basis of attributes of group members. Any number of INDEPENDENT VARIABLES may be tested for effect on the DEPENDENT VARIABLE. It is possible, also, to find the contribution of the independent variables, relative to each other, to the total difference between the scores of the two groups. NONPARAMETRIC.

DISECONOMIES OF SCALE   Disadvantages that may be inherent in company size considered too large for the INDUSTRY. These include poor public image, increased government regulation, and inefficiency produced by cumbersome organization. See: ECONOMIES OF SCALE

DISGUISED-UNSTRUCTURED QUESTIONNAIRE   Same as: UNSTRUCTURED-DISGUISED QUESTIONNAIRE

DISPATCH   A department found in large NEWSPAPERS, although its functions must be performed on any size newspaper, which schedules advertising; processes advertisements; distributes material to the appropriate mechanical departments, e.g., COPY and LAYOUT to the composing room; handles PROOFS for advertiser correction; and delivers TEAR SHEETS.

DISPENSER   (1) A sign or display containing a pocket for literature, or accommodating a tear-off pad. See: TAKE-ONES (2) A merchandise display containing a stock of items arranged for immediate sale.

DISPERSION   (1) The process of moving produce from areas of high supply concentration to centers of DISTRIBUTION closer to the CONSUMER. (2) In statistics, the amount of variability represented in the measurements in the ARRAY. See: MEASURES OF DISPERSION

DISPLACEMENT   Describes the forgetting by the AUDIENCE of one advertising THEME caused by new themes introduced by the same advertiser.

DISPLAY   The POPAI describes a display as "a device or accumulation of devices which in addition to identifying and/or advertising a company and/ or a product, may also merchandise, either by actually offering the product for sale or by indicating its proximity. A display characteristically bears an intimate relationship with the product, whereas a 'sign' is more closely related to the name of the manufacturer, the retailer, or the product.

DISPLAY ADVERTISING   (1) Usually associated with newspapers, this is the advertising which appears in areas other than in classified sections, which have little or no restrictions on LAYOUT or type FACE. See: CLASSIFIED ADVERTISING, CLASSIFIED DISPLAY ADVERTISING (2) ADVERTISING pieces designed to be self-supporting, such as a window display, or to be mounted on a wall or a background.

DISPLAY CARTON   A merchandise carton designed to fold out into a POP display without removing the merchandise.

DISPLAY CLASSIFIED ADVERTISING   Same as: CLASSIFIED DISPLAY ADVERTISING

DISPLAY STORE   A small STORE operated by a firm doing business by mail, in which items are presented for viewing and ordering only. The firm's catalog is the base for the displays. See: CATALOG STORE

DISPLAY TYPE   (1) Any type larger than 14-point.   (2)   Type used for headline or other elements of the ADVERTISEMENT for which emphasis is wanted.

DISPOSABLE INCOME   Money left over after paying taxes, union dues, pension
contributions, and the like.   Not to be confused with DISCRETIONARY IN-
COME.   Same as: PERSONAL DISPOSABLE INCOME

DISPROPORTIONAL SAMPLING   A method of drawing a SAMPLE from a POPULATION
which consists of a number of groups the importance of which to the
VALIDITY of the study is each not directly related to relative size.
The basis for the allocation of numbers from each group must be specially
determined for each study requiring this procedure.

DISSECTION   Often applied to a specific group of merchandise within a department in a RETAIL STORE so that DOLLAR CONTROL may be facilitated.
The relatively small group is accounted for separately from the rest of
the merchandise.

DISSOLVE   An effect for blending scenes in a TELEVISION COMMERCIAL by means
of which one scene is made to fade out even as the next scene fades in.
Used often to denote the passage of time.   See: OPTICALS

DISSONANCE   See: COGNITIVE DISSONANCE

DISSONANCE REDUCTION   See: COGNITIVE DISSONANCE

DISTINCTIVENESS   The degree of serious actual competition existing in the
MARKET for the product or service.   If none can be realistically expected
for five years or more, it is called Lasting.   Otherwise, it is called
PERISHABLE.

DISTRESS MERCHANDISE   That group of items which for any reason must be
sold even at a sacrifice.   Applies to any type of goods in any business.

DISTRIBUTION   (1) Used generally as a synonym for MARKETING, but often
refers in a restricted sense to the activity of physical movement of goods.
(2) Sometimes used to denote DEMAND satisfaction when MARKETING is used
to denote demand generation.   (3) Roughly equivalent to CHANNELS OF
DISTRIBUTION.

DISTRIBUTION ANALYSIS   See: PERFORMANCE ANALYSIS

DISTRIBUTION CENTER   A facility designed for efficient STORAGE, the taking
of orders, and the delivery of merchandise.   Frequently found within the
organization structure of major RETAIL CORPORATE CHAINS.

DISTRIBUTION CHANNEL   Same as: CHANNEL OF DISTRIBUTION

DISTRIBUTION CODE   Same as: DC

DISTRIBUTION CODES, INC.   Same as: DCI

DISTRIBUTION COST ANALYSIS   Same as: DCA

DISTRIBUTION ORDER   An order placed with a supplier for timed and quantity
shipments of a product to multiple destinations, as is frequently done
for some types of merchandise by central buyers for chains, specifying
how many to each store.

DISTRIBUTION SERVICE   An arrangement in which a CARRIER will accept a single
shipment from one shipper to be separated at destination into parts each
of which is to be delivered to a different CONSIGNEE.   See: ASSEMBLY
SERVICE

DISTRIBUTION WAREHOUSE   A STORAGE facility which serves as a transshipment
point for accumulating stocks into larger shipments as units, and for
BREAKING BULK into smaller quantities, or for effecting a transfer from
one type of carrier to another type.   Same as: TRANSIT WAREHOUSE

DISTRIBUTIVE TRADES   Usually refers to SERVICES, RETAILING, and WHOLESAL-
ING, and the activities associated with each of these.

DISTRIBUTOR   Essentially the same as: SERVICE WHOLESALER   See: INDUSTRIAL
DISTRIBUTOR

DISTRIBUTORSHIP   A form of FRANCHISING in which the franchisee takes title
to goods and further distributes them to sub-franchisees. This franchisee
acts as a supply base for the sub-franchisees, whom he usually oversees.

DIVERGENT MARKETING   The establishment of separate organizations to carry
out the MARKETING goals for each of the firm's products or product LINES.
See: CONVERGENT MARKETING

DIVERSIFICATION   The process of adding unrelated products or product LINES
to a firm's stock in trade. May be the result of CUSTOMER demand, or a
deliberate attempt by management to spread RISK. Often accomplished
through MERGER or other form of acquisition. See: SIMPLIFICATION

DIVERSIONARY PRICING   A few PRODUCTS or SERVICES are priced very low and given
great emphasis in all PROMOTIONAL activities to create the illusion that
all prices are low. Considered a deceptive practice when in fact the
prices of other items offered for sale are not low compared with other sources.

DIVERSION IN TRANSIT   A privilege extended by railroads to shippers of carload lots whereby goods may be started in the general direction of MARKETS
without specifying an exact destination, which is to be determined when
the goods reach one of certain junction points. See: RECONSIGNMENT

DIVISIONAL MERCHANDISE MANAGER   See: MERCHANDISE MANAGER

DIY   Trade abbreviation used as a short word for: do-it-yourself. Has particular relevance for those MARKETS in which DIY enthusiasts exist, or in
which a significant number of persons can be induced to become enthusiasts.

DMA   Abbreviation for: DESIGNATED MARKET AREA. Indicated by a map showing
the region in which originating stations have a greater share of the
viewing HOUSEHOLDS than those from any other area. See: ADI

DMAA   Abbreviation for: Direct Mail Advertising Association, an organization
of producers and users of DIRECT ADVERTISING materials.

DMU   Abbreviation for: Decision-Making Unit, a person or number of persons
involved together in the need to make decisions affecting common goals.
The marketer can take much more effective action if he can identify the
DMUs in the MARKET. See: REFERENCE GROUP

DNA   Abbreviation for: Delta Nu Alpha, the national fraternity in the
field of transportation. It is organized on educational principles.
There are about 10,000 members in some 170 chapters, of which some 18
are collegiate. It publishes a monthly magazine mainly concerned with
the fraternity and its members.

DOCKAGE   A charge against a vessel for the use of wharves or mooring facilities. It is generally based on the length of the vessel. The charge usually begins the day after the vessel arrives at the wharf. See: WHARFAGE

DODGER   A circular of advertising intent delivered house-to-house. See:
HANDBILL

DOI DATING   Indicates that the discount period and other elements of the
TERMS OF SALE begin with the date of the invoice. In the absence of any
modifying statement, it is generally assumed that DOI terms prevail.

DOLLAR-BILL SIZE COUPON   A COUPON about the size of paper money. Frequently part of a PRINT MEDIUM ADVERTISEMENT to be cut out and presented at the
store when the item is purchased. See: COUPONING, PUNCH-CARD COUPON

DOLLAR CONTROL   That type of control exemplified by the "open-to-buy" concept. A control in gross dollar amounts. Same as: OPEN-TO-BUY CONTROL, CLASSIFICATION CONTROL

DOLLAR PLAN In RETAILING, a budgeting technique that relates planned sales, planned stocks, and planned profit all in money amounts. See: OPEN-TO-BUY CONTROL

DOMESTIC INTERNATIONAL SALES CORPORATION Same as: DISC

DOMESTICS In RETAILING, a CLASSIFICATION that generally includes sheets, pillow cases, towels, curtains, and the like.

DOMINATION A competitive TACTIC which involves enough concentration of effort or funds in a MARKET area or MEDIUM which enable the firm to be the significant factor there, rather than to compete as just another come-along in an already crowded environment. Often most effective in conjunction with other tactics.

DOMSAT A short term referring to the domestic satellite communications field.

DON'T WANTS COD parcels which customers refuse to accept.

DOOR-OPENER Any interesting item, usually inexpensive, given to a housewife as a PREMIUM by a door-to-door salesperson to induce the housewife to listen to the salesperson's offer.

DOOR-TO-DOOR SELLING Same as: HOUSE-TO-HOUSE SELLING

DOT Abbreviation for: U.S. Department of Transportation

DOUBLE BILLING A practice engaged in by some LOCAL MEDIA of giving the LOCAL ADVERTISER two invoices, one at the LOCAL RATE which he pays to the medium, the other at the ONE-TIME RATE which he uses to support his claim for repayment on a COOPERATIVE ADVERTISING arrangement. Considered by many to be an unethical practice.

DOUBLE-CARDING An arrangement in TRANSIT ADVERTISING whereby two messages of one advertiser are specified for each vehicle. May be available only as a special buy.

DOUBLE-DECKER In OUTDOOR ADVERTISING, one message PANEL erected above another.

DOUBLE-PAGE SPREAD Same as: DOUBLE TRUCK

DOUBLE POSTING See: CENTER SPREAD

DOUBLE SAMPLING A method of obtaining a reasonably precise SAMPLE from a POPULATION of which the researcher can get little advance knowledge. A preliminary sample is taken to obtain only that information needed for taking the more precise second sample, the latter to be used for the intensive data-gathering effort.

DOUBLE SPOTTING In BROADCAST MEDIA, the placing of two COMMERCIALS without any intervening program material. See: CLUTTER, TRIPLE SPOTTING

DOUBLE TRUCK. An advertisement printed on two facing pages of a publication. Same as: Double-Page Spread, but if across the middle pages, called center spread.

DOWNTURN See: BUSINESS CYCLE

DPMA Abbreviation for: Data Processing Management Association, an organization of professionals working in the information processing field, established to facilitate the continuing education of members through publications, seminars, courses, and expositions designed to update and interchange information and ideas. Has over 275 chapters, typically meeting at least once a month.

DRAW   An amount of money allowed a SALESMAN each week to pay his expenses until the results of his efforts are known and his total compensation can be computed, usually on the basis of commissions. Sometimes the draw is guaranteed, in which case it becomes a minimum, non-invadable compensation. Sometimes the draw is nothing more than a non-interest-bearing loan against anticipated earnings. Sometimes called: drawing account.

DRAWING ACCOUNT   See: DRAW

DRAYAGE   Usually applied to local, short-distance hauling of freight. See: CARTAGE

DRIVE   A DESIRE characterized by high intensity and priority, and, often, extreme urgency. See: AFFECTIONAL DRIVES, EGO-BOLSTERING DRIVES, EGO-DEFENSIVE DRIVES, PSYCHOGENIC DRIVES

DRIVE TIME   A PRIME TIME in RADIO consisting of those times of the day when large numbers of people are driving in their own cars to or from work.

DROP-IN   In BROADCASTING, a local COMMERCIAL placed within the time slot of a nationally sponsored NETWORK program.

DROP-OUT HALFTONE   A HALFTONE from which dots have been removed from various areas to achieve greater contrast. Same as: HIGH-LIGHT HALFTONE

DROP SHIPMENT   Essentially the same as DISTRIBUTION ORDER but more frequently applied to a single order and shipment. See: DESK JOBBER

DROP SHIPPER   Same as: DESK JOBBER

DRUG AND TOILET PREPARATION TRAFFIC CONFERENCE   Same as: D&TPTC

DRUMMER   An American salesman of former times who called on RETAILERS or greeted them as they arrived at buying centers. Many of the methods he used are now considered unethical.

DRY REHEARSAL   Same as: DRY RUN

DRY RUN   A television rehearsal without cameras. Same as: DRY REHEARSAL

DUAL DISTRIBUTION   The practice of some manufacturers of planning CHANNELS OF DISTRIBUTION through both wholly owned and independent ESTABLISHMENTS at the same time.

DUAL MERCHANDISING   The offering for sale by an individual firm of products made by others as well as itself. Occurs primarily where the different goods are directly COMPLEMENTARY or their sale results in an expansion of total MARKET coverage.

DUAL PRICING   Essentially the same as: UNIT PRICING (2)

DUBBING   (1) In BROADCASTING, the addition of pictures or sound to the original recording. (2) Sometimes used to indicate duplicate recordings of original material, not necessarily in the same sequence or arrangement.

DUMB BARGE   A river BARGE having no method of self-propulsion.

DUMMY   (1) A mock-up of a publication. (2) An empty PACKAGE used for display.

DUMMY MASTER RECORD   A RECORD put into an ADP system for testing or auditing purposes. Its data is fictitious. See: DUMMY TRANSACTIONS

DUMMY TRANSACTIONS   Transactions introduced into an ADP system to test or audit the system. Such transactions should be confined to DUMMY MASTER RECORDS so that the regular RECORDS in the file will not be compromised.

DUMP BIN   A MERCHANDISER built to contain merchandise as it is literally dumped into it from the shipping case. Only the one product is displayed in it. See: JUMBLE BASKET

DUMPING   Usually refers to the practice of selling in a foreign country below cost to dispose of surplus. More technically, it is the selling in international trade of a commodity at a price below the domestic price of that commodity plus freight, insurance, and other costs incidental to sales in the foreign MARKET.

DUN   To demand payment of an overdue amount. Legal constraints limit the techniques and methods that may be used in this process.

DUPLICATE PLATES   PHOTOENGRAVINGS made from the same negative as the original.

DUPLICATION   In advertising, REACHING the same individual or HOUSEHOLD by two or more MEDIA.

DURABLE GOODS   (1) Same as: HARD GOODS   (2) Same as: CAPITAL GOODS

DUTCH AUCTION   The auctioneer offers the items at a high price and lowers the price gradually until a bidder responds. The concept is used once in a while as a promotion by placing an item in a store window with a sign on which the price is announced with a statement that the price will be reduced by a specified amount each day until someone buys.

DUTCH DOORS   See: GATEFOLD

DYAD   A two-person group. See: REFERENCE GROUP

DYNAMICALLY CONTINUOUS INNOVATION   One of a four-way classification of new PRODUCTS as to degrees of newness, this type has disrupting effects short of generating new buying patterns, although designed to fill new needs brought about by changes in LIFE STYLE. The other three types are: CONGRUENT, CONTINUOUS, and DISCONTINUOUS. Proposed by Thomas S. Robertson.

DYNAMIC RESEARCH   A technique which concentrates on discovering how CONSUMERS react with each other, rather than how they react as individuals, to the idea of a product or service.

DYNAMICS   The process whereby a system continually adapts to change in its own condition or that of its environment.

DYNAMIC SIMULATION   A type of SIMULATION in which FEEDBACK is built into a loop to reflect the outcome of alternative courses of action through time. Uses the same basic diagrammatic techniques as the other two types. See: STATIC SIMULATION, SYMBOLIC SIMULATION

EAGLEBACK   Same as: BIRDIEBACK

EARLY ACCEPTORS   Same as: INNOVATORS   See: ARC OF FASHION, INNOVATION DIFFUSION

EARLY ADOPTERS   Come after INNOVATORS in the INNOVATION DIFFUSION process. SALESPEOPLE and MASS MEDIA are important information sources for this group. May be OPINION LEADERS.

EARLY FOLLOWERS   Same as: EARLY MAJORITY   See: ARC OF FASHION, INNOVATION DIFFUSION

EARLY MAJORITY   Come after the EARLY ADOPTERS in the INNOVATION DIFFUSION process. Usually consider a new PRODUCT or idea only after many early adopters have tried it and found it satisfactory. May take a long time between trial and adoption.

EARMUFF PROBLEM   A condition that occurs when a SALESPERSON becomes so engrossed in dominating the interview that incoming communications from the PROSPECT are blocked, thus destroying effective listening.

EARNED RATE   The amount per unit that an ADVERTISER pays for space or time actually used. See: SHORT RATE

EARS OF A NEWSPAPER   The boxes or announcements in the upper right-hand

and left-hand corners of the front page, alongside the name. Sometimes
sold for advertising space.

EAST AFRICA CUSTOMS UNION   Established in 1967, this market cooperating group
includes Ethiopia, Kenya, Rhodesia, Sudan, Tanzania, Uganda, Zambia.
Turmoil in Africa makes this group unstable.

EAST AFRICAN COMMON MARKET   A smaller group within the EAST AFRICA CUSTOMS
UNION. It is composed of Kenya, Tanzania, and Uganda.

EBI   Abbreviation for: Effective Buying Income, a measure found in Sales
& Marketing Management's "Survey of Buying Power." Equivalent to after-tax
income, it reflects actual CONSUMER purchasing power. Roughly the same as:
DISPOSABLE PERSONAL INCOME

EC   Abbreviation for: European Community. Essentially the same as: EEC

ECC   Abbreviation for: EUROPEAN COMMON MARKET (COMMUNITY)

ECHELON   A level of activity within an organization characterized by the
degree of decision-making assigned. See: BOTTOM MANAGEMENT, MIDDLE
MANAGEMENT, TOP MANAGEMENT

ECONOMETRICS   The organized study of the applications of statistics and
other quantitative techniques to economic problems.

ECONOMICAL ORDER QUANTITY   Same as: EOQ

ECONOMIC COMMUNITY OF WEST AFRICAN STATES   Same as: ECOWAS

ECONOMIC INDICATOR   Same as: BUSINESS INDICATOR

ECONOMIC INDICATORS   A monthly publication of the Council of Economic
Advisors. Contains much general economic data, such as GNP, personal con-
sumption expenditures, and other measurements of general economic activity.
See: BUSINESS INDICATORS

ECONOMIC MAN   The concept of a buyer who makes rational decisions only,
balancing all relevant factors in his objective mind, and who buys only
when the price is right and the quality acceptable. The traditional
concept of the older economics. See: SOCIAL MAN

ECONOMIC QUALITY   Assumes a certain minimum of suitability. It includes
TECHNICAL QUALITY but considers cost and procurability as well. See:
QUALITY

ECONOMIC SHOPPERS   One of a four-way, sociological classification of CON-
SUMERS, the others being APATHETIC SHOPPERS, ETHICAL SHOPPERS, and PER-
SONALIZING SHOPPERS. The economic shoppers are interested in price, quality, VARIETY, and ease in forming decisions. They do not like sales
persons who inhibit or slow down the shopping process. They comprise the
largest group of the four. They are mainly persons from the middle
classes. See: SOCIAL CLASSES

ECONOMIES OF SCALE   Reductions in the cost per unit of output resulting
from efficiencies made possible by increasing the size of the producing
unit. Effective only up to a certain point, which varies with the INDUS-
TRY. This point can usually be set with practical accuracy by the firm's
accountants together with its engineers. Beyond this point costs per
unit begin to rise, producing diseconomies of scale.

ECONOMY PACK   Used in MERCHANDISING, its APPEAL comes from the savings
usually possible when several products are included in one wrapping.
Mainly a producer activity, but may be done by a MIDDLEMAN who finds it
expedient to repackage items.

ECOWAS   Abbreviation for: Economic Community of West African States, a
MARKETING group including Benin, Gambia, Ghana, Guinea, Ivory Coast,

Liberia, Mali Republic, Mauritania, Niger, Nigeria, Senegal, Sierra Leone, Togo, Upper Volta

ECU   Abbreviation for: Extreme Close-up. Refers to a very close camera shot in TELEVISION to show as much detail as possible.

E.D.   Abbreviation for a newspaper INSERTION ORDER directing that an advertisement be run every day. See: E.D.D., E.D.T.F., E.D.W.T.F.

ED&PA   Abbreviation for: Exhibit Designers & Producers Association, the national trade association of professional companies engaged in the design, building and installation of exhibits, and those who supply materials or services associated with the exhibits. It provides many services, including a public relations program, chapter liason, economic surveys, and labor relations assistance.

E.D.D.   A newspaper INSERTION ORDER directing that an advertisement be run every other day. See: E.D., E.D.T.F., E.O.W.T.F.

E.D.D.T.F.   A newspaper INSERTION ORDER directing that an advertisement be run every other day until forbidden. See: E.D., E.D.D., E.O.W.T.F.

EDGE ACT   Originally enacted in 1919 as part of the Federal Reserve Act, it has been broadened by various amendments to permit foreign subsidiaries of United States banks to participate in financing business abroad as well as to engage in the usual commercial banking activities. See: FINANCING

EDGE ACT BANKS   See: EDGE ACT

EDIT   In ADP applications, the review of data to select that which is pertinent, delete unwanted data, insert page numbers, suppress the printing of extraneous zeros, test data for reasonableness, and provide for the machines to arrange and print the data in desired form.

EDITING   The examination of QUESTIONNAIRES or observation forms, and the correction if necessary, to determine whether the data being collected meets the minimum quality standards established for the study. The process may be started in the field where omissions and incorrect procedures may be caught quickly and set right, and then sent to the central office for further critical examination, or the process may involve activity only in the central office. If the latter, problems may be difficult to resolve once the interviewing staff has been disbanded. See: CODING, TABULATION

EDITORIAL MATTER   The entertainment, news, or educational portions of any publication or broadcast, as contrasted with the portion devoted to ADVERTISING.

EDP   Abbreviation for: Electronic Data Processing, the various systems of storing, retrieving, and analyzing quantities of data by the use of computers and other electronic equipment. Essentially the same as: ADP

EEC   Abbreviation for: EUROPEAN ECONOMIC COMMUNITY

EFFECTIVE ADDRESS   The ADDRESS actually used in the execution of a particular computer instruction.

EFFECTIVE BUYING INCOME   Same as: EBI

EFFECTIVE CIRCULATION   In OUTDOOR ADVERTISING, estimated as equalling the total count of automobiles and pedestrians reduced by 50%, and the total fares of public transportation reduced by 75%.

EFFECTIVE DEMAND   The desire by a MARKET to buy, combined with the capacity to pay. See: DEMAND CURVE

EFTA   Abbreviation for: EUROPEAN FREE TRADE ASSOCIATION

EGO   Applies restrictions to the ID through the use of education and experience. Rides herd on the Id so that it expresses itself in a legally acceptable manner. The three concepts indicated here are important to successful SALEMANSHIP. See: SUPEREGO

EGO-BOLSTERING DRIVES PSYCHOGENIC DRIVES characterized by the need to enhance the personality, to gain recognition and prestige, and to satisfy the EGO through domination of others. See: AFFECTIONAL DRIVES, EGO-DEFENSIVE DRIVES

EGO-DEFENSIVE DRIVES PSYCHOGENIC DRIVES characterized by the need to protect the personality, to avoid harm and ridicule, to prevent loss of prestige, and to avoid or get relief from anxiety. A marketer can use an understanding of these DRIVES to good advantage in his communications with his MARKET. See: AFFECTIONAL DRIVES, EGO-BOLSTERING DRIVES

EGO-IDEAL Same as: SUPEREGO

EGOISTIC NEEDS This, the fourth level of MASLOW'S HIERARCHY OF NEEDS, is said to become operative after the SOCIAL NEEDS have been reasonably well satisfied. Includes prestige, self-respect, success, independence, personal satisfaction with achievement.

EGO LOSS RISK See: RISK REDUCTION

EIA Abbreviation for: Equipment Interchange Association, an outgrowth of the National Motor Equipment Interchange Committee which was organized in 1958 by 235 motor carriers after the ICC granted its approval to exempt from the ANTI-TRUST LAWS an association to establish uniform charges for interchange equipment. Today's members include railroads, steamship companies, and as associates, leasing companies, tractor and trailer manufacturers, container manufacturers, and other allied industrial organizations. The Association publishes Equipment Interchange Schedule No. 2 which contains all the rules, regulations, and charges under which participating carriers operate; the International Registry of Equipment, which lists on a voluntary basis the details of intermodal equipments; and various forms and bulletins.

80-20 PRINCIPLE (1) Much empirical evidence points to the fact that most firms get the largest proportion of their business from CUSTOMERS on whom they expend a small proportion of their MARKETING effort, and vice versa. (2) In RETAILING, about 20% of stocked merchandise accounts for about 80% of dollar sales (3) Often applied to any situation in which the preponderance of achievement is accomplished by a relatively few of the people involved.

ELASTIC DEMAND (1) See: ELASTICITY OF DEMAND (2) DEMAND that is sensitive to change in price.

ELASTICITY COEFFICIENT See: PRICE ELASTICITY OF DEMAND

ELASTICITY INDEX The measure of the responsiveness of one variable to changes in another when both variables are expressed in relative terms.

ELASTICITY OF DEMAND DEMAND is generally said to be elastic when a reduction in unit price increases total revenue from a product or service. Demand is said to be inelastic when a reduction in unit price produces a decline in total revenue. Demand is said to be unitary when a reduction in price produces just enough increase in volume so that total revenue from the product or service remains the same. See: INCOME ELASTICITY OF DEMAND, PRICE ELASTICITY OF DEMAND, PROMOTIONAL ELASTICITY OF DEMAND

ELASTICITY OF EXPECTATIONS Technically, the ratio of the future expected percent change in price to the recent percent change in price. Essentially the same as: EXPECTATION EFFECT

ELECTRONIC DATA PROCESSING Same as: EDP

ELECTRONIC VIDEO RECORDING Same as: EVR

ELECTROTYPE   A duplicate of an engraving made by depositing metal electro-
lytically on a wax, lead, or plastic mold made from the original PLATE.

ELEMENTARY UNIT   In statistics, that which carries the CHARACTERISTIC of
interest to be observed. If it is desired to know the BRAND LOYALTY of
housewives, then all housewives who could use the brand are elementary
units. Normally, because of the large size of a POPULATION or the entirety of elementary units, some type of SAMPLING technique must be used.
See: FRAME

ELEVATOR   An ESTABLISHMENT usually run by a MERCHANT MIDDLEMAN, equipped
to store large quantities of grain. See: COOPERATIVE ELEVATOR, COUNTRY
ELEVATOR, INDEPENDENT ELEVATOR, LINE ELEVATOR

ELLIPSIS   A series of three or four periods or asterisks used to indicate
the omission of words or to emphasize the wording which follows them.

EM   The square of any type size. Usually thought of as derived from the
letter m, which is as wide as it is high. Refers to the pica-em, a 12-
point em, which is 1/6 of an inch, unless otherwise specified. See: PICA,
PICA EM POINT

EMBELLISHMENTS   Any letters, figures or mechanical devices attached to a
POSTER or PAINTED BULLETIN to extend beyond the usual borders or to give
a three-dimensional effect. Sometimes called "cut-outs."

EMBOSSING   A method of printing using two dies to raise the printed surface above the rest of the sheet. Sometimes used without ink to raise
a name or a TRADEMARK.

EMC   Abbreviation for: Export Management Company, an independent FIRM that
in effect acts as a manufacturer's export department. Its specialized
services often make possible engaging in international trade when otherwise
a firm would find it impracticable. May be a MERCHANT MIDDLEMAN or a
FUNCTIONAL MIDDLEMAN. Same as: CEM See: FREIGHT FORWARDER (2), SALES
AGENT

EMERGENCY GOODS   Sometimes applied to those items which many CONSUMERS do
not usually consider buying until the requirement is acute, e.g., tire
chains, plumbing or roof repairs, umbrellas, ambulance service.

EML   Abbreviation for: Expected Machine Life. A necessary concept to calculating DEPRECIATION or OBSOLESCENCE.

EMOTIONAL APPROACH   Same as: IMAGINATIVE APPROACH

EMPATHY   The ability to put one's self in another's place in order to understand the other's probable reaction to APPEALS. Every good marketing man
tries to develop this because he can thus gain insights into the feelings,
and ATTITUDES of his PROSPECTS. Most often the result of keen PERCEPTION.

EMPLOYEE DEVELOPMENT   Training of present employees designed to upgrade
them to higher efficiency and PRODUCTIVITY, or for more responsible
positions within the organization.

EMPORIUM   A place of trade, particularly a major center. In the past it
was the name frequently used by the large store in a small town. Not used
much today, but gaining a measure of popularity.

EMULATIVE PRODUCT   A new offering by a competitor of the same general type
of product. As does the ADAPTIVE PRODUCT, it generally appears at a stage
in the PRODUCT LIFE CYCLE in which the original product has reached real
growth, or even later at maturity. Both can succeed only if they introduce an attribute that is perceived by a MARKET SEGMENT as adding some
satisfaction worth having. See: MULTIPLE BRAND ENTRIES

EN   One-half of an EM.

ENABLING ELEMENTS   Those aspects of a firm that indirectly affect the

success of the firm's efforts to satisfy a TARGET MARKET at a profit.
They include financial resources, managerial expertness, information
systems, and the like. Frequently applied to RETAIL STORES.

ENCLOSED MALL   A type of SHOPPING CENTER where all the STORES are arranged
to face an enclosed central walkway. The entire structure is equipped
with year-round air conditioning. See: MALL

END AISLE DISPLAY   Permanent display units situated at the ends of aisles
in a RETAIL STORE. They are usually specialized to hold particular types
of products, such as light bulbs, hosiery, spices, cakes, etc. See:
END DISPLAY

END CAP   A shelf attached to the end of an aisle bank or a GONDOLA, usually
arranged to display the individual pieces of the merchandise contained in
boxed sets immediately below the shelf.

END DISPLAY   A display using a large quantity of merchandise erected
against the end of a store aisle, but not on permanent display units.
Store personnel usually put these up as management determines desirable.

ENDLESS CHAIN METHOD   Same as: CHAIN PROSPECTING

END-OF-MONTH TERMS   Same as: E.O.M.

END-PRODUCT ADVERTISING   Same as: SUBORDINATE PRODUCT ADVERTISING

END RATE   The lowest rate at which a BROADCAST station offers time.

END RUN   A competitive TACTIC by which a firm, having critically examined
its type of business and the possibilities open to it, establishes a new
approach to getting sales which avoids a direct confrontation with a MAR-
KET leader who is firmly established. Often most effective in conjunction with other tactics.

END SIZES   The large and small sizes that determine the range in the LINE
carried by a RETAIL STORE.

ENGRAVING   (1) An original printing plate.   (2) A method of reproducing a
design for printing by cutting or etching a metal plate.

ENGROSSING   Buying up and holding off the market large quantities of goods
until such time as they can be sold at a higher price. Considered a
criminal act in the 16th Century. See: FORESTALLING, REGRATING

ENSEMBLE DISPLAY   In RETAILING, an interior display designed to show together all merchandise which it is suggested be used together (often
called "coordinates").

ENTREPRENEUR   (1) An individual who initiates and operates any type of
business enterprise.   (2) A self-employed proprietor of an unincorporated
business enterprise.

ENUMERATIVE STUDY   Statistical observations made for the purpose of providing a basis for dealing with a situation as it exists. This type of
study deals with a fixed set of observations, called a finite population.
See: ANALYTICAL STUDY

ENVELOPE STUFFER   A piece of direct-mail advertising inserted in mailings
of statements and other correspondence.

ENVIRONMENTAL STIMULI   Same as: EXTERNAL STIMULI

E.O.M.   Abbreviation for: end-of-month terms. Under this type of dating
the cash discount and the full payment (net credit) periods begin on the
first day of the following month rather than on the invoice date. Example:
2/10, n/30, E.O.M. for an invoice dated any date in April indicates that
a 2% CASH DISCOUNT may be taken any time through May 10, and failing that,
the full amount of the invoice must be paid not later than May 30. If no

net period is indicated, it is usually taken to be the end of the month following that in which the purchase was made. See: PROXIMO TERMS

EOQ   Abbreviation for: most economical order quantity. The amount to buy at one time which results in the lowest over-all cost to supply needed materials, all appropriate factors considered. A numer of mathematical formulae have been developed which may prove useful when used with good judgment. Accurate data, properly applied, may point to an economy for the firm if a shortage in some material is allowed to happen occasionally.

E.O.W.T.F.   A newspaper INSERTION ORDER directing that an advertisement be run every other week until forbidden. See: E.D., E.D.D., E.D.D.T.F.

EQUAL STABILIZATION   Same as: FAIR TRADE

EQUAL-STORE CONCEPT   A multi-store RETAILING arrangement in which instead of a FLAGSHIP STORE and BRANCH STORES, all downtown and suburban outlets are considered on a par. This type of organization requires two distinct lines of AUTHORITY, one for the BUYERS responsible for procuring, pricing, and promoting merchandise at all stores, the other for the sales managers who supervise sales and service for customers at their individual locations. There is some evidence that this arrangement is becoming more common among DEPARTMENT STORES.

EQUILIBRIUM   (1) A state of being in which an individual has obtained SATISFACTION of a NEED. See: TENSION   (2) Defined in economics as the condition that prevails for a PRODUCT, company, INDUSTRY, or the economy as a whole when at the time observed, the DEMAND CURVE and the SUPPLY CURVE intersect.

EQUIPMENT INTERCHANGE ASSOCIATION   Same as: EIA

EQUIPMENT INTERCHANGE SCHEDULE NO. 2   See: EIA

EQUITABLE SOCIETY OF PIONEERS   See: ROCHDALE PLAN

EQUITY   (1) A popular usage which confines the meaning to the residual interest of the owners of a business after all obligations to others have been discharged. (2) The meaning as used in accounting practice includes all claims by anyone against the assets of the business. The claims of owners are called "Capital," the claims of others are called "Liabilities." From this is derived the "Balance Sheet Equation" A = L + C.

EQUIVALENT RATE OF SIMPLE INTEREST FORMULA   Used for any credit plan in which there is a service charge or other flat fee. The formula follows:

where a = the number of payments periods <u>possible</u> in one year (12 when payments are monthly, 52 when weekly, etc.)

$$r_{eq} = \frac{2ac}{b(n + 1)}$$

b = the amount borrowed; or put another way, the additional amount which if the buyer had, he could pay cash, not need a credit plan.

c = the amount by which the total payments (cash down, trade-in, and instalments) exceeds the price for cash.

n = the actual total number of instalment payments to be made.

EROSION RATE   Same as: ATTRITION RATE, DECAY RATE

ERRATIC FLUCTUATION   See: TIME SERIES

ERROR-DETECTING AND FEEDBACK SYSTEM   Same as: ARQ

ESCALATOR CLAUSE   In PURCHASING, a clause in a contract between seller and buyer which provides for price increases to be allowed to the seller should certain events occur. This is frequently tied to labor or commodity cost increases imposed on the seller. It is sometimes tied to an index compiled by a reliable source. See: PRICE GUARANTY

ESTABLISHMENT   A general reference to a plant of a place of business without defining its specific type.

ESTABLISH THE DIFFERENTIAL   All of the SALES PROMOTION and PUBLICITY
activities a firm can muster within its budgetary CONTRAINTS to take advantage of a possible DIFFERENTIAL ADVANTAGE.   Sometimes the product makes
an IMPACT on the MARKET so easily that the differential becomes established
without much effort by the firm.

ESTEEM NEEDS   See: MASLOW'S THEORY

ESTEEM VALUE   The value which comes from attributes other than the ability
of something to perform a function reliably.   Of course, few goods can
have esteem value without also having USE VALUE.

ESTIMATING EQUATION   The linear formula, $y = a + bx$.   By using the simultaneous equations for ungrouped available data, the values can be determined.
Then, it is necessary to take statistical significance into consideration
by computing the STANDARD ERROR OF ESTIMATE, the probable margin of SAMPL-
ING ERROR.   PARAMETRIC.

ET   Abbreviation for: electrical transcription, a recording of a radio
program for use in later BROADCASTS.

ETHICAL ADVERTISING   (1) ADVERTISING addressed to physicians as contrasted
with advertising of a similar product to the general public.   (2) advertising that meets the standards of fair, honest, and equitable content.

ETHICAL DRUGS   Medications legally sold only with a physician's prescription.
Same as: Prescription Drugs See: OTC

ETHICAL PRICING   Deliberately refraining from charging all the traffic will
bear in those instances where the PRODUCT is highly PRICE IN-ELASTIC and
the seller is a professional who is considered vested with the responsibí-
lity of not over-charging the client.

ETHICAL SHOPPERS   One of a four-way, sociological classification of CON-
SUMERS, the others being APATHETIC SHOPPERS, ECONOMIC SHOPPERS, PERSON-
ALIZING SHOPPERS.   Ethical shoppers generally feel obligated to support
neighborhood or small stores because they appreciate their availability
and sometimes their distinctiveness.

ETHNIC BUYING HABITS   The particular way a certain ethnic group conducts
its purchasing activities.   It is an outgrowth of the group's CULTURAL
patterns.   Differences of marketing approach are necessitated by these
varying buying habits.

ETHNIC RADIO   A station format directed to a specific ethnic group, sometimes
in that group's home language.

ETHNOCENTRICITY   One of a three-way classification of the POLICIES of firms
engaged in international MARKETING, this one is concerned with the exploita-
tion of a domestic manufacturing base so that foreign business done is considered marginal and incremental accomplished through the exportation of
standard PRODUCTS.   The other two are: POLYCENTRICITY and GEOCENTRICITY

EUROCRAT   An official of the European Economic Community engaged in the
charting of ways to implement economic and monetary union over the intermediate term.

EUROPEAN COMMON MARKET   Same as: EUROPEAN ECONOMIC COMMUNITY

EUROPEAN ECONOMIC COMMUNITY   An organization established by a treaty in
Rome in 1957 by Belgium, France, Italy, Luxembourg, The Netherlands, and
West Germany to integrate the economic activities of the six countries
and to establish a common tariff wall against outside nations.   Since then
Denmark and Great Britain and Ireland have joined.   At one time called
the INNER SIX.   Same as: EEC See: EFTA

EUROPEAN FREE TRADE ASSOCIATION   An organization established in Stockholm in 1959 by Austria, Denmark, Great Britain, Norway, Portugal, Sweden, and Switzerland as a response to the EEC. Also known as the OUTER SEVEN. Iceland and Finland joined later, and other countries have working arrangements with the group. Great Britain and Denmark have become members of the EEC. Same as: EFTA

EVALUATION RIGHTS   In PURCHASING, the AUTHORITY granted managers to assess performance and to reward or punish on the basis of these assessments. See: ALLOCATION RIGHTS, CRITERIA RIGHTS, POLICY RIGHTS, STRATEGY RIGHTS

EVENT   Essentially the same as: ELEMENTARY UNIT, but usually associated with the occurrance of a defined group or collection of entities.

EVOKED SET   The particular group of BRANDS to which a CONSUMER will limit the considerations of choice for purchase. Usually a small number of familiar, remembered, and acceptable brands, even though the total number of brands in the PRODUCT category may be very large. See: SPAN OF RECALL.

EVR   Abbreviation for: Electronic Video Recording. The placing of a message or program on tape in a cartridge which may be played through a television set or a special player. Some companies are using this in their sales training programs. Others consider the potential for CONSUMER use greater than that for business use.

EX   Abbreviation for: (1) Exchange (2) Express (3) Example

EXCESS MATERIAL   An amount of an item in stock determined to be above the reasonable requirement of a plant. This condition usually occurs as the result of errors in judgment regarding the amount forward-bought, or level of production over-optimistically forecast. Same as: SURPLUS MATERIAL See: FORWARD BUYING

EXCHANGE   The entire system by means of which preferences for goods or services are evidenced in the economy through the way work or monetary units are given up in order to acquire goods or services. If exchange did not increase the total satisfactions of all parties, it would not occur. (2) See: COMMODITY EXCHANGE

EXCHANGE EFFICIENCY   One aspect of the concept of marketing efficiency, it is the accomplishment of the trading process itself at the lowest cost possible with present knowledge of MARKETS and technology. Competitive pressure toward providing customer satisfactions with greater exchange efficiency bring about variations in the level and stability of prices, costs, profits, and employment opportunities in MARKETING. See: EXCHANGE, INNOVATIVE EFFICIENCY, TECHNICAL EFFICIENCY

EXCHANGE FLOW   The activities within the network of institutions linking producers and CONSUMERS or INDUSTRIAL USERS which stimulates DEMAND and consummates exchanges of title. See: EXCHANGE, GOODS FLOW

EXCLUSIVE AGENCY METHOD OF DISTRIBUTION   Same as: EXCLUSIVE OUTLET SELLING

EXCLUSIVE DEALING   The DEALER agrees to refrain from handling competing products in consideration for his being supplied with the manufacturer's goods. Such an agreement may not be legal under existing laws if it results in a substantial lessening of competition. See: EXCLUSIVE SELLING

EXCLUSIVE DISTINCTIVENESS   See: PERISHABLE DISTINCTIVENESS

EXCLUSIVE DISTRIBUTION   Same as: EXCLUSIVE OUTLET SELLING

EXCLUSIVE MERCHANDISE   Goods not available in other STORES in that MARKET. See: EXCLUSIVE OUTLET SELLING

EXCLUSIVE OUTLET SELLING   Confining the carrying of a particular service or BRAND in an area to just one RETAILER or one WHOLESALER, usually with some type of contractual agreement. The seller who wishes to use such an arrangement generally anticipates maximum promotional cooperation from his DEALERS. Same as: EXCLUSIVE DISTRIBUTION

EXCLUSIVE SELLING   A manufacturer or other supplier agrees with a particular WHOLESALER or RETAILER not to sell to other wholesalers or retailers in the same MARKET. May not be legal if it can be construed as a restraint of trade. See: EXCLUSIVE DEALING

EXECUTION   In ADVERTISING, the particular style used in the ADVERTISEMENT to direct attention to and involve the AUDIENCE with the PRODUCT. For example, this might be humorous, episode of life, factual, testimonial, etc.

EXECUTION DELAY   A DELAYED RESPONSE EFFECT caused by the making of a MARKETING expenditure in the current period for some presentation to be made to the MARKET in a future period.

EXECUTIVE SALESPERSON   A loose term describing an individual of high technical competence engaged in selling services and/or products to business executives. What is sold by such an individual is not usually used in the manufacturing process although required in the operation of the company. See: SALESPERSON

EXHAUSTIVE   Applied to a list of EVENTS so inclusive that one of the listed events is sure to occur.

EXHIBIT DESIGNERS & PRODUCERS ASSOCIATION   Same as: ED&PA

EXPANSIBILITY OF DEMAND   (1) A concept used to indicate that the use of ADVERTISING or SALESMANSHIP, or both, in the promotion of a product or service will bring about an increase in the total DEMAND for the product or service. See: PROMOTIONAL ELASTICITY OF DEMAND (2) The degree to which the DEMAND CURVE for a PRODUCT can be moved to the right by some technique or the play of natural forces. Such a movement means that the MARKET will accept more product volume at the same price. Compare with: ELASTICITY OF DEMAND

EXPANSION   See: BUSINESS CYCLE

EXPANSIONIST PRICE   Similar to PENETRATION PRICE, but set to anticipate the cost savings projected possible by increased scale of production, such as through the use of automated machinery. Assumes a high PRICE ELASTICITY OF DEMAND.

EXPECTATION EFFECT   A situation of rising prices may precipitate an increase in the DEMAND for an item as buyers hurry to acquire it before the price rises more. The opposite effect may occur, also, where buyers delay buying in a falling price situation. See: LAW OF DEMAND

EXPECTED VALUE   In statistics, the value one would anticipate would occur if chance alone were operating. See: OBSERVED VALUE

EXPEDITER   In purchasing, this title is usually associated with the duties involved in following up on PURCHASE ORDERS so that delivery will be made on time. Duties may include visits to suppliers' plants.

EXPENSE CENTER   A collection of CONTROLLABLE COSTS which are related to one particular job of work or kind of store service. A large number of such centers may be developed in large-scale ESTABLISHMENTS, depending on the amount of detail for each unit that management decides is worth the cost to collect. See: PROFIT CENTER

EXPERIENCE CURVE   Taking into account the combined effect of learning, specialization, investment, and scale, the plot of the decline in PRODUCT cost relative to volume. A broader concept than the LEARNING CURVE.

EXPERIENCE GOODS   Sometimes used to designate that group of PRODUCTS that a user must try before being able to evaluate the claims made for the products. It has particular applicability for such items as candy or

snacks, but in a real sense all products are experience goods. See:
SEARCH GOODS

EXPERIMENT   In MARKETING RESEARCH, the activity of testing an HYPOTHESIS
in such a way that the results will be measurable objectively and be
distinguishable from extraneous variables. See: PAYOFF, SURVEY RESEARCH
DESIGN

EXPERIMENTAL DESIGN   A research study in which the investigator directly
controls at least one INDEPENDENT VARIABLE while changing another variable.

EXPLODED VIEW   Showing the component parts of a product separately but in
realtion to each other. A useful way of developing a better understanding of a product where knowledge of the interior construction is a requisite. Has most significant application in INDUSTRIAL ADVERTISING and
at TRADE SHOWS. Essentially the same concept as: PHANTOM DIAGRAM

EXPLODING THE BILL OF MATERIAL   Multiplying the number of units in each
product by the scheduled output for that product. A record is kept of
this information so that the total requirement for any component may be,
immediately available.

EXPLORATORY RESEARCH   A search for hypothetical solutions to a PROBLEM and
an attempt to state them sufficiently well that the decision maker may determine which to investigate, if any. If the problem is not clear, PRE-
LIMINARY RESEARCH may be necessary before this step in the MARKETING RE-
SEARCH process may be accomplished.

EXPONENTIAL SMOOTHING   See: TIME SERIES

EXPORT AGENTS   BROKERS and other FUNCTIONAL MIDDLEMEN in the domestic MAR-
KET who sell to or buy for foreign customers. See: IMPORT AGENTS

EXPORT COMMISSION HOUSES   Same as: EXPORT AGENTS

EXPORT MANAGEMENT COMPANY   Same as: EMC

EXPORT MANAGERS CLUB OF NEW YORK   See: IEA

EX POST FACTO   A Latin phrase meaning: after the fact. In MARKETING RESEARCH
it indicates a searching for a cause after the observations have been made.

EXPOSURE   How often and how well an ADVERTISEMENT may be read in a MAGA-
ZINE. It is a function of the time between issues, the particular FORMAT,
and the EDITORIAL MATTER of the publication.

EXTENDED FAMILY   The NUCLEAR FAMILY plus all other relatives. See: FAMILY

EXTENDED TERMS   Indicates that a CUSTOMER has been given an additional
period in which to pay.

EXTENDED TYPE   Any type FACE which has CHARACTERS which are wider than
usual, so that fewer will fit on a line. See: CONDENSED TYPE

EXTENSIVE DISTRIBUTION   Same as: INTENSIVE DISTRIBUTION

EXTERNALITIES   All of the environmental relationships to which the firm
reacts. The social issues facing the MARKETING world stem from these
interrelationships. See: PUBLIC RELATIONS

EXTERNAL STIMULI   The forces which shape a part of the behavior of a buying unit in the MARKET as a result of broad developments in the buying
unit's environment brought about by the seller's efforts, changes in LIFE
STYLES, vocational patterns in the economy, and the like. These stimuli
bring about by themselves no change in the characteristics of the buying
unit. See: INDIVIDUAL CHANGE STIMULI, INTERNAL STIMULI, SELLER ACTIVITY
STIMULI

EXTERNAL VALIDITY   A condition of a design of a MARKETING RESEARCH activity
such that the conclusions of the experiment or study can be logically and

properly projected to the real world in which the decision-maker's problem exists. See: INTERNAL VALIDITY, VALIDITY

EXTINCTION PRICE   A price set to eliminate as much of the competition as possible. VARIABLE COSTS are used as a base. Could be interpreted as PREDATORY, in which case it would be illegal.

EXTRA DATING   Under this arrangement the buyer is permitted a specified number of days before ordinary dating begins. Example: 2/10-60 extra indicates that the buyer has 70 days from the invoice date to pay the bill with the discount deducted. Usually no additional time is allowed for payment without discount. See: EXTENDED TERMS

EXTRANEOUS VARIABLE   Any variable other than those which are used to determine the reaction to them of the test unit under EXPERIMENT. See: CONFOUNDED VARIABLE

EXTRAPOLATION   The process of projecting a curve beyond the limits of data or experience, using previous information as a basis for developing the needed values. Only as valid as the assumptions about the environmental factors governing. See: INTERPOLATION

EXTRAS   People willing to work on an irregular schedule or on call.

EXTRINSICALLY BACKED STORE   See: BACKING ACTIVITIES

EXTRINSICALLY MOTIVATED BEHAVIOR   Activity engaged in for the rewards which have no necessary relationship to the activity itself or are independent of the activity, for example, engaging in a job purely for the salary. See: INTRINSICALLY MOTIVATED BEHAVIOR, MOTIVATION

EXTRINSIC CUES   Cues that influence a buyer's PERCEPTION of a PRODUCT, as factors separate from the product itself, such as source image, price, OPINION LEADERS. See: INTRINSIC CUES

EXURBIA   Areas beyond SUBURBIA but still within relative accessibility to major city facilities.

EYEBALL CONTROL   Sometimes used to designate the type of reorder warning system which consists of a mark placed on a shelf-upright in the stockroom or warehouse to indicate minimum inventory point. When the height of the stock falls to the mark, a reorder is initiated.

EYE DIRECTION   Same as: FLOW, GAZE MOTION, MOVEMENT

FA   Abbreviation for: (1) Freight Agent (2) FREE ASTRAY (3) Freight astray

FAAN   Abbreviation for: First Advertising Agency Network, comprising 29 independent, full-service ADVERTISING AGENCIES, each in its own particular MARKET, which is capable of combining all the talents of its members as needed for a task. It has been in operation since 1928.

FABRICATING MATERIAL   RAW MATERIAL which has been processed into a stable form which requires only dimensional changes to permit incorporation into a product. Examples: lumber, leather, cloth. A few liquids, such as mercury and alcohol, may be so classified under certain conditions. See: OPERATING SUPPLIES, PARTS

FACE   (1) The style or design of type. (2) The printing surface of a type CHARACTER or ENGRAVING.

FACILITATING FUNCTIONS   The MARKETING FUNCTIONS of STANDARDIZATION AND GRADING, RISK-TAKING, FINANCING, and MARKET INFORMATION are usually grouped under this classification.

FACING   (1) A shelf stock one unit wide extending to the top and back of a shelf in a display. Used to determine space allocation for packaged items in a RETAIL STORE. Example: a facing for canned asparagus might be two cans high and five cans deep for a total of ten cans. (2) Designates the direction of a POSTER face in relation to the flow of traffic. For example, to be read by westbound traffic, the PANEL must be east facing.

FACING TEXT MATTER   A position in a periodical in which an advertisement is opposite EDITORIAL MATTER.

FACSIMILE BROADCASTING   Same as: FAX

FACT   Empirical reality relevant to a PROBLEM, which is indisputable and manifest, or which experience indicates may be inferred with certainty. See: HYPOTHESIS

FACTOR   A financing organization specializing in lending money with accounts receivable or inventory as a pledge.

FACTOR ANALYSIS   A method for investigating the interrelationships among a number of relevant variables, all treated as INDEPENDENT VARIABLES. Highly complex. Useful in treating the analysis of VARIANCE among the variables in an EXPERIMENTAL DESIGN, and to examine the structure of a cluster of attribute items, especially when the number of original variables is too large to be manageable so that a smaller, workable sub-set must be found. PARAMETRIC.

FACTORY PACK   A DIRECT PREMIUM which comes attached in some way to the product. Includes CONTAINER PREMIUMS, IN-PACKS, and ON-PACKS.

FACTORY SMOKESTACK SELLING   The assignment of a geographically defined territory to an INDUSTRIAL GOODS salesman without any other area description. The SALESMAN is supposed to assume that every smokestack indicates a PROSPECT and proceed accordingly. The incidence of this type of selling is lessening as more sophistication is gained in the gathering and use of detailed information about the prospect group of an area.

FACT TAG   Essentially the same as: INFORMATIVE LABEL

FACTUAL APPROACH   A COPY APPROACH in which the technical facts about a product or service are stressed to prove the logic of the benefits for which the MARKET should buy the product or service.

FAD   A FASHION which has caught on quickly and with a large number of persons, but which has only short-term popularity.

FAIR CREDIT REPORTING ACT   A national law effective April 25, 1971, which is designed to protect people from erroneous credit information exchanged among credit agencies, banks, corporations, and others. The law gives an individual the right to examine the information in his file, to have it deleted if found inaccurate, file a report of his side of the story if re-investigation does not settle the problem, and to have previous recipients of his file informed of any deletions and additions. In general, any adverse information, except bankruptcy, more than seven years old may not be reported.

FAIR PACKAGING AND LABELING ACT   A Federal law authorizing the FTC and the FDA to move against, among other things: use of misleading pictorial or verbal matter on LABELS; omission of ingredients, net quantity and size of serving from labels; misleading package shape and size; and employment of "cents off" deals except on a short term basis. The FTC has issued a guide defining the permissability of the use of "cents off" deals. Same as: TRUTH-IN-PACKAGING ACT

FAIR PRICE REFERENCE REACTION   Among many people there seems to have developed a kind of social learning which causes them to judge the propriety of a price for an item so that they will buy more of it and more willingly at that price than at a lower or higher price. See: COST-PRICE JUDGMENT, PRICE AURA EFFECT, REVERSE-ORDER PERCEPTION

FAIR TRADE LAW   No longer operative, it was a law permitting a manufacturer to establish under certain conditions a minimum resale price for his PRODUCT. Enacted on the state level as authorized by Federal enabling legislation, these laws were in effect in a diminishing number of states when the enabling legislation was repealed. See: McGUIRE-KEOGH FAIR TRADE ENABLING ACT

FAK   Abbreviation for: freight, all kinds. COMMODITY RATES applied on the basis of weight regardless of type of product actually transported.

FALSE CAPS   Capitalizing the first letter of each word. Used as a device to emphasize and fortify the key ideas of a communication.

FAMILY   As defined by the Bureau of the Census it refers to a group of two or more persons related by blood, marriage or adoption who reside together. See: EXTENDED FAMILY, FAMILY OF ORIENTATION, FAMILY OF PROCREATION, HOUSEHOLD, NUCLEAR FAMILY, SUBFAMILY

FAMILY BRAND   One BRAND applied to several or a large number of products of one seller, e.g., White Rose, Heinz, Alcoa, G.E. The major advantage of using this type of brand is that goodwill built up for one product that has caught on may be applied by CONSUMERS or INDUSTRIAL USERS to other products in the family. The major disadvantage is the loss of crisp identity of any one product. See: INDIVIDUAL BRAND

FAMILY HEAD   See: HOUSEHOLD HEAD

FAMILY OF ORIENTATION   The FAMILY into which one was born.

FAMILY OF PROCREATION   A FAMILY established by marriage.

FAMILY OF TYPE   One design of type in a complete range of sizes and variations, e.g., bold, italic, etc. See: FONT

FARM.   (1) A place of 10 or more acres from which annual sales of FARM PRODUCTS amounted to $50 or more. (2) A place of less than 10 acres from which annual sales of farm products amounted to $250 or more. See: COMMERCIAL FARM

FARM COOPERATIVE   An AGRICULTURAL COOPERATIVE on a large scale, buying machinery and supplies needed and selling the crops produced. There are about 7,500 such organizations in the United States. As an example of the size that can be attained, note that Farmland has about 500,000 farmer-members. Some have diversified into ownership of factory sources of requirements. See: SUPPLY COOPERATIVE

FARM PRODUCTS   Those RAW MATERIALS the supply of which is to a large degree controllable by man, at least as to intent. See: NATURAL PRODUCTS

f.a.s.   Abbreviation for: free alongside ship. Indicates that the seller agrees to bear the cost of getting the goods to ship's side. From there on it is the buyer's expense and risk.

FASHION   A STYLE which happens to be popular at a given time with a significant portion of the MARKET. Usually endures for a lengthy period of time. See: FAD

FASHION COORDINATION   In RETAILING, the activity of constant monitoring of FASHION trends to make sure that the merchandise offered is of harmonious STYLE, QUALITY, and APPEAL in the STORE'S various apparel departments that are related.

FASHION COORDINATOR   An expert in the history, dynamics, and current developments of FASHIONS who is employed by a RETAILER to help the

BUYERS and the display staff, and to assist in such PROMOTIONAL activities as fashion shows. See: FASHION COORDINATION

FASHION CYCLE (1) This is a misnomer, implying a regularity or predictability of recurrence or pattern which actually does not exist. Basic STYLES do move in and out of popularity, sometimes very slowly, other times very rapidly, occasionally with lengthy periods between times of popularity. Attempts to chart these movements have but shown how erratic they are. (2) See: ARC OF FASHION, INNOVATION DIFFUSION

FASHION GOODS Frequent change in design is the major appeal of such items. They are in a sense opposite in character to STAPLE GOODS. See: FASHION

FAX Trade shortword for: Facsimile Broadcasting, the transmission of words or pictures by radio waves. Presently, much of this activity is moving over telephone wires using newly introduced equipment.

FCC Abbreviation for: Federal Communications Commission, the government agency that licenses broadcast stations and regulates broadcasting.

FDA Abbreviation for: Food and Drug Administration, the government agency directly charged with controlling the harmful effects of certain foods, drugs, and food additives. Has the authority to forbid interstate commerce in items deemed harmful.

F DISTRIBUTION This distribution describes the frequency of the ratio of two unbiased estimates of the UNIVERSE VARIANCE that can be obtained by chance in drawing two SAMPLES at RANDOM from a normal universe. The computed value of F is compared with the table (expected) value at various CONFIDENCE LEVELS. The NULL HYPOTHESIS is rejected if the computed value is larger than the table value.

FEATHERBEDDING A colloquialism for union rules or practices which require employment in jobs that are not needed in the context established.

FEATURE (1) Some characteristic of a product. In itself usually of little consequence to a PROSPECT unless the benefits which the feature provides are quite obvious. Ordinarily it is the essence of the SALESMAN'S TASK to interpret features into benefits for the prospect. See: PRODUCT DISFEATURE (2) ADVERTISING a BRAND at a reduced price. (3) Give dominant display and space to a product. (4) The product given special SALES PROMOTION.

FEATURES/BENEFITS APPROACH TO SELLING Based on the understanding that a product's FEATURES are of little importance to a PROSPECT unless they can be shown to be a source of benefits to the prospect, this approach insists that the SALESMAN find a way to incorporate this understanding into his presentation. See: AIDCAS, APPEAL, MOTIVE

FEB Abbreviation for: Full-Employment Budget, a measure of the budget surplus or deficit resulting from current national budgetary policy were the economy producing at its full estimated potential. An element of variability in this measure is the estimate of the potential GNP and the level of unemployment at that potential. It does indicate the direction and magnitude of discretionary fiscal activity.

FEDERAL ALCOHOL ADMINISTRATION ACT The producer of alcoholic beverages must obtain from the Internal Revenue Service certificates approving the LABELS he puts on his bottles. These labels must provide adequate information about quality and origin, and must not be deceptive. The same rules apply to the advertising of such beverages.

FEDERAL COMMUNICATIONS COMMISSION. Same as: FCC

FEDERAL CROP INSURANCE CORPORATION This organization, the administrative costs of which are covered by Congressional appropriations, provides all-risk insurance to farmers eligible for coverage. Indemnity payments amount to 90% of the premiums (the rest held in reserve for contingencies), and the premiums are set according to the extent the farmers designate they desire protection.

FEDERAL HIGHWAY BEAUTIFICATION ACT   First enatted in 1965 at the sponsor-ship of Lady Bird Johnson, the then President's wife, and revised in 1970, this Act is designed to preserve whatever esthetic qualities a highway may possess. It exerts a great impact on the OUTDOOR ADVERTISING INDUSTRY by describing as a public nuisance advertising that is not controlled, and provides authority for removal of unauthorized signs. States are encour-aged to pass control laws by making one prerequisite to sharing in Federal highway funds. Some states have enacted strong legislation, e.g., Vermont prohibits all highway advertising and is engaging to pay for removal of signs and loss of business to PLANT OPERATORS; New Jersey's law prohibits signs "within sight of new highways," or within 660 feet of a highway.

FEDERAL MARITIME COMMISSION   Same as: FMC

FEDERAL TRADE COMMISSION   Same as: FTC

FEDERAL TRADE COMMISSION ACT   This Act, together with the CLAYTON ACT both passed in 1914, made the general provision that all unfair methods of com-petition in commerce were declared unlawful. Its major contribution to the force of the law was that now attacks on unfair methods of competition were to be made by public officials financed by public appropriations rath-er than to be left to private suits brought by private parties at their own initiative and expense. See: CELLER-KEFAUVER ANTI-MERGER ACT, ROBINSON-PATMAN ACT, SHERMAN ACT, WHEELER-LEA ACT

FEDERATED ASSOCIATION   This type of cooperative organization is actually an association of associations.

FEE BASIS   An arrangement with an ADVERTISING AGENCY whereby the agency agrees to accept a fixed fee for specific services to be rendered. See: 15 & 2

FEED   To transmit a BROADCAST from one station or location to another. See: NETWORK

FEEDBACK   In SALESMANSHIP, the communication of acceptance or rejection the salesman senses from the PROSPECT'S words, gestures, posture, facial expression, and pertinent acts. It is very important that the salesman proceed in such a way as to make feedback possible, because without it he cannot tell whether the benefits he is presenting are significant to the prospect. In a broader sense, it is any information received by a seller from his customers.

FEEDING THE MARKET   One plan used by COOPERATIVES in the agricultural fields whereby they tried to bring SUPPLY and DEMAND into better balance by re-leasing a storable crop to the MARKET gradually over the storage period. The hoped-for price benefits did not materialize. Studies indicate that in general the rise in prices as the year wears on after harvest is no more than that required to cover carrying charges. Probably the best advantages toward the orderly disposition of seasonally produced goods at higher prices lies in the improvement of MERCHANDISING methods.

FEE OFFICE   A type of RESIDENT BUYING OFFICE which is paid an annual fee by the various SPECIALTY STORES and DEPARTMENT STORES that it represents. The fee is based on the annual volume of the member store. Same as: PAID OFFICE

FERTILITY RATE   The number of children born per 1,000 women aged 15-44. Same as: General Fertility Rate   See: TOTAL FERTILITY RATE

FESTINGER MODEL   See: COGNITIVE DISSONANCE

FIBRE BOX ASSOCIATION   A trade association of producers of corrugated and solid fibreboard. The Association represents over 90% of the production in this $3 Billion industry. Its major services to members are the gathering and dissemination of pertinent statistical and technical information, assistance in cost accounting techniques, legal and marketing advice and training, and representation with appropriate government agencies as liason to develop sound specifications and procurement procedures. The Association does not lobby for specific legislation.

FIELD   In ADP, an area in a RECORD to be used for specific information.
See: CARD FIELD

FIELD CENSUS   Data collected about firms from all possible sources. Some firms such as Dun & Bradstreet conduct ongoing activities designed to provide a variety of information for a fee about any of several hundred thousand companies.

FIELD INTENSITY CONTOUR MAP   A map showing by area the relative reception intensity of television and/or radio stations.

FIELDMAN   An employee working as a rule in some capacity away from the home office in a territory covered by his company. May be a service representative or a SALESMAN.

FIELD SALES FORCE   See: FIELD SALESPERSON

FIELD SALESPERSON   A SALESPERSON who visits PROSPECTS and CUSTOMERS at their homes or places of business. Many firms have well-developed systems for recruiting, training, and then controlling the field sales force.

FIELD WAREHOUSING   A plan in which a marketer leases to a warehousing firm that portion of his plant or BRANCH in which his inventory is stored. The warehousing firm takes legal custodianship of the premises and the goods, issuing WAREHOUSE RECEIPTS to the marketer who can then obtain financing with the warehouse receipts as collateral.

FIFO   Abbreviation for: first-in, first-out, a method of inventory costing and evaluation. Merchandise received first are assumed sold first, leaving in inventory the last received. Generally works to increase the broad effects on profit of a situation in which prices are fluctuating. See: LIFO

15 & 2   In general practice most MEDIA allow an ADVERTISING AGENCY a commission of 15% of the total invoice, which is retained by the agency, and a CASH DISCOUNT of 2% of the net invoice, which is usually passed on to the advertiser. There is an increasing, but rather slow, tendency for agencies to negotiate a flat fee with advertisers.

#50 SHOWING   In OUTDOOR ADVERTISING, the number of PANELS approximating one-half the number included in a #100 SHOWING for the area. Sometimes defined as: a number of POSTERS sufficient to reach about 85% of the people in the MARKET every other day. Other showing levels are available.
Same as: HALF SHOWING

FIGHTING BRAND   A BRAND brought out by a company with which to engage in price competition without injuring the prices of its regular merchandise. It usually has no permanency in the company's LINES, may even be used for a one-run offer. Always suspect as a PREDATORY PRICING device, the use of this STRATEGY must be undertaken with care lest the firm cross the mark into illegal areas.

FILE PROOF   A copy of an ADVERTISEMENT taken usually from a published issue of the MEDIUM used for record purposes rather than for corrections.

FILL IN PRIVILEGE   Permission granted under some conditions to purchase items in small quantities as needed on a discount level established by a previous quantity purchase of those items.

FILL-INS   Items purchased during a period of DEMAND to replace those already sold in order to avoid lost sales of items moving well. See: RUNNERS

FINAL CONSUMER   A redundancy. See: CONSUMER

FINANCIAL RISK   See: CONSUMER-PERCEIVED RISKS

FINANCING   A MARKETING FUNCTION which includes the provision and management of money and credit necessary to get goods to the CONSUMER or user,
excluding those applicable transactions resulting from manufacturing.

FINE-SCREEN HALFTONE   See: HALFTONE

FINISHED GOODS INDEX   A measure of the price of goods just before they are
sold to the CONSUMER. Published by the Bureau of Labor Statistics, it
replaces the WHOLESALE PRICE INDEX which had become outdated. Two other
"stages of processing" will be monitored: crude materials and intermediate materials, and supplies and components.

FINITE POPULATION   See: ENUMERATIVE STUDY

FIRM   Any entity engaged in some business enterprise that conducts its
activities as a unit, whether simple in form as the INDIVIDUAL PROPRIETOR-
SHIP or as complex as the CONGLOMERATE.

FIRM BIDDING   A POLICY of asking for bids for products in which prospective vendors are told that original bids must be final, that revisions
will not be permitted under any circumstances.

FIRM MARKET   Used to describe a condition of stable price in a given MARKET.

FIRST ADVERTISING AGENCY NETWORK   Same as: FAAN

FIRST COVER   See: COVER

FIRST IN, FIRST OUT   Same as: FIFO

FISCAL PERIOD   Any period of time established for accounting purposes at
the end of which the results of operations are put forth to management
in the form of certain reports. Must not be longer than one year except
in the most unusual circumstances. Need not, and often does not, coin-
cide with the calendar year.

FISCAL POLICY   The use of taxation and government spending in various ways
and proportions in an attempt to control the economy. Highly interactive
with MONETARY POLICY.

FISHYBACK   Under this arrangement, loaded vans or trailers are moved by
ship between designated points. See: BIRDIEBACK, PIGGYBACK

FIXED-ALTERNATIVE QUESTION   A form of question used in a QUESTIONNAIRE in
which the RESPONDENTS are allowed but certain response choices. Such
questions may be dichotomous, allowing a choice from but two alternatives,
such as those providing for a "yes" or "no" response. Or they may be
multichotomous, providing for a possible one or a few responses from a
number of given alternatives. Multiple choice questions are multichotomous. See: OPEN-ENDED QUESTION, SCALES

FIXED CHARGES   (1) Obligations which must be met regularly, regardless of
business volume, e.g., interest on bonds, rent. (2) Same as: FIXED COSTS

FIXED COSTS   Those costs which remain essentially the same regardless of
the firm's production level within the relevant range.

FIXED-ORDER-INTERVAL SYSTEM   A method of replenishment of goods in PURCHAS-
ING whereby an order is sent to appropriate VENDORS at regular intervals.
The size of each order varies according to the then relationship between
existing inventory and the maximum amount to be carried. See: EOQ

FIXED POSITION   In BROADCAST MEDIA, a COMMERCIAL delivered at a specific
time agreed on in advance, e.g., 10:27 p.m.

FIXED SLOT LOCATION SYSTEM   A way of placing goods in a WAREHOUSE so that a certain product has a known permanent location. Makes ORDER PICKING easier, but results in much space empty at any particular time. See: VARIABLE SLOT LOCATION SYSTEM

FLAG   (1) In OUTDOOR ADVERTISING, a strip of POSTER paper hanging loose. PLANT OPERATORS generally monitor such problems to replace the strip promptly. (2) A numeral placed in a designated position which an OPTICAL SENSING device can read to identify a DC, a WPC, or any other item wanted identified. (3) The practice of placing some type of marker on an account card to alert a posting clerk of some desired action. (4) The marker used in (3).

FLAGGING AN ACCOUNT   A credit device by means of which a delinquent account may be identified and suspended temporarily. Colored tabs are often used as identification markers.

FLAGSHIP STATION   The main station of a NETWORK.

FLAGSHIP STORE   The PARENT STORE of one or a number of BRANCHES.

FLAMMABLE FABRICS ACT   Under this 1967 Federal law the FTC may institute procedings to enjoin the manufacture of and to confiscate existing stocks of any article of wearing apparel which is "so highly flammable as to be dangerous when worn." The tests for determining whether an article is too flammable have been devised by the National Bureau of Standards, and the testing procedures have been prescribed by the FTC. Producers of flammable products are required to keep swatches of each class sold and to maintain full records of their sales.

FLANNELBOARD   A device used in training and presentation, utilizing a board covered with a flannel-type cloth onto which symbols may be affixed, these symbols being backed with a different type of cloth which adheres readily to the flannelboard.

FLASH APPROACH   When applied to a POSTER, it is a factor for evaluating a position. Generally measured in terms of distance/speed visibility as less than 40 feet to pedestrian traffic, less than 100 feet for vehicular traffic moving at more than 30 miles per hour, or less than 75 feet for vehicular traffic moving at less than 30 miles per hour. See: ANGLED POSTER, HEAD-ON POSITION, PARALLEL POSTER

FLASH REPORT   In RETAILING, the total daily gross sales by departments. Prepared at the end of each day. In smaller STORES the tally is made manually; in larger stores this chore is generally assigned to the computer along with other reporting.

FLAT RATE   In ADVERTISING, a uniform charge per unit of space in a MEDIUM without consideration for amount of space used or for the frequency of insertion. See: BULK DISCOUNT, FREQUENCY DISCOUNT

FLEXFORM   Permitted by some print MEDIA, this permits an ADVERTISEMENT to be shaped in any manner and even be surrounded by EDITORIAL MATTER. May be an attention getter. See: ISLAND POSITION

FLEXIBLE CHARGE ACCOUNT   Same as: ALL-PURPOSE REVOLVING ACCOUNT

FLEXIBLE PRICE POLICY   Same as: VARIABLE PRICE POLICY

FLEXIBLE PRICING   (1) A pricing STRATEGY based on a recognition by a manufacturer of all MARKET forces, as opposed to a POLICY of rigid adherence to a determined ratio of profit to sales. Involves separate considerations of all variables for each PRODUCT. (2) Same as: VARIABLE PRICING

FLEXING SYSTEM   A photomechanical arrangement for resizing ADVERTISING material in PRINT MEDIA which involves a film positive or negative and another sheet of film or paper being moved past a narrow-beam of light source at different speeds. The relative speed determines the amount of reduction. Gives uniform "squeeze." See: ANAMORPHIC LENS

FLEXOGRAPHY   The use of rubber plates in printing. Used mainly where quality is not very critical, although new materials and techniques are raising the quality of this method.

FLIGHT   The period used by an advertiser in BROADCAST MEDIA during which
to run his SPOTS when the total period is less than 52 weeks, e.g.,
June flight, Spring flight, etc.

FLIGHTING SCHEDULE   In ADVERTISING, essentially the same as: PULSATION

FLIGHT SATURATION   The maximum concentration of SPOT ADVERTISING in a short
period of time. See: FLIGHT

FLIP WIPE   An effect used in TELEVISION COMMERCIALS whereby the picture is
turned physically over or around to reveal a new scene. See: OPTICALS

FLONG   A piece of thick, soft cardboard of several pieces of paper pasted
together which is converted into a MAT by pressing it onto and around all
relief elements in the FORM, then curved if desired, and dried.

FLOOR LIMIT   In RETAILING, an amount established as the maximum which a
SALES CLERK may allow a properly identified charge CUSTOMER without special authorization.

FLOOR PLANNING. Any financing arrangement by means of which the borrower
keeps possession of goods which are pledged as security for a business
loan. Widely used in the CONSUMER DURABLE GOODS businesses.

FLOOR STOCK   In general, all merchandise accessible to CUSTOMERS of a store.
Sometimes applied more narrowly to merchandise which is displayed by units
other than shelves, e.g., suits, dresses, refrigerators. See: FORWARD
STOCK, SHELF STOCK

FLOW   Same as: Eye Direction, GAZE MOTION, Movement

FLOW CHART   See: FLOW PATTERN (2)

FLOW PATTERN   (1) One of the significant location determinants, it links
the movement of a group of materials from an original supply source
through one or more locations, in which some processing may be done, to
a location for end use. Various activities and enterprises will come
into existence, and others will be linked in, to support the flow. (2)
The graphic presentation of all the MARKETING institutions involved in
the flow pattern at any one time is called a flow chart. See: CENTRAL-
PERIPHERAL PATTERN

FLUFF   In BROADCASTING, any minor error committed while on the air.

FLUSH   Indicates printed matter set even with the edge of the page, or,
sometimes, even with other material on the page.

FLYING SQUAD   A group of specially trained SALESPERSONS who are able to
work in any STORE department as needed. Most often found in DEPARTMENT
STORES. See: CHINESE WALLS

FM   Abbreviation for: Frequency Modulation. Indicates that the SIGNAL alters the number of waves passing a certain point per second while the
height remains constant. These waves move in a straight line and are
blocked by obstacles on earth. The effective range depends on the height
of the source, but may in general be 40-50 miles. Television sound uses
this type of wave. Used in a significant number of radio broadcasts
where it has the advantage of eliminating most types of static. See: AM

FMC   Abbreviation for: Federal Maritime Commission, an arm of the United
States government established in its present form August 12, 1961, with
authority from previous laws as amended and as to be assigned by future
laws. It licenses ocean freight forwarders, guarantees funds for oil
pollution cleanup, assures funds to cover liabilities to those who use
passenger vessels, guards against unauthorized monopoly in the waterborne

commerce of the United States, fights discrimination or prejudice in United States international trade, and regulates the rates and practices of COMMON CARRIERS by water operating in the domestic offshore or in the foreign commerce of the United States.

F.O.B. Abbreviation for: free on board. Indicates that the seller agrees to pay the cost of placing the goods on board a carrier at a certain point. If the terms are F.O.B destination, it means that the seller pays the freight.

FOCUSED GROUP INTERVIEW A comparatively small number of persons are brought together for discussion and interchange of ideas pertaining to a topic of interest to the marketer, rather than the one-at-a-time process in the DEPTH INTERVIEW.

FOCUS GROUPS Groups of people brought together to engage in open, in-depth unstructured discussion about a relevant subject area. Each group, usually eight to twelve people, are steered in a nondirective manner by a trained moderator. The discussion is tape-recorded so that it can be reviewed for ideas about additional MARKETING RESEARCH, new PRODUCTS or SERVICES, THEMES of ADVERTISING, innovations in PACKAGING, or whatever else may be suggested. The varying nature of the participants' stimuli and inter-actions, combined with the generally too small SAMPLE, make these groups unreliable for CONCLUSIVE RESEARCH.

FOLDER A large, DIRECT MAIL ADVERTISING piece, folded more than once, com-posed to make a more impressive presentation than a LEAFLET. Frequently designed as a SELF-MAILER. Invites quick reading, but makes no image of quality.

FOLKWAYS Those norms for which there are no clearly defined means of en-forcing conformity because they are not considered basic to the welfare of the group. See: MORES

FOLLOWING READING MATTER See: FULL POSITION

FONT A complete assortment of type CHARACTERS in one FACE and one size, including punctuation marks, numbers, etc. See: FAMILY OF TYPE

FOOD AND DRUG ADMINISTRATION Same as: FDA

FOOD BROKER One of the most important categories of FUNCTIONAL MIDDLEMEN, he sells grocery products to those who buy in large quantities. Same characteristics as other BROKERS. **See: NFBA**

FOOD DETAILER Same as: DETAILER

FOOD, DRUG, AND COSMETIC ACT This Act gives the FDA control over defini-tions of adulteration and misbranding of foods, cosmetics and therapeu-tic devices. Amendments have brought chemical additives, pesticides, and herbicides under this jurisdiction. Among the many provisions relating to drugs are the following: manufacturers must apply for approval before placing a drug on the market and must prove that it is safe and effective; all drug factories must be inspected at least biennially; drug LABELS and advertisements must contain information on injurious side effects; the FDA may summarily remove a drug or other material from the market if it has evidence that it carries an imminent threat to health.

FOOD STORE DETAILER Same as: DETAILER

FOR Abbreviation for: (1) Foreign (2) Free on rail, as used in the TRAFFIC field.

FORCED DISTRIBUTION Same as: Pull, in PUSH OR PULL DISTRIBUTION STRATEGY

FORCED SCALE A SCALE which omits a "no opinion" choice, thus forcing RESPONDENTS to select a position. See: SCALING

FORCING METHODS Quick-action stimuli. Methods designed to move CONSUMERS

to immediate action. Usually short-lived. Must be watched closely to determine effectiveness because these can cause negative reactions. See:
CONTEST, PREMIUM

FORECASTING Estimating future magnitudes and TRENDS of elements of business activity on the basis of historical data and/or predictions of coming environmental conditions. Commonly used to h elp plan the sales and
sales-related needs of a business in the following year. May be projections for a five-year period, in which revisions or reviews would be needed periodically. A few firms attempt a ten-year forecast which they review for the next one-year, five-year, and ten-year periods on a rolling
basis. See: BUSINESS CYCLES

FOREIGN TRADE ZONE A port-of-entry area operating under a grant of authority from the United States Government, in which without payment of duty or
taxes foreign and domestic merchandise may be comingled, processed in any
manner, used in the manufacture of other products, exhibited in original
form, or stored indefinitely. FIRMS wishing to use the facilities rent
space from that Port Authority which operates that particular zone.
Merchandise shipped to foreign destinations are not subject to taxes or
duties, but that directed to domestic destinations are subject to import
controls and/or duties.

FORESTALLING (1) the practice of cornering the SUPPLY by buying up goods
on the way to the MARKET, thus putting the merchant in a position to se-
cure a higher price. A criminal offense in the 16th Century. See: EN-
GROSSING, REGRATING (2) In SALESMANSHIP, the anticipation of an OBJEC-
TION by a PROSPECT so that an answer to it may be included in the presentation.

FOREWARD VERTICAL INTEGRATION See: VERTICAL INTEGRATION

FORM Plates and type in LETTERPRESS printing locked in a CHASE ready for
the print operation, making a MAT, or STEREOTYPING.

FORMAL BALANCE A quality an advertisement has when all the elements in it
are of equal optical weight at all points vertically as pairs on opposite
sides of a line drawn from top to bottom through the center of the advertisement. This regularity of LAYOUT is generally less interesting than
that found in INFORMAL BALANCE. Its major effectiveness is found where
it can assist in presenting an image of high worth. Same as: SYMMETRICAL
BALANCE

FORMAL DECISION ANALYSIS A structure of the decision-making process which
divides it into three phases: PRIOR ANALYSIS, PREPOSTERIOR ANALYSIS, and
POSTERIOR ANALYSIS. This process is closely associated with various
MARKETING RESEARCH techniques.

FORMAL GROUP A REFERENCE GROUP which has membership qualifications, dues,
officers, meeting dates, etc. See: INFORMAL GROUP

FORMAL ORGANIZATION The official hierarchy of AUTHORITY flows in the several divisions of a firm as designated by top management. See: INFORMAL
ORGANIZATION

FORMAT All the elements determining the appearance of a print advertisement, or the organization of each element in a broadcast program.

FORMS CLOSE Same as: CLOSING DATE

FORM UTILITY The characteristic of a PRODUCT which makes it possible to
satisfy a human WANT because processing has converted it into a usable
state which makes it desirable for an intended purpose. See: UTILITY

FORWARD BUYING Committing purchases to provide for needs during a time
longer than is necessary for immediate requirements. All firms engage
in this to some extent. Differs from SPECULATION in the degree of involvement and in motive. See: HAND-TO-MOUTH BUYING

FORWARD ORDER   A committment to accept goods to be delivered in the future. Results from the normal operation of a business which must provide LEAD TIME. Sometimes confused with speculative buying, which commits the firm for larger quantities than can be justified by requirements in the foreseeable future. The length of the lead time is an important factor, as well as the EOQ, in deciding about placements of forward orders.

FORWARD STOCK   The merchandise carried in the selling areas of a RETAIL STORE, but not accessible to patrons. See: BACK-UP MERCHANDISE, FLOOR STOCK, SHELF STOCK

FOUNDRY PROOFS   Page composition cast into PLATES for printing. The final step after PAGE PROOFS. Corrections or additions to COPY ordinarily can not be made at this stage. The only reason for a proof now is to be sure that the plate has no flaw caused by the casting process. See: LETTERPRESS

4 A's   Same as: AAAA

FOUR-COLOR PROCESS   The photoengraving process for reproducing color illustrations by a set of four plates, one each for yellow, blue, red, black. The sequence of printing varies with the subject. See: PROCESS PLATES

FOUR P'S   The major ingredients of a MARKETING MIX as designated in one pattern of analysis. They are: Product, the right one for the target MARKET; Place, all the considerations and institutions involved in getting the right product to the target market; Promotion, communication of all sorts to the target market about the product; and Price, determination of the price which is the happy balance of maximum attractiveness to the market and capability of enabling the firm to reach its revenue and profit objectives.

FOURTH COVER   See: COVER

FOUR-WALLING   A technique for MARKETING motion pictures in which a producer will give very heavy ADVERTISING activity to a movie in one city in which he has leased as may theaters (four walls) as possible for a flat fee. The PROMOTION will last but a short time, after which the producer will take his movie to another MARKET, not to return to any one already worked until another movie is to be so treated.

FRAGMENTATION   The current trend of marketers to designate and to isolate portions of the total MARKET as to common characteristics and specialized demand. See: SEGMENTATION, SUBMARKET

FRAME   In statistics, a positive and definite way of identifying all of the ELEMENTARY UNITS to be covered by a study. The resulting list is used to determine whether and how access may be had to the POPULATION so that relevant information may be gathered.

FRANCHISING   An arrangement whereby an organization which has developed a successful RETAIL product or service extends to others for a fee the right to engage in the business, provided they agree to follow the established pattern. It is a special form of EXCLUSIVE DISTRIBUTION. Some abuses have appeared, such as failure by the franchisor to keep his promises of training, MERCHANDISING assistance, and advertising. There have been a few instances of outright fraud. All of these are being attacked through legislation, PUBLICITY, and judicial channels. Anyone contemplating entering into a franchising contract would do well first to investigate fully.

FREE ALONGSIDE SHIP   Same as: f.a.s.

FREE ASTRAY   A shipment misdirected or unloaded at the wrong station is forwarded to the correct station free of additional charges, because of its having been "astray."

FREE FLOW LAYOUT   See: STORE LAYOUT

FREE GOODS   See: DEAL

FREE LANCE   An independent writer, artist, or advertising man who accepts assignments from individual accounts but is not an employee of any of them.

FREE ON BOARD   Same as: F.O.B.

FREE PAPER   Same as: SHOPPER

FREE PORT   An area of a country set apart for customs purposes so that goods entering for local use or re-export are duty-free. See: FOREIGN TRADE ZONE

FREE RESPONSE QUESTION   An inquiry made of a RESPONDENT in such a way that the possible scope of responses is not limited. When the inquiry confines the respondent to a particular category of response (perhaps a product) but leaves it open to full opinion and wording, the inquiry is called a directed-response question.

FREE-STANDING STUFFER   Same as: NEWSPAPER STUFFER

FREE TRADE   Commerce permitted to move freely between nations without tariffs or other restrictions or limitations. See: FREE TRADE ZONE

FREE TRADE ZONE   Same as: FOREIGN TRADE ZONE

FREEZE RATE   The minimum rate which a trucking firm will apply to any shipment whether the shipment qualifies for a lower rate or not. This practice varies from time to time with the same trucker. Same as: RATE STOPS

FREIGHT ABSORPTION   Selling on a prepaid basis where the total price is less than the sum of the product price at the factory plus the freight cost of getting the product to the buyer. Happens often when BASING-POINT PRICING is used, but is present in some degree whenever a common delivered price is quoted for a zone. See: PHANTOM FREIGHT, POSTAGE-STAMP PRICING, MILL NET RETURN

FREIGHT, ALL KINDS   Same as: FAK

FREIGHT ALLOWED   The seller quotes a price which includes delivery cost regardless of the buyer's location. See: POSTAGE-STAMP PRICING

FREIGHT EQUALIZATION.   The distant buyer is quoted a delivered price which consists of the F.O.B. price plus the delivery cost from the seller's competitor nearest the buyer. See: UNSYSTEMATIC FREIGHT EQUALIZATION

FREIGHT FORWARDER   (1) An independent business engaged in consolidating l.c.l. or l.t.l. shipments to one location from many different shippers. His service is usually paid for by the buyer and often is based on a flat fee per package. His service enables the buyer to avoid the extremely high transportation cost attached to many small shipments which would move each at the minimum rate. Thus several shipments may be consolidated to move at no more than the cost for any one. See: CONSOLIDATOR (2) A person or firm acting as agent in the shipment of goods to or from foreign countries, and in the clearing of shipments through customs.

FRENCH DOORS   See: GATEFOLD

FREQUENCY   (1) The number of times an ADVERTISING message is delivered to an AUDIENCE within a set period of time, usually considered for a specified MEDIUM. See: COVERAGE, EXPOSURE, REACH   (2) In BROADCASTING, the number of electromagnetic waves that pass a given point in a second. See: AM, FM   (3) In POP, the number of times an individual sign or display is exposed to persons within a specified period of time.   (4) See: FREQUENCY DISTRIBUTION

FREQUENCY CURVE   A curve on a graph fitted to the data of a FREQUENCY DISTRIBUTION. See: KURTOSIS, SKEWNESS

FREQUENCY DISCOUNT   A reduction in the cost of advertising determined by the number of insetions or broadcasts in a certain period of time. See: BULK DISCOUNT, FLAT RATE

FREQUENCY DISTRIBUTION   A detailed summary of a set of observations showing the ATTRIBUTES of a POPULATION and their frequency of occurrence. It may be presented in a variety of pictorial ánd graphical modes.

FREQUENCY MODULATION   Same as: FM

FRINGE TIME   The approximately one hour adjacent to PRIME TIME.

FRONT   In RETAILING, the selling area of a STORE. The call, "Front," is often used to summon clerks from stockroom activity to service CUSTOMERS. See: FRONT END

FRONT END   In RETAILING, the area or areas where CUSTOMERS pay for the merchandise they have selected. See: FRONT-END CHECKOUT

FRONT-END CHECKOUT   All cash registers and checkout lanes are located near the STORE exit rather than here and there in the various selling-floor areas.

FRONT-END DISPLAY   An outside TRANSIT ADVERTISING display placed on the front of buses or other vehicles. Same as: HEADLIGHT DISPLAY

FRONT-END LOAD   Used to describe a way of assembling a MAGAZINE so that most of the advertisements are placed in the front half of the magazine.

FRUSTRATION   A feeling an individual may get that is brought about by an inability to attain a goal, for whatever reason or obstacle. See: AGGRESSION, AUTISM, IDENTIFICATION, PROJECTION, RATIONALIZATION, REGRESSION, REPRESSION

FTC   Abbreviation for: Federal Trade Commission. Brought into existence by an Act in 1914, it is an independent administrative agency of five commissioners appointed by the President with the advice and consent of the Senate for terms of seven years, the terms overlapping. The President designates the Chairman. No more than three of its members may belong to the same- political party. Its functions include research and publication of reports; promotion of compliance; investigation of unfair methods of competition, deceptive practices, agreements in restraint of trade, and monopolistic mechanisms; and prosecution of violators. Also, it enforces the Wool Products Labeling Act of 1939, the Fur Products Labeling Act of 1951, the Flammable Fabrics Act of 1953, and the Textile Fiber Products Indentification Act of 1958. It received added responsibilities through various congressional enactments in the 1970's.

FTO   Abbreviation for: Foreign Trade Organization, a typical commercial entity of Communist countries through which foreign trade activities are conducted. These state organizations have general responsibility for conducting negotiations with foreign firms and have specific power to sign contracts. See: CT

FTZ   Abbreviation for: FOREIGN TRADE ZONE

FULL-CAPACITY OUTPUT   The greatest output achievable while operating on usual schedules and using existing plant, equipment and other resources applicable to manufacturing.

FULL COLOR   Same as: FOUR-COLOR PROCESS

FULL COSTING   A way of applying costs to products based on the principle that each product should bear its fair share of all the costs involved in making it. At the end of a period all of the costs incurred during that period will have been applied to the products worked on during the period. See: DIRECT COSTING

FULL DISCLOSURE   The requirement by law that manufacturers of certain

PRODUCTS must provide specified kinds of information about them, often on LABELS and in ADVERTISEMENTS.

FULL-EMPLOYMENT BUDGET   Same as: FEB

FULL-FUNCTION WHOLESALER   Same as: SERVICE WHOLESALER

FULL LINE   A CLASSIFICATION of goods which includes every possible variation of style, color, size, and material that a CUSTOMER may reasonably expect to find at a given price. See: BROAD-LINE STRATEGY

FULL-LINE FORCING   The practice of requiring the buyer to take the less desirable items of a seller's LINE in order to get the more desirable items. This practice is increasingly thought to have negative consequences for the seller. See: CHERRY PICKING

FULL-LINE STRATEGY   Same as: BROAD-LINE STRATEGY

FULL MARK   In RETAILING, a reference to a 100% MARKUP.

FULL POSITION   A position for newspaper advertisements either next to or following reading matter, or top of column next to reading matter. Usually charged for extra when demanded because it is considered a PREFERRED POSITION.

FULL-PROGRAM SPONSOR   A SPONSOR who pays the full cost of time and production of a program, whatever the length of time it uses, so that only his COMMERCIALS are run. See: ALTERNATE SPONSOR, PARTICIPATING PROGRAM

FULL RUN   Same as: FULL SHOWING

FULL RUN SHOWING   Same as: FULL SHOWING

FULL SERVICE   Same as: FULL SHOWING

FULL SERVICE AGENCY   An ADVERTISING AGENCY that will handle the planning, developing, production, and placement of ADVERTISING for its clients. Such agencies frequently are able to accomplish various research projects.

FULL-SERVICE WHOLESALER   Same as: SERVICE WHOLESALER

FULL SHOWING   (1) In TRANSIT ADVERTISING, a message of the same advertiser in each car or other unit of the system. (2) Used loosely to refer to a #100 SHOWING of OUTDOOR ADVERTISING.

FUNCTIONAL APPROACH   A way of studying MARKETING which looks at the whole as the sum of the activities embodied in the MARKETING FUNCTIONS. See: COMMODITY APPROACH, INSTITUTIONAL APPROACH

FUNCTIONAL COST ANALYSIS   Based on a classification of expenses according to the business functions for which they were incurred, this analysis is directed to the control of internal operations. Costs are directly related to specific areas of MARKETING activity. A SERVICE UNIT is selected for each function. See: NATURAL EXPENSES

FUNCTIONAL DISCOUNT   A reduction in price granted to a BUYER based upon the MARKETING activities performed by that buyer or his firm. Same as: Trade Discount

FUNCTIONALIZATION   Where many persons are required to accomplish a task, the breakdown of the task into manageable units, and the assignment of appropriate units to each person. See: SPECIALIZATION

FUNCTIONAL MIDDLEMAN   An independent business the major operations of which are to assist in the passing of title to goods without taking title to the goods in the process. Same as: AGENT MIDDLEMAN   See: AUCTION RECEIVER, BROKER, COMMISSION AGENT, MANUFACTURERS' REPRESENTATIVE, RESIDENT BUYING OFFICE, SELLING AGENT

FUNCTIONAL RISK   See: CONSUMER-PERCEIVED RISKS

FUNCTIONS OF EXCHANGE   The MARKETING FUNCTIONS of BUYING and SELLING are often grouped under this classification.

FUNCTIONS OF PHYSICAL SUPPLY   The MARKETING FUNCTIONS of TRANSPORTATION and STORAGE are often grouped under this classification.

FUR PRODUCTS LABELING ACT   Requires sellers to use the true English names of furs as determined by the FTC. LABELS must show these and state whether the furs are new or used, dyed or bleached, and whether from bellies, tails, or paws. Country of origin is to be disclosed.

FUTURES   Transactions in the FUTURES MARKET. All COMMODITY EXCHANGES have rules governing the agreements by means of which the transactions are effected.

FUTURES MARKET   That part of the MARKET for a commodity in which contracts to buy or sell the commodity at some determinable future date are traded. The existence of this market makes possible such activities as HEDGING. See: COMMODITY EXCHANGE

GAFF or GAFFO   Abbreviation for a store classification group which includes the General Merchandise, Apparel and Accessory, and Furniture and Home Furnishings and Appliance stores. RETAILING management is using the sales of this group more and more as a standard of comparison for measuring changing competitive market positions.

GAIN OPPORTUNITY   The difference between a firm's objective in a MARKET and the actual sales achieved. If the objective was set realistically, the difference indicates how much more sales the firm may expect to realize in that market.

GALLEY PROOFS   Proofs on sheets printed from the type as it stands in the galley trays before being separated into pages. Errors are correctable most easily at this stage.

GAMBLER   One who assumes RISKS based almost entirely on the laws of probability or on personal hunch without specific foundation. The risks assumed are contrived for the purpose and do not exist naturally in the MARKET. See: SPECULATOR

GANG   (1) A group of engravings, type pages, or other printing units assembled together for printing at a single impression. (2) Multiple reproduction of art work in PHOTOENGRAVING.

GANGING UP   The activity involved in working with and using a GANG.

GANG PRINTING   Essentially the same as: GANGING UP

GARBAGE   In ADP, meaningless information in a computer's memory. Usually the incorrect input by humans, but may be the result of machine complications. See: GIGO

GATEFOLD   A MAGAZINE page of extended size, folded over. If it is so arranged that the folds are set so that the page opens at top and bottom, it is called dutch doors. If the page opens from side to side, it is called french doors. If it is part of the COVER, it is called a gatefold cover.

GATEFOLD COVER   See: GATEFOLD

GATEKEEPER   A member of a group who keeps the channels of communication open, mainly by controlling the flow of discussion of interest to marketers, because of their general influence in the group.

GATT   Abbreviation for: General Agreement on Tariffs and Trade, an organization which includes most of the major trading nations of the free world, established in 1948 to negotiate among themselves for reductions in tariffs. It meets every two years.

GAZEBO   A display fixture, often free-standing, used to show various types of fashion accessories.

GAZE MOTION   That quality of the LAYOUT which draws the eye from part to part.   Same as: Eye Direction, Flow, Movement

GCMI   Abbreviation for: The Glass Container Manufacturers Institute, an organization whose members produce in about 100 plants nearly 90% of all glass containers made in the United States.   The Institute conducts ADVERTISING PROGRAMS on behalf of the glass container industry, coordinates with the FDA, and provides a range of technical, research and traffic services to members.

GENERAL ACCEPTORS   Same as: LATE MAJORITY   See: ARC OF FASHION, INNOVATION DIFFUSION

GENERAL ADVERTISING   NATIONAL or other non-local advertising in NEWSPAPERS.

GENERAL AGREEMENT ON TARIFFS AND TRADE   Same as: GATT

GENERAL FERTILITY RATE   Same as: FERTILITY RATE

GENERALIZED SYSTEM OF PREFERENCES   Same as: GSP

GENERAL LINE DISTRIBUTOR   An INDUSTRIAL DISTRIBUTOR classified as a GENERAL-LINE WHOLESALER

GENERAL LINE HOUSE   Same as: GENERAL LINE DISTRIBUTOR

GENERAL-LINE WHOLESALER   A MERCHANT WHOLESALER characterized by his attempting to carry a complete stock of merchandise within a given field.

GENERAL MERCHANDISE WHOLESALER   A MERCHANT WHOLESALER who carries goods in a number of unrelated lines.

GENERAL RATE   Same as: ONE-TIME RATE

GENERAL STORE   A RETAIL STORE that handles a large number of LINES of merchandise without any significant degree of departmental organization.   It is usually small-scale and heavily oriented toward groceries.

GENERIC LABEL   An innovation in the food INDUSTRY in which the PRODUCT'S undecorated PACKAGE carries a LABEL identifying the contents without BRAND connection.   The label is usually unadorned, with minimum required data.

GENERIC NAME   The name by which a certain type of product is identified, as distinguished from its BRAND NAME, e.g., petroleum jelly is generic, Vaseline petroleum jelly is a brand name.   Unless precautions are taken, brand names may become generic, in which case anyone may use them because they then are considered the identifier of the type of product.   In this way the word "aspirin" which was the property of Bayer became generic and may now be used by anyone to describe the basic chemical.   See: USTA

GEOCENTRICITY   One of a three-way classification of the POLICIES of FIRMS engaged in international MARKETING, this one focuses on the methods of accomplishing an understanding of the economic, cultural, and legal conditions which are different among the countries considered as a global target, and the means by which they can be managed.   The other two are: ETHNOCENTRICITY and POLYCENTRICITY.

GEOGRAPHIC SEGMENTATION   See: SEGMENTATION

GEOGRAPHIC SKEW   A situation in which an ADVERTISER, usually because of insufficient analysis of MARKETS, seriously overspends in one area while underspending in another.

GFA   Abbreviation for: General Freight Agent.   Used in the TRAFFIC field.

GHOST DIAGRAM   Same as: PHANTOM DIAGRAM

GHOST VIEW   Same as: PHANTOM DIAGRAM

GIANT INSERT   Same as: NEWSPAPER STUFFER

GIGO   A word used in the computer field to denote the inability of a computer to convert invalid inputs into valid outputs in the form of usable data. It is made up of the first letters of the words: garbage in, garbage out. See: GARBAGE

GIMMICK   (1) Any unusual and clever slant in the presentation of a PRODUCT. (2) Any clever device or feature of a device.

GIVE-AWAY   A low cost item handed out freely to customers without charge. May be a TRAFFIC-BUILDER or an ADVERTISING NOVELTY. Sometimes used to refer to any DIRECT PREMIUM.

GLASS CONTAINER MANUFACTURERS INSTITUTE.   Same as: GCMI

GLITCHES   Surprise failures of things that were expected to succeed. The lack of success of things that were not supposed to fail.

GLOBAL MARKETING PROGRAM.   Same as: GMP

GLOSSY   Commonly used to denote a black and white photograph which has been reproduced on high gloss paper. Especially indicated for reproduction in PRINT MEDIA.

GMP   Abbreviation for: Global Marketing Program, managed by the Bureau of International Commerce of the U.S. Department of Commerce. The pattern is for the Bureau to determine by international survey in which foreign countries there exists a competitive edge for American products not now being supplied by American exporters. Through the GMP the Department then tries to stimulate American firms to step up sales efforts in the neglected areas. The hope is that this program will help offset any deficit in the balance of international payments, increase employment in the discovered industries, and strengthen the dollar as the world's international currency. See: DISC

GNP   Abbreviation for: Gross National Product. Equals the total market value of the output of goods and services of the nation's economy at "final" prices.

GOAL CONGRUENCE   Identifies the managerial PRINCIPLE that all of the subgoals of a FIRM must work together to achieve one central set of objectives. See: MARKETING CONCEPT

GOFFMAN MODEL   See: THEORY OF ROLE ENACTMENT

GOING-RATE PRICING   Using the average price level charged by the INDUSTRY to set the price charged by a firm. Same as: Imitative Pricing

GOING TO MARKET   Same as: VISITING THE MARKET

GOLDEN SHOWCASE   In OUTDOOR ADVERTISING, two POSTER PANELS used as one unit, either side by side or one atop the other. Makes possible a message on twice the usual size surface. See: CENTER SPREAD

GONDOLA   An island of shelving, usually open on two sides but may be open all around. Generally used in RETAIL STORES.

GOOD   (1) In economics, any tangible thing which people consider useful and which is a benefit within the meaning of that concept in our society. (2) Widely used to mean the same as merchandise or product.

GOODNESS OF FIT   See: CHI-SQUARE TEST

GOODS FLOW   The activities within the network of institutions linking producers and CONSUMERS or INDUSTRIAL USERS, which are concerned with PHYSICAL DISTRIBUTION.

GPA   Abbreviation for: General Passenger Agent. Used in the TRAFFIC FIELD.

GRADE LABELING   Indicating on the LABEL the grade of the PRODUCT as determined by qualified comparison of the product's characteristics with those of an unvarying standard.

GRADING   The activity of comparing GOODS with a previously established criterion as to the acceptability of certain aspects of the goods. Combined with STANDARDIZATION, one of the MARKETING FUNCTIONS.

GRAPHICS   Generally, all visual elements of communication associated with the presentation of a PRODUCT or SERVICE to a MARKET. Includes art, color effects, photographs, COPY, etc.

GRAVURE   A form of INTAGLIO.

GREEN CROSS   See: NSC

GREEN RIVER ORDINANCE   A local law restricting a SALESPERSONS house-visits to those where the resident has invited the salesperson.

GREETERS   Representatives of WHOLESALERS in the United States during the early 1800s period of territorial expansion, who met boats and stage coaches on which buyers from the rural areas were arriving on their annual or biennial visits to the large centers to fill orders or to replenish their basic stock items. Over a period of time these greeters anticipated buyers farther and farther from the city, until they eventually went to the buyers' establishments, thus becoming travelling salesmen.

GRID CARD   A station's RATE CARD in which the COMMERCIAL times are priced individually, Spot by SPOT.

GRID PATTERN   See: STORE LAYOUT

GROSS DOMESTIC PRODUCT.   GNP minus net foreign investment.

GROSS MARGIN   The difference between the quantity of goods sold at net selling prices in total and the same quantity of goods at total cost.

GROSS NATIONAL PRODUCT.   Same as: GNP

GROSS PROFIT   (1) The entire difference between the purchase price of an item and the sale price of that item. (2) The total of the differences in (1) for all the items a firm sells.

GROSS RATING POINT BUY   (1) In general, the number of ADVERTISEMENTS required in a MEDIUM to achieve the desired percent of exposure of the message to the population of a MARKET. See: GROSS RATING POINT (2) In OUTDOOR ADVERTISING, the number of PANELS needed to deliver in one day the desired percent of exposure opportunities, an 100 buy being considered that which would reach the entire population. See: 100-SHOWING

GROSS RATING POINTS   (1) A method used to compare shows in BROADCAST MEDIA by measuring the total impression being delivered by a particular schedule, ignoring AUDIENCE duplication. An important, but controversial, factor in buying time. Until more valid ways are developed of measuring broadcast advertising's effect in delivering purchases of the advertised items, doubts will remain as to just what significance to an advertiser a certain rating may have. See: RATING POINT   (2) In OUTDOOR ADVERTISING, the base is the number of people passing a sign in one day, even if more than once. Percent is calculated on population of a particular MARKET. See: GROSS RATING POINT BUY

GROSS TON   2,240 pounds. Used in the concept of DEADWEIGHT TONNAGE. See: SHORT TON

GROUPING   The tendency of individuals to arrange STIMULI into pieces of data together forming a unified impression, rather than into discrete, unassociated bits of information. It appears to be an automatic phenomenon. See: CLOSURE

GROUP INTERVIEW   See: DEPTH INTERVIEW, FOCUSED GROUP INTERVIEW

GROUP MAILING Same as: COOPERATIVE MAILING

GROUP MARKING The practice of placing low-priced or small, odd-shaped items in a bin without individual pricing, the bin ticket indicating the price. Not practical with self-service or central check-out arrangements. Same as: Nonmarking

GROUP PLAN Same as: PARTY SELLING

GROUP PURCHASE PLAN A selling plan whereby a RETAILER offers purchase incentives to a group or organization. Each participating individual is usually given an identification card.

GROUP RATE Same as: BLANKET RATE

GROWTHS Commodities classified according to area where grown. May refer to country, district, or place of semi-manufacture.

GRP Same as: GROSS RATING POINT

GSP Abbreviation for: GENERALIZED SYSTEM OF PREFERENCES, an arrangement whereby the PRODUCTS originating in developing countries are granted special TARIFF treatment by developed countries.

GUARANTEED DRAW A method of compensating SALESPEOPLE by allowing them a DRAW which is not repayable should the commissions earned in a given period be less than the draw.

GUARANTY A statement by a seller in which he promises to do certain things should the item bought not perform as specified or prove to be defective in some way within a certain time after being put into use. Now generally used to mean the same as warranty. Federal legislation is needed to make consistent among all guarantors the elements to be publicized. Some progress toward this end has been achieved.

GUARANTY AGAINST PRICE DECLINE Same as: PRICE GUARANTY

GUTTER The two inside margins of facing pages.

HABIT A pattern of behavior that occurs consistently and without specific consideration. Once established, usually requires repetition in order to persist for any significant period of time.

HALF-LIFE The period of time when half the responses to a mailing have been received of the total which will ultimately come in. Attempts have been made to predict this mathematically, with uncertain success thus far. It appears that the period is brief after returns start arriving until half-life as compared with the total time during which returns will continue to arrive. Some researchers have set this period at as little as two weeks.

HALF RUN In TRANSIT ADVERTISING, a CAR CARD placed in every other unit of the transit system used. Same as: Half Service

HALF SERVICE Same as: HALF RUN

HALF SHOWING Same as: #50 SHOWING

HALFTONE A photoengraving plate photographed through a glass screen inserted in the camera to break the picture into dots. Screens vary from 45 to 300 lines to the inch. The more lines in the screen, the finer the reproduction of the subject's pictorial values. Coarse screens, 65- to 85-line, are used on rough paper such as is found in NEWSPAPERS. The finer screens are used in MAGAZINES using smooth papers. The dots, massed in the denser parts of the picture and scattered in the lighter parts, permit the printing of tones such as are found in a photograph. Used for color as well as black-and-white. See: DROP-OUT HALFTONE, HIGHLIGHT HALFTONE, OUTLINE HALFTONE, SILHOUETTE HALFTONE, SQUARE HALFTONE, VIGNETTE HALFTONE

HALO EFFECT   The extension from an impression, favorable or unfavorable, to an individual's PERCEPTION and interpretation of STIMULI which may not be relevant, but which because of an experience not necessarily informative enough, seem to apply.

HANDBILL   A circular of promotional intent passed out to shoppers in the store or on the street. Sometimes used to include the term DODGER.

HAND-TO-MOUTH BUYING   The buying policy which dictates acquisition of only enough quantity to meet very immediate requirements.

HAPPENINGS   A type of FEEDBACK to the MIS that comes from continuous monitoring of the FIRM'S environment. See: UNCONTROLLABLE VARIABLES

HARBOR   Essentially a haven, an area of water where vessels can find relative safety from wind and heavy seas. Sometimes used in the same sense as, but should be distinguished from, PORT.

HARD COPY   The typewritten copy on ordinary paper usually produced simultaneously with the paper or magnetic tape by the keyboard action of a PHOTO-COMPOSITION device.

HARD GOODS   Usually refers to CONSUMERS' durable goods, but may refer to any goods of a durable nature. See: SOFT GOODS

HARDSHIP POINT   As applied to a SALES TERRITORY, a CUSTOMER or PROSPECT who is situated at a point isolated and difficult to reach.

HARD SELL   Same as: HIGH-PRESSURE SELLING

HARDWARE   In ADP, the physical equipment forming a computer and its peripheral devices. See: SOFTWARE

HARDWARE INSTITUTE FOR RESEARCH AND DEVELOPMENT   Same as: HIRD

HARMONY   That essence an advertisement has when it contributes to the PRODUCT IMAGE desired and to the objectives of the message.

HASH TOTAL   In ADP, a total of one or more data FIELDS for all the RECORDS in a BATCH, used as a control device. This total merely checks for deviations from one operation to the next; a deviation may indicate the loss of an item of data or of a punched card. The total usually will have no real significance, e.g., it may be the sum of all customer account numbers.

HAUL BACK ALLOWANCE   Same as: HAULING ALLOWANCE

HAULING ALLOWANCE   Essentially a discount allowed a CUSTOMER for picking up his own order where customarily the order would be delivered without extra charge. In order to be legal as generally interpreted today, the difference should not exceed the amount the seller saves by this action.

HAZARD LOSS RISK   See: RISK REDUCTION

HAZARDOUS SUBSTANCES LABELING ACT   A Federal law requiring that warnings be printed on the LABELS of household products if they contain substances which are toxic, corrosive, irritating, flammable, or likely to generate pressure through heat or decomposition, and if they can cause personal injury in normal handling or use. Goods lacking the labels can be seized and withdrawn from use or sale.

HEAD END   The electronic control center of a CATV system where incoming SIGNALS are amplified, filtered and converted to appropriate cable system channels.

HEADER   A sign or identification piece at the top of a display, MERCHANDISER, or exhibit.

HEADLIGHT DISPLAY   Same as: FRONT-END DISPLAY

HEADLINE   An opening statement in a print advertisement which presents what the advertiser hopes will be an idea of interest to the reader.

Usually in a distinctive type style or size. See: COMMAND HEADLINE, CURI-
OSITY HEADLINE, DIRECT PROMISE HEADLINE, NEWS HEADLINE, SELECTIVE HEADLINE

HEAD OF HOUSEHOLD   See: HOUSEHOLDER

HEAD OF STOCK   In a large RETAIL department, the key SALES CLERK or specialized individual given the responsibility for maintaining front stocks
and for advising the BUYER currently of imminent outages both on the sales
floor and in the stock rooms or warehouse.

HEAD-ON POSITION   An OUTDOOR ADVERTISING location in which the message directly faces traffic, rather than at an angle or from a parallel view.
See: ANGLED POSTER, FLASH APPROACH, PARALLEL POSTER

HEAVISIDE LAYER   A region of ionized air beginning about 60 miles above
the earth's surface.   It has no effect on FM BROADCASTS, and little effect on AM broadcasts during the day, but reflects AM broadcasts back to
earth at night.   Same as: Kennelly-Heaviside Layer

HEAVY BUYER   Same as: HEAVY-HALF USER

HEAVY EQUIPMENT   Almost always used to mean the same as INSTALLATIONS, but
occasionally applied to expensive ACCESSORY EQUIPMENT used in the manufacturing process.

HEAVY-HALF USER   The people in the MARKET for a PRODUCT who account for
more than 50% of the total volume of sales of the product.   They are usually less than half of the number of users of the product.   Same as:
Heavy Buyers, Heavy Users

HEAVYING UP   An expression used in the ADVERTISING field to denote an increase in the use of a MEDIUM by an already long-time user.

HEAVY MARKET   A condition of a MARKET characterized by the existence of
more orders to sell commodities or goods than corresponding orders to buy.

HEAVY SPECIALIZED CARRIERS CONFERENCE   Same as: HSCC

HEAVY USERS   Same as: HEAVY-HALF USERS

HEDGING   (1) A simultaneous purchase and sale of equal quantities of a commodity, one in the SPOT MARKET and one in the FUTURES MARKET.   A hedge is
opened by the first set of transactions, and closed by a reverse set.
The proper function of hedging is to preserve the normal operating profit
by minimizing the effects of adverse price changes in the commodity that
enters the finished goods.   In this process, the hedger exchanges for the
protection the possibility of a windfall profit from a possible favorable
price change in the commodity.   In practice, a very complex activity.   (2)
Used frequently to apply to the building of inventory in a commodity in
anticipation of a shortage due to an impending strike or other reason
for limitation to SUPPLY. See: LONG HEDGE, PERFECT HEDGE, SHORT HEDGE

HERTZ   The electronic term for: cycles per second, most frequently abbreviated to Hz.   Used internationally.

HEURISTIC   Any device or procedure used to reduce the effort of arriving
at a reasonable solution to a problem.   A "rule of thumb" is an example.
See: HEURISTIC PROGRAM

HEURISTIC IDEATION TECHNIQUE   Same as: HIT

HEURISTIC MODEL   Appropriate for a PROBLEM which cannot be set in a compu-
tational routine or ALGORITHM, this technique is a search pattern which
will lead step-by-step to a feasible solution.   No optimum is guaranteed,
which is usually the case with a DETERMINISTIC MODEL.   The search pattern
may contain trial-and-error steps as well as mathematical formulae.   See:
HEURISTIC PROGRAM

HEURISTIC PROGRAM   A combination or collection of HEURISTICS used for solving a particular type of problem.

HGCB   Abbreviation for: Household Goods Carriers' Bureau, primarily a rate publishing organization filing rates with the ICC for the accounts of its members.

HGFAA   Abbreviation for: Household Goods Forwarders Association of America, an organization of firms engaged in the movement of household goods in the door-to-door through container method. The Association attempts to encourage high standards of service, provides various types of assistance to members, and acts as a clearinghouse for applicable information.

HIDDEN OFFER   A special offer incorporated inconspicuously in the COPY of a print advertisement as a test of readership. Same as: BURIED OFFER

HIGH DENSITY   Compression of a bale of cotton to about 32 pounds per cubic foot. See: STANDARD DENSITY

HIGH END   The most expensive merchandise in a CLASSIFICATION. See: LOW END

HIGH FASHION   At one time referred to the preferences of the wealthy. Now refers to the FASHION preference of the INNOVATORS. See: FASHION CYCLE

HIGHLIGHT HALFTONE   Same as: DROP-OUT HALFTONE

HIGH-PRESSURE SELLING   A selling situation in which the PROSPECT is conscious at all times that the SALESPERSON is in control of the sale and that the prospect is making the purchase because of the salesperson's insistence. Although most often thought of in a negative frame of reference, this type of selling is quite acceptable when the results bring real benefits to the buyer. It may even be indicated where the buyer can undoubtedly benefit from the salesman's offering but is too insecure or timid to make the decision. See: LOW-PRESSURE SELLING

HIGH SPOT   In OUTDOOR ADVERTISING, a location of extra heavy traffic at which a showing is possible.

HIGHWAY SIGN   A large, elevated identification sign for service stations, located on or adjacent to interstate highways, expressways, or freeways.

HIGHWAY USERS FEDERATION FOR SAFETY AND MOBILITY   A national organization bringing together highway users and highway related industry and business groups dedicated to the advancement of sound, safe, and economical highway use and development in the public interest. It sponsors the 23,000 member Auto Dealers Traffic Safety Council which operates at the community level. Its aims are to increase public information on highway matters and to assure sound policies relative to highway development and safety.

HIRD   Abbreviation for: Hardware Institute for Research and Development, an organization of about 50 WHOLESALERS and 50 manufacturers of hardware items, devoted to research in DISTRIBUTION, improvement in ROI, and communication among members.

HI-SPOTTING   Same as: CHERRY-PICKING (2)

HISTOGRAM   A form of BAR CHART in which the occurrence frequency of the variable is indicated on one axis and the values of the variable are indicated on the other axis.

HISTORICAL DESIGN   A design of a MARKETING RESEARCH activity which uses data recorded in the past. Such a design may be statistical as in a TIME SERIES, or may be a descriptive case study. See: EXPERIMENT, SURVEY RESEARCH DESIGN

HISTORICAL STATISTICS OF THE UNITED STATES FROM COLONIAL TIMES TO 1957   See: STATISTICAL ABSTRACT OF THE UNITED STATES

HIT   Abbreviation for: Heuristic Ideation Technique, a procedure for generating PRODUCT ideas by locating all rules of thumb that have been successful in producing useful solutions to certain problems, developing a list of all pertinent factors, and then subjecting the list to the basic questions What? How? When? Why? The answers should develop various relevant ideas about product form and content, PACKAGING, CUSTOMER use related to place and time, and what customers may perceive as benefits.

HITCHHIKE   A COMMERCIAL at the end of a program, within the SPONSOR'S time, which features a sponsor's product not shown in the program's other commercials. See: COWCATCHER

HOARDING   An early POSTER of commercial import usually put up near a poster of political or legislative import. Really an early form of BILLBOARD.

HOLD   Same as: KEEP STANDING

HOLDING COMPANY   A firm formed to own and control other firms, all of which remain separate entities. The INTEGRATION is often accomplished through an exchange of capital stock.

HOLDING POWER   In BROADCASTING, the degree to which a program keeps its AUDIENCE for the entire program time.

HOLD ORDER   Same as: KEEP STANDING

HOLD-OVER AUDIENCE   In BROADCASTING, the AUDIENCE which remains to watch at least the beginning of a succeeding program over the same NETWORK or station.

HOLLOW LUMBER   Square cardboard tubes for use in constructing displays in a store.

HOLOGRAPHY   A photographic technique using laser technology to code film without using lenses, so that a light beam applied at the proper angle will show a three-dimensional image. Some use of this technique is being made to produce illustrations for advertisements, but this has the disadvantage of requiring a source of a relatively small beam of light to make the picture understandable to the human eye. Some plans are said to be in the making for producing 3-D movies using this technique, and for television applications relative to more effective showing of products.

HOLOGRAM   A photograph produced by HOLOGRAPHY. See: XOGRAPH

HOMEOSTASIS   A term borrowed from biology, it is used in the business world to denote the coordination of all of its elements so as to restore a healthy balance should any element get out of alignment with the rest. Thus, the MARKETING elements in the body of a healthy economy adapt as necessary to contribute to the well-being of the whole.

HOME PREFERENCE LAW   A law dealing with local purchasing with reference to government and public institution goods acquisition. Involves a wide spectrum of diverse POLICIES.

HOMES USING RADIO   Same as: HUT, except for RADIO instead of TELEVISION.

HOMES USING TELEVISION   Same as: HUT

HORIZONTAL BUY   (1) An ADVERTISING schedule using MAGAZINES with varying AUDIENCE APPEALS so as to achieve the widest COVERAGE of different groups of people. (2) Sometimes applied to any use of numerous units of the same MEDIUM.

HORIZONTAL COMPETITION   Competition among firms on the same side of the SUPPLY-DEMAND relationship, e.g., buyers against buyers and sellers against sellers. See: INTERTYPE COMPETITION, VERTICAL CONFLICT

HORIZONTAL CONCURRENCE   See: CONCURRENCE

HORIZONTAL INTEGRATION   Acquisition by one company of another in the same or related lines of business and on the same level of the CHANNEL OF DIS-

TRIBUTION, the CONSUMER considered as the base. See: CONGLOMERATE INTE-
GRATION, VERTICAL INTEGRATION

HORIZONTAL MARKET   A condition of a MARKET in which a manufacturer's product may be sold to BUYERS in many INDUSTRIES. See: VERTICAL MARKET

HORIZONTAL PUBLICATION   An INDUSTRIAL or TRADE PUBLICATION which reaches
management men at a certain level in all industries. See: VERTICAL PUB-
LICATION

HORIZONTAL SATURATION   (1) Same as: SATURATION   (2) A heavy schedule of
COMMERCIALS placed at about the same time for several consecutive days.

HORSE TRADING   A term usually used in a derogatory fashion to.describe the
type of bargaining or "negotiation" which is designed to gain a one-sided
advantage only, whether price or other benefits are involved. This
activity resorts to trickery, deception, and other unethical practices.
True negotiation involves planning and analysis by all the parties to
reach a mutually beneficial agreement. The latter process usually includes
review and compromise of many factors of common interest.

HOUSE ACCOUNT   A CUSTOMER, usually large, reserved for handling by a company executuve. SALESMEN may not call on such an account and usually receive no commissions on business done with it.

HOUSE AGENCY   Same as: HOUSE SHOP

HOUSE BRAND   Same as: PRIVATE BRAND

HOUSEHOLD   A dwelling unit occupied by one or more persons living together
under a single roof which constitutes a HOUSING UNIT. A household may
contain more than one FAMILY.

HOUSEHOLDER   Formerly: "head of household." The continuing increase in
working women made this change necessary in order that the Census of
Population would not be biased toward men in the count of who is the
support of the HOUSEHOLD or the breadwinner of the FAMILY.

HOUSEHOLD GOODS CARRIERS' BUREAU   Same as: HGCB

HOUSEHOLD GOODS FORWARDERS ASSOCIATION OF AMERICA.   Same as: HGFAA

HOUSEHOLD HEAD   Two types are recognized by the Bureau of the Census:
family head, living with one or more persons who are related to the family
head; primary individual, living alone or with non-relatives only. Census
rules require that each HOUSEHOLD must have a head: the number of "household heads" is always the same as the number of "households."

HOUSEKEEPING   In ADP, the operations required for a RUN, usually before
actual processing begins.

HOUSE ORGAN.   A PUBLICATION issued periodically by firm to one or more of
its publics to strengthen its relationships with those PUBLICS. Same as:
COMPANY MAGAZINE, COMPANY NEWSPAPER

HOUSE SHOP   An ADVERTISING AGENCY owned and controlled by an advertiser.
Sometimes a group within a firm which decides upon and coordinates advertising bought from independent creative entities. It usually cannot pass
the acid test imposed by many ADVERTISING MEDIA for the recognition that
entitles it to the 15% commission: an entity capable of preparing COPY
for publication, which performs services for advertisers, and which pays
with its own check. Some PUBLICATIONS consider a house shop as merely a
subterfuge designed to circumvent recognized advertising agencies in order
to buy time or space for less than the amount otherwise necessary.

HOUSE-TO-HOUSE SELLING.   A form of DIRECT RETAILING in which employees are
engaged to solicit business by COLD CANVASS from door-to-door. See:
HUCKSTERING, PARTY SELLING

HOUSING UNIT   A single room or a group of rooms occupied or intended for occupancy by persons who do not live and eat with any other persons in the structure.   It must access either through a common hall or directly from the outside, or have a kitchen or cooking equipment for the exclusive use of the occupants.   The key idea is separate occupancy.

HSCC   Abbreviation for: Heavy Specialized Carriers Conference, founded in 1949, it is the national association of heavy specialized haulers and crane operators.   Its main objectives are to promote consistency in state requirements for sizes, weights, permits, etc.; to provide continuing activities for informing and improving members; and to be active with regard to pending and existing legislation.   It is an affiliate of the American Trucking Associations and the 50 state trucking association.   It publishes a monthly magazine and a variety of technical manuals.

HUCKSTERING   A method of house-to-house selling ordinarily used by farmers in which the goods are brought with the seller for immediate delivery.

HUE   In color, the quality which distinguishes one color from another. The other dimensions of color are CHROMA and VALUE.

HUMAN INTEREST APPROACH   Same as: IMAGINATIVE APPROACH

HUMAN RESOURCES MANAGEMENT   A more elegant name for Personnel Management, it includes that part of administration that has the responsibility for recruiting, selecting, hiring, and training employees.   May include the evaluating activity as well.   Same as: Personnel Management

HUR   Same as: HUT, except for RADIO rather than TELEVISION.

HUT   Abbreviation for: Homes Using Television.   It is the percent of TELEVISION HOMES where viewers are watching a television program during a given time period.   It can be stated for a particular MARKET.   "HOME" here is equivalent to HOUSEHOLD.

HYPERMARCHE   A combination of SUPERMARKET and DISCOUNT HOUSE under one roof on a very large scale (200,000 sq. ft. and larger).   Such STORES often have merchandise shipped from source directly to the store in CONTAINERS that then serve as instore displays.   Originated in Europe.   Much study is now being conducted in the United States to evaluate the effect of very large stores on CUSTOMER patronage.

HYPERMARKET   Same as: HYPERMARCHE

HYPOTHESIS   A provisional explanation adopted conjecturally to guide the investigation of FACTS that might generally prove or disprove the hypothesis.   See: THEORY

HYPOTHESIS TESTING   The process of determining whether an assumed PARAMETER is correct.   Usually based on SAMPLE data, it involves the techniques of statistical inference.   See: SAMPLING

HZ   See: HERTZ

IATA   Abbreviation for: International Air Transport Association, the world association of scheduled airlines.   Its work begins after governments have agreed on an exchange of traffic and other rights and have licensed airlines to perform the service.   Subject to each government's approval, it establishes fares and rates by unanimous consent of its members, registered in about 100 nations.   Through its auspices an international traveler can move through many countries on a ticket bought at home in one currency.   To facilitate the clearance of cross-claims among airlines, the IATA operates a clearinghouse.   Less than 10% of the claims finally require settlement by a transfer of funds.   It is very involved with all air travel problems and cooperates with all international organizations having powers related to civil aviation.   In the United States, because of its regulatory position, The CAB exerts great influence on the final decisions resulting from IATA activities.

ICA   Abbreviation for: International Coffee Agreement. See: INTERNATIONAL
COFFEE ORGANIZATION

ICC   Abbreviation for: Interstate Commerce Commission, the government agency directly involved in the establishment of rules and transportation
rates for COMMON CARRIERS.

ICEBERG PRINCIPLE   Commonly used in sales analysis to indicate that gross
numbers may hide the bulk of the important, decision-assisting data which
finer breakdown into detail would reveal. How far to go is a matter for
executive consideration. Usually thought to be a minimum is a division
that shows sales by geographical regions, individual customers, individual
salesmen, and, probably, individual product.

ICO   Abbreviation for: INTERNATIONAL COFFEE ORGANIZATION

ICONIC MODEL   In MARKETING RESEARCH, a representation of the real world in
greatly reduced proportions, such as a small model of the St. Lawrence
Seaway constructed for a child to play with, or a scale-model of the
AMTRAK route between New York City and Washington, D.C.

ICONOCLASM   A competitive TACTIC which calls for an unorthodox, creative
solution to prosaic problems. It requires a complete willingness to make
a full break with existing ideas and procedures, at best not an easy accomplishment. Often most effective in conjunction with other tactics.

ID   Basic, unconscious passions and urges of man live here. Craves satisfaction without regard for means, side effects, or consequences. See:
EGO, SUPEREGO

I.D.   An abbreviation used to designate a brief COMMERCIAL between programs
on television which has about eight seconds to identify a PRODUCT. May
accommodate a SLOGAN. See: CHAINBREAK

IDEA ADVERTISING   The type of ADVERTISING in which the ADVERTISER'S purpose
is to communicate its positions on public issues. If properly done, it
may have all the advantages of INSTITUTIONAL ADVERTISING and more by
creating the role of the firm as a serious, credible citizen.

IDEAL OTHER   How one _wants_ other people to think of him/her. Has an effect
on buying behavior in an attempt to create the wanted impression. See:
REAL OTHER, SELF-CONCEPT

IDEAL SELF   The way a person would like to be. See: LOOKING-GLASS SELF,
SELF-IMAGE

IDENTIFICATION   (1) The recognition of common aspects between one person and
another as to situation, problems, etc., so that the one person may believe he could easily be in the same circumstances as the other. Important to take into account so that APPEALS may be believable. (2) A way
of coping with FRUSTRATION by subconsciously emulating other persons or
situations considered relevant. See: AGGRESSION, AUTISM, PROJECTION,
RATIONALIZATION, REGRESSION, REPRESSION, SLICE-OF-LIFE COMMERCIAL

IEA   Abbreviation for: International Executives Association, founded in
1917. It has been a major factor in the export program of the United
States. Its name was changed in 1960 from the original Export Managers
Club of New York. It conducts a wide variety of informational, educational, advisory, and reporting activities.

IH   Abbreviation for: International House, founded in 1943 by New Orleans
civic leaders to give practical effect to the Good Neighbor Policy. It
has become a clearinghouse for international trade, travel and communications.

ILLUSION MIRROR   Same as: CHINESE MIRROR

IMAGE ADVERTISING   Same as: INSTITUTIONAL ADVERTISING

IMAGINATIVE APPROACH   A COPY APPROACH in which the emphasis is on the possibilities for life enrichment of the reader through the attributes of
the product or service.   See : FACTUAL APPROACH

IMBRICATIVE MARKETING   A term coined to indicate that the MARKETING CON-
CEPT, in order to be implemented literally, requires an understanding of
the capabilities of the firm, the real requirements of the MARKET, a determination of the real market, a realization of the total system within
which the organization exists, and a dedication to resolving the interrelationships in the orderly overlapping of all aspects of the firm's marketing efforts.

IMF   Abbreviation for: International Marketing Federation, an organization
for the advancement of the scientific approach to marketing. It is composed of 27 member marketing organizations from 24 countries representing
virtually all of the free world. The permanent address of its Secretariat
is The Hague, Netherlands.

IMITATIVE PRICING   Same as: GOING-RATE PRICING

IMMEDIATE ADDRESS   An ADDRESS in ADP designated to be used as data by the
instruction of which it is a part.

IMMEDIATE DATING   Same as: COD

IMMEDIATE PURPOSE   The communication is intended to get at once some wanted response from the receiver, perhaps ideas or feelings. See: ULTERIOR
MOTIVE

IMPACT   The degree to which an advertising message, or campaign, affects
the AUDIENCE receiving it.

IMPACT COMPOSITION   The production of text material on a typewriter. Same
as: Direct Impression Composition, Strike On Composition

IMPERFECT COMPETITION   Used to refer either to OLIGOPOLY or to MONOPOLISTIC
COMPETITION, both situations in which FIRMS have some degree of control
over the MARKET PRICE of their PRODUCTS.

IMPLICIT PRICE DEFLATOR   See: IPI

IMPLICIT PRICE INDEX   Same as: IPI

IMPORT AGENTS   BROKERS and other FUNCTIONAL MIDDLEMEN in the domestic MAR-
KET who arrange to sell merchandise there for foreign firms. See: EXPORT
AGENTS

IMPORT COMMISSION HOUSES   Same as: IMPORT AGENTS

IMPRESSION OPPORTUNITY   The occasion provided by a TRANSIT ADVERTISING display for a passenger or passer-by to become exposed to the message.

IMPROVEMENT CURVE   Same as: LEARNING CURVE

IMPROVEMENT FUNCTION   Same as: LEARNING CURVE CONCEPT

IMPULSE BUYING   An act of purchasing, made on the spur-of-the-moment, im-
pelled by some thing or happening in a store. See: PLANNED IMPULSE BUY-
ING, PURE IMPULSE BUYING, REMINDER IMPULSE BUYING, SUGGESTION IMPULSE
BUYING

IMPULSE ITEM   A product which has a high appeal for a customer but which
is an unplanned purchase. There is really no such thing as a group of
impulse items, but only IMPULSE BUYING, because any item may be subject
to this by some customer at any time. Alert RETAILERS try to arrange
their merchandise in such a way as to encourage impulse buying. See:
MERCHANDISING

INAE   Abbreviation for: International Newspaper Advertising Executives, an
association representing more than 90% of the daily CIRCULATION of NEWS-

PAPERS in the United States and Canada. The Association attempts to increase the effectiveness of newspaper advertising by issuing a monthly bulletin, running two annual conventions followed by appropriate verbatim accounts of the proceedings, publishing Sales and Idea Books containing the top ideas from the newspaper advertising industry, and making a special effort to involve teachers of advertising as privileged members.

IN BOND   (1) If permitted by a store's policies, merchandise shipped several months ahead of normal selling season with ADVANCE DATING, or sometimes without this, is not charged against the department's OPEN-TO-BUY until moved to FORWARD STOCK. Until that time it is said to be "in bond." (2) Applies to the procedure for postponing customs clearance of CARGO until a specified inland point is reached, the cargo moving under the bond of the CARRIER until released by customs.

INCENTIVE   (1) A reward offered to inspire a desired performance. (2) same as: PREMIUM

INCENTIVE AGENCY   A firm offering a variety of INCENTIVE items, usually on the basis of representing as a FUNCTIONAL MIDDLEMAN a large number of manufacturers, producers, and travel organizers. Provides excellent help in setting up incentive awards rules structures and in preparing PROMOTIONAL materials. See: DIRECT SELLING HOUSE, PREMIUM JOBBER, PREMIUM REPRESENTATIVE

INCENTIVE ITEMS   Same as: INCENTIVE

INCH   Same as: COLUMN-INCH

INCOME   (1) Everything accruing to an individual which contributes to his standard of living. See: REAL INCOME (2) Total sales of a business.

INCOME EFFECT   An increase in REAL INCOME occurs for those HOUSEHOLDS which experience a substantial price reduction on an item purchased in significant quantities. This may lead them to switch to more expensive products instead of using more of the same product. The opposite may occur, also. See: LAW OF DEMAND

INCOME ELASTICITY OF DEMAND   Other factors remaining constant, the percent change in quantity demanded which may be expected to result from a percent change in INCOME. See: PRICE ELASTICITY OF DEMAND

INCREASING RETURNS TO SCALE   See: RETURNS TO SCALE

INCREMENTAL ANALYSIS   The process of comparing alternatives by the changes they effect in operating data rather than by their total impact on operating results. An appropriate decision criterion and rule is prerequisite to the satisfactory use of this process. See: DECISION RULE

INCREMENTAL COSTS   Those costs which increase or decrease as the direct result of a particular decision. They are relevant for determining EOQ because they represent the most accurate picture of the cost of a change in the order quantity.

INCREMENTAL PRICING AGREEMENT   A pricing arrangement between seller and buyer that uses a schedule of price which varies with the cumulative increment bought. Differs from QUANTITY DISCOUNT or CUMULATIVE DISCOUNT in that clauses may be inserted to permit LEAD TIME considerations, minimum quantities per time period, minimum quantities per shipment, and other special provisions. See: BLANKET PRICING AGREEMENT

INDENT   In international trade, an offer to purchase at a price and under specified conditions a given quantity of a particular PRODUCT. In actual practice, an indent frequently is treated in all significant respects as an order.

INDEPENDENT BUSINESSMAN   Any person owning and conducting a business who

controls it himself rather than having the control imposed from outside.
See: ENTREPRENEUR, INDEPENDENT STORE

INDEPENDENT ELEVATOR   An ELEVATOR which is a single one operated as a private business enterprise.

INDEPENDENT EVENT   One which does not depend upon the occurrence of another EVENT in order to happen.

INDEPENDENT GOODS   See: COMPLEMENTARY GOODS

INDEPENDENTS   Businesses owned and operated by private individuals. See:
ENTREPRENEUR

INDEPENDENT STORE   A RETAIL STORE controlled by its individual ownership.
It may enter into limiting agreements, such as that of a VOLUNTARY CHAIN,
without impairing its status as an independent. In a basic way, the same
as: INDEPENDENT BUSINESSMAN

INDEPENDENT VARIABLE   In a cause-and-effect system, any one of the causes
that will produce an outcome that is the DEPENDENT VARIABLE. Same as:
INPUT VARIABLE   See: CONFOUNDED VARIABLE

INDEX NUMBER   A measure, expressed as a percent, of the change in a statistical series over time as compared to a base period. For example, if the
price of a product was $20 in 1950 and is $30 in 1972, then, using 1950
as the base period, the price index will be 150 (100 x 30 ÷ 20 = 150).
Many major business indexes involve refinements such as the weighting of
various quantity factors and the combining of several series.

INDEX OF SALES ACTIVITY   A relative measure of RETAILING sales performance
in a given MARKET, published by Sales & Marketing Management magazine.
For the nation as a whole the ISA = 100. Significant only if used in conjunction with some indicator of market size. See: QUALITY INDEX

INDIRECT-ACTION ADVERTISING   The goal here is to create a favorable attitude toward the product or service through long-range planning of frequent EXPOSURE over a period of time, so that at a particular time when
the PROSPECT is ready, the IMPACT already made will impel a decision
favorable to the seller. See: DIRECT-ACTION ADVERTISING

INDIRECT CHANNEL   A CHANNEL OF DISTRIBUTION characterized by the presence
of many MIDDLEMEN. In general, the opposite of DIRECT CHANNEL. See:
INDIRECT DISTRIBUTION, SEMI-DIRECT CHANNEL

INDIRECT COSTS   Those costs which can be charged to a product only on the
basis of some type of allocation. See: DIRECT COSTS

INDIRECT DISTRIBUTION   Selling by a manufacturer through MIDDLEMEN. Usually, INDIRECT DISTRIBUTION will be the choice when the manufacturer has
few LINES, needs financing, has a WIDE MARKET, requires service at the
CUSTOMER level, and/or is in a situation where inventories are an important factor to the users of his offerings. If the opposites prevail, the
manufacturer will generally prefer DIRECT DISTRIBUTION. See: DIRECT CHAN-
NEL, INDIRECT CHANNEL, SEMI-DIRECT CHANNEL

INDIRECT RETAIL OUTLET   A RETAILER that buys its offerings through WHOLE-
SALERS.

INDIVIDUAL BRAND   A distinctive identification for a single product. In
contrast to FAMILY BRAND. Its major advantage is the sharpness of its recall to a CONSUMER, once established. Its major disadvantage is that it
can get little or no help from other products of the same firm which have
gained consumer acceptance.

INDIVIDUAL CHANGE STIMULI   The forces which shape a part of the behavior
of a buying unit in the MARKET as the result of changes in the characteristics of the buying unit, such as family size, aging, education, and

other DEMOGRAPHIC changes over time. See: EXTERNAL STIMULI, INTERNAL STIMULI, SELLER ACTIVITY STIMULI

INDIVIDUAL SUPPLEMENT   A SUPPLEMENT edited and published by the NEWSPAPER which distributes it, e.g., The New York Times Sunday Magazine.

INDOOR PANEL   A POSTER placed within a structure frequented by a large number of individuals, such as one placed on the fence of a ball park, visible to the spectators. See: STATION POSTER

INDUCED INVESTMENT   Investment made primarily in response to actual or expected increase in DEMAND. See: AUTONOMOUS INVESTMENT, DERIVED DEMAND

INDUCTION   A system of reasoning that results in a general PRINCIPLE derived from a study of particulars. See: DEDUCTION

INDUSTRIAL ADVERTISING   ADVERTISING addressed to people in the business world to instruct and to convince them of the merits of the advertiser's product or service as it may be used in manufacture or to facilitate the operation of the business.

INDUSTRIAL CONSUMER   A misnomer except in the economic sense of one engaged in CONSUMPTION. See: CONSUMER

INDUSTRIAL DISTRIBUTOR   A MERCHANT MIDDLEMAN primarily engaged in selling INDUSTRIAL GOODS. See: METAL WAREHOUSE, MILL SUPPLY HOUSE

INDUSTRIAL DYNAMICS   A system for tracing the effects of inventory policy. These effects are traced and analyzed all the way from RETAIL outlet back to the producer. Possible improvements can often thus be discovered.

INDUSTRIAL GOODS   Any goods bought for motives other than personal or household satisfactions.

INDUSTRIAL PUBLICATION   A PERIODICAL devoted to helping solve the problems associated with producing goods. Those to whom such publications appeal are in the main production managers, plant superintendents, purchasing agents, engineers, and research and development men. See: HORIZONTAL PUBLICATION, VERTICAL PUBLICATION

INDUSTRIAL STORE   Same as: COMMISSARY STORE

INDUSTRIAL TRUCK ASSOCIATION   Same as: ITA

INDUSTRIAL USER   Anyone or any firm buying goods or services for purposes other than personal or household satisfactions. In contrast to: CONSUMER

INDUSTRY   (1) A group of companies related in competition for the same type of products, which usually exhibit a high degree of substitutability among the products made. See: SIC (2) Often used to refer generally to all manufacturing done in the economy. (3) Sometimes used to refer to all business transactions in the economy.

INELASTIC DEMAND   (1) See: ELASTICITY OF DEMAND (2) DEMAND that is relatively insensitive to changes in price.

INERTIA   The natural resistance to change which is found in every organization. If a firm is to adapt to necessary changes, means must be found to overcome inertia and to gain the cooperation of personnel in accomplishing the changes with a minimum of disruption.

INFINITE POPULATION   See: ANALYTICAL STUDY

INFLATION   A condition of the economy characterized by continually rising prices. See: DEFLATION

INFORMAL BALANCE   A method of LAYOUT in which the ADVERTISEMENT is pleasing to the eye, yet the elements comprising the advertisement are not evenly spaced or weighted. Same as: ASYMMETRICAL BALANCE See: FORMAL BALANCE

INFORMAL BUYING GROUP   Same as: POOLED BUYING

INFORMAL GROUP   A REFERENCE GROUP with which an individual associates because of nearness, e.g., neighbors; or because of some other common bond
such as commuting to work. These groups form without a regular organization to govern the relationship. See: FORMAL GROUP

INFORMAL ORGANIZATION   If decisions, or requests for information, or coordination of various activities had to wait the travel time up and down
the FORMAL ORGANIZATION lines, the firm could not function with real effectiveness. Those who must accomplish the tasks form liasons with those
whose cooperation will be necessary. Contacts are freely made in other
parts of the firm across the formal lines and activities are thus speeded.

INFORMATIVE INSTITUTIONAL ADVERTISING   Same as: INSTITUTIONAL ADVERTISING

INFORMATIVE LABEL   An affix to a PRODUCT telling about the product.

INFORMATIVE PRODUCT ADVERTISING   ADVERTISING in the PIONEERING STAGE.

INHERITED AUDIENCE   Same as: HOLD-OVER AUDIENCE

IN-HOME RETAILING   RETAILING in which the transaction takes place in a CON-
SUMER'S home. See: HOUSE-TO-HOUSE RETAILING, PARTY PLAN

IN-HOUSE AGENCY   An arrangement in which the ADVERTISER ASSUMES THE ADVERTIS-
ING AGENCY functions by making direct commitments for the individual services
of creation, MEDIA selection, and placement as the need for these arises.
Compensation to suppliers of required services is usually on a negotiated
basis.

INITIAL MARKUP   The money difference in the RETAIL field between merchandise cost and the price originally placed on the merchandise. See:
MAINTAINED MARKON

IN-LINE   Same as: ON-LINE

INNATE NEEDS   Same as: PRIMARY NEEDS

INNER-DIRECTEDNESS   The condition of man motivated by his individualistic,
inner drives. Primarily applicable where each person is largely self-
sufficient, giving major attention to his own requirements. See: OTHER-
DIRECTEDNESS

INNER SIX   See: EEC

INNOVATION   See the following types: CONGRUENT, CONTINUOUS, DISCONTINUOUS,
DYNAMICALLY CONTINUOUS

INNOVATION DIFFUSION   The general process by which anything in the MARKET
perceived as new by some group becomes adopted for regular use. Sometimes
this process is divided into the stages of awareness, interest, evaluation,
trial, and adoption. Note that people differ greatly in their willingness
to try new products, and may be classified on this basis as innovators,
early adopters, early majority, late majority, and laggards.

INNOVATIVE EFFICIENCY   One aspect of the concept of marketing efficiency,
it is the offering of products and services demanded by and supplied to
the MARKET by activities which together with the offerings are the most
appropriate which can be brought into being under our present knowledge
of markets and technology. It involves constant choice-making among alternatives. Competitive pressure results in two effects besides better
choices: 1) it makes total marketing in some way easier for users, and
2) it provides for a psychological change in the perspective applied to
alternative choices. See: EXCHANGE EFFICIENCY, PRODUCT IMAGE, TECHNI-
CAL EFFICIENCY

INNOVATORS   The first to adopt a new PRODUCT or idea. Tend to have high
economic and social status. Rely much more on impersonal sources and
other innovators than on personal SALESPEOPLE. See: INNOVATION DIFFUSION

INPA Abbreviation for: International Newspaper Promotion Association, an association of daily and weekly member newspapers and allied organizations, devoted to sharing ideas and enhancing the art of promotion. It publishes a number of monthly newsletters and a handbook of newspaper promotion and research and other books, and runs one international and several regional conferences annually.

IN-PACK A DIRECT PREMIUM enclosed in a product PACKAGE. Same as: PACKAGE ENCLOSURE

INPUT-OUTPUT ANALYSIS The use of tables showing the quantity or monetary value of goods flowing from one INDUSTRY to another. Very useful in some types of MARKETING planning.

INPUT VARIABLE Same as: INDEPENDENT VARIABLE

INQUIRY PRODUCTIVITY The power of an ADVERTISEMENT to produce responses. Particularly useful in DIRECT RESPONSE ADVERTISING. See: INQUIRY TEST

INQUIRY TEST A method of deciding the relative efficacies of advertisements or MEDIA by comparing the number of inquiries received through each medium from readers, listeners, or viewers. See: KEYING AN ADVERTISEMENT

INSATIABILITY CONCEPT The belief that there can never be an end to the different human WANTS that will require satisfying. Same as: INSATIABILITY THEORY

INSATIABILITY THEORY The idea that human wants can never be fully satisfied inasmuch as new inventions produce a new set of wants, a cycle resulting in an ever-expanding desire for more satisfactions.

INSERT (1) A special page or ADVERTISING unit, often on special paper or cut to a special shape, printed by an advertiser and forwarded to a publisher for binding into a PUBLICATION. (2) See: ENVELOPE STUFFER (3) A special advertisement included loose within a NEWSPAPER. (4) Promotional material included in a mailing, such as a COUPON or a sample of the product. (5) Interchangeable COPY or art signs which fit into a holder.

INSERTION ORDER An authorization from an advertiser or agency for a publisher to print an advertisement of a specified size on a given date at an agreed rate.

INSIDE-OUT A method of getting data about the readers of a MAGAZINE by using the publisher's information about his readers' buying and living habits and other DEMOGRAPHIC details. Publishers usually search out this information to prove what good MEDIA they are for certain products. See: OUTSIDE-IN

INSIDE PANEL In OUTDOOR ADVERTISING, any PANEL in a group of ANGLED PANELS except the one nearest to the traffic line. Not to be confused with INDOOR PANEL.

INSIDE SALESMAN Mainly found in INDUSTRIAL and in WHOLESALE firms, this SALESMAN remains in a central office location to take calls from CUSTOMERS. Frequently, he acts as a consultant to a customer regarding a special requirement. In general he must have a broader, more specialized, and more current acquaintanceship with the firm's products and services than does a FIELD SALESMAN.

INSTALLATIONS In a plant, the major equipment which determines the product to be produced, and which sets the scale of operations. See: ACCESSORY EQUIPMENT

INSTALLMENT CREDIT ACCOUNT Same as: ALL-PURPOSE REVOLVING ACCOUNT

INSTITUTE FOR CERTIFICATION OF COMPUTER PROFESSIONALS See: ACM (2)

INSTITUTIONAL ADVERTISING ADVERTISING intended to build goodwill for the ADVERTISER rather than to stimulate immediate purchase of a PRODUCT. See:

ADVERTISING COUNCIL, PATRONAGE INSTITUTIONAL ADVERTISING, PROMOTIONAL ADVERTISING, PUBLIC RELATIONS INSTITUTIONAL ADVERTISING, PUBLIC SERVICE INSTITUTIONAL ADVERTISING

INSTITUTIONAL APPROACH   An approach to the study of MARKETING which considers the various MIDDLEMEN and facilitating agencies which perform the MARKETING FUNCTIONS.   See: COMMODITY APPROACH, FUNCTIONAL APPROACH

INSTRUCTION   In ADP, a set of symbols which defines an operation, the applicable ADDRESSES, and the operations which the computer should perform on the indicated quantities.

INSTRUMENTAL PURPOSE   The consumption of the message is intended to produce behavior at some later time.   Any one message may have elements of CONSUMMATORY PURPOSE as well as instrumental purpose.   Important in that often it is necessary to effect changes in ATTITUDES before purchase can be persuaded.

INTAGLIO   A process of printing from a depressed surface.   GRAVURE is an intaglio form.   See: LETTERPRESS, LITHOGRAPHY

INTEGRATED COMMERCIAL   A time slot used by an advertiser to present more than one product in a single COMMERCIAL with a unified theme and a single announcer.   See: PIGGYBACK

INTEGRATION   The extension through ownership by a firm of the control of a formerly separate business so that it becomes part of a single business unit.   See: CONGLOMERATE INTEGRATION, HOLDING COMPANY, HORIZONTAL INTEGRATION, MERGER, VERTICAL INTEGRATION

INTENSITY   In OUTDOOR ADVERTISING, the extent to which the advertiser's message is displayed to the MARKET, or the number of POSTERS in a SHOWING.

INTENSIVE DISTRIBUTION   Maximum exposure of goods to BUYERS in the MARKET. Uses as many different types of RETAILERS and retail locations as possible. See: EXCLUSIVE DISTRIBUTION, FRANCHISING, SELECTIVE DISTRIBUTION

INTENTIONS   Future behavior planned or anticipated, as expressed by an individual.   So far no techniques have been developed which can use intentions in a CORRELATION with actual future behavior sufficiently reliable for decision-making, except in unusual circumstances.

INTER-AMERICAN CONVENTION   Including most of the Latin American countries and the United States, it provides protection very much the same as does the PARIS UNION.

INTERCUT   In TELEVISION, the abrupt transfer of the camera from one scene to another.

INTERMEDIARY   Same as: MIDDLEMAN

INTERMEDIATE CUSTOMER   Anyone who is a purchaser but not a CONSUMER.

INTERMEDIATE SORT   The process which consists chiefly of ASSEMBLING from a variety of sources a large inventory of products and then dividing this into small lots for resale.   Typical of the activity of the MERCHANT WHOLESALER.   A major economic contribution of the merchant wholesaler in a mature society and economy.

INTERMERCHANT   An independent businessperson in the foreign trade arena whose function is to arrange for the payment of goods exported from a hard-currency country to a soft-currency country.   Knowledge of foreign MARKETING and international finance is the basis for this service which involves a switch of currencies or a multilateral deal.

INTERNAL STIMULI   The forces at work within even a stable buying unit which determine a part of its behavior in the MARKET.   These are the result of individual preferences, the wearing out of products being used, the recognition through experience of how to achieve greater benefits, and the like, all within a fixed set of characteristics and behavior patterns. The marketer must take these into account, ideally to discover their direction so that he may cater to them rather than inadvertently oppose them. See: EXTERNAL STIMULI, INDIVIDUAL CHANGE STIMULI, SELLER ACTIVITY STIMULI

INTERNAL VALIDITY   A condition of a design of a MARKETING RESEARCH activity such that there will be no other sensible cause of the observed results except that tested. See: EXTERNAL VALIDITY, VALIDITY

INTERNATIONAL AIR TRANSPORT ASSOCIATION   Same as: IATA

INTERNATIONAL CHAMBER OF COMMERCE   An organization which since 1920 has worked across national lines to improve conditions for international business. Its policies favor the free movement of persons, goods, services, and capital between countries, at all levels of development. It has members in more than 80 countries, comprising about 6,000 companies and some 1,600 economic organizations, some of which themselves represent more thousands of companies. Among its practical services are a Court of Arbitration, the International Council on Advertising Practice, and work on standardization of documents and practices. It cooperates and coordinates with hundreds of government and international associations. It issues many publications.

INTERNATIONAL COFFEE AGREEMENT   Same as: ICA See: INTERNATIONAL COFFEE ORGANIZATION

INTERNATIONAL COFFEE ORGANIZATION   The institutional arm of the International Coffee Agreement, signed in 1962, under which the producer and consumer nations meet yearly to determine mutually satisfactory coffee quotas as well as price ranges for various coffee types. Its objective is to regulate the coffee supplies to world markets and to hold prices at a level more beneficial to producer nations.

INTERNATIONAL COUNCIL ON ADVERTISING PRACTICE   An organ of the INTERNATIONAL CHAMBER OF COMMERCE, it examines alleged cases of unfair international and sometimes national advertising practice. If determined unfair according to its Code, and the practice is not stopped, the plaintiff can quote the decision of the Council in proceedings in national courts.

INTERNATIONAL EXECUTIVES ASSOCIATION   Same as: IEA

INTERNATIONAL FIRM   A FIRM that produces goods in one country, sells in that country and exports the goods to other countries. May maintain distribution organizations in the other countries. See: MULTINATIONAL FIRM

INTERNATIONAL FORWARDING AGENT   See: FREIGHT FORWARDER (2)

INTERNATIONAL FREIGHT FORWARDER   See: FREIGHT FORWARDER (2)

INTERNATIONAL HOUSE   Same as: IH

INTERNATIONAL MARKETING FEDERATION   Same as: IMF

INTERNATIONAL NEWSPAPER ADVERTISING EXECUTIVES   Same as: INAE

INTERNATIONAL NEWSPAPER PROMOTION ASSOCIATION   Same as: INPA

INTERNATIONAL REGISTRATION OF TRADEMARKS   See: MADRID CONVENTION, INTER-AMERICAN CONVENTION, PARIS UNION

INTERNATIONAL REGISTRY OF EQUIPMENT   See: EIA

INTERNATIONAL UNION OF ADVERTISERS ASSOCIATIONS   Same as: IUAA

INTERPOLATION   The process of establishing a value for a point between two points of known values. Based on the assumption that there is a constant relationship between the two known points for the entire distance and for the factors involved. See: EXTRAPOLATION

INTERPRET   In ADP, to translate non-machine language into a LANGUAGE by which a machine will understand and be able to carry out INSTRUCTIONS. See: COBOL, FORTRAN

INTER-SELLING   Essentially the same as: CROSS-SELLING

INTERSTATE COMMERCE COMMISSION   Same as: ICC

INTERSTATE TRAFFIC   Shipments moving between points in two or more states, or between two points in the same state that goes by a route that passes through another state.   See: INTRASTATE TRAFFIC

INTERTYPE COMPETITION   The competing for business by firms using different methods of DISTRIBUTION.   See: HORIZONTAL COMPETITION, VERTICAL CONFLICT

INTERURBIA   Same as: MEGALOPOLIS

INTERVAL SCALE   A result of a system of SCALING which provides information not only about identification and simple ranking, but also indicates specific intervals between data points which can be quantified.   This is a continuum without an absolute zero point.   See: NOMINAL SCALE, ORDINAL SCALE, RATIO SCALE

INTRANSIT STORAGE   A rate privilege by which a shipper may forward carload lots of mixed goods directly to a central storage facility where the goods are stored until orders are received from CUSTOMERS.   The carload of mixed goods is then sent to the final destination.   Maximum flexibility is achieved and the rate is the through rate plus a small added charge for the privilege.   See: TRANSLOADING

INTRASTATE TRAFFIC   Shipments moving between points within one state only. See: INTERSTATE TRAFFIC

INTRINSICALLY BACKED STORE   See: BACKING ACTIVITIES

INTRINSICALLY MOTIVATED BEHAVIOR   Activity engaged in for the pleasure which the activity itself provides.   See: EXTRINSICALLY MOTIVATED BEHAVIOR, MOTIVATION

INTRINSIC CUES   Cues that influence a buyer's PERCEPTION of a PRODUCT, as factors of physical characteristics of the product itself.   See: EXTRINSIC CUES

INVENTORY ANALYSIS   The process of determining for a multi-location FIRM the most advantageous level of stock to have on hand at each location and the most advantageous size of each order for a specific item.   See: EOQ

INVENTORY COSTING   See: COST OR MARKET, FIFO, LIFO

INVENTORY POLICY   The relationship desired between the amount of stock on order and the amount on hand, and the rate of use.   Usually expressed as a number of days' supply, although it is always to be kept in mind that the critical aspect is a matter of dollars.   May vary widely among firms, and among types of goods within a single firm.

INVENTORY SHORTAGE   Same as: SHORTAGE

INVENTORY TURNOVER   See: TURNOVER

INVENTORY VALUATION   See: COST OR MARKET, FIFO, LIFO

INVERSE DEMAND PATTERN   A situation typical of certain status-associated GOODS, characterized by increasing DEMAND as price increases until a certain level is reached, after which as price continues to increase demand will gradually recede.   For most goods the situation is that the lower the price, the more the MARKET will absorb.

INVISIBLE HAND   A term used by Adam Smith in his classic The Wealth of Nations (1776) to describe the idea that economy guided by the ethical, enlightened self-interest of its business individuals leads to the increased general welfare of that society.

INVISIBLE SUPPLY   Generally refers to uncounted stocks in the hands of middlemen, manufacturers, and CONSUMERS.

INVITATION POINT THEORY   An attempt to explain why new MARKETING forms appear and what course they run until newer forms appear. Its thesis is that existing forms are forced by CONSUMER demands for services to increase their MARGINS as they grow until a point is reached where it interests someone to conceive a way of providing the activity at a lower margin and still make a satisfactory profit. See: RETAIL INSTITUTION CYCLE, WHEEL OF RETAILING

IOA   Abbreviation for: Institute of Outdoor Advertising, the research, marketing and promotional organization of the OUTDOOR ADVERTISING field. It is much involved with educational work. It merged in 1970 with the OAAA but retains its identity and functions as the Marketing Division.

IPI   Abbreviation for: Implicit Price Index, a relative measure of changes in the general level of the prices of all "final" goods and services produced by the economy during a given period (GNP). It is the most comprehensive price index compiled. Sometimes referred to as the implicit price deflator. See: CPI, WPI

IPSO FACTO   A Latin phrase meaning "by the fact itself" or "by the mere fact."

ISA   Abbreviation for: INDEX OF SALES ACTIVITY

ISLAND DISPLAY   A STORE display fixture centered in an open space.

ISLAND POSITION   (1) A NEWSPAPER position in which the advertisement is entirely surrounded by EDITORIAL MATTER. Not usually offered by most newspapers. Occasionally available in some MAGAZINES. See: PREFERRED POSITION   (2) A COMMERCIAL placed with program content on each side.

ISOLATED LOCATION   A STORE located by itself in a residential district. Usually a CONVENIENCE GOODS store such as a SUPERETTE.

ISSUE DATE   The date which appears on the cover of a magazine. See: CLOSING DATE, ON SALE DATE

ISSUE LIFE   The time it takes for a PUBLICATION to REACH its largest measurable AUDIENCE. For a weekly, this is generally thought to be about five weeks; for a monthly, about twelve weeks.

IT   Abbreviation for: Immediate Transportation. Used in the TRAFFIC field.

ITA   Abbreviation for: The Industrial Truck Association, a trade association of firms manufacturing powered INDUSTRIAL lift trucks and associated items and components. It publishes a variety of technical and educational materials in cooperation with the Materials Handling Institute and with the College-Industry Committee on Material Handling Education.

ITEM   See: RECORD

ITEM MERCHANDISING   The special planning and control effort to discover and take advantage of the sales opportunities presented by those items that are in greatest customer demand. Such items out of stock even for a day may result in considerable lost sales volume and adverse customer relations. This is an activity well worth attention and effort. See: RUNNER

ITERATION   A trial and error system for finding a mathematical solution to a problem for which a formula cannot be constructed in advance. Useful in finding which of a given list of MEDIA will give the widest REACH at the lowest cost. See: HEURISTIC MODEL

IUAA   Abbreviation for: The International Union of Advertisers Associations, an organization devoted to joint study of problems relating to advertising

in all of its forms, to joint study of the national advertisers associations and their positions relative to public authorities and other professional organizations, to centralization for the benefit of members all informative materials and the results of experiments, and to cooperation with
all parties concerned with promoting and improving advertising. Organized
in 1953 by advertising associations from Belgium, France, Italy, Sweden
and Switzerland, in 1970 it included Australia, Britain, Denmark, Finland,
Germany, India, Ireland, Israel, Japan, Mexico, Netherlands, New Zealand,
Norway, Spain, South Africa, and the United States (ANA joined in 1965).

JAPAN INDUSTRY FLOATING FAIR Same as: JIFF

J-HOOK A device which, when attached to a shelf or a shelf moulding, holds
a small amount of a product on display. Commonly used to present an item
in a section not normally associated with that type. Often a good acti-
vator of IMPULSE BUYING. Sometimes called a spindle.

JIFF Abbreviation for: Japan Industry Floating Fair, a ship specially out-
fitted to display products of Japanese industry at various ports throughout the world.

JINGLE A set of lyrics alone in print advertising or set to music in broadcast advertising, designed to be a pleasing, memory-inducing device for presenting the selling message. Although the jingle should be short, it
should for maximum effectiveness mention the product more than once and
should recite the SLOGAN. It helps if the slogan can itself be the jingle,
or at least part of the jingle so described.

j.n.d. Abbreviation for: JUST NOTICEABLE DIFFERENCE See: DIFFERENTIAL
THRESHOLD

JOBBER Generally same as: WHOLESALER. Sometimes more narrowly used to designate a MIDDLEMAN who buys in relatively small lots and sells to a RE-
TAILER. A firm may be so called in an industry as a matter of long-stand-
ing custom.

JOB-LOT An incomplete ASSORTMENT of odds and ends of merchandise, bought
as a unit usually at an exceptionally low price. See: BROKEN LOT

JOB PRICE PROTECTION A guarantee of quoted prices on sufficient material
to complete the particular project in which the buyer is engaged.

JOINT DEMAND The DEMAND which occurs because one PRODUCT is used in conjunction with or as a prerequisite to the use of another product. Such
a condition results in both products being demanded jointly, or neither
may be demanded at all. Very common among INDUSTRIAL GOODS.

JOINT PROBABILITY The measured chance that two or more EVENTS will all
occur.

JOINT PROMOTION A special sale sponsored by a group of FIRMS as contrasted
with that by a single RETAILER, such as a sidewalk sale or a special
PROMOTION in a SHOPPING CENTER or MALL.

JOINT RATE A TRANSPORTATION rate which applies to a shipment over the
lines of more than one carrier.

JUDGMENT SAMPLE A SAMPLE in which the elements of the POPULATION are chosen on the basis of the experience and considered judgment of the selector. As with the CONVENIENCE SAMPLE, the degree of accuracy of the measurements derived from this type of sample cannot be specified statistically. See: PROBABILITY SAMPLE

JUMBLE BASKET See: JUMBLE DISPLAY

JUMBLE DISPLAY A display of merchandise created by simply throwing products helter-skelter into a bin or onto a counter. A MERCHANDISER made
to contain this type of display of a number of different products is often
called a jumble basket. The DUMP BIN contains only one product.

JUNIOR UNIT An advertisement size that allows the advertiser to use the same plates for large-size and for small-size-page MAGAZINES. On the large page, the advertisement appears with EDITORIAL MATTER on two or more sides, while in the small magazine the advertisement appears as a full page.

JUNK MAIL See: DIRECT MAIL ADVERTISING

JUSTIFY TYPE. To arrange type so that the letters are spaced for best eye-appeal and so that the lines are of equal length. Machine-set type is justified automatically.

JUST NOTICEABLE DIFFERENCE See: DIFFERENTIAL THRESHOLD Same as j.n.d.

KAMERALISM The German form of MERCANTILISM. More attention was devoted to fiscal problems as a whole than to foreign trade alone. Supposedly derived from the word Kamer, denoting a room, hence the treasure room of the King.

KBI Abbreviation for: Key Buying Influence, the individual in an organization who is the decision-maker regarding the purchase of particular items. Sometimes this function is divided by product. For some products the KBI may be a group of people or a committee. With the cost of a sales call averaging over $90 in 1978, it is easy to understand that firms are focusing ever more attention on teaching their SALESMEN how to reach the right influence without making the usually fatal mistake of trying to by-pass the PROSPECT'S bureaucracy. See: MULTIPLE PURCHASE INFLUENCE

k.d. Abbreviation for: KNOCKED-DOWN

KEEP-OUT PRICE Same as: PREEMPTIVE PRICE

KEEP STANDING An order to a printer to hold type forms for future use. Same as: HOLD, HOLD ORDER

KENNELLY-HEAVISIDE LAYER. Same as: HEAVISIDE LAYER

KEY ACCOUNT In any area, a large CUSTOMER who accounts for a significant part of the volume done by a seller in that area. See: 80-20 PRINCIPLE, RESIDENT SALESMAN

KEY BUYING INFLUENCE Same as: KBI

KEYING AN ADVERTISEMENT Identifying an advertisement with a number or letter so that the source of an inquiry may be determined. Sometimes the key is a variation of the address or the name or the box number to which the inquiry is to be sent. See: INQUIRY TEST

KEY ITEMS (1) Those in greatest CONSUMER acceptance. (2) Those PRODUCTS which determine the acceptance of a LINE of merchandise.

KEYNOTE IDEA The single idea to be presented in an ADVERTISEMENT that will be the most important to a PROSPECT. Once decided upon, it may be the continuing THEME for the CAMPAIGN.

KEY PLATE In color process printing, the plate with the greatest detail to which the other plates must be REGISTERED. See: FOUR-COLOR PROCESS

KEYPUNCH A special device used in ADP to record information in cards or tape by punching holes to represent letters, digits, or special characters. See: PUNCH-CARD EQUIPMENT

KEY STATION The station which originates the principal program of a BROADCAST NETWORK. See: BASIC NETWORK

KEYSTONE MARKUP See: KEYSTONING

KEYSTONING The practice of doubling the maker's prices to determine RETAIL prices.

KINESCOPE   (1) The tube in a television receiver on which the picture
appears.   (2) A filmed recording taken directly from the picture tube
for rebroadcast or storing for reference.

KINKED DEMAND CURVE   A characteristic DEMAND CURVE in a MARKET situation
of OLIGOPOLY, this curve is down-sloping at about the expected angle
until a certain price-quantity relationship is reached, after which the
angle changes sharply and becomes very steep.   The kink represents that
point beyond which competition will not allow any one competitor to drop
the price in an attempt to increase MARKET SHARE without immediately
meeting the new price in an effort to retain CUSTOMERS.   Knowledge of
this likely reaction among the few sources of supply common in an oligopoly
is one of the factors operating to discourage acts which could lead to
a price war.

KNOCKED DOWN   (1) Indicates that an article has been packaged unassembled,
but with all the parts necessary to the assembly at the place of use.
Same as: k.d.   (2) May indicate that the item shipped has been entirely
or partially taken apart.

KNOCKOFF   An imitation of a design of a clothing or textile product.   Usually a close duplication which has been altered in some way to permit selling at a lower price than the original.

KOLMOGOROV-SMIRNOV TEST   An alternative to the CHI-SQUARE TEST for GOODNESS-
OF-FIT which has two advantages over the chi-square: 1) it treats individual observations separately so there is no loss of information through
combining categories to meet the size requirement of the chi-square, and
2) it can be used with very small SAMPLES.   If the computed value is greater than the table value at the significance level desired, the NULL
HYPOTHESIS should be rejected.   The two tests are often used to verify each
other.   NONPARAMETRIC.

KURTOSIS   The degree of peakedness of a FREQUENCY CURVE.   See: LEPTOKURTIC,
MESOKURTIC, PLATYKURTIC, SKEWNESS

LAA   Abbreviation for: League of Advertising Agencies, an association of
qualified, recognized ADVERTISING AGENCIES, organized to issue information designed to help an advertiser find the right agency for his needs,
and in general to promote the use of advertising agencies.

LABEL   That part of the product as it is sold which conveys verbal information about the product or the seller.   It may be affixed directly to the
product itself, may be a part of the PACKAGE, or may be a tag securely
attached to the product.   See: DESCRIPTIVE LABELING, GRADE LABEL, INFORM-
ATIVE LABELING, PERFORMANCE LABEL

LABOR INTENSIVE INDUSTRY   An INDUSTRY in which the requirement for labor
is high in relation to the requirement for plant and equipment.   Most of
the construction industry may be so classified.   See: CAPITAL INTENSIVE
INDUSTRY

LADING   That which constitutes a load, or the freight in a car or vessel.

LAFTA   Abbreviation for: LATIN AMERICAN FREE TRADE ASSOCIATION

LAGGARDS   Come after the LATE MAJORITY in the INNOVATION DIFFUSION process.
Very conscious of tradition.   Lowest economic and social status.

LAGGED EFFECTS   Same as: CARRYOVER EFFECTS

LAGGING INDICATOR   See: BUSINESS INDICATOR

LAISSEZ FAIRE   A philosophy of government in which it is held that the interference of government in business affairs should be at a minimum consistent with protection to contracts, the physical premises, and the
physical safety of society.

LANDBRIDGE   A TRANSPORTATION arrangement which substitutes a trans-
continental train movement for an all-water route for CONTAINERS to and
from the Far East and Europe. Adds to United States ports volume; MINI-
BRIDGE tends to lessen United States ports volume.

LANDED COST   Cost of merchandise and transportation charges of all types
as a total to get the goods to the buyer's dock or place of business.

LANGUAGE   A means by which data may be precisely described and any ADP
equipment made to perform operations on them. The usual machine is a computer which is constructed especially to understand and use a particular
set of symbols. Some computers understand several languages. See: COBOL,
FORTRAN, INSTRUCTION

LANHAM ACT   The Federal statute governing TRADEMARKS and other symbols
identifying products sold in interstate commerce.

LARGE-SIZE PAGE   Same as: STANDARD SIZE PAGE

LASH   Abbreviation for: LIGHTER aboard ship, a means of transporting goods
in water-bourne carriers especially designed to hold fully-loaded BARGES,
with BULK or CONTAINERIZED loads. Such vessels are capable of carrying
38 barges each with a capacity of 850 LONG TONS of CARGO. Today's vessels
are over 800 feet long. A LASH vessel can carry over 70% more cargo than
a conventionally designed vessel, and take only one-half the time in port.

LAST CHANCE METHOD   Same as: STANDING ROOM ONLY

LAST IN, FIRST OUT   Same as: LIFO

LASTING DISTINCTIVENESS   See: DISTINCTIVENESS

L-A STORE   Same as: LIMITED-ASSORTMENT STORE

LATE MAJORITY   Come after the EARLY MAJORITY in the INNOVATION DIFFUSION
process. Usually below average in economic and social status. Make
little use of MASS MEDIA and SALESPEOPLE. Adoption generally follows
quickly after trial.

LATENT DEMAND   A situation within a MARKET in which a significant segment
of that market exhibits a preference for a PRODUCT which is not being
offered. Usually represents a MARKETING opportunity if the segment is
large enough to make the offering economically sound.

LATERAL DIVERSIFICATION   The movement of a firm outside the INDUSTRY in
which it is placed to enter activities far removed from its present market
structure. Generally results in CONGLOMERATE INTEGRATION.

LATIN AMERICAN FREE TRADE ASSOCIATION   Formed in 1960 by Argentina, Brazil,
Chile, Mexico, Peru, Paraguay, and Uruguay, and later included Columbia
and Ecuador, to emulate the EEC. Same as: LAFTA

LATIN SQUARE   A device used in a controlled EXPERIMENT so that the variable
to be tested is randomly rotated by rows and columns in order that the
effect of other variables can be eliminated, leaving only the effect of
the variable to be measured. Statistical interpretation is complex.

LAW OF DEMAND   A basic relation in economics which states that the quantity
demanded per period is negatively related to price. It is based on these
assumptions: a rational CONSUMER with full knowledge of alternative goods,
limited purchasing power, and a drive to maximize the UTILITY accruing to
him. For exceptions which slope the DEMAND CURVE positively see: BAND-
WAGON EFFECT, EXPECTATION EFFECT, INCOME EFFECT, QUALITY EFFECT, SNOB
EFFECT, VEBLEN EFFECT

LAW OF DIMINISHING MARGINAL PRODUCTIVITY   Same as: LAW OF DIMINISHING
RETURNS

LAW OF DIMINISHING MARGINAL UTILITY   This states that the ownership or

CONSUMPTION of each succeeding unit of a good will, after a certain point has been reached, adds less to total satisfaction than did the preceding unit; technically, that total UTILITY will increase at a decreasing rate. Probably explains the reason why systems of EXCHANGE work as they do.

LAW OF DIMINISHING RATE OF FACTOR SUBSTITUTION   As the quantity of any factor of production is increased relative to the quantity of another factor of production, the number of units of the second necessary to replace a unit of the first and maintain output falls, because the marginal product of the first factor falls relative to the second.   See: MARGINAL RATE OF FACTOR SUBSTITUTION.

LAW OF DIMINISHING RETURNS   This states that in most business situations, after a certain point has been reached, successive applications of input factors will add less to total product than each preceding application. If this progresses far enough, total product may decrease absolutely as well as relatively.   The point at which total product begins to increase at a decreasing rate is known as the Point of Diminishing Returns.   Same as: LAW OF DIMINISHING MARGINAL PRODUCTIVITY

LAW OF DISUSE   One of the LAWS OF LEARNING, it states that if a response to a stimulus is not to be lost, the stimulus must continue to recur.   Of real significance to advertisers.   See: LAW OF USE, LAW OF EFFECT

LAW OF EFFECT   One of the LAWS OF LEARNING, it states that when a response or series of responses leads to a satisfying state, the connection between the situation and the response is strengthened, while other responses not so satisfying are weakened and made less probable of recurrance.   Important to marketers as an insight into how BRAND LOYALTY may be built.   See: LAW OF USE, LAW OF DISUSE

LAW OF EXERCISE   See: LAW OF EFFECT

LAW OF READINESS   One of the LAWS OF LEARNING, it states that no learning can occur unless the subject has the ability and the willingness to attempt a solution to a PROBLEM.

LAW OF RETAIL GRAVITATION.   A formula for determining the interchange of RETAIL trade between cities.   Formulated in 1931 by William J. Reilly, it purports to tell at what distance from one city a CONSUMER would be indifferent to going to either city.   Applicable to cities of rather large size and quite far apart.   Does not apply to cities where the population characters differ widely, nor to situations where travel is not considered by consumers to be an economic factor.   Several other formulae have since been constructed based on more data and theoretical refinements.

LAW OF THE UNATTAINABLE TRINITY.   This states that in the production of PRINT ADVERTISING three objectives are prime and are not in conflict with one another only fortuitously: low price, fast delivery, and proper quality.   This "law" is a way of stressing that the advertiser must decide which of the three is overriding in importance, and then accomplish the best he can with the other two in priority order.

LAW OF USE   One of the LAWS OF LEARNING, it states that as a given situation is frequently followed by a response or group of responses, the bond between the stimulus and the response becomes stronger as it is exercised. Leads to habit formation and the remembering of ideas conveyed.   Useful in ADVERTISING and in SALESMANSHIP applications.   See: LAW OF DISUSE, LAW OF EFFECT

LAWS OF LEARNING   See: LAW OF DISUSE, LAW OF EFFECT, LAW OF READINESS, LAW OF USE

LAY-AWAY SALE   The CUSTOMER makes a small down-payment on an item which is held by the seller until the price has been paid. The customer is usually permitted to make payments from time to time. Sometimes the item will be released to the customer when the balance has been brought low enough that the customer qualifies for a credit arrangement.

LAYOUT   (1) A working drawing showing how an advertisement or a publication is to look. (2) The appearance of the finished advertisement as a whole. (3) The arrangement of fixtures or departments in a STORE. (4) The arrangements of units in an office. (5) In TRANSIT ADVERTISING, A line drawing of the COPY scaled to fit the differently proportioned POSTERS being used.

LAZY SUSAN DISPLAY   A POP unit turned by hand or operated by a push-button motor on a turntable base.

LBL   Abbreviation for: less-than-bargeload. FREIGHT FORWARDERS specializing in water transportation can consolidate such smaller-quantity shipments into the larger quantity required to earn the minimum rates applicable to 100, 150, and 200 tons.

l.c.   Abbreviation for: Lower Case. Letters which are not capitals.

l.c.l.   Abbreviation for: less-than-carload. Denotes railroad rates higher than those for carloads (c.l.).

LEADED MATTER   MATTER which has been spaced extra between lines by the insertion of leads.

LEADER   A DEALER offer conditioned by a unit volume-purchase.

LEADER OFFERINGS   See: LOSS LEADER

LEADER PRICING   See: LOSS LEADER

LEADERS   A series of dots, dashes, or other marks used to guide the reader's eye across a page. See: ELLIPSIS, GAZE MOTION

LEADING   Insertion of metal strips between lines of type to provide more white space. The purpose is to achieve greater readability and better appearance. Pronounced "ledding."

LEADING INDICATOR   See: BUSINESS INDICATOR

LEADING NATIONAL ADVERTISERS   Same as: LNA

LEADS   (1) Clues to the finding of PROSPECTS. May come from a variety of sources, such as newspaper accounts, friends, former customers, present customers, COLD CANVASSING. Pronounced "leeds." See: BIRD DOG (2) Strips of metal inserted between lines of type to provide more white space and make reading easier. Pronounced "ledds."

LEAD TIME   The expected time interval between the day of placing an order and the day of arrival of the items. An important consideration in purchasing, especially from the point of view of the control of inventory level. **Same as:** Order Cycle

LEAFLET   A small, single sheet printed on one or both sides and usually folded not more than once. An economical form of DIRECT MAIL ADVERTISING, it is very adaptable to many uses, especially to accompany a letter or a statement of account in the same envelope.

LEAGUE OF ADVERTISING AGENCIES   Same as: LAA

LEAPFROGGING   Designates the practice of bringing in SIGNALS from distant stations for distribution on a CATV system that could not be picked up with ordinary home antenna equipment.

LEARNING CURVE CONCEPT This is the rationale that if there is some knowledge of how labor's time usage decreases as the worker becomes more experienced in his task, then to that extent the decline in unit cost can
be predicted over increased volume for an initial time period. A useful
tool in purchasing to help in the analysis of labor cost estimates when
negotiating with vendors for new items. Same as: IMPROVEMENT FUNCTION

LEASE-BACK ARRANGEMENT Used frequently where the site is important to the
supplier or franchisor, it is an arrangement whereby the party of major
interest signs the primary lease on the property and then sub-leases the
property to the DEALER or FRANCHISEE.

LEASED DEPARTMENT A business operated within the physical space of another
business, usually on a rental agreement based on sales. Sometimes called
concession.

LEASING An increasingly popular plan whereby a FIRM may acquire the use
of equipment without the necessity of taking title. Of particular import
where rapid changes in technology are taking place, highly specialized
services may be required, or where the firm may employ its CAPITAL more
advantageously in some other investment.

LEGEND The title or description under an illustration. See: CAPTION

LEPTOKURTIC Descriptive of a FREQUENCY CURVE in which the measurements
charted are quite closely concentrated around a particular number. Such
a curve is characterized by a high peak. See: KURTOSIS

LETTERPRESS Printing from raised surfaces. See: INTAGLIO, LITHOGRAPHY

LETTER SPACING Putting QUADS between type CHARACTERS to extend them over
a greater width. See: EXPANDED TYPE

LEVERAGED MARKETING The process whereby INDUSTRIAL GOODS firms diversify
into high profit CONSUMER GOODS by taking basic industrial products or
processes and applying them to consumer uses. The DIVERSIFICATION is thus
accomplished without costly acquisitions or new-product development
programs.

LEVERAGE FACTOR The increase in the rate of profit which follows an increase in the volume of sales or production when FIXED COSTS are spread
over more units.

LIFE CYCLE ANALYSIS The study of changes in DEMAND that may be related
to changes in age or stage in the LIFE CYCLE OF POPULATION.

LIFE CYCLE OF POPULATION A popular division by age groups is as follows:
through 5 years, Preschool Children; 6 through 12 years, Gradeschool Children; 13 through 18 years, Adolescents; 19 through 24 years, Young Adults
or Young Marrieds; 25 through 44 years, Acquisitive Years or Full Nest;
45 through 64 years, Empty Nest; 65 years and over, Golden Age or Soli-
tary Survivor. See: LIFE CYCLE ANALYSIS

LIFE CYCLE OF PRODUCT The pattern of the sales volume of a PRODUCT as competition and natural processes (such as the introduction of a new or better product) bring the product through maturity to decline and, eventually, extinction. The time extent of the life cycle has varied greatly
among products in the past and may be expected to continue to vary in the
future. Increasing emphasis is being placed on the use of this concept
to guide decision-making about capital investment planning, advertising
and promotion planning, the probability of acceptable ROI for new products,
the elimination of certain products based on a rationale, and to assist
in integrating management's thinking in all functional areas. It is increasingly recognized that all of these vary greatly according to each
product's progress through the stages of its life cycle. See: SATURATION

LIFE CYCLE PURCHASING A concept that would require marketers promoting
CONSUMER GOODS to deemphasize acquisition cost as the major factor, and

focus instead on four factors: acquisition, operating costs, servicing costs, and disposal.

LIFE STYLE   The characteristic mode of living in its broadest sense of a segment of or the whole of a society, especially as it is concerned with those unique qualities which distinguish one group or CULTURE from others.

LIFETIME GUARANTEE   A promise by the maker of a PRODUCT to repair or exchange the product should any defect appear during the period the purchaser retains the product. See: TWO-LIFETIME GUARANTEE

LIFO   Abbreviation for: last-in, first-out. A method of inventory valuation and costing in which the assumption is that merchandise received last is always sold first. Generally works to decrease the broad effects on profit of a situation in which prices are fluctuating. See: FIFO

LIGHT CAR   Sometimes used to denote a company-owned automobile.

LIGHTER   A large BARGE commonly used to transport freight about a harbor, especially to facilitate the loading and unloading of ships not lying at wharves. See: LASH

LIGHTER ABOARD SHIP   Same as: LASH

LIGHTERAGE   A charge made for the conveyance of goods by water, either in a BARGE or a LIGHTER.

LIGHT-FACE TYPE   A type FACE designed with thin lines, giving it a light look. Contrast with: BOLDFACE TYPE

LIGHT STEALER   A POP display which has no illumination of its own, but appears to be illuminated because it is made of materials which reflect light derived from other sources in the STORE.

LIMEN   See: SUBLIMINAL AWARENESS

LIMITED-ASSORTMENT STORE   An innovation of the late 1970s, this modification of the CONVENIENCE STORE carries only 600 to 1,000 food items, mainly PRIVATE LABELS or packer labels. Little choice in any one type of food is offered. CUSTOMERS bring their own bags. An apparently growing form, the about 200 in operation in 1979 are expected to increase to total about 500 in 1980.

LIMITED DISTRIBUTION   Selection of the number of DEALERS in an area that a firm considers will produce maximum profitability, taking into account all factors. No more dealers are accepted when that number have been activated. Same as: SELECTIVE DISTRIBUTION See: INTENSIVE DISTRIBUTION, EXCLUSIVE DISTRIBUTION, FRANCHISING

LIMITED-FUNCTION WHOLESALER   The general category applied to WHOLESALERS who do not grant credit, or who do not carry stock, or who do business only by mail. Some one or more services ordinarily supplied by the REGULAR WHOLESALER are lacking. See: CASH-AND-CARRY WHOLESALER, DESK JOBBER

LIMITED-LINE STORE   A non-departmentized RETAILER handling but one major LINE of merchandise.

LIMITED-LINE STRATEGY   The decision of a firm to concentrate on only a small number of variations of a product. See: BROAD-LINE STRATEGY

LINAGE   The total number of LINES of space used by an advertisement or a series of advertisements. See: RATE CARD

LINE   (1) In ADVERTISING, a unit of space measure equal to one-fourteenth of a COLUMN-INCH. See: RATE CARD (2) In RETAILING, generally associated with goods of a related type bought to resell at a single, predetermined price. (3) In INDUSTRY, the group of items related in use which are offered for sale by a firm. See: BREADTH OF LINE (4) In a firm's organization, those positions assigned the responsibilities and the AUTHORITY to act directly to achieve the defined goals of the firm.

LINEAR SYSTEM   A MARKETING system which is merely adjunct to a factory. If the goods are not right for the MARKET, they will pile up at the factory. Few firms today dare to make things without first examining to a reasonable degree what likelihood exists that the market will accept them. See: CLOSED-CIRCUIT SYSTEM, OPEN-CIRCUIT SYSTEM

LINEAR TARIFF CUT   A reduction in all TARIFFS by the same percent. Usually determined via GATT talks.

LINE CHART   A graph usually constructed so that one variable is shown on one axis and another variable is shown on the other axis. Time is often one of the variables. See: BAR CHART, HISTOGRAM, PICTOGRAM, PIE CHART

LINE CUT   An engraving made without a screen so that the reproduction is in solid lines without shades or tones such as in a HALFTONE. Same as: LINE PLATE

LINE DRAWING   A pen or brush drawing consisting of solid lines without tonal gradations. Used as the source for a LINE CUT.

LINE ELEVATOR   An ELEVATOR which is one of those controlled by a private company which operates two or more.

LINE-HAUL RATE.   The basic transportation rate from which adjustments are made up or down for services or privileges given or not wanted.

LINE PLATE   Same as: LINE CUT

LINE TINT PATTERNS   Essentially the same as BENDAY   See: LINE TINT PLATE

LINE TINT PLATE   Essentially the same as the tint plate produced by using BENDAY, but probably more involved with patterns made with lines.

LINE YARD   One of a CHAIN of lumber yards organized by a milling company to sell its lumber without the use of MIDDLEMEN outside its organization. Usually a form of FORWARD INTEGRATION.

LINKING PHRASE   Any short series of words in SALESMANSHIP that serves to connect a FEATURE with a benefit in a directed, smooth, logical manner. See: OBJECTION

LINOTYPE   A machine capable of mechanical type-setting by casting a single complete line of type at a time and assembling these in sequence.

LIP SYNC   Trade shortword for the synchronization of an actor's or a singer's lip movements with the sound from a recording.

LIQUID WEALTH   Cash, bank accounts, marketable securities, and other assets that may be converted quickly, if not immediately, into cash. See: WEALTH

LIST   In DIRECT MAIL ADVERTISING, the completed assembly of the names and addresses of the persons to whom the advertiser wishes to send his message. Very critical to the success of the CAMPAIGN. The composition must be done with care after analysis of the desired PROSPECT characteristics.

LIST BROKER   An independent businessman who arranges the rental to one advertiser of the LISTS compiled by another advertiser. He is paid a fee or a commission for his services.

LIST PRICE   (1) The full price before any applicable discounts. (2) The suggested selling price set by a manufacturer. (3) A price set to be the permanent base from which percent deductions are allowed to various BUYERS who qualify for different FUNCTIONAL DISCOUNTS. In many instances the simplest way of reflecting price fluctuations affecting an extensive CATALOG.

LIST SUPPLIER   A FIRM the business of which is to compile and furnish to DIRECT MAIL ADVERTISERS the names and addresses of groups of persons

identified by some common characteristic. Some list suppliers are
equipped to do the entire mailing operation for clients. See: LIST BROKER

LITHOGRAPHY   A method of printing from a flat surface. Can accommodate
HALFTONES. See: INTAGLIO, LETTERPRESS

LIVE MATTER   MATTER which is to be used again, to be preserved. See:
DEAD MATTER

LIVE MERCHANDISE   Products on display and offered for sale for which there
is an active demand. See: RUNNER

LME   Abbreviation for: London Metal Exchange, a very important factor in
the market mechanism relating to world supplies of metal, copper and gold
in particular.

LNA   Abbreviation for: Leading National Advertisers, a compilation service
which tabulates expenditures of advertisers in various MEDIA.

LOAD   (1) In ADP, to put data into a REGISTER or STORAGE. (2) Also in ADP,
to put magnetic tape on a drive, or to put punched cards into a card
reader or other TAB EQUIPMENT.

LOADER   A DEALER offer tied to a single, volume purchase. May take a variety of forms, such as trips, gifts, or additional merchandise. A rather
derogatory way of referring to a DEALER PREMIUM.

LOADINGS   Usually used to mean the same as: CARLOADINGS, but in some contexts may apply to trucks or planes.

LOCAL ADVERTISING   ADVERTISING paid for by a RETAILER at a LOCAL RATE.
The message of such advertising is usually "Buy this product here!"

LOCAL BRAND   Any BRAND used in a limited geographic area by either a manufacturer or a MIDDLEMAN. See: NATIONAL BRAND, MANUFACTURER'S BRAND,
PRIVATE BRAND

LOCAL BROADCAST   A program sent out by a local advertiser over a station
in his community. See: SPOT

LOCALIZED TIME   Same as: SPOT RADIO or SPOT TELEVISION

LOCAL MARKET   An area in which the first steps are taken in ASSEMBLING
products from a number of farmers. Same as: PRIMARY MARKET

LOCAL PLAN   A MEDIA selection plan governed by the advertiser's limitation
of sale of his products in one town and its immediate TRADING AREA. The
media for this plan are confined to the specific geographic area of interest. CIRCULATION outside this area would be wasted almost in its entirety. See: REGIONAL PLAN, NATIONAL PLAN, SELECTIVE PLAN

LOCAL RATE   (1) A transportation rate that applies when a shipment is handled completely over the lines of one carrier. See: JOINT RATE (2) An
advertising rate applied to regular advertisers in a newspaper as contrasted with TRANSIENT RATE.

LOCAL STATION   A RADIO station authorized to use power not exceeding 250
watts, which gives it generally a range of about 25 miles. Many may broadcast only during day hours. Frequencies are shared by these stations inasmuch as assignments are made by the FCC so that there will be no interference. See: CLEAR-CHANNEL STATION, REGIONAL STATION

LOCAL WHOLESALER   A WHOLESALER who confines his activities to an area within roughly 75-100 miles around his place of business. See: NATIONAL
WHOLESALER, SECTIONAL WHOLESALER

LOCATION   A STORAGE position in an ADP system which can store one WORD.
it is usually identified by an ADDRESS.

LOCATION HABIT   Refers to a purchaser's preconceived idea as to the
particular type of MARKETING ESTABLISHMENT he ought to use as a source
of supply for certain items.

LOCKUP   Same as: FORM

LOG   In BROADCAST MEDIA, the accurate, chronological record of all programs and COMMERCIALS aired by a station. Required by law.

LOGIC   In ADP, the scheme which defines the inter-connections and the interactions of signals entering into the design of a complete system. Unless all parts of the system interlock properly, the outputs will not be reliable.

LOGICAL FLOW MODEL   Consists of geometric figures, symbols, and directional arrows to trace the sequence of events or operations. Usually a DESCRIPTIVE MODEL. See: MODEL

LOGISTICS SYSTEM   The establishment of physical distribution as an operating subsystem within the larger system of the company's entirety of activity. Recognized as affording the opportunity for significant savings through more adequate coordination. See: TRANSPORTATION

LOGO   (1) Musical or sound signature used by an advertiser to identify himself to the AUDIENCE of a BROADCAST MEDIUM. (2) Brief form for: LOGOTYPE

LOGOTYPE   The signature plate or standard name plate of an advertiser. Same as: LOGO, NAME SLUG

LOLLIPOP DISPLAY   A large round ADVERTISEMENT mounted on a pole. A form of OUTDOOR ADVERTISING.

LONDON METAL EXCHANGE   Same as: LME

LONG   Same as: LONG POSITION, but is used also to refer to the individual who is in the position.

LONG HEDGE   A HEDGE in which the contract to buy commodity is in the FUTURES MARKET.

LONG POSITION   Present ownership of commodity, or making a contract to take delivery in the future at a fixed price. A firm or SPECULATOR may take this position when there is a firm belief in the company or by the speculator that the price of the commodity will rise. See: SHORT POSITION

LONG RUN   A period of time sufficient to permit all the costs of production of a firm to be variable. Generally considered to be longer than one year; may extend for many. See: SHORT RUN

LONG SHOT   Same as: LS

LONG TON   Same as: GROSS TON

LOOKING-GLASS SELF   The way a person thinks he/she is regarded by others. See: IDEAL SELF, SELF-IMAGE

LOOSE MARKET   Same as: BUYERS' MARKET

LOSS LEADER   An item offered by a MERCHANT at an unusually low price with the full intention of selling it to all who wish to buy. The purpose is to induce a larger customer traffic than would be possible at the normal price. The loss factor is now not legal in those states having UNFAIR TRADE PRACTICES ACTS. Use of this promotional device results in a continuing situation of special sales.

LOWER CASE   Same as: l.c.

LOWER-LOWER CLASS   See: SOCIAL CLASSES

LOWER-MIDDLE CLASS   See: SOCIAL CLASSES

LOWER-UPPER CLASS   See: SOCIAL CLASSES

LOW-PRESSURE SELLING   A technique often used by an experienced SALESMAN by means of which the PROSPECT is lead to make the purchase by adroit questioning and seeming reluctance by the salesman. The entire activity is calculated to create the impression to the prospect that he has been in control of the sale at all times. Not for beginning salesmen. See: HIGH-PRESSURE SELLING

LOYALTY   See: BRAND LOYALTY

LS. Abbreviation for: Long Shot   In TELEVISION, a full view of the background or set and the models or actors.

l.t.l. Abbreviation for: less-than-truckload. Indicates a shipment moving at a higher rate than a truckload. See: l.c.l.

LTR   Abbreviation for: LIGHTER

MAAN   Abbreviation for: Mutual Advertising Agency Network, a group of independent ADVERTISING AGENCIES whose objectives are to increase managerial efficiency, raise the standards of service to clients, simplify and standardize agency operations, exchange information on common problems, assist one another when requested, and develop carefully planned literature designed to promote the welfare of all members.

MAB   Abbreviation for: Magazine Advertising Bureau, a part of the MPA which acts to promote the sale of advertising space in CONSUMER MAGAZINES. Name changed in 1972 to: Magazine Association of Canada.

MAC   Abbreviation for: Magazine Association of Canada. See: MAB

MACRO-MARKETING   MARKETING from the overall view of the aggregate activity in the economy for meeting society's objectives of a proper flow of goods and services. See: MICRO-MARKETING

MACROSALES MODEL   A way of portraying the sales process by letting sales be represented by a single variable consisting of units or dollars, and then studying this in relation to other pertinent variables. See: MICROANALYTIC SALES MODEL, MICROBEHAVIORAL SALES MODEL, MICROCOMPONENT SALES MODEL

MADRID CONVENTION   The 22 member countries in Europe have agreed to automatic TRADEMARK protection for all members through the Bureau for International Registration of Trademarks. The United States is a participant only to the extent that a subsidiary of a United States company located in one of the member countries can effect protection for its company in all member countries. See: PARIS CONVENTION

MAGAZINE   A print PUBLICATION, usually issued regularly, devoted to a certain category of EDITORIAL MATTER, sometimes classified broadly as consumer, farm, and business, designed to appeal to certain groupings of the MARKET. Provides the best possibility for graphic reproduction. Not good for narrow geographic uses. Essentially the same as: PERIODICAL

MAGAZINE ADVERTISING BUREAU   Same as: MAB

MAGAZINE ASSOCIATION OF CANADA   See: MAB

MAGAZINE PUBLISHERS ASSOCIATION   Same as: MPA

MAGAZINE SUPPLEMENT   See: SUPPLEMENT

MAGNESIUM PLATES   Lightweight, low cost originals flexible enough for direct printing on rotary presses, they are used with PHOTOCOMPOSITION, having a light-sensitive plastic coating over a metal base on which the image is hardened by exposure to ultraviolet light.

MAGNETIC INK CHARACTER RECOGNITION   Same as: MICR

MAGNUSON-MOSS FTC IMPROVEMENTS ACT   A 1975 federal law designed to broaden the powers of the FTC, especially with respect to misleading PACKAGING and ADVERTISING of toys. Included in the new powers is one permitting the assessment of money fines.

MAGNUSON-MOSS WARRANTY ACT   A federal law passed in 1975 requiring that all CONSUMER PRODUCTS distributed in interstate commerce and sold with a

written warranty must have the warranty designated as "full" or "limited."
These are the only designations permitted. To be eligible for designation as a "full warranty," it must promise to remedy any defect or malfunction within a stated, reasonable time after notice, by refund or free
repair or replacement with an identical or substantially equivalent
product. If the product is functional only when attached to some other
product, a full warranty must provide installation without charge. The
CONSUMER must not be required to do anything more than give notification
of the defect or malfunction. There are other details imposed on the
marketer by FTC regulations interpreting the Act.

MAILER Any PROMOTIONAL literature sent through the mail. Examples are
solicitations for funds for charities, announcements of sales, distributions of political appeals.

MAIL-IN Any PREMIUM offered which must be requested by mail, sometimes
free for boxtops or labels, but generally a SELF-LIQUIDATOR.

MAILING LIST Same as: LIST

MAIL-ORDER A way of selling goods by receiving and filling orders by mail.
This type of MARKETING system owes its stimulus to the origination of the
parcel post service. See: DIRECT MAIL ADVERTISING, DIRECT MARKETING

MAIL-ORDER HOUSE A business firm specializing in the sale of goods through
orders received by mail. May be a RETAILER or a WHOLESALER. See: MAIL-
ORDER

MAIN STORE Same as: PARENT STORE

MAINTAINED MARK-ON The difference between net sales and gross cost of
goods sold. See: MARGIN, MARKUP

MAINTAINED MARKUP Same as: MAINTAINED MARKON. May be expressed as a
percent or a dollar amount.

MAJOR APPLIANCES Electrical housewares of relatively large size and price,
such as refrigerators, washers, television sets, freezers, etc. See:
TRAFFIC APPLIANCES, WHITE GOODS

MAJORITY FALLACY The belief that the thrust of PROMOTION must be toward
the majority of the MARKET. See: SEGMENTATION, TARGET MARKET

MAJOR RETAIL CENTER This class of PLANNED SHOPPING CENTER is a concentration of RETAIL STORES in a STANDARD METROPOLITAN STATISTICAL AREA but outside the CENTRAL BUSINESS DISTRICT, which has annual sales of at least
$5 million and at least 10 retail establishments, one of which is a
DEPARTMENT STORE.

MAKE-BULK CENTER Essentially the same as: FREIGHT FORWARDER

MAKE-GOOD A free run of an advertisement in which in the first run there
was an error made by the publisher.

MAKE OR BUY A dilemma faced by many manufacturing firms. In general the
decision will be to make the needed item when capacity is available, demand is large and relatively stable, the cost is lower within the firm,
the item is critical and requires very close quality control, and/or facilities are not available at suppliers. In general the decision will be to
buy when company capital can be more profitably invested in other opportunities, necessary skills are not available within the company, legal barriers stop the firm from making, and/or the demand for the item is temporary or seasonal.

MAKE-READY The activity involved in mounting and preparing artwork and/or
COPY for photographing or reproduction.

MAKE-UP. The appearance of a NEWSPAPER page. Most newspapers require advertisements to have a minimum depth, usually as many inches as columns

wide, in order to prevent unusual-shaped advertisements which would complicate the make-up to the disadvantage of other advertisements.

MALL. An increasingly popular type of shopping center which may be a number of shopping blocks closed to vehicular traffic; or more recently, a shopping center of the usual type but with walkways entirely closed against the weather and airconditioned, or the same in the form of a building with inside parking provided, sometimes near a particular department area. See: SHOPPING PLAZA

MANAGED OBSOLESCENCE   Same as: PLANNED OBSOLESCENCE

MANAGEMENT BY EXCEPTION   Contrary to the popular but uninformed notion that such a system generates exceptions, it is rather a means by which the attention and energies of management are brought to bear on those activities where performance is significantly different from goals, to establish why, and to attempt corrective measures. See: MANAGEMENT BY OBJECTIVES

MANAGEMENT BY OBJECTIVES   Usually considered to be a process directed at setting goals that can be compared with some previously established criteria. Supervisors on all levels are drawn into the process, and a mechanism is arranged so that any superior and his subordinates may contribute mutually discussed inputs. Four aspects are generally regarded as fundamental: the objectives must be stated clearly, the time factor must be set as an established schedule of events to occur, subordinates must be given a significant participatory role in designing the objectives, and MOTIVATION must be activated by providing a high level of job satisfaction through all of the foregoing.

MANAGEMENT INFORMATION SYSTEM   See: MIS (2)

MANCHESTER MAN   Same as: BAGMAN

MANDATORY COPY   The COPY specified by certain laws to appear in the ADVERTISING or on the LABEL of indicated PRODUCTS, such as cigarettes or medications.

MANN-WHITNEY TEST   See: U TEST

MANPOWER MANAGEMENT   Same as: HUMAN RESOURCES MANAGEMENT

MANUFACTURERS' AGENT   A FUNCTIONAL MIDDLEMAN characterized by his rendering services similar to those of a SALESMAN, by his restriction to a limited territory, by limited authority to make terms, and by offering to finance his PRINCIPALS only under unusual circumstances. Same as: MANUFACTURERS' REPRESENTATIVE

MANUFACTURER'S BRAND   Same as: NATIONAL BRAND

MANUFACTURER'S COOPERATIVE ADVERTISING   Same as: COOPERATIVE ADVERTISING

MANUFACTURERS' REPRESENTATIVE   (1) Same as: MANUFACTURERS' AGENT (2) An elegant title for a manufacturer's salesperson.

MANUFACTURER'S SALES BRANCH   An ESTABLISHMENT owned and operated by a manufacturer apart from his plants out of which his SALESMEN may work, and which houses STOCKS from which deliveries may be made to CUSTOMERS.

MANUFACTURER'S SALE OFFICE   Except that no STOCK is housed, essentially the same as a MANUFACTURER'S SALES BRANCH.

MARAD   Acronym for: Maritime Administration, United States

MARCONAFLO   An innovation which has permitted the adaptation of SLURRY transportation via PIPELINE to the constraints of transportation in ocean-going vessels. It offers the potential of very significant reduction in overseas transportation costs.

MARGIN. The percent of selling price which gross profit is. Used generally by RETAIL ESTABLISHMENTS. Distinguish from: MARKUP

MARGINAL BUYER   The buyer whose willingness to buy is just enough to cause him to pay a given price.

MARGINAL COST   The addition to total cost occasioned by the manufacture of one additional unit of **PRODUCT**. See: MARGINAL REVENUE

MARGINAL CUSTOMER   A buyer judged by the seller to be at the border between providing profit enough to be continued as a CUSTOMER by the seller and profit so little as to merit being dropped as a customer.

MARGINAL RATE OF FACTOR SUBSTITUTION   The number of units of one factor of production necessary to replace a unit of another factor of production and maintain the same level of output. See: LAW OF DIMINISHING RATE OF FACTOR SUBSTITUTION

MARGINAL RETURN TO SPACE   The addition to gross profit occasioned by the addition of one unit of shelf FACING for a product. Profit maximization for the firm occurs when marginal returns to space are the same for all items.

MARGINAL REVENUE   The addition to total revenue resulting from the sale of one additional unit of product, considered from the point of view of sliding down the DEMAND CURVE. See: MARGINAL COST

MARGINAL UTILITY   (1) The satisfaction added to one's total satisfaction from acquiring one additional unit of a particular item. See: LAW OF DIMINISHING MARGINAL UTILITY (2) The increase in satisfaction derived from an additional expenditure. See: UTILITY, VALUE

MARGINAL WORKER   The value of his work just equals his wages.

MARK   A blanket term which includes any TRADEMARK, SERVICE MARK, COLLECTIVE MARK, or CERTIFICATION MARK entitled to registration under the law, whether registered or not. See: ABANDONMENT OF MARK, PRINCIPAL REGISTER

MARKDOWN   (1) A reduction in the retail price of merchandise. (2) In the RETAIL METHOD, a reduction from the price at which the merchandise was offered originally. See: MARKDOWN CANCELLATIONS

MARKDOWN CANCELLATIONS   In the RETAIL accounting method, decreases in MARKDOWNS that do not raise the prices of merchandise above ORIGINAL RETAIL.

MARKET   The totality of those who can benefit from the producer's product or service and who can afford to buy it. More technically: a sphere within which price-making forces operate, and in which exchanges of title tend to be accompanied by the actual movement of the goods affected.

MARKET BASKET PRICING   A philosophy of setting price applicable to a situation where the sale of one product stimulates the sales of other products. It is generally characterized by the use of specials, as in a SUPERMARKET, or by equipment and maintenance contracts. TIE-IN SALES are also examples of this type of pricing, but the legality of tie-in sales are now open to question.

MARKET CLEAVAGE   Same as: MARKET SEGMENTATION

MARKET DELINEATION   The determination of who are PROSPECTS and CUSTOMERS, and finding their identifying characteristics. See: MARKET, MARKET SEGMENTATION

MARKET DEMAND   Used variously to mean essentially the same as DEMAND, or MARKET POTENTIAL.

MARKET DEMOGRAPHY   The science of DEMOGRAPHICS applied to a market.

MARKET GRADE   A standard for a commodity generally accepted as a basis for description of the commodity for trade purposes, e.g., "prime" for meats, "AA" for butter, "93 octane" for gasoline, "#2" for home fuel oil.

MARKET GRID   A way of dividing a MARKET by cross-hatching a square or
rectangle on the basis of relevant market characteristics on the different
axes. Really a device for determining the various possible market segments by using a number of dimensions such as size or age groups on one
axis and a number of characteristics on the other, and then checking all
the boxes corresponding to those dimensions for which the characteristics
are applicable. Usually a two-dimensional figure, it may be expanded to
a cube if there are enough relevant classifications of dimensions, in
which case it may provide a basis for innovations. By varying color in-
tensities, a sort of four-dimensional grid may be devised.

MARKETING   All business activities necessary to effect transfers of ownership of goods from producers to CONSUMERS except those normally regarded
as manufacturing operations. An examination of the MARKETING FUNCTIONS
will reveal that these activities begin long before the offerings are put
into the actual supply mode, and to insure the CUSTOMER'S satisfaction
they continue long after the actual sale has been closed. In the field
of SERVICES, all those activities required to make the services desirable
and available to those who can benefit from their use and have the
purchasing power to acquire them. In recent years the same activities
as those used for goods and services have been applied to ideas, political candidates, and social philosophies. Because of the dynamic nature
of marketing, all techniques employed are necessarily under continuous
development. See: MARKETING FUNCTION

MARKETING AUDIT   A rigorous review of the MARKETING system within a firm
to determine the strengths and weaknesses of the system's parts and how
well the parts are performing their assigned tasks.

MARKETING CHANNEL   Same as: CHANNEL OF DISTRIBUTION

MARKETING CONCEPT   Focusing of all company activity on what will best serve
the CONSUMER, within ways compatible with the objectives of the company.
Requires an internal marketing organization in which all MARKETING
activities are consolidated under the leadership of one executive placed
in top management. See: GOAL CONGRUENCE

MARKETING COOPERATIVE   An organization formed by a group of farmers who
have joined together to sell their produce more efficiently. As a group
they can hire specialized managers, advertise and promote with greater
IMPACT, and control handling and grading quality so that consumer demand
may be enhanced. The California Fruit Growers Association, through the
common BRAND NAME Sunkist, is an example of one which has been very
successful in accomplishing its goals.

MARKETING EFFICIENCY   See: EXCHANGE EFFICIENCY, INNOVATIVE EFFICIENCY,
TECHNICAL EFFICIENCY

MARKETING ERA   The period of time beginning about 1950 and extending into
the future in which the MARKETING CONCEPT has achieved a significant
amount of acceptance in most INDUSTRIES.

MARKETING FUNCTION   A major economic activity which is inherent in the
MARKETING process, and which tends to become specialized through a con-
tinuous division of labor. Generally classified into: BUYING, SELLING,
STORAGE, TRANSPORTATION, STANDARDIZATION AND GRADING, RISK TAKING,
FINANCING, MARKET INFORMATION.

MARKETING INFORMATION   A MARKETING FUNCTION characterized by the accumulation and dissemination of intelligence concerning MARKET developments and
other market data. See: MARKETING RESEARCH, MARKETING RESEARCH CONCEPTS

MARKETING INFORMATION AND ANALYSIS CENTER   Same as: MIAC

MARKETING INFORMATION SYSTEM   Same as: MIS

MARKETING INTELLIGENCE   MARKETING INFORMATION, however acquired, which has been evaluated, classified, and organized for use by management in developing marketing STRATEGY.

MARKETING INTELLIGENCE SYSTEM   The mechanisms which induce the organized reporting of all data relevant to a firm's MARKETING goals, and which maintain these data reporting flows in continuously working order. See: MARKETING RESEARCH

MARKETING MIX   The total complex of the firm's MARKETING effort. The central problem in planning this is to find that combination which will produce the maximum net cash inflow. Usually considered to include: Personal Selling, Advertising, Delivery, Pricing, Quality, Promotion, Special Jobs, and Technical Service. See: FOUR P's

MARKETING PHILOSOPHY   Same as: MARKETING CONCEPT

MARKETING PLANNING   A process by means of which a carefully worked out, detailed account, most frequently in writing, is developed that prescribes the company's self-image, the company's objectives, the MARKETING PROGRAMS designed to achieve the objectives, and the methods to be used to measure the degree of success of the planning effort. Many firms divide the effort into short term (one or two years into the future) and long term (more than two years into the future).

MARKETING PROGRAM   Coordination of all the elements of the MARKETING MIX for the company as a whole toward the attainment of a particular goal. See: MARKETING PLANNING

MARKETING RELATIVISM   A PRINCIPLE OF MARKETING, especially appropriate to marketing activities in foreign lands, which emphasizes that experience, the basis for MARKETING STRATEGIES, is interpreted by each marketer in the light of his own CULTURE.

MARKETING RESEARCH   The use of the scientific method in the solution of MARKETING problems. A tool for management, not a substitute for experience and judgment. It involves the gathering, organization, and analysis of MARKET data as a branch of a MARKETING INTELLIGENCE SYSTEM which makes studies of specific PROBLEMS for the guidance of management in the making of marketing decisions of lowest RISK. See: CONSTRAINT, PAYOFF, PRELIMINARY RESEARCH

MARKETING RESEARCH CONCEPTS   See the following: ALPHA ERROR, ANALYTICAL MODEL, ARRAY, BETA ERROR, CONDITIONAL PROBABILITY, CONFOUNDED VARIABLE, CONSUMER RESEARCH, CORRELATION, CORRELATION COEFFICIENT, COVARIANCE, CRITICAL VALUE OF t, DEGREES OF FREEDOM, DELPHI TECHNIQUE, DICHOTOMOUS QUESTION, DISCRIMINANT ANALYSIS, DISPERSION, EXTERNAL VALIDITY, FACTOR ANALYSIS, F DISTRIBUTION, GOODNESS OF FIT, INTERVAL SCALE, MATHEMATICAL MODEL, MEAN, MODE, NOMINAL SCALE, NONPARAMETRIC, NONSAMPLING ERROR, OPEN-ENDED QUESTION, POISSON PROBABILITY DISTRIBUTION, POPULATION, POSTERIOR ANALYSIS, PREPOSTERIOR ANALYSIS, PRIOR ANALYSIS, PROJECTIVE TECHNIQUES, QUESTIONNAIRE, RATIO SCALE, REGRESSION, RORSCHACH TEST, SAMPLING, SAMPLING PRECISION, STANDARD DEVIATION, STANDARD ERROR OF ESTIMATE, TABLE OF RANDOM NUMBERS, t DISTRIBUTION, TEST OF RANDOMNESS, THEMATIC APPERCEPTION TEST, TIME SERIES, t VALUE, TYPE I ERROR, TYPE II ERROR, UNIVERSE, U TEST, VARIANCE

MARKETING RISKS   These are the various ways in which losses may be incurred by a marketer. They include: OBSOLESCENCE, WASTE, damage, physical deterioration, shoplifting and other thefts, CREDIT, discontinuity of supply, discontinuity of demand, changes in suppy and demand factors resulting in price declines, and "acts of God." To a varying degree these may be passed on to others through insurance, HEDGING, and SYSTEMS CONTRACTING. Others may be minimized only through the effects of good management action.

MARKETING SCIENCE INSTITUTE   Same as: MSI

MARKETING SERVICES DIRECTOR   Very frequently used as a title to designate the expanded duties now assigned to the position which used to be called Advertising Manager.

MARKET-MINUS PRICES   In RETAILING, an attempt consistently to price similar merchandise for less than does competition in the area. See: AT-THE-MARKET PRICES, MARKET-PLUS PRICES, VARIABLE PRICING

MARKET-MINUS PRICING   The producer starts with a RETAIL price thought possible because of MARKET RESEARCH or visual perusal of existing products, and then removes in succession all the MARGINS of MIDDLEMEN in the anticipated CHANNEL OF DISTRIBUTION and his own. This leaves him with an estimate of the maximum-cost-to-produce allowable for the product. The kind of product he can offer for this cost and the resulting retail price depends on his efficiency at the forecast sales volume. Same as: DEMAND-BACKWARD PRICING

MARKET PLACE   Essentially the same as MARKET, but may have more geographic implications.

MARKET-PLUS PRICING   In RETAILING, this way of setting prices fixes them higher where wanted than for similar merchandise at competitors in the area, as in gourmet shops vs SUPERMARKETS. See: AT-THE-MARKET PRICES, MARKET-MINUS PRICES, MARKET-MINUS PRICING, VARIABLE PRICING

MARKET POTENTIAL   The total sales of all manufacturers of a PRODUCT that a MARKET is estimated to be able to deliver during a given period.

MARKET POWER   The ability of a firm to control the activities in which it engages in the MARKET, e.g., buying at lowest prices, acquiring interested sources of supply, controlling that part of the TRADE CHANNEL which is its concern, etc. The Justice Department is alert to new evidence that may indicate market power in excess of what is considered normal, or the improper use of market power. See: COUNTERVAILING POWER

MARKET PRICE   The price at which a GOOD is exchanged in the MARKET from day to day. (2) The current ruling price of a commodity in the market.

MARKET PROFILE   A DEMOGRAPHIC description of the people or the HOUSEHOLDS or both, of a product's MARKET. Sometimes includes the economic information applicable to a geographic area.

MARKET RATIO   The power of one product or service to command another in exchange for itself in a free market. Usually accomplished and calculated in money, but may be on a BARTER basis.

MARKET SEGMENTATION   Same as: SEGMENTATION

MARKET SHARE   One firm's proportion of the INDUSTRY'S total actual volume. Sometimes the base is potential volume rather than actual volume.

MARKET-SHARE ANALYSIS   See: PERFORMANCE ANALYSIS

MARKET SKIMMING   Using a SKIMMING PRICE as a STRATEGY when introducing a new PRODUCT. The objective is to recover the investment as quickly as possible.

MARKET STRETCHING   A competitive TACTIC which involves narrow SEGMENTATION where others are aiming broadly, or perhaps SIMPLIFICATION where a MARKET has been unduly FRAGMENTED. The aim is to mine the market more intensively. Often most effective in conjunction with other tactics.

MARKET STRUCTURE   The features of a MARKET that are so significant economically that they affect the behavior of the firms in the INDUSTRY supplying the market. The important elements are the number and size distribution of buyers and sellers, the type and importance of PRODUCT DIFFERENTIATION, and the conditions of entry of new sellers.

MARKET TARGET   Same as: TARGET MARKET

MARKET TEMPER   The general feeling which exists among buyers in the MARKET regarding the near future: optimistic or pessimistic outlook. See: BUYERS' MARKET, SELLERS' MARKET

MARK-ON   The difference between the cost, and the retail price of an item as originally established. Sometimes called INITIAL MARKUP. See: ORIGINAL RETAIL

MARKOV CHAIN   A system wherein the probabilities associated with a set of events creates a new set of probabilities of subsequent events. A Markov chain process may continue over several stages. It is frequently used to assist decision-makers in choosing among several alternatives. Because the charting of the process produces a tree-shaped diagram with branches, the finished diagram is often called a decision tree.

MARKOV PROCESS   Same as: MARKOV CHAIN

MARKUP   (1) The percent of cost which gross profit is. (2) Sometimes used by definition to mean the percent of selling price which gross profit is. See: MARGIN, MARK-ON

MARKUP CANCELLATIONS   In the RETAIL accounting method, decreases in ADDITIONAL MARKUPS that do not reduce the sales prices of merchandise below ORIGINAL RETAIL.

MASLOW'S HIERARCHY OF NEEDS   Psychologist Dr. Abraham H. Maslow postulated a rank order of importance in human needs of five levels, suggesting that individuals seek to satisfy lower-level needs before higher-level needs become active. MOTIVATION at any time comes from the lowest level of need that is dominant because of a deprivation, which may be temporary. The five are physiological, safety, social, egoistic, and self-actualization. Also see: The TRIO OF NEEDS, power, affiliation, and achievement, which are often considered independent of the other five, although they may be subsumed within the other five. See in addition: MASLOW'S THEORY

MASLOW'S THEORY   Psychologist Dr. Abraham H. Maslow has advanced a THEORY, now quite generally accepted, that all behavior is the result of the unsatisfied needs which create TENSION and then activity to satisfy the needs. He has defined a five-level hierarchy as follows: 1- Physiological needs, or those most basic, necessary to sustain life and well-being; 2- Safety needs, or protection from the world around us, physical and mental security, and a fair chance in life; 3- Social needs, or love, friendship, companionship, and acceptance by others; 4- Esteem needs, or recognition, self-confidence, self-respect, appreciation; 5- Self-actualization needs, or the fulfillment of one's potential in life. See: MASLOW'S HIERARCHY OF NEEDS

MASS COMMUNICATION   The delivery of a large number of an identical message simultaneously by various MEDIA. In contrast to personal or individual communication.

MASS DISPLAY   A display off-shelf, made up of a large quantity of product arranged to attract attention and to induce customer SELF-SERVICE.

MASSED RESERVE   A special case of POSTPONEMENT which says that, CETERIS PARIBUS, MARKETING costs are minimized by deferring the commitment of a unit of material to a specific use for as long a time as possible. Involves STOCKS of goods held for a group of MIDDLEMEN or users by a few selected agencies rather than each firm itself.

MASS MAGAZINE   A MAGAZINE of large CIRCULATION, not directed toward a select, specific AUDIENCE and which is widely accepted by all types of people. See: CLASS MAGAZINE

MASS MEDIUM   An ADVERTISING MEDIUM widely accepted by all types of people.

MASS MERCHANDISER   A subject of continuing study by the A.C. Nielsen Company, which specifies it to be an outlet presenting a discount image, handling at least three merchandise LINES, and having a floor space of 10,000 or more square feet.

MASTERPAK   A PACKAGE containing a certain number of smaller or individual packages.

MASTHEAD   That part of a page in a PUBLICATION which contains the official heading of the publication, names of key personnel, and in some instances information about the publication's POLICIES.

MAT   Short form for: Matrix. An advertisement or a portion of an advertisement in mold form that the MEDIUM can use to reproduce the advertisement in a form suitable for printing. It resembles baked cardboard in appearance. See: FLONG, MAT SERVICE, STEREOTYPE

MATERIALS CONTROLLER   This title is usually given to the person who is charged with the physical custody of all reserve stocks. It is his responsibility to be sure issuance is properly authorized and that correct records are maintained. Usually initiates REQUISITIONS that lead to the purchase of stock items   Same as: TOOL-CRIB SUPERVISOR

MATERIALS HANDLING INSTITUTE, INC.   See: MHI

MATERIALS MANAGEMENT   In a typical company this would probably include all activities involving materials of all sorts except design, manufacture, or facilities for repair and maintenance. Inspection of goods received may or may not be included, but a strong argument can be made for the efficiency which comes from inclusion. Today generally encompasses PURCHASING.

MATERIALS REQUIREMENTS PLANNING   A technique for safely controlling inventory balance under conditions of discontinuous production caused by DEMAND that is virtually unpredictable, so that EOQ formulae are not efficient or even practical. Same as: MRP

MATERIALS USAGE CURVE   A curve used to chart and to depict more readily what improvement may be expected as buying economies occur and as experience in the manufacturing process reduces SCRAP rates.

MATHEMATICAL MODEL   Usually an attempt to construct an experimental situation for analytical purposes by proposing the quantification of key variables. May be used as an aid to FORECASTING when the values of the appropriate PARAMETERS are determinable. See: ANALYTICAL MODEL, MODEL

MATRIX   (1) Same as: MAT. (2) A device for problem-solving by placing data in rows and columns for mathematical treatment.

MAT SERVICE   A service supplied by some commercial organizations making available for a fee ready-made MATS on a large variety of subjects in verbal and pictorial form.

MATTER   Type or other elements, assembled for printing. See: DEAD MATTER, LEADED MATTER, EDITORIAL MATTER, LIVE MATTER, SOLID MATTER, STANDING MATTER

MAXIMAX CRITERION   The directive to select that alternative which maximizes the maximum PAYOFF. See: MAXIMIN CRITERION

MAXIMIL RATE   A newspaper's MILLINE RATE calculated by using its highest line or space rate. See: MINIMIL

MAXIMIN CRITERION   The directive to select that alternative which maximizes the minimum PAYOFF. See: MAXIMAX CRITERION

MAXIMUM OPERATING STOCK   The largest quantity of an item that theoretically should ever be on hand under ordinary circumstances. See: EOQ

McCLELLAND MODEL   See: THEORY OF ACHIEVEMENT MOTIVATION

McGUIRE-KEOGH FAIR TRADE ENABLING ACT   Now repealed, it was an amendment to the FEDERAL TRADE COMMISSION ACT. In addition to exempting from all ANTI-TRUST LAWS any interstate contract fixing retail prices in states where intrastate contracts are allowed, confining this exemption to products in open competition and forbidding agreements among competitors, it permitted enforcement of interstate contracts against all the DEALERS in a state where such a contract had been signed by any one of them. See: FAIR TRADE

MDS   Abbreviation for: Multidimensional Scaling, a recent development in MARKETING RESEARCH which uses the PRODUCT SPACE concept but with actual PRODUCTS rather than characteristics or ATTRIBUTES, attempting to infer from the similarities found among the products and their relative positions in the space what it is that CONSUMERS prefer. As a numerical procedure, it lends itself well to computer techniques. While not much has been done in an applicational way as yet, there appears to be some promise for the future in this approach to ordering and analyzing consumer preferences.

MEAN   See: AVERAGE (1), MEDIAN, MODE

MEASUREMENT RATE   Involves the ship's option to define a ton of freight as 2,240 pounds or 40 cubic feet, whichever produces the greater revenue.

MEASURES OF CENTRAL TENDENCY   See: MEAN, MEDIAN, MODE   Compare with: MEASURES OF DISPERSION

MEASURES OF DISPERSION   Methods for measuring the extent of DISPERSION in a collection of measurements. See: COEFFICIENT OF VARIATION, RANGE, STANDARD DEVIATION

MEAT INSPECTION ACT   A Federal law which requires that the slaughtering, packing, and canning plants shipping meat across state lines be inspected by veterinarians from the Department of Agriculture. Animals are inspected before, and carcasses after, slaughter. Pure meat is stamped "U.S. Government Inspected" and released for sale. For a fee, meat packers may also have official grades stamped on the carcasses.

MECHANICAL RECORDER METHOD   A means of measuring BROADCAST AUDIENCE size by program which uses a device affixed to the set with the consent of the set owner, which automatically registers when the set is on to what station it is tuned and how long it stays there. It can be hooked in directly to a recording center for fast counts. While not subject to human error, such devices are not only costly to install, but tell only that the set is on, not how many viewers are involved, if any. Yet, many advertisers seem to find the results definitive. Often used in a MARKET in conjunction with DIARY or TELEPHONE COINCIDENTAL METHODS in other markets. Called AUDIMETER by the A.C. Nielsen Company, ARBITRON by ARB. See: PERSONAL INTERVIEW METHOD

MECHANIZATION   The substitution of machines for manual labor.

MEDIA BUYING SERVICE   An organization which specializes in purchasing print space or broadcast time for a SPONSOR according to the sponsor's plan. A relatively new specialist, it is becoming generally accepted as frequently more efficient than a department in the sponsor's organization. It is usually given a requirement to fill, such as 200 POINTS in FRINGE TIME. See: BOUTIQUE, RATING POINTS

MEDIA COVERAGE   Same as: REACH

MEDIA MIX   The combination of the various MEDIA to be used in an ADVERTISING CAMPAIGN.

MEDIAN   The middle number in an ARRAY. Divides the distribution into two halves. See: MEAN, MODE

MEDIA SUPPORT   The entire complex of ADVERTISING MEDIA which may be used to back up a promotion. See: MEDIA MIX

MEDIUM (1) Any class of vehicle, or the vehicle itself, used to deliver an ADVERTISING message. See: ADVERTISING MEDIUM (2) The method and tools used by an artist. See: ARTIST'S MEDIUM

MEGALOPOLIS The area created by the merger of adjacent METROPOLITAN AREAS. The result is really a Supercity with many social and economic problems. The Atlantic Seaboard Megalopolis extends from Boston to Norfolk, over 600 miles, and is beginning to merge with the Great Lakes Megalopolis. Same as: Interurbia

MEGASELLING Newly preferred terminology for "Big Ticket Selling." Generally means any selling involving orders of relatively large money amounts.

MEMBERSHIP GROUP A REFERENCE GROUP of which an individual is actually a member, e.g., family, club, team.

MEMORANDUM TERMS A special form of FUTURE DATING in which the title to the merchandise passes to the BUYER who assumes all the risks of ownership, but any unsold portion of the merchandise may be returned to the seller without payment. Frequently found where items are to be introduced on an experimental basis. See: CONSIGNMENT TERMS

MENTAL SET See: SET

MERCANTILE CREDIT Deferred payment arrangements between seller and buyer, both of whom are MERCHANT MIDDLEMEN. See: CREDIT, TERMS OF SALE

MERCANTILE CUSTOMER Any MERCHANT MIDDLEMAN.

MERCANTILISM A political end economic philosophy prevalent until about the 19th Century, but now discredited, that precious metals are the most important form of wealth and that an excess of exports over imports is the way to increase the inventory of such metals held by a country. To achieve this goal public control was necessary over prices, wages, place of work, type of work, etc. Many historians attribute to this philosophy importance as a factor resulting in the loss of the Colonies by England. See: KAMERALISM

MERCHANDISE-ACCEPTANCE CURVE Same as: ARC OF FASHION

MERCHANDISE BROKER Essentially the equivalent of: BROKER

MERCHANDISE BUDGET Used mainly in RETAILING, this denotes a plan in dollar terms of specified activities involving merchandise for a definite period of time. Usually includes a projection of sales, inventories, markdowns, discounts, stock shortages, expenses, returns, and controllable net profit. Provides not only a course for future action, but also a yardstick for evaluating performance as it progresses.

MERCHANDISE CAR A railroad car containing several LESS-THAN-CARLOAD shipments.

MERCHANDISE MANAGER An executive responsible for the MERCHANDISING activities of one or a number of different types of goods in various selling departments in RETAILING. If the STORE or CHAIN is large, there may be an individual position of supervising even unrelated departments. Such a position is often called "Divisional Merchandise Manager."

MERCHANDISE MART A permanent building devoted to continuous display of merchandise by vendors, but not usually open to CONSUMERS. May be specialized to one type of goods, such as furniture or toys.

MERCHANDISER Any display unit designed to present certain merchandise for immediate sale. Usually offered by manufacturers to RETAILERS to assist them in MERCHANDISING specific products. An effective merchandiser will have been designed for most advantageous storage/display of the products. See: POP ADVERTISING

MERCHANDISE RESOURCE Used in RETAILING to denote a source of supply from

which salable and reliable merchandise can be bought on a recurring basis
with a minimum of complications over a lengthy period of time. May be
a manufacturer, farmer, or MIDDLEMAN. See: RESOURCE

MERCHANDISING   The activities of manufacturers and MIDDLEMEN which are designed to adjust the merchandise produced or offered for sale to achieve
maximum customer acceptance.

MERCHANDISING BUS   A regular transit bus converted into a mobile showcase
to display products. Especially useful during the height of an ADVERTIS-
ING CAMPAIGN because it permits the presentation directly to the AUDIENCE,
thus tying the IMPACTS of the various MEDIA together.

MERCHANDISING GROUP   A number of the members of a COOPERATIVE CHAIN joined
together under a common name to facilitate advertising and promotion.
Full benefit of this arrangement is achieved when the group members identify with one another with like store appearance, and join fully in price
and product programs.

MERCHANDISING THE ADVERTISING   Informing the trade and the firm's SALES-
MEN and departments when and where the ADVERTISING will appear, usually
accompanied by reprints. Sometimes salespersons are given elaborate
promotion folders to use in informing customers of the nature of coming
campaigns. See: CAMPAIGN PLAN

MERCHANTISM   The concept which stresses the merchants' obligations to the
customers, the what they must do _for_ rather than _to_ their customers. Involves services in a major way, especially with respect to product knowledge. See: CONSUMERISM, MERCHANDISING

MERCHANT MIDDLEMAN   A MIDDLEMAN who takes title to GOODS while performing
MARKETING FUNCTIONS.

MERCHANT WHOLESALER   A MIDDLEMAN who, on his own account, buys and then
sells GOODS mainly to those who buy for resale or to facilitate the operating requirements of a business. See: RETAILER, WHOLESALER

MERGER   A type of acquisition in which one company is absorbed into another,
thereby ceasing to exist as a separate entity. See: CELLER-KEFAUVER
ANTI-MERGER ACT

MESOKURTIC   Descriptive of a FREQUENCY CURVE in which the measurements
charted are only moderately concentrated around a particular number.
Such a curve is characterized by a modest height and a well-rounded shape.
See: KURTOSIS

METAL SERVICE CENTER   See: METAL WAREHOUSE, STEEL SERVICE CENTER

METAL WAREHOUSE   A specialized type of INDUSTRIAL DISTRIBUTOR which accounts
for about 20% of the total steel tonnage. It operates on the differential
between mill prices for standard lots and smaller quantities. It deals
primarily in shapes, plates, bars, tubing, and tool steel. Usually able
to deliver on a next day basis. It will cut and shear to order. There
is a trend toward maintaining supplies in other metals too, such as brass,
copper, and aluminum. About 1,400 locations service metals users.

METAMARKETING   An approach to the study of MARKETING as a field by focusing all social, ethical, scientific, and business experience on marketing,
thus forming an integration of experience with the human personality.

METRIC TON   See: CARGO TONNAGE

METROMARKET   CENTRAL CITY and SUBURBIA from which a RETAIL STORE attracts
a major proportion of its CUSTOMERS

METROPOLITAN AREA   See: SMSA

METROPOLITAN RING   Same as: BALANCE OF AREA

MG   Abbreviation for: MAKEGOOD

MHI   Abbreviation for: Materials Handling Institute, Inc., a national trade association of United States manufacturers of materials handling systems, equipment, and/or components. Founded in 1945 to promote education in the use of materials handling equipment, its more than 320 members support trade shows, conferences, financial grants to teachers of related matters, and a wide assortment of literature and films. Its College-Industry Committee on Materials Handling Education is financed by the Institute and receives staff assistance, but is otherwise an independent organization cooperating with and acting jointly with a number of other professional societies and organizations.

MIAC   Abbreviation for: Marketing Information and Analysis Center, a separate unit often established within a firm to gather, evaluate, edit, index, abstract, analyze, search out, program, and cause to be stored for retrieval, pertinent data for management's various uses.

MICR   Abbreviation for: Magnetic Ink Character Recognition, a process whereby a computer system can read letters and numbers printed in a stylized type face and with a special magnetic ink. Widely used by banks for automated check handling.

MICROANALYTIC SALES MODEL   A way of portraying the sales process by letting total sales be the product of the number of buyers in the MARKET, the percent who buy from the firm, and the average rate of purchase. Numerous STRATEGY alternatives may be exposed using this approach. See: MACRO-SALES MODEL, MICROBEHAVIORAL SALES MODEL, MICROCOMPONENT SALES MODEL

MICROBEHAVIORAL SALES MODEL   A way of portraying the sales process by focusing on the individual customer's knowledge, ATTITUDES, behavior toward products, and environmental factors affecting him so that the probability of his purchase may be projected. See: MACROSALES MODEL, MICROANALYTIC SALES MODEL, MICROCOMPONENT SALES MODEL

MICROBRIDGE   A shortened version of MINIBRIDGE, introduced in 1977. It involves import-export shipments which originate or terminate at specified inland United States points. See: LANDBRIDGE, MINIBRIDGE

MICROCOMPONENT SALES MODEL   A way of portraying the sales process by showing sales made up of additive components, each of which may be subjected to separate analysis. Such variables may be sales by product, or by customer, or by SALESMAN, etc. See: MACROSALES MODEL, MICROANALYTIC SALES MODEL, MICROBEHAVIORAL SALES MODEL

MICRO-MARKETING   MARKETING from the marketing manager's point of view, the specific objectives and activities of the individual firm. See: MACRO-MARKETING

MIDDLEMAN   Any individual or business firm operating between the producer or seller and the CONSUMER or INDUSTRIAL USER for the purpose of passing title to GOODS and being paid for this service. See: FUNCTIONAL MIDDLE-MAN, MERCHANT MIDDLEMAN

MIDDLE MANAGEMENT   Consists of those ECHELONS in the organization where significant decisions are expected of all types short of those establishing POLICIES. These are usually reserved to TOP MANAGEMENT. See: BOTTOM MANAGEMENT

MIDDLE-OF-MONTH DATING   Same as: M.O.M.

MIDDLE-OF-MONTH TERMS   Same as: M.O.M.

MILESTONES OF LIFE   Said to occur when a person passes from one stage of the LIFE CYCLE to another stage.

MILITARY RETAILER   Same as: COMMISSARY STORE, but operated on a military base by the military.

MILL BASE SYSTEM   A pricing system in which prices are quoted for delivery at the point of production with the buyer to pay freight from that point. Differs from FOB in that sometimes the buyer may have to pay charges to get his purchase loaded on the carrier which is to do the transporting.

MILLINE RATE   Used only to compare the relative cost of ADVERTISING among alternative MEDIA units, it is the cost of presenting one AGATE LINE to one million readers. The formula is:

$$\frac{1,000,000 \times \text{line rate}}{\text{Quantity of CIRCULATION}} = \text{milline rate}$$

MILLING IN TRANSIT   A privilege offered by TRANSPORTATION companies which allows materials to be halted for processing on their way to a destination without any or a very small increase in the through rate.

MILL MARKET   Same as: SPINNER'S MARKET

MILL NET RETURN   The amount the factory receives for an item sold on a DELIVERED PRICE basis after the actual freight cost to the factory is deducted from the price. See: FREIGHT ABSORBED, PHANTOM FREIGHT

MILL SUPPLY HOUSE   A type of INDUSTRIAL DISTRIBUTOR handling as many as 20,000 items in over 600 product lines such as fasteners, bearings, fittings, tools, beltings, valves, and metal rods, bars, and tubing.

MINERALS YEARBOOK   See: CENSUS OF MINERAL INDUSTRIES

MINIBRIDGE   An arrangement by which shippers in CONTAINERS from the East Coast of the United States to the Far East send the items by rail to the West Coast where the containers are transferred to ships for the journey across the Pacific Ocean. Cost to shippers is the same as the all-water route through the Panama Canal, but is a few days quicker, and pickup is more frequent to most PORTS. See: LANDBRIDGE

MINI-LANDBRIDGE   Same as: MINIBRIDGE

MINI-LASH   Small, feeder-type BARGE-carrying vessel. See: LASH

MINIMAX REGRET CRITERION   The directive to select that alternative which offers the minimum opportunity loss.

MINIMIL   A MILLINE RATE based on a NEWSPAPER'S lowest rate. See: MAXIMIL

MINI UNIT TRAINS   UNIT TRAINS of 12 to 25 cars moving between two points while by-passing intermediate TERMINALS. Permits a two-day turnaround on equipment as compared with 10 days to two weeks in regular service, thus reducing costs.

MIRROR RESPONSE TECHNIQUE   A SALESMANSHIP technique used in dealing with OBJECTIONS. The SALESPERSON restates what the PROSPECT is understood to have said. This allows the prospect to reconsider the statement and turns up any deviations in mutual understanding. Also called: Repeating Technique

MIS   (1) Abbreviation for: Total-Marketing Information System, the putting of incoming raw data into computers or other electronic data processing devices in such a way that it can easily be retrieved as needed, and so that individual, detailed bits of data can be combined for special reports. Many firms are already using models to help in decision-making. Some students of this activity predict that the biggest value in the future will be at the line management level where decisions are extremely critical to make or break the profit goals set in the higher management levels. (2) Abbreviation for: Management Information System, similar in function to that in (1) but more inclusive.

MISREDEMPTION   Applied to the incidence of error and fraud in offering for redemption to the manufacturer COUPONS presented to or obtained by RETAILERS as the result of a COUPONING program.

MISSIONARY SALESMAN   An employee of a manufacturer who often works with a

MIDDLEMAN'S SALESMEN for the purpose of assisting them in introducing new products or to render technical advice. Frequently works alone through a territory when primarily engaged in persuading the use of various DEALER AIDS, leaving samples, or explaining the use of his firm's products. See: DETAIL MAN

MIT   Abbreviation for: MILLING IN TRANSIT

MIXED CAR   Shipped in the same car are commodities to which otherwise a variety of rates would apply, as in a POOL CAR, but the whole shipment moves at the highest c.l. rate applicable to any of the commodities.

MLM   Abbreviation for: Multi-Level Merchandiser, any organization which is VERTICALLY INTEGRATED as to MIDDLEMEN, whether it is RETAIL- or WHOLESALE-directioned. The MARKET POWER of such an organization is stronger to the extent that final users accept goods by GENERIC name rather than BRAND.

MNA   Abbreviation for: Multi-Network Area, a group of 30 MARKETS where programs from the three major NETWORKS can be received live. This includes about 50% of the population in TELEVISION HOMES.

MNC   Abbreviation for: MULTINATIONAL CORPORATION

MOBILE FRANCHISE   A conventional FRANCHISE except that the franchisee dispenses his products or service from a vehicle which is moved from place to place.

MODE   That number which occurs most frequently in an ARRAY. An array is said to be unimodal when there is but one number which occurs with more frequency than any other, bimodal when two different numbers have equal and maximum frequencies, and multimodal when more than two numbers have equal and maximum frequencies. See: MEAN, MEDIAN

MODEL   A representation of a specific reality, usually chosen to be broadly relevant in portraying some aspect in which the model constructor will be interested as an ongoing device. Examples: organization chart, behavior patterns, forces affecting GNP. See: ANALYTICAL MODEL, DESCRIPTIVE MODEL, LOGICAL FLOW MODEL, MATHEMATICAL MODEL, PROSE MODEL, SIMULATION MODEL

MODEL STOCK   Applicable mainly to SHOPPING GOODS requiring a degree of selection at each stock control point, it is an outline of the composition of an ideal stock stated as to factors of characteristics or ASSORTMENTS, e.g., size and color, usually indicating optimum quantities which reflect a balance as compared with expected sales. Used generally for FASHION GOODS, for which a BASIC STOCK often cannot be set because of the speed of change present.

MODIFIED REBUY   A purchase which would be a STRAIGHT REBUY were it not for the need for additional information or analysis which experience has shown to be necessary. May take as much of a BUYER'S time, or even more, as NEW-TASK BUYING.

MODULAR FIXTURES   Showcases, wall cases, desks with various work places attached, wall shelving, and the like, constructed in units of standard dimensions. Because the units, called modules, fit together and are moved easily, use of these gives great flexibility of arrangement.

MODULAR SERVICE AGENCY   Same as: A LA CARTE AGENCY

MODULES   See: MODULAR FIXTURES

MOM   Abbreviation for: middle-of-the-month dating. The 15th and the last day of the month are used as cut-off dates. All invoices dated before the 15th of the month are considered dated the 15th; for invoices dated on and after the 15th, the credit period begins with the last day of the month. Discount and due dates are counted as from one of the two cut-off dates.

MOM AND POP STORE   A small RETAIL STORE generally operated by a husband-wife team with restricted capital. Often applied as a generic term to any very small, neighborhood RETAILER, especially in the food business.

MONETARY POLICY   The various techniques employed at any one time to control the money supply in its several forms, and the level of interest rates both long-period and short-period, in an attempt to control the economy's rate of progress. Highly interactive with FISCAL POLICY.

MONEY INCOME   Cash flow in over a period of time. See: REAL INCOME

MONEY LOSS RISK   See: RISK REDUCTION

MONOPOLISTIC COMPETITION   A structure of a MARKET in which many FIRMS offer items of a similar but not identical nature. Each firm tries to differentiate its offering in such a way as to win acceptance over competitors. Generally characterized by a down-sloping DEMAND CURVE. See: MONOPOLY, OLIGOPOLY

MONOPOLY   A condition of the MARKET in which there is but one source of supply for a given good or class of product, and there are no acceptable substitutes. See: MONOPOLISTIC COMPETITION, MONOPSONY, OLIGOPOLY

MONOPSONY   A MARKET condition in which there is but one buyer for a certain product or class of products. See: MONOPOLY, OLIGOPSONY

MONOTYPE   A typesetting machine which casts each CHARACTER separately and assembles them into lines. See: LINOTYPE

MONTAGE   (1) The combining of a number of photographs or drawings into a single illustration. (2) In television, a series of scenes shown in rapid succession by using DISSOLVE techniques.

MONTHLY LABOR REVIEW   This monthly publication of the Bureau of Labor Statistics includes data on labor turnover, earnings and hours worked, wholesale and retail prices, strikes and other work stoppages, and employment and unemployment.

MONTHLY RETAIL TRADE   See: CENSUS OF BUSINESS

MONTHLY SELECTED SERVICES RECEIPTS   See: CENSUS OF BUSINESS

MONTHLY WHOLESALE TRADE   See: CENSUS OF BUSINESS

MORALE   A mental attitude that leads employees freely and eagerly to subordinate their personal objectives to effect the cooperation necessary to the achieving of the company's objectives.

MORES   Those NORMS which, embodying a group or a society's basic moral values, specify behavior enforced by the society through legal action or a system of social sanctions. See: FOLKWAYS

MORPHOLOGICAL BOXES   Three-dimensional matrices designed to force breakdown of MARKETS into all relevant elements so that combinations may be discerned. Essentially the same as a cubical MARKET GRID.

MORTISE   An area cut out of a printing plate to permit insertion of other elements.

MOTIVATION   (1) The psychological manifestation that appears to an observer as activity directed toward a goal. (2) All the forces that activate human behavior. See: MOTIVE

MOTIVATION RESEARCH   The study of why people respond as they do to various MARKET situations. Understanding is sought through the use of psychiatric and psychological techniques. Its findings are not yet accepted in full as valid. See: DYNAMIC RESEARCH

MOTIVE   Anything which makes a person act as he does, such as the need for peer approval, fear, love of family, etc. See: APPEAL, PATRONAGE MOTIVES, PHYSIOLOGICAL MOTIVES, PRIMARY MOTIVES, PRODUCT MOTIVES, SECONDARY MOTIVES, SOCIAL MOTIVES

MOTOR VEHICLE MANUFACTURERS ASSOCIATION OF THE UNITED STATES, INC.
Same as: MVMA

MOVEMENT   Same as: Eye Direction, Flow, GAZE MOTION

MOVERS' & WAREHOUSEMEN'S ASSOCIATION OF AMERICA   An organization of about
600 small, independent movers in interstate commerce, comprising around
half the number registered with the ICC. Its primary function is to pub-
lish rate tariffs for its membership with the object of maintaining these
tariffs in accordance with the regulations of the ICC. It renders varied
services to its members.

MPA   Abbreviation for: Magazine Publishers Association, the organization
of CONSUMER MAGAZINE publishers.

MR   Abbreviation for: MOTIVATION RESEARCH

MRO ITEMS   Abbreviation for: MAINTENANCE, REPAIR, and OPERATING SUPPLIES
items.

MRP   Abbreviation for: MATERIALS REQUIREMENTS PLANNING

MSEC   Abbreviation for: Millisecond, 1/1,000 of a second. Applications in
ADP.

MSI   Abbreviation for: Marketing Science Institute, a nonprofit, research
organization in the field of MARKETING, founded in 1962 by a group of
national business leaders and associated in 1968 with the Harvard Business
School, it now includes member companies, academicians, and professionals.
Its research programs cover all areas of the marketing field, generally on
a project basis, and the findings are made known. Besides the research
activity it sponsors mini-conferences, workshops and other activities in
cooperation with interested organizations. It publishes a newsletter, a
series of Research Briefs, and numerous books and reports on major issues
in the marketing discipline.

MULTICHOTOMOUS QUESTION   See: FIXED-ALTERNATIVE QUESTION

MULTIDIMENTIONAL SCALING   Same as: MDS

MULTI-LEVEL MERCHANDISER   Same as: MLM

MULTIMODAL   See: MODE

MULTINATIONAL FIRM   A FIRM that maintains production and distribution
facilities in more than one country for the purpose of getting the most
advantageous entry into the MARKETS of the host and other countries.
See: INTERNATIONAL FIRM

MULTINATIONALISM   Sometimes applied to the activities of FIRMS engaged in
international trade by means of which they operate some or many of their
manufacturing and distribution facilities abroad to take advantage of
foreign labor, executive talent, and more favorable financial climate.

MULTI-NETWORK AREA   Same as: MNA

MULTIPLE BRAND ENTRIES   A competitive STRATEGY which aims to exclude others
from a MARKET by producing the same product or the applicable variants of
the product under different BRANDS. Often most effective in conjunction
with other strategies. See: PRODUCT DIFFERENTIATION

MULTIPLE CORRELATION   An analysis of the effect of several INDEPENDENT
VARIABLES on one DEPENDENT VARIABLE. Similar in purpose to simple
CORRELATION but the statistical calculations are much more complex. The
COEFFICIENT OF MULTIPLE CORRELATION (R) is obtained by expanding the
equation. The complexity comes from the necessity to weight the factors
included in the equation to determine their varying degrees of influence.
The tedious calculations are made managable by the speed of the computer's
operation. Significant as a tool in MARKETING RESEARCH. PARAMETRIC.
See: CANONICAL CORRELATION ANALYSIS, DISCRIMINANT ANALYSIS

MULTIPLE PURCHASING INFLUENCE   The general situation in the INDUSTRIAL MARKET in which a number of persons must approve the buying of an important item. See: KBI

MULTIPLE-SOURCE PURCHASING   The practice of buying from more than one supplier those items considered to be of major significance to the FIRM.

MULTIPLE-UNIT PACKAGING   The practice of combining a number of units of a product into one wrapping or container so that the buyer will be encouraged to take the number as a unit item. Example: six-packs. Intended to build home inventories in the belief that what is on hand will be used.

MULTIPLE-UNIT PRICING   The practice of pricing items so many for a price, e.g., 3 for 98¢, 7 for $1, etc. Once the most common practice in SUPERMARKETS, it is generally used now for special offerings. See: UNIT PRICING

MULTIPLIER EFFECT   The amplified effect of business investment on national income which results from the fact that an increase in net investment will increase national income by an amount greater than the increase in net investment: it "multiplies" by some numerical coefficient. This is because a round of spending touches off a series of rounds of spending inasmuch as the money spent moves through many hands, but in decreasing amounts as the chain progresses as some is set aside for savings here and there. See: PROPENSITY TO CONSUME

MULTI-STAGE SAMPLING   See: CLUSTER SAMPLING

MULTI-VISION SIGN   Similar in general to the PAINTED BULLETIN, but arranged in louvres turned simultaneously by electric motors to deliver different messages about the advertiser's product or service. Usually the louvres are three-sided. Same as: Tri-Vision Sign

MUTUAL ADVERTISING AGENCY NETWORK   Same as: MAAN

MVMA   Abbreviation for: Motor Vehicle Manufacturers Association of the United States, Inc., the trade association for U.S. car and truck makers. Its member companies produce over 99% of all domestic vehicles. The Association's interest deals with all the issues that are central to the economic health of this country and the personal mobility of every American. During the Association's over 75 years of existence it has represented the motor vehicle INDUSTRY on a wide range of topics to the general public, the academic community, and to local, state, Federal, and foreign governments.

NAB   (1) Abbreviation for: National Association of Broadcasters, the organization of RADIO and TELEVISION stations and NETWORKS. (2) Abbreviation for: Newspaper Advertising Bureau, Inc., an organization devoted to developing research data, training programs, creative suggestions, workshops and publications in the NEWSPAPER field.

NAFB   Abbreviation for: National Association of Farm Broadcasters, whose members consist of those radio stations which have a full-time farm director. Member stations, about 150, cover 75% of U.S. counties and about 83% of the farm operators. The Association's major purposes are to promote this MEDIUM to advertisers, to provide the FARM operator with a respected, reliable source of pertinent information to help improve farm operation, and to run many events designed especially to be a forum for farm operators and farm suppliers.

NAFTA   Abbreviation for: New Zealand-Australia Free Trade Agreement, originally signed in 1965 and renewed for another ten years in 1976.

NAILED DOWN   Merchandise ADVERTISED at an extremely low price but which the STORE makes every effort not to sell. See: BAIT ADVERTISING

NAM   Abbreviation for: National Association of Manufacturers, a voluntary organization of industrial and business FIRMS of various sizes devoted to

supporting and encouraging individual freedom. Through its Marketing
Committee it works to preserve a competitive, free-choice market system and
to promote improvement in manufacturer-CONSUMER relationships.

NAMA   Acronym for: National Agri-Marketing Association, an organization of
over 2,000 people directly and indirectly involved in marketing products
and services to America's farm community. It began over 25 years ago as
the CAAAA (Central Area Agriculture Advertising Association). Its name
was changed as its interests widened beyond ADVERTISING to include FORE-
CASTING, educational activities, communications to the CONSUMER, and various
regular publications and career development coordination programs with
colleges, including scholarships and summer internships.

NAMBO   Acronym for: National Association of Motor Bus Owners, the national
trade association for the intercity bus INDUSTRY. Established in 1926,
its members today provide over 90% of the intercity bus transportation in
the United States. It also has numerous associate members engaged in the
manufacture of buses and related lines. Its main objectives are to improve the transportation service rendered by its members, to promote BUS
PACKAGE EXPRESS and mail, to promote the construction of better-routed
and graded roads made with improved materials, and to influence uniform
and equitable legislation and regulation affecting the industry.

NAME ADVERTISING   Same as: REMINDER ADVERTISING, RETENTIVE ADVERTISING

NAME SLUG   Same as: LOGOTYPE

NANOSECOND   One billionth of a second. Applications in ADP. Same as: NSEC

NAPA   Acronym for: North Atlantic Ports Association, Inc., organized in
1950 as an outgrowth of its precursor, the Association of Maritime Terminal Operators, Atlantic Ports. Its prime objective is the development of
its member ports along sound economic lines. It includes various interests
involved with marine terminals in the North Atlantic Range: Eastport, Maine,
to Hampton Roads, Virginia. Frequent mailings keep members informed of
rate changes by all CARRIERS, innovations in pier and WAREHOUSE design,
FOREIGN TRADE ZONE developments, and new regulations by government bodies.

NAPM   Abbreviation for: National Association of Purchasing Management, an
association of more than 100 affiliated local associations in the United
States through which the membership totals about 20,000. Organized in
1915 (until 1968 known as the National Association of Purchasing Agents),
its main objectives are to provide a forum for interchange of purchasing
ideas and to disseminate practical and authoritative information on purchasing policies, procedures, and related topics. The Association offers
a variety of services including training programs, publications, a liason
program with colleges and universities to help the academic fraternity
keep up with developments in the purchasing world, and regular reports of
surveys to reflect the trends of production and prices. It recently
introduced a certification program including courses and examinations
leading to the designation Certified Purchasing Manager (C.P.M.).

NARB   Abbreviation for: NATIONAL ADVERTISING REVIEW BOARD

NARRATIVE   In ADP, the written description of the flow of information in
the system.

NARRATIVE COPY   Usually verbal, but may be a combination of verbal and pictorial elements, this is an IMAGINATIVE APPROACH to the reader, listener,
or viewer which presents a story about how the product or service played
an important role in the life of someone with whom a member of the
AUDIENCE can IDENTIFY. This type of COPY generally consists of four parts:
the predicament or problem being faced, the discovery of the solution (provided by the product or service), the happy ending, and the transition
which ends with a direct suggestion to the audience. Once again the product or service has resolved a conflict! This technique is much used in
television COMMERCIALS. Essentially the same as: SLICE-OF-LIFE COMMERCIAL

NARROW MARKET   A MARKET condition in which DEMAND for a PRODUCT is restricted to a few firms or to a limited geographic area. See: BROAD MARKET

NARUC   Abbreviation for: National Association of Regulatory Utilities Commissioners, an organization of men and women in federal and state positions of regulatory responsibility who have joined for the purposes of
keeping regulation in step with the economics of the MARKET, promoting
uniformity of regulation among the commissioners, and cooperating with
each other. Over 65 Commissions and 230 Commissioners are included.

NARW   Abbreviation for: National Association of Refrigerated Warehouses,
an organization of about 500 members most of whom are PUBLIC REFRIGERATED
WAREHOUSES. Started in 1891, it now provides serious long-range planning,
training of personnel, and many other services including a PALLET exchange
program. It helps to support The Refrigeration Research Foundation, a
group of scientists who since 1940 have worked continuously to improve refrigeration techniques, and lately have contributed importantly to the expansion of the frozen foods INDUSTRY.

NATC   Abbreviation for: National Air Transportation Conferences, whose members are partners in service with major airlines so that passengers and
CARGO may be routed to destination from point of origin. All members are
also members of one or more of the following: Air Taxi Conference, whose
members operate small aircraft anywhere as needed and are called Air Taxi
Charter Operators; Commuter Air Carrier Conference, whose members operate
small aircraft on scheduled service between specific points and are known
as Commuter Air Carriers; and/or Cargo & Mail Conference, whose members
carry all sorts of things on small aircraft to places the major airlines
do not serve. It renders a wide variety of technical, legal, and promotional services to members.

NATIONAL ACCOUNT   (1) Used by some firms to designate a CUSTOMER which has
locations in more than one MAJOR TRADING AREA.   (2) Essentially the same
as: HOUSE ACCOUNT

NATIONAL ADVERTISING   (1) That kind of ADVERTISING the basic message of
which is "Buy my product (or service) somewhere." (2) Advertising placed
in newspapers by firms who present the message as in (1) and who are most
often charged a higher rate than firms who are in business locally. Same
as: General Advertising See: LOCAL ADVERTISING, OPEN RATE, PROMOTIONAL
ADVERTISING

NATIONAL ADVERTISING REVIEW BOARD   A self-regulatory mechanism of the advertising industry which will use the Better Business Bureau organization
to implement its intent to work with the CONSUMERISM movement. $10 mil-
lion was subscribed in 1972 by major advertisers to back this program.
Four national organizations are the sponsors: American Advertising Federation, Association of National Advertisers, American Association of Advertising Agencies, and the Council of Better Business Bureaus. Its board
consists of 50 members, 30 from among the advertisers, 10 from agencies,
and 10 from the public. It will review matters of fact, truth and accuracy; adequate and relevant disclosure; deception, intentional or uninten-
tional; and precedents set by the FTC. These have all been in the various advertising codes for a long time, but now more serious attention
will be given to policing. If unable to get voluntary compliance with
its decisions, the Board will publicize its findings. See: ADVERTISING
REVIEW BOARD

NATIONAL AGRI-MARKETING ASSOCIATION   Same as: NAMA

NATIONAL AIR TAXI CONFERENCE   See: NATC

NATIONAL AIR TRANSPORTATION CONFERENCES   Same as: NATC

NATIONAL ASSOCIATION OF BROADCASTERS   Same as: NAB

NATIONAL ASSOCIATION OF ELECTRICAL DISTRIBUTORS   Same as: NAED

NATIONAL ASSOCIATION OF EXPORT MANAGEMENT COMPANIES   Same as: NEXCO

NATIONAL ASSOCIATION OF FARM BROADCASTERS   Same as: NAFB

NATIONAL ASSOCIATION OF FINISHERS OF TEXTILE FABRICS   See: ATMI

NATIONAL ASSOCIATION OF MANUFACTURERS   **Same as: NAM**

NATIONAL ASSOCIATION OF MOTOR BUS OWNERS   **Same as: NAMBO**

NATIONAL ASSOCIATION OF PURCHASING·AGENTS   See: NAPM

NATIONAL ASSOCIATION OF PURCHASING MANAGEMENT   Same as: NAPM

NATIONAL ASSOCIATION OF REFRIGERATED WAREHOUSES   Same as: NARW

NATIONAL ASSOCIATION OF REGULATORY UTILITIES COMMISSIONERS   Same as: NARUC

NATIONAL ASSOCIATION OF WHOLESALER-DISTRIBUTORS   Same as: NAW

NATIONAL BRAND   (1) A BRAND owned by a manufacturer. Same as: Manufacturer's
Brand (2) Popularly, but inaccurately, a brand familiar to CONSUMERS
because of its distribution throughout the country.

NATIONAL BUREAU OF ECONOMIC RESEARCH   Same as: NBER

NATIONAL BUSINESS AIRCRAFT ASSOCIATION, INC.   **Same as: NBAA**

NATIONAL BUSINESS COUNCIL FOR CONSUMER AFFAIRS   Same as: NBCCA

NATIONAL BUSINESS PUBLICATIONS GROUP   See: ABP

NATIONAL CABLE TELEVISION ASSOCIATION   Same as: NCTA

NATIONAL CANNED FOODS AND DRIED FRUIT BROKERS ASSOCIATION   **See: NFBA**

NATIONAL COMMITTEE ON INTERNATIONAL TRADE DOCUMENTATION   Same as: NCITD

NATIONAL COUNCIL OF PHYSICAL DISTRIBUTION MANAGEMENT   Same as: NCPDM

NATIONAL COUNCIL OF PRIVATE MOTOR TRUCK OPERATORS   See: PTC

NATIONAL FEDERATION OF TEXTILES   See: ATMI

NATIONAL FOOD BROKERS ASSOCIATION   **Same as: NFBA**

NATIONAL FOREIGN TRADE COUNCIL   Same as: NFTC

NATIONAL HIGHWAY USERS CONFERENCE   See: HIGHWAY USERS FEDERATION FOR
SAFETY AND MOBILITY

NATIONAL HOUSEWARES EXPOSITION   See: NHMA

NATIONAL HOUSEWARES MANUFACTURERS ASSOCIATION   Same as: NHMA

NATIONAL INDUSTRIAL TRAFFIC LEAGUE   Same as: NITL

NATIONAL MARKETING ADVISORY COMMITTEE   See: NBCCA

NATIONAL MICROGRAPHICS ASSOCIATION   **Same as: NMA**

NATIONAL MOTOR EQUIPMENT INTERCHANGE COMMITTEE   **See: EIA**

NATIONAL OFFICE MANAGEMENT ASSOCIATION   **See: AMS**

NATIONAL OUTDOOR ADVERTISING BUREAU   Same as: NOAB

NATIONAL PAPER BOX ASSOCIATION   Same as: NPBA

NATIONAL PLAN   A geographic plan for using MEDIA in which the intent is
to REACH the largest number of different buyers over the entire country
at the lowest cost per thousand. Used where the seller has national TRADE
CHANNELS for his product. All media can be included in the considerations
for this plan. See: LOCAL PLAN, REGIONAL PLAN, SELECTIVE PLAN

NATIONAL PREMIUM SALES EXECUTIVES   Same as: NPSE

NATIONAL RAILWAY LABOR CONFERENCE   Established in 1963 with the basic concept of improving relations between the railroads and their employees who
are represented by 34 unions. 162 railroads comprise the conference,

which speaks for them with the unions, various federal and state officials, the United States Departments of Labor and Transportation, the National Mediation Board, and the labor departments of the states. It cooperates with but is separate from the Association of American Railroads. The establishment of AMTRAK has necessitated some adjustments.

NATIONAL RAILWAY PASSENGER CORPORATION Better known as Amtrak, this public service corporation was established by Congress to sustain passenger rail service. It went into operation in May, 1971. It was given complete monopoly power until 1973, after which the ICC may delay reductions in service. Amtrak's fares are not subject to any regulation. The arrangements between Amtrak and the existing railroads for the assumption of passenger responsibility are quite complex. Whether this is the way the deteriorating train service to passengers will be improved will not be seen for some time to come. It appears that Amtrak will continue to be greatly underfunded. Its most notable success has been with the Metroliner, a 100 mph+, luxury rail service in the Northeast MEGALOPOLIS, especially in the New York City-Washington corridor, where it seems to have more acceptance than plane service. It has recently started a PACKAGE EXPRESS service. See: CONRAIL

NATIONAL RATE Same as: ONE-TIME RATE

NATIONAL SAFETY COUNCIL Same as: NSC

NATIONAL SOCIETY OF ART DIRECTORS Same as: NSAD

NATIONAL TANK TRUCK CARRIERS Same as: NTTC

NATIONAL WATERWAYS CONFERENCE An organization of persons from many kinds of businesses, it sponsors economic research, meetings, newsletters, and studies in pursuit of its objective of bettering the understanding of the public value of water transportation and water resource programs and the importance of these to the American economy.

NATIONAL WEALTH See: WEALTH (1)

NATIONAL WHOLESALER A WHOLESALER whose activities reach all or most of the nation. There are very few such wholesalers. A small number have been successful at mail order operation. See: LOCAL WHOLESALER, REGIONAL WHOLESALER

NATIONAL WOODEN PALLET & CONTAINER ASSOCIATION Same as: NWPCA

NATIONAL YELLOW PAGES SERVICE ASSOCIATION Same as: NYPSA

NATURAL COST ANALYSIS One of the cost and profit analysis techniques used in PERFORMANCE RESEARCH, it is based on NATURAL EXPENSES. Has limited capacity to reveal the profit PAYOFF of MARKETING activities.

NATURAL EXPENSES A firm's expense items classified according to the nature of the cost rather than the reason for which it was incurred. This is the simplest type of cost analysis and requires an Income Statement. See: FUNCTIONAL COST ANALYSIS

NATURAL FOLD A method of folding a DIRECT ADVERTISEMENT so that the continuity of the message is emphasized as the piece is unfolded.

NATURAL PRODUCTS Those RAW MATERIALS the supply of which is fixed fundamentally by nature. See: FARM PRODUCTS

NAW Abbreviation for: National Association of Wholesaler-Distributors, an organization of over 40,000 MERCHANT WHOLESALERS and over 100 affiliated national associations, from its founding in 1946 devoted to making and distributing studies pertinent to WHOLESALING, to representing the INDUSTRY in legislative matters pertaining to DISTRIBUTION both PHYSICAL and MARKET, to publishing regular informational newsletters, and to running meetings of various sorts both general and specific. Over 3,300 companies are individual FIRM members. Because it involves so many commodity LINES, its activities are very broad. Through its subsidiary, Distribution Codes, Inc., the Association has been instrumental in developing standard product numbering throughout the economy.

NBAA Abbreviation for: National Business Aircraft Association, Inc., started in 1947. This organization of FIRMS operating aircraft as an aid in the conduct of their businesses has worked successfully for numerous regulatory improvements. It provides many services to its members including pertinent bulletins and manuals, training meetings and conferences, and representation before government agencies regarding the effects of proposed legislation.

NBCCA Abbreviation for: National Business Council for Consumer Affairs, successor to the Commerce Department's National Marketing Advisory Committee (NMAC). It is planned to have 50 chief business executives who will apply themselves to the problems of LIFE STYLES and environmental challenges as they may be reflected in advertising and promotion; packaging, labeling and information; warranties and terms of sale; product safety; performance and service; and complaints and remedies. Its exact powers and scope will be determined gradually.

NBER Abbreviation for: National Bureau of Economic Research, a private, non-profit research organization which has been preparing BUSINESS CYCLE indicators for more than 50 years. It sets the official dates of the peaks and troughs of business cycles.

NCITD Abbreviation for: National Committee on International Trade Documentation, a research organization dedicated solely to the simplification and elimination of trade documentation. Its membership includes firms and individuals from every area of business interested in international trade. It is having considerable success in getting a standard BILL OF LADING which could serve as a through bill from origin to final destination regardless of transportation modes or government involvement.

NCPDM Abbreviation for: National Council for Physical Distribution Management, an organization mainly concerned with increasing the professional dialogue in the field, developing the theory and understanding of the PHYSICAL DISTRIBUTION process, and improving the skills of its members in the industry. It publishes a quarterly bulletin and various studies, operates a volunteer speaker clearinghouse and a summer intern program, and makes two research grants available to doctoral candidates in this field.

NCTA Abbreviation for: National Cable Television Association. With a membership exceeding half of all CATV systems in the United States, this organization represents the industry in promotional, educational, political, and self-regulatory matters. It supplies interested parties with regular bulletins outlining current developments.

NEED (1) The lack of any useful thing. One is often not aware of something which could be a benefit to him. MARKETING tries to make him aware. "Need" should not be confused with "necessity." (2) Internal forces that cause activity toward specific satisfaction. Applies to persons and institutions.

NEED HIERARCHY See: MASLOW'S HIERARCHY OF NEEDS

NEGATIVE AUTHORIZATION A system of credit approval in which a list is maintained of delinquent accounts. If the customer's name is not on the list, his request for credit is approved. See: FLOOR LIMIT

NEGATIVE DEMAND A situation within a MARKET in which a significant segment of that market dislikes a PRODUCT so much that it will take measures to avoid the product.

NEGATIVE EFFECTS OF ADVERTISING See: CDNPA

NEGATIVE GROUP   Same as: NEGATIVE REFERENCE GROUP

NEGATIVE OPTION SELLING   A practice in which the CONSUMER must tell the seller by a certain date <u>not</u> to send him merchandise that he does not want. A popular procedure among book-club and record-club companies. Under current attack by consumerists who insist that it takes advantage of basic human inertia and is therefor an unfair practice. Little complaint has come from consumers.

NEGATIVE REFERENCE GROUP   A REFERENCE GROUP whose LIFE STYLE or behavior patterns one wishes to avoid.

NEGATIVE SELLING   A selling technique in which the SALESPERSON uses suggestions which would seem to discourage buying but which actually stimulate the DESIRE of the PROSPECT. Requires considerable experience before it can be used effectively. See: LOW-PRESSURE SELLING

NEGOTIATED PRICE SYSTEM   Essentially the same as: VARIABLE PRICE POLICY

NEGOTIATION   The process of give-and-take in PROCUREMENT by means of which the parties come to a mutually beneficial agreement from which a contract springs. See: HORSE TRADING

NEIGHBORHOOD CLUSTER   A group of several STORES in an otherwise residential district of a city. Mainly found are CONVENIENCE GOODS stores such as grocery, drug, and baked goods stores, and service establishments such as dry cleaners and barber shops. Patronage comes essentially from residents of the area immediately surrounding the location. See: SHOPPING CENTER

NEMO   A term used to indicate a broadcast which did not originate in the station sending it.

NETBACK   The sale of a product less OUT-OF-POCKET COSTS to move it from the manufacturing plant to the point of sale. These costs include such expenses as freight, agents' commissions, and duties. A term probably used more in export than in domestic commerce.

NET CREDIT PERIOD   The maximum time a FIRM may take to pay a bill according to the TERMS OF SALE. For example, 1/20, n/60 provides a net credit period of 60 days. After the twentieth day no discount may be taken; the bill is payable net.

NET PURCHASES   The invoice cost of goods bought plus transportation charges applicable to them, minus the sum of returns, allowances, and CASH DISCOUNTS TAKEN.

NET SALES   Total (gross) sales minus the sum of customer returns, allowances and CASH DISCOUNTS taken by customers.

NET TERMS   The TERMS OF SALE call for the billed amount of the invoice to be paid in full. No CASH DISCOUNT is to be allowed.

NET TON   Same as: SHORT TON

NETWORK   A group of broadcast stations usually affiliated by contract although some may have common ownership. They are interconnected for simultaneous broadcast of the same programs. See: BASIC STATION, BASIC NETWORK

NETWORK BROADCAST   A program sent out over a series of connected stations. See: SPOT

NEUTRAL PHILOSOPHY   A philosophy of competitive behavior under which a company chooses to exert only a moderate, but steady, competitive pressure just adequate to maintain MARKET SHARE. See: AGGRESSIVE PHILOSOPHY, PASSIVE PHILOSOPHY

NEVER-OUT LIST   A check-list of items that a firm intends must never be allowed to run out of inventory. See: BASIC STOCK, MODEL STOCK

NEW-BUYER HOLDOVER EFFECT   Essentially the same as: CUSTOMER HOLDOVER EFFECT, but with the refinement that no additional marketing expenditure is made,

yet the number of customers is higher in future periods than if no marketing expenditure is made initially.

NEW ENGLAND PAPER & PULP TRAFFIC ASSOCIATION   An organization of manufacturers of paper, paper articles, and/or woodpulp, to develop good relations
with CARRIERS so that they and its members may cooperate for maximum
efficiency. The association also provides individual services involving
adjustments, traffic patterns, tracing, claims, etc. It publishes a monthly traffic bulletin, and numerous letters of current importance.

NEWS HEADLINE   A HEADLINE communicating specific information about an innovation, or indicating that such information is to be found in the COPY.

NEWSPAPER   Issued frequently (daily or weekly), this is a timely MEDIUM,
devoted to the printed reporting of the latest developments. AUDIENCES
may be selected on a sharply geographic base or on a religious, labor,
college, Black, foreign language, financial, commercial, trade, or professional base. A daily newspaper comes closer to reaching all customers
in its area than any other ADVERTISING MEDIUM. It is also the most flexible for the advertiser.

NEWSPAPER ADVERTISING BUREAU, INC.   Same as: NAB (2)

NEWSPAPER AUDIENCE RESEARCH DATA BANK   See: ABC DATA BANK

NEWSPAPER MAGAZINE   Same as: SUPPLEMENT

NEWSPAPER STUFFER   An ADVERTISING piece that is inserted loose in a Sunday SUPPLEMENT section of a newspaper. May be a single card or may be
in book form with many pages. Same as: Free-Standing Stuffer, Giant Insert, Sheridan Stuffer, Stuffer

NEW-TASK BUYING   Occurs when a firm discovers a new requirement. The process involves the entire ramification of getting information, establishing specifications, selecting sources of supply, and creating an order
routine. See: MODIFIED REBUY, STRAIGHT REBUY

NEW ZEALAND-AUSTRALIA FREE TRADE AGREEMENT   Same as: NAFTA

NEXCO   Abbreviation for: National Association of Export Management Companies, organized in 1965 at the request of the U.S. Department of Commerce to promote the expansion of U.S. exports. Its membership must meet
strict eligibility requirements as professional international marketing
specialists experienced in all phases of export sales. It renders a
variety of services, including the development of a proposed standard contract, dissemination of information, and acting as spokesman for the members before government agencies charged with enforcing legislated export
restrictions.

NEXT TO READING MATTER   See: FULL POSITION

NFBA   Abbreviation for: National Food Brokers Association, an organization
of over 2,100 FOOD BROKERS in the United States and other countries, founded
in 1904 to provide a means of disseminating information among members and
of setting a strict member code of ethical standards. It conducts a broad
educational and informational program with colleges and other PUBLICS.
From 1904 to 1921 it was known as the National Canned Foods and Dried
Fruit Brokers Association.

NFTC   Abbreviation for: National Foreign Trade Council, a private, non-
partisan organization of U.S. companies engaged in international trade
and investment. Its continuing main objectives since its start in 1914
have been to promote American private initiative in furthering competition and free enterprise in foreign trade; to serve as an authoritative
voice of the broad spectrum of international interests represented by its
members; and to develop in consultation with business and government the
practical measures to achieve its objectives. It sponsors the annual
National Foreign Trade Convention.

NHMA Abbreviation for: National Housewares Manufacturers Association, established in 1938 with the still-major goal of providing buyers with the best possible INDUSTRY exhibits at the lowest feasible costs consistent with good management. It conducts the twice-annual National Housewares Exposition, the world's largest single-industry TRADE SHOW. It has inaugurated an every-other-year Housewares Design Award program, and conducts a series of research studies of all phases of the housewares industry.

NIELSEN RETAIL INDEX A measure of the MARKET SHARE in each geographic area for various packaged goods, derived by the A.C. Nielsen Co. from regular audits of about 1,600 food stores and about 750 drug stores.

NIELSEN STATION INDEX Reports produced by the A.C.Nielsen Company to provide measurements of AUDIENCE in individual television MARKETS. Same as: NSI

NIELSEN TELEVISION INDEX Reports prepared by the A.C.Nielsen Company that measure national AUDIENCES of all NETWORK programs.

NIFO Abbreviation for: next in, first out. A relatively new concept in the valuation of inventories, it is an attempt to reflect replacement cost more specifically in current financial statements than has been practicable in the past. See: LIFO

NITL Abbreviation for: The National Industrial Traffic League, an organization of any individual or FIRM units engaged in shipping and receiving. Founded in 1907, it has consistently advocated beneficial legislation. Presently it keeps its membership informed and updated through several regular publications, reports from numerous working committees, and special meetings. Its promulgation of "Transportation Policies" for the information and use of members has gained wide acceptance and practice in modern commerce.

NITTY-GRITTY The substantive details of a PROBLEM, as opposed to generalities regarding its essence.

NIXIE A piece of mail which cannot be delivered for whatever reason. Classes of mail which are not returnable to the sender are destroyed by the Post Office.

NMA Abbreviation for: National Micrographics Association, an organization founded in 1943 to provide continuous information and education to its members regarding new micrographics technology of all types. Its over 5,000 members receive a variety of reports and can purchase from among many specialized publications pertaining to diverse uses.

NMAC See: NBCCA

NOAB Abbreviation for: National Outdoor Advertising Bureau, an organization owned and used cooperatively by ADVERTISING AGENCIES for servicing OUTDOOR ADVERTISING CAMPAIGNS and TRANSIT ADVERTISING CAMPAIGNS.

NO DEMAND Same as: ABSENCE OF DEMAND

NOISE (1) An unanticipated variation in the message. It is an interference in communication and results in a fuzzy or even erroneous PERCEPTION of the message. (2) In ADP, random electrical signals introduced by circuit components or natural disturbances, which tend to degrade the performance of a communications channel.

NOMINAL SCALE Separates data into categories by naming only. Provides no relative measures such as degree of preference or opinion regarding desirability. See: INTERVAL SCALE, ORDINAL SCALE, RATIO SCALE, SCALING

NONADOPTERS Fit into the same general group as the LAGGARDS in the INNOVATION DIFFUSION process. May try the PRODUCT but do not become regular users.

NONCOMMERCIAL ADVERTISING   ADVERTISING placed by government agencies, charitable institutions, religious organizations, or by political groups for informational purposes or in order to attempt to create support for causes or for persons running for office. See: INSTITUTIONAL ADVERTISING, PROMOTIONAL ADVERTISING

NONMARKING   Same as: GROUP MARKING

NONPARAMETRIC   Applied to a statistical measure in connection with which no assumptions have been made about the UNIVERSE from which the SAMPLE is taken. See: PARAMETRIC

NONPREEMPTIBLE TIME   BROADCAST MEDIA time sold with the promise that the program scheduled for that time will not be removed in favor of any other program. Commands a higher amount per time unit. See: PREEMPT

NON-PRICE COMPETITION   Generally, any competitive activity except price reduction. Trading stamps, games, advertising of BRANDS, and PACKAGING innovations are examples.

NON-PRODUCT   A product offered to what was thought to be a discovered segment of a MARKET which would appreciate its benefits, only to find that the segment did not exist. Really a product which turns out to be an instant failure.

NONRESPONSE ERROR   A form of NONSAMPLING ERROR that represents the magnitude of data error caused by failure to obtain data from RESPONDENTS who were designated part of the SAMPLE.

NONRESULTANT PRODUCTS   See: COUNTERPURCHASE

NONSAMPLING ERROR   Deviation from correct data that arises in MARKETING RESEARCH because of faulty logic; misinterpretation of responses; statistical or arithmetic miscalculations or wrong methods; errors in CODING, EDITING, or TABULATING; or mistakes in the reporting of results. See: CHEATING, NONRESPONSE ERROR, NOT-AT-HOME, OBSERVATION ERROR, OVERCOVERAGE ERROR

NON-SIGNER CLAUSE   See: McGUIRE-KEOGH FAIR TRADE ENABLING ACT

NONSTORE RETAILING   Includes the activities of VENDING, MAIL ORDER, and HOUSE-TO-HOUSE.

NONTARIFF BARRIERS   Same as: NTB

NONVARIABLE PRICE POLICY   Same as: ONE-PRICE POLICY

NORAZI AGENT   A reputed MIDDLEMAN who deals in transactions closed to normal trading channels. Supposedly able to operate in the black market in countries where it is profitable to do so. Alleged to be heavily involved in smuggling to avoid payment of high import duties.

NORMAL CURVE   Same as: NORMAL PROBABILITY CURVE

NORMAL PROBABILITY CURVE   The graphic presentation of the Normal Probability Distribution, which plots symmetrical and MESOKURTIC. A normally distributed set of measurements will have about 34% of the measurements within one STANDARD DEVIATION above the MEAN and the same below the mean, or about 68% within a RANGE of one standard deviation around the mean. Similarly, about 95% of the measurements will fall within two standard deviations above and below the mean. Because collections of SAMPLE data tend to be normally distributed even though the POPULATION is not, the probability may be inferred that a chosen measurement lies within a given distance from the mean. Of great importance in determining the degree of RISK involved that the data will not have VALIDITY. This deviation from the mean in terms of the standard deviation is given the symbol Z and is available as a table usually titled "Table of Areas Under the Normal Curve."

NORMATIVE JUDGMENT   As applied to a buyer of goods or services, the result of his sense of obligation or duty. Based on his knowledge of the facts as he understands them to be, what he believes he ought to do. See: COGNITIVE JUDGMENT, CONATIVE JUDGMENT, VALUE JUDGMENT

NORMATIVE THEORY   The type of THEORY, using DESCRIPTIVE THEORY and PREDIC-TIVE THEORY to build on, which guides decisions toward the maximization of the firm's objectives, considering its environmental constraints. Eco-nomics and OPERATIONS RESEARCH provide the concepts and tools with which to construct normative theory. The range of variables which must be taken into account is very broad, and the variables themselves tend to have very complex structures. While much work has been done in this area, much more is yet necessary; understandings are improving constantly.

NORMS   Rules or standards delineating the boundaries of acceptable behavior in normal circumstances, adopted by a group or a society as a whole. See: FOLKWAYS, MORES

NORTH ATLANTIC PORTS ASSOCIATION   Same as: NAPA

NOSE-TO-NOSE SELLING   Same as: BELLY-TO-BELLY SELLING

NOT-AT-HOME   A unit of the SAMPLE who could not be reached by the researcher because this RESPONDENT was not at home on each of the designated number of tries. A source of NONSAMPLING ERROR.

NOTING DELAY   A DELAYED RESPONSE EFFECT brought about by a time lag between the end of the EXECUTION DELAY and the reception of the particular stimulus by the MARKET. In the instance of a SALESMAN'S presentation, the noting delay almost always is zero.

NOVELTY   Same as: ADVERTISING NOVELTY

NPBA   Abbreviation for: National Paper Box Association, an organization of those involved in the manufacture and sale or rigid, or set-up, boxes made of any of various types of paper. The Association provides numerous services to members, including meetings, a plant layout kit, technical data, vocational training help, and a newsletter. It sponsors an annual Rigid Paper Box Competition to encourage innovation in packaging.

NPSE   Abbreviation for: National Premium Sales Executives, the professional society in the field of INCENTIVES. Limited to 300 leading professionals in the premium-merchandising area. Pronounced: Nipsie

n.r.   Abbreviation for: next to reading matter

NRDGA   Abbreviation for: National Retail Dry Goods Association. Name changed to: National Retail Merchants Association. See: NRMA

NRMA   Abbreviation for: National Retail Merchants Association, the organi-zation to which belong many DEPARTMENT STORES and SPECIALTY SHOPS sell-ing apparel, shoes, dry goods, etc. It publishes many valuable aids for RETAILERS, including continuing reports of studies concerned with operat-ing expense data in various classifications by store size. It invites membership from colleges and college professors.

NSAD   Abbreviation for: National Society of Art Directors, a professional organization of art directors for MEDIA, ADVERTISERS, ADVERTISING AGENCIES, and advertising suppliers.

NSC   Abbreviation for: National Safety Council, a nonprofit, non-govern-mental, privately supported, public service organization founded in 1913 and chartered in 1953 by the United States Congress. Dedicated to re-ducing the number and severity of accidents in all types of environments, including the home, members receive books, magazines, newsletters, and other literature, and can draw on the Council's research program and library. It runs an annual National Safety Congress and an Exposition the major focus of which is accident prevention and education regarding products and de-vices proven useful toward this purpose. It has adopted the Green Cross as its registered MARK.

NSEC   Abbreviation for: NANOSECOND

NSI   Abbreviation for: NIELSEN STATION INDEX

NTB   Abbreviation for: Nontariff Barrier, any measure other than a tariff public or private, that significantly distorts international trade flows. Government forms may be: artificial restriction of imports through quotas or agreements, assisting domestic firms in competing with imports, and subsidizing exports. An NTB can have more far-reaching effects than were anticipated. GATT rules include a number of NTB's; negotiations about them continue among the countries.

NTI   Abbreviation for: NIELSEN TELEVISION INDEX

NTTC   Abbreviation for: National Tank Truck Carriers, an organization of for-hire tank truck companies which transport liquids and dry flowables. Established in 1945, it has consistently worked for the benefit of the industry without losing sight of responsibility to the public. It cooperates closely with the ATA. It publishes a directory of this type of carrier in the United States, Canada, Australia, England, Europe, Japan, and Mexico, together with traffic executives in petroleum, chemical, and other industries shipping and receiving liquid and dry commodities in bulk.

NUCLEAR FAMILY   With a few exceptions, refers to a group of at least two adults of opposite sex living in a socially approved sexual relationship. Children may or may not be present. If present, may be own or adopted. Usually the smallest kinship group recognized by society as a separate unit. See: FAMILY

NULL HYPOTHESIS   This HYPOTHESIS states that there is no difference between the assumed PARAMETER of the POPULATION and the computed amount based on a randomly selected SAMPLE from the population. This test is used when the population hypothesis cannot be tested directly, usually because of the population's very large size. If a difference appears, it is then necessary to evaluate the significance of the size of the difference. Statistical methods are available to help determine this significance.

NUT   A colloquialism for: uneliminatable operating costs. Very often used as the equivalent of VARIABLE COSTS.

NVOCC   Abbreviation for: Non-Vessel-Owning COMMON CARRIER.

NWPCA   Abbreviation for: National Wooden Pallet & Container Association, an organization that publishes technical literature and industry standards on wooden pallets and containers, sponsors an INDUSTRY-wide quality control Grade Mark system, and assists pallet and container users to lower materials handling and distribution costs.

NYPSA   Abbreviation for: National Yellow Pages Service Association, an organization of directory publishers established to provide one-contract, one-contact convenience for those who wish to use National Yellow Pages Advertising Programs. It publishes a monthly rate and data release and DEMOGRAPHIC data of various sorts. It offers assistance in creating LAYOUT and COPY. Its Advisory Council includes distinguished persons from the fields of ADVERTISING and MEDIA.

O   A symbol used in EXPERIMENTAL DESIGN to denote observation or measurement of the DEPENDENT VARIABLE in the test. See: X

OAAA   Abbreviation for: Outdoor Advertising Association of America. See: IOA

O and O   (1) A service station owned and operated by an oil company. (2) A station owned and operated by a NETWORK. (3) In general, any integrated facility which is owned and operated by another firm.

OAPEC   Abbreviation for: Organization of Arab Petroleum Exporting Countries, the members of which produce about one-third of the world's oil. From its formation in 1968 it has been a medium for the formulation of member energy POLICIES, economic cooperation, and manpower training. This organization, not OPEC, was the initiator of the Arab oil embargo in October, 1973. Its ten members are Saudi Arabia, Kuwait, Qatar, the United Arab Emirates, Iraq, Libya, Algeria, Egypt, Syria, and Bahrain. The first seven are members also of OPEC in which they constitute a majority. Since 1978 it appears that there may be something less than unity in objectives among the members. See: OPEC

OBJECTION   Any reason given by a PROSPECT for not accepting the offering of a SALESPERSON. It may be valid, such as a true lack of purchasing power, or merely an excuse, such as wanting to think over the offering. Often the prospect has a reason which he does not consider acceptable to others, such as that caused by a prejudice, and will consciously or unconsciously cover this up with other reasons. The salesperson's task is to uncover the real reasons and then to present verbal and/or pictorial solutions to the prospect so that the objection may be overcome. A DEMONSTRATION is quite often effective. An objection anticipated can be provided for in the salesperson's presentation. 100% success is not to be expected. See: TRIAL CLOSE

OBJECTIONS, TECHNIQUES FOR DEALING WITH   See: BOOMERANG TECHNIQUE, DIRECT DENIAL TECHNIQUE, MIRROR RESPONSE TECHNIQUE, YES-BUT TECHNIQUE

OBJECTIVITY   The quality data have when they are free of researcher's BIAS. See: VALIDITY

OBSERVABILITY   With respect to the DIFFUSION RATE, the ease with which the potential MARKET can observe and become aware of the benefits from accepting the INNOVATION. See: CHARACTERISTICS OF INNOVATION

OBSERVATION ERROR   A source of NOSAMPLING ERROR that arises when erroneous information is obtained from RESPONDENTS.

OBSERVED VALUE   In statistics, the actual value(s) obtained from the SAMPLE(S) taken from the relevant POPULATION(S). In order to draw inferences based on the laws of probability, the samples must be RANDOM. See: EXPECTED VALUE

OBSOLESCENCE   The loss in value of an asset due to the advent of superior technology, a better product, or a change in FASHION. See: DEPRECIATION

OBSOLETE MATERIAL   Items in inventory which there is little or no likelihood will be used in the future. This classification usually comes about because of design changes in the product, or abandonment of some products as the result of a SIMPLIFICATION program.

OC   Abbreviation for: Operating Characteristics Curve, a mathematical relationship between the percent of defects in a given lot with the statistical probability that the incoming lot will be accepted by a given SAMPLE plan. If the elements are correct, such a curve indicates to the user how well his sample plan discriminates between good and bad lots. Used as a tool for the inspection activity, mainly in manufacturing firms.

OCCUPANT LIST   A LIST containing only the addresses to which DIRECT MAIL is to be sent. The MAILER carries the word "occupant" in place of a specific name.

OCCUPATIONAL SAFETY AND HEALTH ACT   Same as: OSHA

OCR   Abbreviation for: Optical Character Recognition, a system whose devices are capable of capturing text in machine-readable form without the cost of operating another machine keyboard. OCR devices can read typewritten material at up to 20,000 words a minute. As compared with typical manual keyboard composition of about 50 words per minute, the significance to the publishing industry is apparent. Combining these computer capabilities with high-speed printing devices permits newspaper and other print

MEDIA services which would otherwise be cost-prohibitive. Applications have been developed for use at check-out stations in RETAIL STORES to read the price tags on merchandise.

ODDBALL PRICING Applied to the practice of selling an ASSORTMENT or a group of related items at the same price which does not necessarily relate to cost, desired MARKUP or MARGIN, or CUSTOMARY PRICE of any of the individual items.

ODD-ENDING PRICING Same as: ODD PRICING

ODD-NUMBER PRICING Same as: ODD PRICING

ODD PRICING A form of psychological pricing in which the prices are set at any amount except even dollars or even cents.

O.E. Abbreviation for: ORIGINAL EQUIPMENT

OECD Abbreviation for: Organization for Economic Cooperation and Development, composed of 18 European nations, Japan, Canada, and the United States, evolved from the OEEC in 1960 to work toward a common solution to economic problems while retaining full national sovereignty. It is a consultant agency without power to bind any of its members.

OEEC Abbreviation for: Organization for European Economic Cooperation, formed by 17 European nations in 1948, and which evolved in part as OECD in 1960.

OEM (1) Abbreviation for: Original Equipment Manufacturers (2) Abbreviation for: Other Equipment Manufacturers, especially as applied to data processing users.

OFF-EVEN PRICING Same as: ODD PRICING

OFF-FACTOR A CHAIN DISCOUNT resolved to a single percent. The complement of the ON-FACTOR.

OFF-LINE In ADP, descriptive of a system in which the operation of the equipment is not under the control of a central processing unit. See: ON-LINE

OFFSET A printing method whereby the image is transferred from a flat surface. A type of LITHOGRAPHY.

OFHA Abbreviation for: Oil Field Haulers Association, Inc., an organization of motor carriers of oilfield equipment and other heavy and cumbersome commodities. Its purposes have been consistent since its founding in 1936. They are: to render assistance to members and the INDUSTRY generally through the publication and filing of interstate and intrastate tariffs, and the provision of instruction in safety, tax, accounting, and other matters in connection with Federal and State laws and regulations. It is closely associated with ATA.

OIL FIELD HAULERS ASSOCIATION, INC. Same as: OFHA

OIL JOBBER An independent WHOLESALER who sells petroleum products to service stations in quantity lots.

OLIGOPOLY A condition of a MARKET in which there are only a few sources of supply for a given product or class of products. See: KINKED DEMAND CURVE, MONOPOLISTIC COMPETITION, MONOPOLY, OLIGOPSONY

OLIGOPSONY A condition of a MARKET in which there are only a few BUYERS for a particular product or class of product. See: MONOPSONY, OLIGOPOLY

OMA Abbreviation for: Outstanding Merchandising Achievement, an annual award of POPAI. See: WOODEN INDIAN

OMNIBUS COOPERATIVE ADVERTISEMENT A full-page advertisement placed by a RETAILER over his own name, which consists in MATS supplied by manufacturers of different products. The retailer will bill each manufacturer a pro rata share of the cost of the whole advertisement in accordance with the provisions of the various COOPERATIVE ADVERTISEMENT agreements with the manufacturers. Applies also to agreements with WHOLESALERS.

OMNIBUS PANEL   A PANEL in which the RESPONDENTS are measured again and again but on different variables each time. See: TRUE PANEL

100% LOCATION   That location within a given shopping district that is the best possible site for a particular type of STORE.

#100 SHOWING   The number of POSTERS considered enough in a given area to expose the message to nearly every mobile person during a 30-day period. Sometimes defined as: a sufficient number of posters to reach nearly 90% of the people in a given MARKET something over once a day during a 28-day period. See: #50 SHOWING, OUTDOOR ADVERTISING, POSITION MEDIA

ONE-PRICE POLICY   A POLICY of pricing whereby goods are offered for sale at a given time at the same price to all similar buyers who purchase in comparable quantities. Distinguish from: SINGLE-PRICE POLICY   Same as: NON-VARIABLE PRICE POLICY

ONE-SHOT PROMOTIONS   A one-time PROMOTION usually involving merchandise which cannot be re-ordered. Sometimes a supplier may be induced to provide merchandise manufactured especially for a particular event.

1-3-5-10 FORMULA   Establishing the customer circulation areas of a store as a base, this formula sets lighting requirements for merchandising areas, showcases and shelves, and feature displays, approximately doubling foot-candle ratios with each step. The General Electric Company has made data available which the following table reflects.

Store Area	Foot-Candle Ratio	Typical Number of Foot-Candles	Common Range of Foot-Candles
Customer Circulation	1	20	15–30
Merchandising areas	3	50	30–70
Showcases, shelves	5	100	70–150
Featured Displays	10 plus	200, 500, 1,000	150–1,500

ONE-TIME RATE   The rate paid by an advertiser who does not use enough space or time to qualify for a VOLUME DISCOUNT. It is the highest rate, on which all discounts are based. See: BASIC RATE, NATIONAL RATE, OPEN RATE, TRANSIENT RATE

ON-FACTOR   The difference between 100% and the single discount representing a CHAIN DISCOUNT. Example: chain discount of 40% and 10% = single discount of 46%. The on-factor is 100% - 46% = 54%.

ON-LINE   In ADP, descriptive of a system in which the operation of the equipment is under control of the central processing unit. Frequently made possible by REAL TIME PROCESSING. Same as: In-Line

ON-PACK   A PACKAGE consisting of a display card, suitable for hanging on hooks, to which the product has been affixed without any covering.

ON-PACK PREMIUM   Same as: BANDED PREMIUM

ON-SALE DATE   The date on which a MAGAZINE appears on the newsstands, or is mailed. It is almost always earlier than the ISSUE DATE. See: CLOSING DATE

ON TRACK   A sale practice used by COUNTRY ELEVATORS in which not only has a definite price been agreed upon between the elevator and the buyer, but the buyer accepts all further responsibility once the grain has been contracted for. The buyer makes the transfer arrangements. Relatively little grain is sold this way. Eliminates for the seller the risk of price change during the transportation period. See: TO ARRIVE

OPEC   Abbreviation for: Organization of Petroleum Exporting Countries, an association mainly of Arab countries, but includes Iran, Venezuela, and

some others. As with any CARTEL, its activities and membership will vary
with economic pressures. As at the end of 1978 the membership included
Algeria, Ecuador, Gabon, Indonesia, Iran,Iraq, Kuwait, Libya, Nigeria,
Qatar, Saudi Arabia, United Arab Emirates, and Venezuela. See: OAPEC

OPEN ACCOUNT   The seller does not require the buyer to provide written
proof of the indebtedness and promise to pay. The TERMS OF SALE are
understood. Same as: Open Credit

OPEN AD   A WANT AD which indicates both the job and the employer's name
and address. See: BLIND AD

OPEN ASSORTMENT   An ASSORTMENT in which the CONSUMER does not have at hand
all the PRODUCTS normally required. Usually a function of LIFE STYLE and
standard of living, it is subject to much flexibility over time. See:
CLOSED ASSORTMENT

OPEN ASSORTMENT DISPLAY   See: ASSORTMENT DISPLAY, OPEN DISPLAY

OPEN AUDIT PLAN   Run by the ARF, companies which provide continuing ADVER-
TISING and MARKETING RESEARCH studies may register voluntarily and without cost to permit professional examination and evaluation of their services. Those who do will be permitted to use a distinctive symbol. Such
objective reporting should be a great help to those firms that use large
quantities of these studies and services.

OPEN-CIRCUIT SYSTEM   A MARKETING system which provides for FEEDBACK from
all the influences which affect the firm. Information generally is taken
into account quickly, so that efficiency is maximized. See: LINEAR SYS-
TEM, CLOSED-CIRCUIT SYSTEM

OPEN CODE DATING   Same as: OPEN DATE LABELING

OPEN CREDIT   Same as: OPEN ACCOUNT

OPEN DATE LABELING   A clearly printed date marked on a PRODUCT of limited
SHELF LIFE to designate the last day that the product can safely be sold
by the STORE without danger of deterioration in some way. Same as: Open
Code Dating

OPEN DATING   The practice in the RETAILING of foods in which PACKAGED items
subject to deterioration are marked in a way that the CONSUMER can readily
understand with the date after which the items should not be sold for consumption. A few retailers make code books available so that the often
complex codes used by manufacturers to designate such dates may be interpreted. Because this practice is relatively recent, its full effect is
not known. Consumers seem to react toward this practice differently according to the food, ranging from careful perusal to a general faith in
the store. See: OPEN DATE LABELING

OPEN DISPLAY   Merchandise is placed where it can be handled and examined
by customers. See: CLOSED DISPLAY

OPEN-END COMMERCIAL   A COMMERCIAL which is designed to accomodate a DEAL-
ER TAG at its conclusion.

OPEN-ENDED QUESTION   A form of question, used in a QUESTIONNAIRE, characterized by its general nature so that RESPONDENTS are free to reply in their
own words without the restriction of a limited set of alternatives as in
a FIXED-ALTERNATIVE QUESTION. "What effect do you think a President can
have in settling labor disputes?" is an example of an open-ended question.

OPEN-END ORDER   Same as: BLANKET ORDER

OPEN-END PRICING   A situation in purchasing in which a PURCHASE ORDER is
issued without a fixed price agreed upon. Occurs where the price is
established by a free market and the supply is more critical to the firm
than is a fixed price.

OPEN-END PROGRAM   Any BROADCAST program designed to permit the insertion of LOCAL COMMERCIALS.

OPENING PRICE POINT   In the RETAIL field, the lowest price LINE of a given kind of merchandise, such as the least costly of several BRANDS of paint.

OPEN INTEREST   The total number of contracts in a commodity outstanding at any one time, usually as reported by the COMMODITY EXCHANGE pertinent. See: LONG POSITION, SHORT POSITION

OPEN PRICING   Marking goods with shelf life expiration dates clearly shown in common symbols so everyone can interpret them. See: OPEN DATING

OPEN RATE   Same as: ONE-TIME RATE

OPEN STOCK   Perhaps the best explanation of this concept is found in the following sign taken from a DEPARTMENT STORE display. "When we describe a pattern of dinnerware or glassware as 'open stock,' we mean that you may buy items singly or in the service you desire. This does not mean that we will always carry the pattern in stock. However, we will gladly order any item for you as long as the manufacturer makes it."

OPEN-TO-BUY CONTROL   A way of limiting the amount which a BUYER for a RE-TAILER may spend in any one period. It usually involves the establish-ment of maximum inventory levels, planned period purchasing figures, and the institution of a MERCHANDISE BUDGET system. The dollar amount of allowable purchasing for the period, resulting from the calculation in-herent in the above, is known as the OPEN-TO-BUY. See: DOLLAR CONTROL

OPERATING CHARACTERISTICS CURVE   Same as: OC

OPERATING SUPPLIES   Materials of relatively short life used up during manu-facturing and which do not enter physically into the final product.

OPERATIONAL DIVERSIFICATION   Broadening the firm's offerings on the basis of some sort of gain of MARKET advantage, such as the lowering of cost through ECONOMIES OF SCALE, or the increasing of the customer family. See: CONGRUENT PRODUCTION DIVERSIFICATION

OPINION   Generally refers to topical judgments relating to the SHORT TERM.

OPINION LEADERS   Members of a group who are able in a given situation to exert personal influence on the group. Of interest to marketers because successful APPEALS to these people have the effect of successful appeals to the group, thereby reducing the cost of the promotional campaign and the time of securing acceptance for the product. It is not always easy to identify these people. See: REFERENCE GROUP

OPPORTUNISTIC SAMPLE   Same as: CONVENIENCE SAMPLE

OPTICAL CENTER   In an advertisement, a point on a vertical, imaginary line dividing the page equally from side to side, about 3/8ths of the distance from top to bottom. Studies reveal that the eye appears to favor this spot first. Advertisements which have an interesting element in this area generally achieve higher readership ratings than those which have not.

OPTICAL CHARACTER RECOGNITION   Same as: OCR

OPTICALS   Visual effects added to a television film in the laboratory after it has been shot. These serve as part of the editing process to give con-tinuity to the COMMERCIAL as a whole. All the devices developed by the motion picture industry are available plus a few made possible by new electronics techniques. Probably the most frequently used are: CUT, FLIP WIPE, DISSOLVE, SUPERIMPOSE, WIPE, ZOOM

OPTICAL SCANNER   See: OCR

ORACLE   Acronym for: Optional Reception of Announcements by Coded Line Electronics, a news service offered by Independent Television in Britain which also displays ADVERTISING of a CLASSIFIED sort. Subscribers pay a fee for the service and the decoder. The competition with NEWSPAPERS can be direct. See: CEEFAX

ORBITAL STRUCTURE   Refers to those MARKETING institutions that are not fixed in space, e.g., a traveling SALESMAN, a TRUCK JOBBER.

ORDER CYCLE   In PURCHASING, the same in effect as LEAD TIME, but is used to include the activity of the VENDOR.   It is usually divided into four distinct parts: order transmittal, what takes place and how long it takes to get the order to the vendor from the instant of initiation; order processing, what the vendor does and how long it takes from the moment of receipt of the order to the notification of the appropriate WAREHOUSE to get the order ready for shipment; order picking, what happens at the warehouse and how long it takes to prepare the order for pickup and to put the shipment into the custody of the selected CARRIER; order delivery,what happens and how long it takes during the process of pickup and final delivery to the CUSTOMER.

ORDER DELIVERY   See: ORDER CYCLE

ORDER GETTER   A SALESPERSON using highly developed skills of SALESMANSHIP to conduct activities which are generally considered CREATIVE SELLING. See: ORDER TAKER

ORDERLY MARKETING   See: FEEDING THE MARKET

ORDER PICKING   See: ORDER CYCLE

ORDER PROCESSING   See: ORDER CYCLE

ORDER TAKER   Applied to a "SALESMAN" who merely makes calls and accepts whatever business is offered to him.   Rarely involves himself in either CREATIVE SELLING or SERVICE SELLING.

ORDER TRANSMITTAL   See: ORDER CYCLE

ORDINAL SCALE   In addition to the simple naming provided by the NOMINAL SCALE, this scale adds the attribute of ranking on a non-quantified order mechanism. See: INTERVAL SCALE, NOMINAL SCALE, RATIO SCALE, SCALING

ORGANIZATIONAL LEARNING   See: SEARCH

ORGANIZATION FOR ECONOMIC COOPERATION AND DEVELOPMENT   Same as: OECD

ORGANIZATION FOR EUROPEAN ECONOMIC COOPERATION   Same as: OEEC

ORGANIZATION OF ARAB PETROLEUM EXPORTING COUNTRIES   Same as: OAPEC

ORGANIZATION OF PETROLEUM EXPORTING COUNTRIES   Same as: OPEC

ORIGINAL EQUIPMENT   Refers to items such as tires or batteries sold to automobile manufacturers for use in equipping their units. Same as: O.E.

ORIGINAL RETAIL   In the RETAIL accounting method, the sales price of merchandise which is the total of cost plus the original MARKON.

OSHA   Abbreviation for: Occupational Safety and Health Acts of 1970 and 1971, effective August 27, 1971, the declared purpose of both of which is to assure working conditions that are safe and healthful for every working man and woman. The Secretary of Labor is authorized to set standards, has a rather vast enforcement structure, and there is provision for monetary penalties for violations. Much controversy has been generated about the type of regulations that have been issued and the nature of the citations for alleged violations.

OTB   Abbreviation for: OPEN-TO-BUY

OTC   Abbreviation for: over-the-counter. Frequently used to apply to those items of medicinal use which may be sold without prescription. Advertising for this type of item is under attack as misleading, and even harmful

in that people may be induced to use preparations which may have no real
help for them while delaying proper medical attention. The FDA is very
close to this situation, already having removed many products from sale.

OTHER-DIRECTEDNESS The condition of man motivated primarily by the demands
of his CULTURE and his associates, exercising his own preferences only to
the extent that they harmonize with the other directions in his life.
Generally applicable to a modern, sophisticated society. See: INNER-
DIRECTEDNESS

OTO Abbreviation for: one-time-only. Denotes a COMMERCIAL that runs only
once.

OUTDOOR ADVERTISING An ADVERTISING MEDIUM in which the message is not delivered to the AUDIENCE as it is with those media which enter the home,
but the units are, rather, placed in strategic locations where they can
be seen by an audience on the move. Messages in this medium must be brief
and easy to read and grasp because the average viewer is exposed to the
message for a few seconds only. See: APPROACH, FEDERAL HIGHWAY
BEAUTIFICATION ACT, PAINTED BULLETIN, POSTER, SPECTACULAR

OUTER SEVEN Same as: EFTA

OUTGOING A POSTER or PAINTED BULLETIN which exposes the advertiser's message to traffic leaving the CENTRAL BUSINESS DISTRICT of a city.

OUTLINE HALFTONE A HALFTONE from which all of the background has been removed, usually right around the illustration of the product. Same as:
Silhouette Halftone

OUT-OF-POCKET COSTS The additional cash outlay that would be made in
order to achieve an additional amount of product. See: VARIABLE COSTS

OUT-PACK A PREMIUM fastened to the outside of a PACKAGE.

OUTPOST DISPLAY Merchandise placed with appropriate signs at traffic
points in a STORE away from the regular selling department of the goods.

OUTSERT Separate printed matter attached to the outside of a PACKAGE.
Same as: Zip Ad

OUTSHOPPER One who goes outside the natural local area to purchase certain
items. See: OUTSHOPPING

OUTSHOPPING (1) The number of SHOPPING trips made outside the TRADE AREA
by CONSUMERS within a given time span. (2) The proportion of total dollar
purchases made out of town, rather than the frequency of such trips. The
types of this shopping may vary with the POPULATION LIFE CYCLE, LIFE STYLE,
MOBILITY SCALES, and the SOCIOECONOMIC COMPOSITION of the area's population. See: OUTSHOPPER

OUTSIDE-IN A way of finding out about the readers of MAGAZINES by going
to CONSUMERS or INDUSTRIAL USERS to determine for what MEDIA they are
AUDIENCE. Much research is done to try to match as closely as possible
the product, the readers, and the media. See: INSIDE-OUT

OUTSIZES Same as: END SIZES

OUTTAKES Scenes taped or filmed during the making of a show or a
COMMERCIAL which are not used in the final production, usually because
of errors or peculiar episodes.

OVERBOUGHT (1) A condition which exists when some element in the planning
process has not materialized as expected, resulting in a zero OPEN-TO-
BUY. (2) A condition in RETAILING in which a STORE finds itself with a
quantity of merchandise in excess of DEMAND.

OVERCOVERAGE ERROR A source of NONSAMPLING ERROR injected into a study in
MARKETING RESEARCH when some of the units in the SAMPLE are duplicated
on the lists given to different interviewers.

OVER-DOOR DISPLAY   Same as: TOP-END DISPLAY

OVERHEAD   In accounting, may refer to those expenses of a general nature which apply to the business as a whole. Basically the same as: FIXED COSTS

OVERLAY   A strip of COPY pasted over a POSTER to add something special or current to the message. Same as: SNIPE

OVERPRINT   A COMBINATION PLATE produced by superimposing a LINE PLATE negative on a HALFTONE negative. The result appears to be an illustration on which words or a line drawing have been printed.

OVERRUN   The number of pieces of printed matter in excess of the quantity ordered. Unless otherwise specified, it is customary for an advertiser to accept up to 10% overrun at pro rata cost. See: UNDERRUN

OVERSTORED CONDITION   A situation in a MARKET in which more RETAIL STORES are opened than existing demand warrants. This overinvestment causes stress until the condition is corrected either by population increase or by bankruptcy.

PAAA   Abbreviation for: Premium Advertising Association of America, a trade association for the PREMIUM incentive industry, representing the principal segments and interests of the industry. It offers its members a variety of publications, programs, and aids.

PACKAGE   (1) That which serves as a protective device for the product as well as a vehicle to carry the BRAND and the LABEL. A container.   (2) In BROADCAST MEDIA, a combination assortment of time units, sold as a single offering at a set price. (3) In broadcast media, a program that includes all components ready for the addition of commercials. It is bought as a unit for a lump sum.

PACKAGE BAND   Same as: BANDED PREMIUM

PACKAGE CAR   A carload of a VARIETY of merchandise sent to a number of BUYERS located in one city and moving at l.c.l. rates.

PACKAGE CONSOLIDATING AGENCY   Same as: FREIGHT FORWARDER

PACKAGE DESIGNERS COUNCIL   Same as: PDC

PACKAGE ENCLOSURE   Same as: IN-PACK

PACKAGE EXPRESS   Same as: BUS PACKAGE EXPRESS

PACKAGE FREIGHT   Merchandise shipped in l.c.l. quantities.

PACKAGE GOODS   A general reference to merchandise produced in some sort of container designed for practical display and handling by a RETAILER. Examples include cereals, laundry detergents and bleaches, paper goods, many stationery items, and the like.

PACKAGE INSERT   (1) Advertising material put into a PACKAGE with the product, usually to promote a different product. (2) Printed material inclosed with the product to explain its operation or care.

PACKAGE PLAN   Same as: PACKAGE (2)

PACKAGE PROGRAM   In BROADCASTING, a program complete with all elements except commercials, sold as a unit. May be live or on film or tape.

PACKAGING INSTITUTE   Same as: PI

PACKAGING MACHINERY MANUFACTURERS INSTITUTE   Same as: PMMI

PACKING HOUSE   Same as: FREIGHT FORWARDER

PACK PEDDLER   Same as: YANKEE PEDDLER

PAGE PROOF   A rendering of type and plates arranged by pages as they are to appear finally. Usually made after the GALLEY PROOF has been shown and corrected.

PAID OFFICE   Same as: FEE OFFICE

PAINTED BULLETIN   Similar in type to POSTERS, but painted directly on the surface. Can be done on the walls of buildings. May be individualized. Provides considerable flexibility. See: OUTDOOR ADVERTISING

PAINTED DISPLAY   Same as: PAINTED BULLETIN

PAIRED COMPARISON QUESTION   A form of question designed to elicit a ranked opinion from a RESPONDENT. The respondent is asked to indicate which of two presented alternatives is considered the choice according to criteria enumerated at the start. A QUESTIONNAIRE may have a long series of such questions in which certain alternatives are paired with many different ones.

PALLET   A small, portable platform designed to hold a quantity of product during movement by CARRIER or while in storage. Commonly fitted for lifting by fork-lift truck. May be constructed of wood, corrugated paper, light metals, or a combination of these.

PALLETIZE   The process of placing material on a PALLET in such a way that it forms a reasonably stable load. If the load is to be moved several times in conditions which may cause it to tilt, it is usually strapped to the pallet or shrink-wrapped to form a UNIT LOAD.

PANEL   (1) A group of people used to get comparable data on product acceptance, use and suggestions over a period of time. Frequently used as a MARKETING RESEARCH tool. See: OMNIBUS PANEL, TRUE PANEL (2) That part of an outdoor sign on which the message is pasted or painted. (3) One of the printed sections which comprise the entire advertisement on an outdoor sign.

PAPERLESS PURCHASING   Same as: CHECK PAYMENT ORDERING SYSTEM

PARALLELISM   Same as: CONSCIOUS PARALLELISM

PARALLEL POSTER   A POSTER so situated that its ends are within six feet of a line parallel to the traffic flow. While it can be seen by traffic moving in both directions, the possible time of viewing is less than for an ANGLED POSTER. See: FLASH APPROACH

PARAMETER   A descriptive measurement of a POPULATION, such as a STANDARD DEVIATION. When populations must be measured through SAMPLES, a certain amount of error must be taken into account. Models purporting to describe certain MARKETING elements or processes often assume the accuracy of the parameters used when these are not measurable within acceptable limits of error, and thereby provide decision data that is not VALID. Caution should be exercised in using models until the model has been proven acceptable under varying conditions.

PARAMETRIC   Applied to a statistical measure about which it is assumed that the POPULATIONS from which SAMPLES are drawn are normal in configuration, that the VARIANCE is homogeneous, and that the sample selection has been RANDOM. See: NONPARAMETRIC, NORMAL PROBABILITY CURVE

PARASITE STORE   A store depending entirely on traffic originating from conditions outside those generated by the store itself, which is usually negligible compared with the total traffic flow.

PARENT STORE   The main store of a RETAILER operating one or more BRANCHES. See: FLAGSHIP STORE

PARIS CONVENTION FOR THE PROTECTION OF INDUSTRIAL PROPERTY   Same as: PARIS UNION

PARIS UNION   The common name for the Paris Convention for the Protection of Industrial Property, an agreement among a group of 50 nations to recognize the same rights of all members in the protection of TRADEMARKS, PATENTS, and other property rights as are granted by the home country. The United States is a member.

PARITY PRICE   The basis for governmental price support of a commodity according to a formula which is intended to prevent the farmers' purchasing
power from falling below his REAL INCOME as it was in a period of years
considered as a standard, usually 1910-1914. Many plans have been implemented to put supply and demand factors for FARM PRODUCTS into balance,
but none have worked well to date. There is considerable evidence to indicate that a sound solution to the farmers' problem lies in some program
to eliminate the about 70% of all FARMS, almost all non-economic in size,
which produce only 30% of farm output. Perhaps a retirement plan could
be effected; or perhaps providing for mergers into larger units so that
PRODUCTIVITY might be increased through the use of more mechanization.
Any such solution is presently not politically palatable.

PARTIAL VISUAL MERCHANDISE CONTROL   An automatic RETAIL reorder system
based on designing each fixture to hold a supply of merchandise enough
to cover the reorder interval. Visual inspection indicates how much
should be reordered. See: DOLLAR CONTROL, OPEN-TO-BUY CONTROL, PERPETUAL
MERCHANDISE CONTROL, ROTATED MERCHANDISE CONTROL, UNIT CONTROL, WANT-SLIP
SYSTEM

PARTICIPATING PROGRAM   A BROADCAST program sponsored by more than one advertiser. See: ALTERNATE SPONSOR, FULL-PROGRAM SPONSOR, SPOT

PARTICIPATION   In contrast to an I.D., an ANNOUNCEMENT delivered within the
time frame of a program on television or radio.

PARTICIPATION GROUP   A REFERENCE GROUP in which an individual actually
takes active part. May be small, such as a FAMILY, or large, such as a
political party. See: ANTICIPATORY GROUP. AUTOMATIC GROUP, NEGATIVE
REFERENCE GROUP

PARTS   Unit components of a product which are complete without further
processing but are useful only when incorporated into the product. Motor
switches, Tv tubes are examples. See: FABRICATING MATERIALS, OPERATING
SUPPLIES, RAW MATERIALS

PARTY PLAN SELLING   Same as: PARTY SELLING

PARTY SELLING   A form of house-to-house selling in which a hostess is persuaded through the promise of a gift to invite her friends to an after-
noon or evening gathering at which the SALESMAN can DEMONSTRATE his wares.

PASS-ALONG CIRCULATION   See: PRIMARY CIRCULATION

PASS-ALONG DEAL   A DEAL in which the intent is that the RETAILER will be
encouraged to reduce the price of the product to the CONSUMER, thereby increasing volume and perhaps SHARE OF MARKET for the manufacturer.

PASS-ALONG READERSHIP   While technically this term applies to total people
who read a publication through having acquired access to it by means other
than as the purchaser, this term is often used to mean essentially the
same as: PASS-ALONG CIRCULATION.

PASSIVE PHILOSOPHY   A philosophy of competitive behavior under which a
firm engages in only enough competitive TACTICS to survive in the MARKET.
See: AGGRESSIVE PHILOSOPHY, NEUTRAL PHILOSOPHY

PASTE-UP   A LAYOUT in which illustrations, type material, and other elements of an advertisement are pasted on a single sheet for reproduction
as an engraving.

PATENT INSIDES   Same as: BOILER PLATE

PATENT MEDICINE   Same as: OTC

PATRONAGE DISCOUNT   A type of discount allowed on the basis of the amount
of business done with one firm.

PATRONAGE DIVIDEND   Earnings in excess of an amount needed by the business returned to members of a cooperative in accordance with the proportions which each member's dealings with the cooperative bears to the total business done by all members with the cooperative.

PATRONAGE INSTITUTIONAL ADVERTISING   The thrust of this type of INSTITUTIONAL ADVERTISING is to persuade the AUDIENCE to use the SPONSOR as the source of supply for reasons other than the specific merit of the offering.   See: PUBLIC RELATIONS INSTITUTIONAL ADVERTISING, PUBLIC SERVICE INSTITUTIONAL ADVERTISING

PATRONAGE MOTIVES   The considerations explaining why customers make their purchases from certain sources.   See: PRODUCT MOTIVES

PAYOFF   What it is that one seeks as a quality in the solution to a PROBLEM or the answer to a question prerequisite to decision-making.   This may be in the area of profit, SHARE OF MARKET, ROI, probability of acceptance of a new product, etc.   See: CONSTRAINT

PAY-TV   See: CATV

PCC   Abbreviation for: Private Carrier Conference, an affiliate of ATA but independent and autonomous.   Its purpose is to preserve the basic rights of firms to operate their own trucks for their own account, free from restraint and regulation.   Its about 4,000 members receive a monthly trade publication, a number of guides and handbooks, and many pieces of instructional material.

PCM   In ADP, abbreviation for: Punch-Card Equipment, commonly used for tabulating data as input for various machines, including computers.   Also called: Tab Equipment.

PDC   Abbreviation for: Package Designers Council, the professional organization of industrial design consultants who specialize in PACKAGE DESIGN and other visual expressions of the corporate image.   It has since its founding in 1952 promoted recognition for creative work, stimulated free flow of ideas and technical information, intercommunicated with other interested organizations, conducted meetings, sponsored an awards program for outstanding designer-client packaging over an extended period, cooperated with government agencies, maintained a speakers' bureau, encouraged young talent, and brought the latest developments of materials suppliers to the attention of the design profession.

PD CONCEPT   Same as: PHYSICAL DISTRIBUTION CONCEPT

PDM   Abbreviation for: Physical Distribution Management, the control mechanism which governs the implementation of the PHYSICAL DISTRIBUTION CONCEPT.

PEAK   See: BUSINESS CYCLE

PEAK SEASON   That particular time of the year when an item or LINE of merchandise is in the greatest acceptance by a FIRM'S CUSTOMERS.

PEDDLER   (1) A petroleum WHOLESALER operating one or two trucks who services small accounts.   (2) The name still used in some areas for door-to-door sellers who carry their wares with them.   See: HUCKSTER

PEGGED PRICES   Prices held artificially at a given level below which they are not permitted to fall regardless of market forces.   Usually involves government action, often in the form of a subsidy to affected producers.

PENETRATION   Used to denote the degree of effectiveness of ADVERTISING in terms of its impact on the public at large.

PENETRATION PRICE   A price set deliberately low to insure maximum acceptance of a new product by its MARKET.   A price set low enough to insure a mass market.   See: EXPANSIONISTIC PRICE

PENNYSAVER   Same as: SHOPPER

PEOPLES' GALLERY   See: TRIOSK

PERCEIVED REALITY   Especially applied to the effects of ADVERTISING as
they convey the image of a PRODUCT to a CONSUMER. Courts are tending to
decide whether a particular ADVERTISEMENT or CAMPAIGN is misleading by
what the AUDIENCE perceives as real about the product, rather than by
the literal meaning of the words in the message. See: PERCEPTION

PERCENTAGE OF LAST YEAR'S SALES METHOD   A method of arriving at an ADVER-
TISING BUDGET which uses a specific predetermined proportion of last
year's total sales to determine the next year's advertising expenditure.
Easy to use, but does not provide for addition to promotional effort.
May be applied as well to the development of the budget for the total
MARKETING MIX. See: ASSESSMENT METHOD, PERCENTAGE OF NEXT YEAR'S SALES
METHOD, PLUNGE METHOD, TASK METHOD

PERCENTAGE OF NEXT YEAR'S SALES METHOD   A method of arriving at an ADVER-
TISING BUDGET by using a predetermined proportion of estimated sales for
the coming year as that year's advertising expenditure. Requires regular
review to be sure it stays in line with expectations. May be applied as
well to the development of the budget for the total MARKETING MIX. See:
ASSESSMENT METHOD, PERCENTAGE OF LAST YEAR'S SALES METHOD, PLUNGE METHOD,
TASK METHOD

PERCENTAGE VARIATION METHOD One of the four primary methods used by
RETAILERS for STOCK PLANNING. Especially useful when STOCKTURN is
greater than six per year, it supplies the BOM stock level by this
formula: BOM stock level = average stock $[h(1 + \frac{\text{sales for month}}{\text{average monthly sales}})]$.
The $\underline{h}$ in the formula is a fraction determined by experience. It is
ordinarily less than 1, reflecting the general knowledge that sales
increase or decrease by less than the percent change in stocks.

PERCENTILE   Found in the same general manner as the MEDIAN, except that
percentiles divide the ARRAY into one hundred equal parts.

PERCEPTION   How one interprets what one sees. The process by which people
select and organize sensory stimuli. Important for SALESMEN and ADVER-
TISERS to understand; for example, does the PROSPECT who looks at a car
see a means of transportation economical or dependable, or a status symbol
for ego building, or a means of easier access to romance? Significant
in deciding upon APPEALS. See: HALO EFFECT, PRODUCT IMAGE, SYMBOL

PERCEPTUAL BLOCKING The protection individuals give themselves against
the bombardment of STIMULI by preventing them from reaching conscious
awareness. The process is popularly called "tuning out." See:
PERCEPTUAL DEFENSE

PERCEPTUAL DEFENSE   Subconscious screening out of STIMULI that are
important to the individual not to sense, usually because such stimuli
will be damaging to a cherished idea, value, or belief. See: PERCEPTUAL
BLOCKING

PERCEPTUAL DISTORTION   The tendency of each individual to make objective
information consistent with his own experience, knowledge, and expectation by interpreting it in accordance with his own goals and value systems.
The result is selective distortion and selective retention of available
information. See: PERCEPTION, SEARCH

PERCEPTUAL MAPPING Constructing a graph of BRAND attributes as seen by
CONSUMERS on a scale of low to high. It usually is done for two relevant
characteristics, one on each axis, and is for one PRODUCT at a time.
Such a graph may reveal gaps in the POSITIONING of all brands in that
product class where consumer preferences are not being well provided for.

PER DIEM   A Latin phrase meaning: by the day. A popular way of paying the expenses of SALESMEN, it involves simply granting each man a fixed amount for each day on the road. No supporting expense documents are required.

PERFECT HEDGE   A HEDGE in which the gain or loss on the commodity transaction exactly equals the loss or gain on the finished goods transactions.

PERFORMANCE ANALYSIS The comparatively regular examination of data, mainly internal supplemented by external, to provide management with better understandings of trends, outcomes, and results. The main types are: sales analysis, providing cross-classifications by product, territory, salesperson, element in the CHANNEL OF DISTRIBUTION, or any combination, on the basis of units or money amounts; market-share analysis, often using data compiled by trade groups, government agencies, or syndicated services, to determine MARKET SHARE by BRAND; distribution analysis, an examination of the quality and number of outlets for the FIRM'S products, frequently involving continuous reviews of inventory levels and distributor support of PROMOTION; salesforce performance analysis, a careful focus on each member with regard to assigned duties such as new account development, distributor assistance and training, and various checks as well as relative expense generated in getting of orders; cost and profit analysis, financial analysis of all of the foregoing to determine strong and weak elements so that through proper cost accounting techniques the firm's profits can be optimized.

PERFORMANCE LABEL   An affix to a PRODUCT describing the operating characteristics and making disclosures of the performance of that product in use. See: LABEL

PERFORMANCE RESEARCH   An investigation to find out whether an instituted course of action is producing anticipated results, and to discover what changes have resulted as caused by the course of action. See: CONCLUSIVE RESEARCH, MARKETING RESEARCH

PERIODICAL   Same as: MAGAZINE

PERIODIC REORDERING   Same as: P-SYSTEM

PERISHABLE DISTINCTIVENESS   Describes a product for which serious actual competition may be realistically expected in the MARKET in less than five years. At first this will be Exclusive Distinctiveness. When competition appears and yet as a result of the momentum resulting from initial acceptance MARKET SHARE increases, this will be Preferential Distictiveness. Finally, however, innovators will capture a larger and larger share of the market and the product will enter a stage of Declining Distinctiveness. If charted, the Curve of Distinctiveness will show an inverse relationship with the Sales Curve.

PERK   Taken from "perquisite" which is defined by Webster as "an incidental gain or profit in addition to regular salary or wages," this today includes all privileges or advantages given an executive for which his company pays, such as a villa in Bermuda, a helicopter for commuting to and from the office, and the general use of a company plane. The structure of the tax laws makes these less expensive ways for an executive to be rewarded than an equal amount in cash. Also, they are often more effective in keeping an executive with a firm or in enticing a good one in. The use of perks has been faulted on the basis of uneven use, no relationship between use and executive performance, and the creation of poor MORALE within the firm. They are defended on the basis that top executives enjoy them and thus produce better. Some are questionable practices being looked at closely by the Internal Revenue Service.

PERMISSIVE COMPETITION   Some firms are allowed by the established sellers to remain in a competitive posture, usually to prevent the INDUSTRY from becoming concentrated to the point that the attention of government agencies will be drawn to it and ANTI-TRUST action brought against it. This type of competition exists only because the important sellers want it to exist. See: WORKABLE COMPETITION

PERPETUAL INVENTORY SYSTEM   A way of keeping track of a firm's inventory by continuous recording of the movement of items into and out of the firm. The system usually provides for recording order and receipt quantities, and requisition or sale quantities.

PERPETUAL MERCHANDISE CONTROL   Same as: PERPETUAL INVENTORY SYSTEM, but adapted particularly to RETAILING. See: CLASSIFICATION CONTROL, DOLLAR CONTROL, OPEN-TO-BUY CONTROL, PARTIAL VISUAL MERCHANDISE CONTROL, ROTATED MERCHANDISE CONTROL, UNIT CONTROL, WANT-SLIP SYSTEM

PER SE   A latin expression used to denote something which is characteristic in and of itself. See: PER SE VIOLATION

PER SE VIOLATION   A rule at law in which the subject action is illegal in and of itself, requiring no proof of motive or intent. For example, under our ANTI-TRUST LAWS price fixing agreements among competitors are per se illegal. See: RULE OF REASON

PERSONAL CARE GOODS   All merchandise designed to help improve a CONSUMER'S appearance. Includes various electrical appliances for use with hair grooming, shaving, manicuring, and complexion clearing.

PERSONAL CREDIT   See: CREDIT

PERSONAL DISPOSABLE INCOME   PERSONAL INCOME after the payment of income taxes. See: DISPOSABLE INCOME

PERSONAL INCOME   The total MONEY INCOME received by all individuals in an economy during a given period of time. See: DISCRETIONARY INCOME

PERSONAL INTERVIEW METHOD   A technique of MARKETING RESEARCH, often used to analyze a broadcast AUDIENCE, which involves having an interviewer call at the HOUSEHOLDS selected by one of several SAMPLING methods to ask questions related not only to what is being attended at the time, but of a much more DEMOGRAPHIC nature. Used mainly for special surveys because of its generally high cost. See: DIARY METHOD, MECHANICAL RECORDER METHOD, TELEPHONE COINCIDENTAL METHOD

PERSONALIZING SHOPPERS   One of a four-way sociological classification of CONSUMERS, the others being APATHETIC SHOPPERS, ECONOMIC SHOPPERS, and ETHICAL SHOPPERS. The personalizing shopper seeks STORES in which he feels comfortable. He is inclined to rate stores in terms of the closeness of his relationships with sales personnel. Most of this group is from the lower SOCIAL CLASSES.

PERSONAL TRADE FILE   Same as P.T. File

PERSONNEL MANAGEMENT   Same as: HUMAN RESOURCES MANAGEMENT

PERSUASION VEHICLES   Same as: ADVERTISING MEDIA

PERSUASIVE PRICING   Any form of psychological pricing which tends to convey a sense of extra-good value to the customer. See: ODD-PRICING

PERT   Abbreviation for: Program Evaluation and Review Technique. A more elaborate form of CPM.

PHANTOM DIAGRAM   A way of VISUALIZING by means of a cut-away picture showing the inner construction of the product. Same as: Ghost Diagram

PHANTOM FREIGHT   A freight cost that is not actually incurred, although paid for. Arises when a DELIVERED PRICE is computed by adding to the unit price, freight from a BASING POINT, regardless of the actual origin of the shipment, and the freight paid is more than it would have been F.O.B. See: FREIGHT ABSORPTION, MILL NET RETURN

PHANTOM MARKET   A MARKET presumed to exist but which when closely examined or analyzed is found to be actually nonexistant or too small to warrant attention.

PHANTOM SHOPPERS Sellers' representatives who pose as CUSTOMERS to evaluate the techniques of DEALERS in selling certain PRODUCTS. They often give on-the-spot awards if preferred techniques are being used.

PHARMACEUTICAL MANUFACTURERS ASSOCIATION An association representing 95% of the production of U.S. prescription drugs. It has become heavily involved in the general effort to combat drug misuse.

PHOTOCOMPOSING To photomechanically arrange continuous tone, line, or HALFTONE COPY for reproduction. Not the same as PHOTOCOMPOSITION.

PHOTOCOMPOSITION Producing images on film or paper which the engraver can transfer to metal or other printing surfaces. Claimed advantages over usual LETTERPRESS typesetting are: improved sharpness and clarity, wider choice of type FACES, and faster production at lower cost. The computer applications are many, including expanding or contracting the type size and spacing.

PHOTODISPLAY Composition of HEADLINES and other display matter on paper or film either by manual process lettering or automated equipment.

PHOTOLETTERING Sometimes used as a synonym for PHOTODISPLAY, but more specifically descriptive of the system of assembling film positive images of letters into words for subsequent PHOTOCOPYING to produce film or paper prints.

PHOTOTEXT Text matter composed or set onto film or paper by means of keyboard-operated or computer-tape-driven PHOTOCOMPOSITION machines.

PHOTOTYPESETTING Same as: PHOTOCOMPOSITION

PHOTOTYPOGRAPHY A general reference to the entire field of composing, makeup, and processing PHOTODISPLAY and PHOTOTEXT, or type converted to film form, for the production of image carriers by platemakers and printers.

PHYSICAL DISTRIBUTION A term employed in manufacturing and commerce to describe the entire range of activities associated with the efficient movement of goods from producer to CONSUMER. Sometimes used to refer only to the movement of materials from sources of supply to producers. It includes various modes of freight transportation, warehousing, materials handling, protective packaging, inventory control, plant and warehouse site selection, order processing, market FORECASTING, and customer service.

PHYSICAL DISTRIBUTION CONCEPT Frequently referred to as the PD concept, it is a business theory which requires that all physical handling and the TRADE CHANNEL system be considered parts of one total system in the firm. A rather old idea, but as yet adopted by few firms in spite of demonstrable advantages, because it requires special and rare managerial talent able to coordinate all the aspects of a business into a unified system. See: LOGISTICS SYSTEM, PHYSICAL DISTRIBUTION

PHYSICAL DISTRIBUTION MANAGEMENT Same as: PDM

PHYSICAL RISK See: CONSUMER-PERCEIVED RISKS

PHYSIOLOGICAL MOTIVES Those MOTIVES whose satisfaction is essential to survival, according to the standards of a particular LIFE STYLE. See: SOCIAL MOTIVES

PHYSIOLOGICAL NEEDS The first and lower-most level of MASLOW'S HIERARCHY OF NEEDS. Includes all of the biogenic needs, such as food, water, shelter, clothing, and sex. Dominant when chronically unsatisfied. Essentially the same as: PRIMARY NEEDS

PI   Abbreviation for: The Packaging Institute, a national professional society of people whose careers and personal motivations are linked to the field of packaging. The Institute's primary purpose is to advance the technology and increase the MARKET value of packaging and packaged products. It runs an annual National Packaging Forum, publishes a great many technical papers, keeps its members current on governmental matters, and conducts its own Evening Course Program to educate its members in all phases of the field.

PIB   Abbreviation for: Publishers Information Bureau, an organization that supplies reports on the expenditures of national advertisers in MAGAZINES and NETWORK TELEVISION.

PICA   The measuring unit of width in printing. There are six picas to the inch. Sometimes used also as a vertical measure, especially with reference to a book page. See: EM, POINT

PICA EM   An EM that is 12 POINTS wide and 12 points deep.

PICTOGRAM   A form of BAR CHART which employs figures of varying sizes instead of bars to show the relative values of the variables, e.g, outlines of people-figures for population, car outlines for automobile sales, etc. See: HISTOGRAM, LINE CHART, PIE CHART

PIE CHART   A graph in the form of a circle representing the total, divided into segments depicting the components of the whole so that each segment is shown proportionate in size to its portion of the whole. See: BAR CHART, HISTOGRAM, PICTOGRAM

PIECE GOODS   Fabrics which may be bought in required lengths for home sewing of personal and household items.

PIGGYBACK   (1) A TRANSPORTATION arrangement in which truck trailers with their loads are moved by train to a destination. See: BIRDIEBACK, COFC, FISHYBACK, TOFC   (2) In broadcast advertising, a SPOT by an advertiser for two or more of his products in which each is shown as a separate COMMERCIAL.

PILFERAGE   In essence the same as SHOPLIFTING but generally applied to that done by employees.

PIMS   Abbreviation for: Profit Impact of Marketing Strategies, a data pool on the MARKETING experiences of its about 120 members with respect to more than 650 PRODUCT LINES, it provides a means of simulating by computer the probable result of MARKET STRATEGIES as tested against real experiences of many comparable FIRMS. Members pay a fee per year and may receive a number of reports and analyses. All activities are confidential.

PIONEERING STAGE   The stage a product or service is in, according to a certain classification, when PROSPECTS for it either do not know of its existence or are not yet convinced that there are benefits to them in adopting it. Most often applied where a completely different type of benefit is offered. Any offering may skip this stage if the benefits are obvious to a significant number of prospects. See: SPIRAL

PIPE LINE   A system of TRANSPORTATION using pipe as the means. May be a PUBLIC CARRIER or a PRIVATE CARRIER. The items moved may be in liquid, gaseous, or SLURRY state. Requires very large capital investment to establish, but operating costs are very low. Innovative uses of pipe line transport are just beginning to appear.

PIRATE PARTS   Replacement parts made and sold by producers who specialize in these alone. Such producers are firms other than the makers of the machines which the pirate parts fit.

PIRATING   The practice of a non-subscriber to rating reports to persuade a subscriber to those reports to allow the non-subscriber to use them. Such unauthorized use has been subjected to legal action.

PIT   An area within a COMMODITY EXCHANGE in which actual trading takes place. Some pits are elaborately laid out on several levels for better visibility of the traders. See: RING

PITTSBURGH PLUS PRICING   A former BASING POINT system for pricing steel, now an illegal system, in which all steel of all producers was sold at a delivered price which assumed shipment from Pittsburgh regardless of where the shipment actually originated.

PLACE UTILITY   The characteristic of a GOOD which makes it possible to satisfy a human WANT based on geographical considerations, i.e., the item has been moved to where it is desired as distinguished from where it was made or grown or mined. TRANSPORTATION creates place utility. See: UTILITY

PLANNED IMPULSE BUYING   A seeming misnomer, this type of IMPULSE BUYING occurs when the customer intends to use the store's stock as a shopping list. A significant portion of RETAIL sales is traceable to this habit of many CONSUMERS in the MARKET. See: PURE IMPULSE BUYING, REMINDER IMPULSE BUYING, SUGGESTION IMPULSE BUYING

PLANNED OBSOLESCENCE   While this concept is a fully acceptable one as applied to business investment, in the sense that a firm should not provide a facility that will last longer than it is anticipated will be useful because resources are wasted thereby, in recent years this term has become associated with the idea of change for CONSUMPTION'S sake, as in the practice of frequent model changes in CONSUMER GOODS. In the latter sense this is a controversial issue. Sometimes called: MANAGED OBSOLESCENCE

PLANNED PROFIT   See: DOLLAR PLAN

PLANNED SALES   See: DOLLAR PLAN

PLANNED SHOPPING CENTER   A concentration of a number of STORES, usually of different types, developed as a unit and located in suburban areas or in outlying areas of large cities. Same as: CONTROLLED SHOPPING CENTER

PLANNED STOCK   See: DOLLAR PLAN

PLANNING   The entirety of the STRATEGIES involving all elements necessary to accomplish an objective. The activity which is the determinant of a future course of action. See: ACTION PLANNING, STRATEGIC PLANNING

PLANNING HORIZON   The number of future years for which management estimates the financial consequences of alternative MARKETING POLICIES. This may be for three, five, or even ten years. Management usually finds it of little consequence to project beyond the planning horizon because of rapid DEPRECIATION or OBSOLESENCE that makes many assets worthless in a relatively short time, and because the great uncertainty about future events reduces the probability of a useful estimate below that which can be accepted as a basis on which to plan dollars to be earned then.

PLANOGRAPHIC PRINTING   Same as: LITHOGRAPHY

PLANT   In OUTDOOR ADVERTISING, the company in an area that erects and maintains the POSTER PANELS and other appropriate structures in that area. Same as: Plant Operator, Poster Plant

PLANT CAPACITY   The number of message structures under the control of a PLANT in OUTDOOR ADVERTISING. See: SHOWING

PLANT OPERATOR   Same as: PLANT

PLASTICITY OF DEMAND   A concept that assumes that CONSUMER choices may be partially influenced around a given point on the DEMAND CURVE. See: PRICE ELASTICITY OF DEMAND, PROMOTIONAL ELASTICITY OF DEMAND

PLASTIC PLATE   A positive printing PLATE, similar to an ELECTROTYPE, but made by a complex process, lighter in weight, and less expensive.

PLATE   A term applied in a general way to any unit used to make a printed impression, usually of an illustration with its accompanying CAPTIONS, by any method of printing. See: INTAGLIO, LETTERPRESS, LITHOGRAPHY

PLATEAUING   The tendency of SALESPERSONS of some limited ambition to relax their efforts after they have reached the particular level of sales or income that satisfies them.

PLATYKURTIC   Descriptive of a FREQUENCY CURVE in which the measurements charted are widely dispersed. Such a curve is characterized by a broad, very flat top. See: KURTOSIS

PLUG   A commercial message, usually without charge. Sometimes appears in unexpected contexts.

PLUNGE METHOD   Essentially the same as: TASK METHOD

PM   Abbreviation for: PUSH MONEY, PREMIUM MONEY

PMMI   Abbreviation for: Packaging Machinery Manufacturers Institute, chartered in 1933 to help member companies, makers of packaging machinery and packaging-related converting machinery, solve common problems. It provides technical information and current guidance through a weekly bulletin, confidential statistics, periodic surveys, a program to train mechanics, and an annual TRADE SHOW. Its directory of members, showing the products and capabilities of each, is widely distributed.

PNS   Abbreviation for: POTENTIAL NEED SATISFIER

POINT   (1) A unit of vertical measurement for type and print. There are 72 points to the vertical inch. Type is specified by point size as well as FAMILY, e.g., 12 pt., 18 pt., 24 pt. New use is to designate horizontal spacing in points in applications heretofore usually reserved to PICAS. (2) In BROADCAST MEDIA, same as: RATING POINT

POINT OF DIMINISHING RETURNS   See: LAW OF DIMINISHING RETURNS

POINT OF INDIFFERENCE   In RETAILING, a geographic distance between two cities at which CONSUMERS would have no preference for shopping in either city. See: LAW OF RETAIL GRAVITATION

POINT OF NEGATIVE RETURNS   See: LAW OF DIMINISHING RETURNS

POINT-OF-ORIGIN PRICING   Same as: F.O.B.

POINT-OF-PURCHASE ADVERTISING   Signs and displays at the point of final sale. POP is very flexible as to permanency, FORMAT, position, location. Its greatest problem is persuading the DEALER to use it. Much of this problem is caused by the advertiser's failure to determine in advance the realistic probability of the dealer's being <u>able</u> to use the piece as the advertiser intends.

POINT-OF-PURCHASE ADVERTISING INSTITUTE   Same as: POPAI

POISSON PROBABILITY DISTRIBUTION Useful in those classes of business PROBLEMS characterized by the small probability of success for any one of the many trials of an EXPERIMENT, e.g., analysis of the formation of waiting lines at service facilities, the demand for inventory items, and counting the number of defects in a manufactured item. The EVENTS must be units so small that no more than one success will occur in a given trial, and the probability of success is the same for all trials and is independent of the outcomes of any previous or future trials. The computed values may be used as good estimates of the process PARAMETERS. The CHI-SQUARE TEST can be used to check the HYPOTHESIS that the events of a process are distributed according to the Poisson Distribution. NONPARAMETRIC.

POLE DISPLAY   A POP display mounted on a footed pole, designed to be visible above the MASS DISPLAYS with which it is used. See: CROW'S FEET

POLICY   A rule of action adopted by an operating organization to insure uniformity of procedures under similar, recurring circumstances.

POLICY RIGHTS   In PURCHASING, the AUTHORITY granted managers to set procurement objectives. See: ALLOCATION RIGHTS, CRITERIA RIGHTS, EVALUATION RIGHTS, SAMPLING RIGHTS, STRATEGY RIGHTS

POLYCENTRICITY   One of a three-way classification of the POLICIES of FIRMS engaged in international MARKETING, this one emphasizes the legal, cultural, and DEMOGRAPHIC differences and similarities among MARKETS, each one considered unique so that only local managers can comprehend and deal with local conditions. The other two are ETHNOCENTRICITY and GEOCENTRICITY.

POOL CAR   A carload of similar goods made up of the combined shipments of several BUYERS, loaded by a single shipper who also arranges for unloading and delivery at destination, and which moves at carload rates. See: MIXED CAR, PACKAGE CAR

POOLED BUYING   A number of independent MIDDLEMEN combine their orders informally. The group may change membership from time to time. Same effect as: Informal Buying Group

POOLED MARKETING   An arrangement between two or more manufacturers whereby one offers the PRODUCTS of another as a PREMIUM when buying a certain number of units of the first's product. See: SYMBIOTIC MARKETING

POOLED SYSTEMS PROCUREMENT   Same as: PSP

POOLING   Combining various producers' product without any attempt to keep separated the contribution from any one producer. Typically used by ELEVATORS and selling cooperatives where the goods fall into a limited number of well-defined classes.

POP   Abbreviation for: point-of-purchase, although probably most often used to mean: POINT-OF-PURCHASE ADVERTISING

POPAI   Abbreviation for: POINT-OF-PURCHASE ADVERTISING INSTITUTE, the organization of advertisers, agencies, and producers of POP materials.

POPULATION   In statistics, the entirety of all observations that might be made which are relevant to a certain PROBLEM. Same as: UNIVERSE   See: SAMPLE, SAMPLING

POPULATION LIFE CYCLE   See: LIFE CYCLE OF POPULATION

POP-UP BIN   A display bin so constructed that it can be erected from a flat state in one motion.

PORT   A place for loading and discharging the CARGO of vessels. It has facilities for handling both cargo and personnel, and includes a HARBOR.

PORTABLE REEFER   A refrigerator on wheels which permit moving it about the store to various locations as desired.

POS   Abbreviation for: point-of-sale. Same as: POP

POSITION   See: LONG POSITION, SHORT POSITION

POSITIONING   See: PRODUCT POSITIONING

POSITION MEDIA   A blanket term applied to both OUTDOOR and to TRANSIT ADVERTISING MEDIA, but includes POP and nonstandardized signs.

POSITIVE CONVERSION   Same as: BOOMERANG TECHNIQUE

POSSESSION UTILITY   The characteristic of a good or service which makes it possible to satisfy a human WANT based on the need to have the right to use the good as required. MARKETING creates possession utility through its title-passing activities. See: UTILITY

POSTAGE STAMP PRICING   Same as: FREIGHT ALLOWED

POSTER   An OUTDOOR ADVERTISEMENT characterized by pasting up a series of printed sheets on a smooth surface to form an advertising message. Same as: BILLBOARD. Also, a large-size BANNER to be placed on interior walls or on windows. See: ANGLED POSTER, FLASH APPROACH, PARALLEL POSTER

POSTER BENCH   Some form of seat or bench in a public place on which an advertising message has been painted.

POSTERIOR ANALYSIS   The main purpose of this analysis is to provide for the revision of decisions on the basis of new information. The techniques of MARKETING RESEARCH and various statistical measures come into use here. See: FORMAL DECISION ANALYSIS, PRIOR ANALYSIS, PREPOSTERIOR ANALYSIS

POSTER PANEL   A structure in one of several standard sizes on which POSTERS are pasted.

POSTER PLANT   A local organization which builds and maintains OUTDOOR ADVERTISING FACILITIES. See: POSTER PANEL, PLANT OPERATOR

POST EXCHANGE   Same as: PX

POSTPONEMENT   A principle in the activity of minimizing risks which requires that changes in form and identity occur at the latest possible point in the MARKETING flow, and that changes in inventory location take place at the latest moment in time. Its basic aim is to permit the greatest possible SORTING while the product is relatively undifferentiated as it stands.

POST-PURCHASE DOUBT   See: COGNITIVE DISSONANCE

POTENTIAL COMPETITION   The possibility of entry into the MARKET of new firms, or of substitute products or materials of superior benefits or lower price. Recognition of this possibility is a potent factor in spurring firms toward bettering products and services, even as a real competitor would be, perhaps even more potent, for the unknown is often vested with characteristics of power not attributed to the known.

POTENTIAL COMPETITION DOCTRINE   A way, long established, of interpreting our ANTI-TRUST LAWS which holds that no company may legally acquire another company if it could reasonably be supposed that the acquiring company would or could have been a competitive factor in the INDUSTRY had it not been for the acquisition which eliminated it as a "potential competitor."

POTENTIAL NEED SATISFIER   Any PRODUCT, SERVICE, or consideration which is seen by a CONSUMER as a possible source of satisfaction to a need. Same as: PNS See: EVOKED SET, MASLOW'S HIERARCHY OF NEEDS, RISK REDUCTION

POULTRY PRODUCTS INSPECTION ACT   A Federal law which requires the Department of Agriculture to examine all poultry sold in interstate commerce, before and after slaughter, and to supervise sanitation and processing.

POWER NEED   One of the TRIO OF NEEDS, it involves an individual's desire to control his environment, including things and people. It appears to be associated with self-enhancement. See: EGOISTIC NEEDS

PPI   Abbreviation for: PRODUCER PRICE INDEX

PREAPPROACH   In SELLING, all of the activities which take place before the PROSPECT is contacted. Involves prospect analysis, developing a sales STRATEGY for that prospect, and planning the presentation.

PRECISION   See: STANDARD ERROR OF ESTIMATE

PRECISION IN SAMPLING   Same as: SAMPLING PRECISION

PRECLUSIVE BUYING   The purchase of something to keep someone else from having it, rather than for one's own use.

PRECLUSIVE SPECIFICATION   A specification so written that only one or a

very few suppliers qualify to bid. Good purchasing practice would provide for a maximum of potential suppliers. Any limitation should be
avoided except where it can be justified adequately.

PREDATORY PRICING   Setting prices so low that competitors will be driven
out of business. Illegal where intent can be shown, whether proved or
inferred from flagrant actions. It is usually quite difficult to draw
the line between normal acts of price competition in an active MARKET,
designed to draw business to one competitor rather than another, and
those acts of pricing designed to destroy competitors so as to gain a
monopoly position, which are identifiable as predatory. See: EXTINCTION
PRICE

PREDICTIVE THEORY   That type of THEORY which attempts to tell, using DE-
SCRIPTIVE THEORY as a platform, what will happen under a given set of
circumstances. The difficulty here lies in getting adequate data on the
INDEPENDENT VARIABLES that influence the pattern of the system. A base
for NORMATIVE THEORY.

PREDICTIVE VALIDITY   An attribute of an ATTITUDE measurement mechanism,
such as a QUESTIONNAIRE, when the behavior predicted from the mechanism
has a high CORRELATION with the observed actual behavior. See: CONTENT
VALIDITY, CONSTRUCT VALIDITY, VALIDITY

PREDICTOR VARIABLE   Same as: INDEPENDENT VARIABLE

PREEMPT   In BROADCAST MEDIA, the removing of one program from the air so
that another may be presented in its place.

PREEMPTIVE PRICE   A price set so low that the MARKET is made unattractive
to potential entrants, who might become formidable competitors. Same as:
KEEP-OUT PRICE, STAY-OUT PRICE

PREFERENTIAL DISTINCTIVENESS   See: PERISHABLE DISTINCTIVENESS

PREFERRED OPERATING RATE   The proportion of CAPACITY that a FIRM would
like to use to maximize profit or achieve another objective. Assumes
inputs available as required and output salable as anticipated.

PREFERRED POSITION   Any position for an advertisement in a print MEDIUM for
which the advertiser must pay an additional amount when ordered specifically. The advertiser may be willing to pay the premium if he believes
that the position may have proportionally greater effectiveness. See:
FULL POSITION, PRIME TIME

PREFERRED RESOURCE   A seller established by a BUYER as the first choice
source of supply for a particular kind of goods.

PRELIMINARY RESEARCH   When the PROBLEM or its area need clarification, a
study should be initiated which may be diagnostic, to define the problem
stressing the depth of root causes; or to find the problem's relevant environment, stressing the breadth of the area of information desired.
Without a good understanding of the problem, further study to discover a
solution would be haphazard and likely unproductive. See: CONCLUSIVE
RESEARCH, EXPLORATORY RESEARCH, PERFORMANCE RESEARCH

PRE-MARKETING   Same as: PREPRICING

PREMARKING   A service afforded by some producers by which the merchandise
can have the buyer's selling price put on it at the factory.

PREMIUM   An article of merchandise offered as an INCENTIVE to the perform-
ance of a specified action in the MARKET. May be used to induce
CONSUMERS to try a PRODUCT, or to inspire SALESPERSONS to exceed quotas.
See: DIRECT PREMIUM, INCENTIVE AGENCY, PREMIUM JOBBER, PREMIUM REPRESENTA-
TIVE, REFERRAL PREMIUM, SELF-LIQUIDATOR

PREMIUM ADVERTISING ASSOCIATION OF AMERICA   Same as: PAAA

PREMIUM JOBBER   WHOLESALER of INCENTIVE merchandise, frequently with extensive range of items. May offer a degree of help with plans and literature. See: INCENTIVE AGENCY, PREMIUM REPRESENTATIVE

PREMIUM MONEY   Same as: PUSH MONEY

PREMIUM REPRESENTATIVE (REP)   (1) A specialized MANUFACTURERS' REPRESENTA-
TIVE serving PREMIUM users. Often the key to dealing with manufacturers
or other manufacturers' agents. Offers factory price, back-up support,
knowledge of the INCENTIVE field, and personal service. Each has rather
narrow ASSORTMENT and VARIETY. See: INCENTIVE AGENCY, PREMIUM JOBBER
(2) A commission SALESPERSON serving several manufacturers on a direct-
factory-price basis.

PRE-PALLETIZED FREIGHT   A number of UNIT LOADS mounted on a PALLET for
movement as one piece, eliminating the need for cartons. May weigh about
one ton and occupy about 140 cubic feet. Especially applicable to shipments by water.

PREPOSTERIOR ANALYSIS   The main purpose of this analysis is to determine
whether additional information may be worth the cost of generating it.
Should be done before the MARKETING RESEARCH design is initiated and
refined. See: FORMAL DECISION ANALYSIS, PRIOR ANALYSIS, POSTERIOR
ANALYSIS

PREPRICING   The manufacturer prints the retail price (sometimes as "suggested") on the item or the item's PACKAGE. The effect of this, while it
saves the DEALER the cost of pricing if he sells for the marked price, is
to lock him into a situation where he cannot sell the item for a higher
price despite the willingness of his customers to pay. Indeed, the item
might be more acceptable at the higher price in that location. Sometimes
criticized for the infrequent, unethical practice of putting fictitious,
extra-high prices on items so that a reduction in price seems to indicate
a bargain, which is not true. See: LAW OF DEMAND, QUALITY EFFECT

PREPRINT   A reproduction of an ADVERTISEMENT in advance of its running
in a PRINT MEDIUM.

PREPURCHASE ACTIVITY   The stage that ensues after the buyer has become
aware of the benefits to be had from acquiring a PRODUCT. It involves
the search for information, sources of supply, and reduction of uncertainty,
accompanied by continuing evaluations at each step. The time element at
this stage may be brief or lengthy.

PRERETAILING   A POLICY of requiring that retail prices be established prior
to or at the time of purchase of goods for resale. In many stores the retail prices are placed on a copy of the PURCHASE ORDER at the time the
goods are bought and this copy is used as a price authorization for marking when the goods reach the marking stage in the flow to the selling area.

PRESCRIPTION DRUGS   Same as: ETHICAL DRUGS

PRESS RUN   (1) The number of copies printed. (2) The actual printing of
a particular job.

PRESSURE SENSITIVE TAPE COUNCIL   Same as: PSTC

PRESTIGE PRICING   Setting the price of an item high to attract those who
find satisfaction in owning expensive and relatively exclusive items, or
those who equate high quality with high price. If the DEMAND is enough
and the product lives up to expectations for the buyer, this practice
may prove successful.

PRETEST   The measurement of the acceptance of an idea of a product or service presented to potential buyers. Usually accomplished through interviews with Prospects to determine the strengths and weaknesses of the
ideas or perhaps advertisements either alone or in comparison with others

or a norm. If done properly, this can be of real value in establishing
effective selling STRATEGY.

PRE-TICKETING   Same as PREPRICING

PRE-WRAP   Merchandise wrapped before being placed on sale. May be done in
the STORE or by the source of supply. Used with regular wrapping materials
for normal, high-volume sales items, and with special wrapping materials
for occasions and holidays, such as the gift-wrapping usual to Easter and
Christmas.

PRICE   The amount of something for which something-else can be acquired.
In our modern society the something is the legal tender in the form of
money. In more primitive societies it may be and has been expressed in
cows, horses, wives, beads, etc.

PRICE ANALYSIS   Investigation by a BUYER of a supplier's costs to make an
item with the objective of assisting the buyer to negotiate a price closely parallel to the supplier's cost to produce.

PRICE-AURA EFFECT   Inasmuch as a customer usually buys an assortment of
satisfaction bundles at the same time and place, he tends to judge the
suitability of the price of any one item by his judgment of the prices
of other items of high importance to him which are in the assortment purchased. Each MARKET SEGMENT has its own hierarchy of purchasing priorities and will tend to pay closest attention to the items at the top of
the list. PERCEPTIONS made over a period of time develop into quick judgments regarding present prices. See: COST-PRICE JUDGMENT, FAIR PRICE
REFERENCE REACTION, REVERSE-ORDER PERCEPTION

PRICE DISCRIMINATION   See: ROBINSON-PATMAN ACT

PRICE ELASTICITY OF DEMAND   Other factors remaining constant, the percent
change in quantity demanded of the product or service of interest which
may be expected to result from a percent change in price. The elasticity
between any two points on the DEMAND CURVE may be measured by this
formula:

$$\frac{P + P_1}{P - P_1} \cdot \frac{Q - Q_1}{Q + Q_1} = E$$

Where: P is the price at Q quantity
P_1 is the price at Q_1 quantity

The numerical value of E, called the elasticity coefficient, indicates
the relative increase or decrease (as E is larger or smaller than 1) in
the total revenue effected by changes incorporated into the formula. It
is customary to express this value as a positive number, regardless of
the sign. See: ELASTIC DEMAND, INELASTIC DEMAND, UNITARY DEMAND

PRICE EQUALIZATION   A competitive pricing POLICY that results in a FIRM'S
delivered price to a CUSTOMER consisting of the price of the PRODUCT at
the factory plus the freight cost to the customer as though the shipment
originated from the shipping point of the firm's competitor nearest to the
firm's customer.

PRICE FIXING   See: SHERMAN ACT

PRICE GUARANTY   An agreement on the part of the seller to make a proportionate refund to the BUYER on all applicable items in the buyer's inventory at the time of a price reduction. Usually qualified for a specified
time after purchase.

PRICE LEADERSHIP   Other sellers fix their prices by accepting the price
announced by a leading firm. The leadership may change from time to time.
See: BAROMETRIC PRICE LEADERSHIP, CONSCIOUS PARALLELISM

PRICE LINING   Buying merchandise to sell at a limited number of predetermined selling prices. See: PRICE ZONE

PRICE MIX   The total pattern of a firm's POLICY regarding raising and lowering prices to meet competition, and the LINES on which it will take actions.

PRICE PROTECTION   Same as: PRICE GUARANTY

PRICE SETTING   See: FAIR TRADE LAWS

PRICE STRUCTURE   The integration of the MARKETING system through the inter-relationships and interactions of the myriad individual prices by means of which exchanges are effected in a MARKET economy. Wide variations in price responsiveness may occur over time. See: HOMEOSTASIS

PRICE ZONE   A series of price LINES that appeal to one group of a given RETAIL STORE'S CUSTOMERS. See: PRICE LINING

PRICING   See these types: ADMINISTERED, BALLPARK, BASING POINT, COST-ORIENTED, COST-PLUS, CTO, CUSTOMARY, DELIVERED, DEMAND-ORIENTED, ETHICAL, EQUALIZATION, EXPANSIONIST, EXTINCTION, LIST, MARKET-MINUS, MARKET-PLUS, MULTIPLE-UNIT, ODD, ODDBALL, OPEN-END, PENETRATION, POSTAGE STAMP, PREEMPTIVE, PRESTIGE, PSYCHOLOGICAL, SKIMMING, STAY-OUT, UNIT, ZONE
See also: FREIGHT ALLOWED, FREIGHT EQUALIZATION, ONE-PRICE POLICY, OPEN, SINGLE-PRICE POLICY, PRICE ELASTICITY OF DEMAND, PRICE GUARANTY, PRICE LEADERSHIP, PRICE LINING, PRICE MIX, VARIABLE PRICE POLICY

PRICING ERROR   Although buying and selling techniques have been adequate, the wrong price was selected at the first offering of the goods, necessitating a MARKDOWN in order to move the merchandise. See: BUYING ERROR, SELLING ERROR

PRIMARY BUSINESS TEST   A provision of the Interstate Commerce Act designed to distinguish PRIVATE CARRIAGE from for-hire carriage by motor vehicles. Under this test, persons engaged in any other business enterprise may not transport property by motor vehicle in interstate or foreign commerce for business purposes unless such transportation is within the scope, and the furtherance of, the primary business enterprise other than transportation operated by such persons. The rules have recently been relaxed to permit contracting services. Some commodities are exempted. See: BUY-AND-SELL TRANSPORT

PRIMARY BUYING MOTIVE   A PRODUCT MOTIVE applicable to a product the concept of which is new to the MARKET or which has not yet been generally accepted. For example, when commercial air travel was first introduced, it was necessary to convince people that benefits were to be found in flying that were superior to those found by using other means of personal transportation. To this day, the vast majority of people in the United States have never flown. Much work remains toward activating primary motives with respect to air travel. See: PIONEERING STAGE, SELECTIVE BUYING MOTIVE

PRIMARY CENTRAL MARKET   An area in which the concentration of available supply of agricultural CONSUMERS' GOODS is at a maximum. See: LOCAL MARKET

PRIMARY CIRCULATION   The number of residents of HOUSEHOLDS who buy a publication. In contrast to: PASS-ALONG CIRCULATION

PRIMARY DATA   Those data gathered by the firm itself by going directly to the source. Includes internal data, i.e., data available currently from company records. When the gathering of primary data is done outside the company, the process is most often called MARKET RESEARCH. See: SECONDARY DATA

PRIMARY DEMAND   Refers to the DEMAND for a class of PRODUCT, such as washing machines. See: SELECTIVE DEMAND

PRIMARY DEMAND ADVERTISING   ADVERTISING intended to create PRIMARY BUYING MOTIVES within the AUDIENCE. See: SECONDARY DEMAND ADVERTISING

PRIMARY GROUP   Any group in which an individual finds face-to-face associa-

tion and very high cooperation among members, for example, car pools.
See: SECONDARY GROUP

PRIMARY INDIVIDUAL   In census data, a HOUSEHOLD HEAD living alone or with
non-relatives only. The number of primary individuals living alone equals
the number of one-person HOUSEHOLDS. See: SECONDARY INDIVIDUAL

PRIMARY MARKET   Same as: LOCAL MARKET

PRIMARY NEEDS   Basic physiological needs such as hunger, thirst, shelter,
sex. Same as: BIOGENIC NEEDS, INNATE NEEDS, PHYSIOLOGICAL NEEDS

PRIMARY PROCESSED GOODS   A CLASSIFICATION used by THE CONFERENCE BOARD when
reporting on manufacturing CAPACITY. The goods include: lumber; stone,
clay, and glass; blast furnace and steel work products; nonferrous and
other primary metals; fabricated metals; textiles; paper; chemicals;
petroleum; and rubber. See: ADVANCED PROCESSED GOODS

PRIMARY READERSHIP   Essentially the same as: PRIMARY CIRCULATION

PRIMARY STAGE   Same as: PIONEERING STAGE

PRIMARY TRADING AREA   The particular geographic boundary within which a
MARKETING institution has buying and/or selling dominance. See: AREA
STRUCTURE, SECONDARY TRADING AREA, ZONE OF INDIFFERENCE

PRIME TIME   In BROADCAST MEDIA, the several hours during the day that attract the largest AUDIENCES. Different for RADIO than for TELEVISION.
Not the same for all products, e.g., an advertiser of toys might prefer
Sunday mornings. Most stations do not accept 1-minute SPOTS in this time
but do accept 10- and 20-second spots. See: DRIVE TIME, FRINGE TIME

PRINCIPAL   One who designates another to act as his agent or representative.

PRINCIPAL REGISTER   MARKS, with certain exceptions and with proper qualifications, may be registered on this in the U.S. Patent Office. Such
registration is constructive notice of the registrant's claim of ownership and prima facie evidence of the validity of the registrant's exclusive right to use the mark in commerce. It also gives the right to sue
in the United States courts and to prevent importation of goods bearing
an infringing mark. Marks must have been in lawful use in commerce for
at least one year to be eligible. See: SUPPLEMENTAL REGISTER

PRINCIPLE   An exploratory statement of general truth, derived from a study
of FACTS set up in a cause and effect relationship, that always applies
under given conditions or assumptions.

PRINCIPLE OF MARKETING RELATIVISM   Same as: MARKETING RELATIVISM

PRINTER'S INK MODEL STATUTE   A law, drawn up and sponsored vigorously by
this advertising TRADE MAGAZINE since 1911, designed to prevent deceptive
and misleading advertising. Only six states have no law of this kind.
Printer's Ink is now known as Marketing/Communications.

PRINT MEASUREMENT BUREAU   Created and supported by advertisers, agencies,
and national print MEDIA to take accurate measurements of Canadian MAGA-
ZINE AUDIENCES. The planned result is to provide dependable figures with
which planners may operate. Started in 1972.

PRINTOUT   The document produced by a computer when ordered to report the
data accumulated or calculated as a result of certain inputs.

PRIOR ANALYSIS   The main purpose of this analysis is to provide a basis for
choosing among alternative courses of action based on existing information.
Allows for the use of DECISION TREES. See: FORMAL DECISION ANALYSIS,
PREPOSTERIOR ANALYSIS, POSTERIOR ANALYSIS

PRIVATE BRAND　A BRAND NAME owned by a MIDDLEMAN.　Sometimes called: PRIVATE LABEL

PRIVATE CARRIER　A TRANSPORTATION agency owned and operated by the FIRM using it.　It is not available to anyone else.　There are complex legal provisions which determine the permissable operating mechanics of a private carrier.　These rules are in process of being relaxed in order to be consistent with the government's deregulation activities.　See: PRIMARY BUSINESS TEST

PRIVATE CARRIER CONFERENCE　Same as: PCC

PRIVATE LABEL　Same as: PRIVATE BRAND

PRIVATE TRUCK COUNCIL OF AMERICA　Same as: PTC

PRIVITY OF CONTRACT RULE　A rule in common law, which became undisputed legal dogma in this country, that the maker of an item could not be held liable for damages caused by his product unless he sold directly to the user.　Where he sold to a reseller, he was effectively immunized against liability.　This rule has been totally eroded since the landmark case of MacPherson vs Buick Motor Co. in New York in 1916.　By 1966 all the states had adopted laws which had made privity no longer a requirement.　In addition, many cases have been interpreted on this basis: that a manufacturer or seller has strict liability, requiring only proof by the injured party that the item had a defect which damaged him during use that should have been reasonably anticipated.　In general, under the present status of "products liabilities" law, employees, members of the buyer's family, subsequent buyers, users of the product, persons in the vicinity of the product's probable use, and mere bystanders can recover for injuries proved to have been caused by the product as the result of defects. Among those who can be sued are manufacturers of PARTS, those who place PRIVATE LABELS on another's products, RETAILERS, repairmen, and contractors.　The recent rash of product recalls was prompted in large part by this current legal thinking away from CAVEAT EMPTOR.　See: PRODUCT LIABILITY

PROBABILITY SAMPLE　A SAMPLE chosen by a procedure which results in every element of the POPULATION having a known, and usually equal, chance of being selected.　This quality makes possible the use of the techniques of statistical inference to determine the degree of accuracy of the data derived from the sample.　See: CLUSTER SAMPLING, SIMPLE RANDOM SAMPLING, STRATIFIED SAMPLING, SYSTEMATIC SAMPLING

PROBLEM　The situation which exists when the decision-maker is faced with a question which must be answered and the answer involves uncertainty. It should not necessarily be associated with "trouble."　See: DECISION, PROBLEM SOLVING, SYMPTOM

PROBLEM SOLVING　All phases of action undertaken to resolve doubt or to reduce the RISK to acceptable levels of probability in order to lead to a course of activity designed to attain desired objectives.　See: MARKETING RESEARCH, PAYOFF, PROBLEM

PROCESS AVERAGE　A term used in PURCHASING to denote the average percent of defective PARTS submitted in a supplier's shipments.　It is sometimes used as part of a formula designed to help in determining the necessity for inspection where inspection is to be accomplished by SAMPLE.

PROCESSED MATERIALS　Essentially the same as: FABRICATING MATERIALS

PROCESS MACHINERY　Same as: INSTALLATIONS

PROCESS PLATES　See: FOUR-COLOR PROCESS

PROCUREMENT　That activity within a firm which carries out the BUYING function.　It involves organization, personnel, VALUE ANALYSIS, description of requirements, sources of supply, analysis of vendor and price, deter-

mination of acceptability, FORWARD BUYING, SALVAGE operations, and procurement budgeting. Often includes inventory control and analysis. In
general the same as: PURCHASING

PRODUCER PRICE INDEX   Essentially the same as WHOLESALE PRICE INDEX, but
with a few minor revisions. The new name was adopted in 1978.

PRODUCERS' GOODS   See: CAPITAL

PRODUCER'S RISK   Used sometimes in PURCHASING to denote the probability
of rejecting a SAMPLE of a lot which is actually satisfactory. See:
CONSUMER'S RISK

PRODUCT   The totality of every aspect of a firm's offering which the PROS-
PECT perceives as giving VALUE. May involve psychological as well as
physical aspects. See: DESIRE-SET, USE-SYSTEM

PRODUCT ANALYSIS   Investigation by a BUYER of the performance of a purchased item with the objective of determining an adequate QUALITY at the
lowest final cost. See: VALUE ANALYSIS

PRODUCT BUY-BACK AGREEMENT   Same as: BUY-BACK

PRODUCT DELETION   Essentially the same as: SIMPLIFICATION, but may take
place on a slower, more piece-by-piece basis.

PRODUCT DEVELOPMENT   A very complex MARKETING activity, not with characteristics common to many companies, but generally encompassing initial
development, subsequent change to reflect new ideas, and the determination of new applications.

PRODUCT DIFFERENTIATION   The situation in which two products of similar
characteristics and end use, usually made by different producers, acquire
divergent IMAGES in the minds of SEGMENTS of the MARKET. Ordinarily comes
about through promotional activities by the respective producers. See:
MULTIPLE BRAND ENTRIES

PRODUCT DISFEATURE   Something about a PRODUCT that a PROSPECT does not like.
Price is often such a thing, except for PRESTIGE goods and services.
See: FEATURE

PRODUCT FEATURE APPROACH   A way of determining CHANNELS OF DISTRIBUTION by
assuming that size, unit value, perishability, requirement for service,
and the like, should be used to fit the product into a channel set to
handle them. The process is incorrect theoretically and potentially dangerous because it gives little or no thought to the requirements or buying
habits of the potential users, and there is no necessary correlation between product features and channel features.

PRODUCT IMAGE   How the CONSUMER perceives the characteristics of a PRODUCT.
What really counts for the marketer is not what the product really is, but
what the consumer thinks of it as being. See: BRAND IMAGE, PERCEPTION,
PRODUCT POSITIONING

PRODUCTION   (1) Creation of UTILITY. (2) In everyday language, the same
as: manufacturing.

PRODUCTION FUNCTION   A statement of the varying amounts of output per time
period which may be expected to result from the application of different
levels and combinations of resources, e.g., more or less labor combined
with more or less equipment. A firm should aim at that combination which
provides the required result at the lowest unit cost. Requires attention
because the relationship among the factors may change over time.

PRODUCTION INVENTORY   The stock of goods that will be used up in manufacturing. It consists of RAW MATERIALS, PARTS, FABRICATING MATERIALS, and
SUPPLIES. Usually of such great importance that this be attended properly that it is worth being the primary, if not the sole, responsibility of
one person placed in the firm's policy-making echelon.

PRODUCTION-ORIENTED DIVERSIFICATION   Same as: CONGRUENT PRODUCTION DIVER-
SIFICATION

PRODUCTIVITY   Output units per man-hour expended.   It is redundant to
preface this definition with the word "useful."

PRODUCT LIABILITY   Whereas negligence by manufacturers and DISTRIBUTORS
was formerly held to be the required grounds for damages, recent court
cases have introduced the concept of STRICT LIABILITY, which holds manufacturers, sellers, WHOLESALERS or RETAILERS, equally liable for customer
injury without the need by the complainant to prove negligence.   See:
PRIVITY OF CONTRACT RULE

PRODUCT LIFE CYCLE   Same as: LIFE CYCLE OF PRODUCT

PRODUCT LINE   Same as: LINE (3)

PRODUCT MANAGER   In a FIRM organized according to the MARKETING CONCEPT, a
person charged with planning and coordinating all activities pertinent to
the successful introduction and continuous profitable sale of one PRODUCT,
or a series of very closely related products, to the TARGET MARKET.   Because this person is not vested with AUTHORITY, he can discharge his
responsibilities only through his powers of persuasion, backed by the
implied edict of higher ECHELONS for the necessary interdepartmental
cooperation.   Essentially the same as: Brand Manager, Project Manager

PRODUCT MIX   A firm's entire PRODUCT complex.

PRODUCT MOTIVES   The considerations explaining why customers buy certain
products.   See: PATRONAGE MOTIVES

PRODUCT PLANNING   The company activity which involves the screening and
appraisal of an idea, analysis of the MARKET, and the development and
testing of a product before production is committed.   Although specific
organization for this effort varies from company to company, it is almost uniformly recognized as belonging in the top management echelons.

PRODUCT POSITIONING   The attempt by marketers to achieve the acceptance by
TARGET MARKETS of their PRODUCTS as better fulfilling specific wants, or
having specific characteristics superior to competing BRANDS.   See:
PERCEPTUAL MAPPING, PRODUCT SPACE

PRODUCT POSTCARD AUDIT   See: CCAB

PRODUCT PROTECTION   In ADVERTISING, the spacing of advertisements of competing products so that either a certain period of time (as in BROADCAST
MEDIA) or a certain number of pages (as in PRINT MEDIA) separates the advertisements.   Subject to negotiation between advertiser and medium.   Same
as: COMMERCIAL PROTECTION, SEPARATION

PRODUCT REPUTATION ADVERTISING   Same as: COMMERCIAL ADVERTISING, PROMOTIONAL
ADVERTISING

PRODUCT RESEARCH   Same as: QUALITATIVE MARKET ANALYSIS

PRODUCT SPACE   The totality of all the dimensions of a PRODUCT as they might
be arranged on continuums of ATTRIBUTES, such as softness, status-giving,
economy, size, price, etc.   The closer two competing products are in the
product space, the more alike they will be perceived by the MARKET.   See:
PRODUCT POSITIONING

PRODUCT SPLITTING   A practice in the motion-picture INDUSTRY in which competing theaters agree not to show any one picture at the same time.
Suspect under our ANTI-TRUST LAWS.   See: BLIND BIDDING, BLOCK BIDDING

PRODUCT SPOTTER   A small, attention-getting device or sign placed on or
attached to a shelf to emphasize a particular BRAND or PACKAGE.   Often
used as part of the effort to introduce a new product.

PRODUCT USAGE SEGMENTATION   One of a four-way classification of the

STRATEGIES of SEGMENTATION, this tries to relate observed factors of use to the ways in which users with certain characteristics react to particular MARKETING MIXES. The other three are: BENEFIT SEGMENTATION, STATE-OF-BEING SEGMENTATION, and STATE-OF-MIND SEGMENTATION

PROFESSIONAL ADVERTISING   ADVERTISING directed by the maker of a product or producer of a service to someone who can specify it for use by those whom he advises. See: PROFESSIONAL PUBLICATION

PROFESSIONAL PUBLICATION   A PERIODICAL addressed to those persons who are able to influence the use of the advertiser's offering in connection with discharging the duties of their callings, e.g., physicians, dentists, teachers, bankers. See: PROFESSIONAL ADVERTISING

PROFIT ANALYSIS   See: PERFORMANCE ANALYSIS

PROFIT CENTER   A unit of a business sufficiently self-contained so that a useful measure of its contribution to the profit of the firm may be developed for it. DECENTRALIZATION is fostered when a firm is divided into profit centers. See: EXPENSE CENTER

PROFIT IMPACT OF MARKETING STRATEGIES   Same as: PIMS

PROGRAM   (1) The sequence of operating INSTRUCTIONS given to a computer system to obtain a desired result. See: SOFTWARE   (2) To compile and put into logical sequence all the INSTRUCTIONS necessary to solve a problem, using a computer system for the operations. (3) See: PACKAGE

PROGRAM LOADING ROUTINE   In ADP, a routine able to bring the remainder of the PROGRAM into the computer's memory from whatever type of memory unit is being used. Such a routine must itself be in the computer's memory.

PROGRAM MANAGER   Essentially the same as: PRODUCT MANAGER

PROGRAMMED MERCHANDISING   A concentration on top management executives of a RETAIL organization in joining with its BUYERS to develop a key resource for significantly increasing the amount of business done with that LINE. The plan will include commitments for all forms of PROMOTIONAL effort.

PROGRAMMING   The art and science of converting the plan for the solution of a PROBLEM into INSTRUCTIONS which a machine, usually a computer, can understand and use.

PROJECTION   (1) Essentially the same as: FORECASTING   (2) A way of coping with FRUSTRATION by transferring to objects or other persons the blame for one's failures or inabilities. See: AGGRESSION, AUTISM, IDENTIFICATION, RATIONALIZATION, REGRESSION, REPRESSION

PROJECTIVE METHODS   Same as: PROJECTIVE TECHNIQUES

PROJECTIVE TECHNIQUES   See: SENTENCE COMPLETION, STORYTELLING, THEMATIC APPERCEPTION TEST (TAT), WORD ASSOCIATION

PROJECT MANAGER   Essentially the same as: PRODUCT MANAGER

PROMOTIONAL ADVERTISING   ADVERTISING intended to stimulate immediate purchase of a certain product. See: INSTITUTIONAL ADVERTISING, LOCAL ADVERTISING, NATIONAL ADVERTISING   Same as: PRODUCT REPUTATION ADVERTISING

PROMOTIONAL ELASTICITY OF DEMAND   Other factors remaining constant, the percent change in quantity demanded which may result from a percent change in promotional activity. See: PRICE ELASTICITY OF DEMAND

PROMOTIONAL KIT   A collection of materials, plans, ideas, and suggestions supplied as one piece to RETAILERS by a source of supply which may be a manufacturer, an importer, or a WHOLESALER.

PROMOTIONAL MIX   The combination of all means used to effect sales. It should be recognized that a great deal of substitutability exists among the various means. Traditional mixes may not produce the greatest efficacy at the lowest cost, usually a desired outcome.

PROMOTIONAL PACKAGE   An assortment of special materials sent to a DEALER to help him tie in with the ADVERTISING THEME of a product's manufacturer. Usually consists of such materials as BANNERS, window streamers, INSERTS, etc.

PROMOTOOLS   Any of the various MEDIA used in the PROMOTIONAL MIX. Includes such activities and units as demonstrations, contests, trade exhibits, free samples, catalogs, trading stamps.

PROOF   (1) an inked impression of type or PLATE for inspection or filing. (2) An impression taken during the engraving or etching process to determine the condition of the illustration at some stage of the work. See: PULLING A PROOF

PROPENSITY TO CONSUME.   Measured by the percent of DISPOSABLE INCOME that CONSUMERS may be expected to spend.

PROPRIETARY DRUGS   Same as: OTC

PROSE MODEL   Consisting mainly of verbal matter, it is usually a descriptive model, but may be analytical in nature. When the latter, it is relatively cumbersome as compared with a MATHEMATICAL MODEL. See: ANALYTICAL MODEL, MODEL

PROSPECT   Anyone not now using a firm's product or service, who can benefit from owning it, who has the purchasing power to acquire it, who has the authority to make the decision, and who is available. Someone who is not qualified as indicated above should not be subjected to a selling effort. In the industrial field where MULTIPLE PURCHASING INFLUENCE is a significant factor, persons who can influence the purchasing decision are often called prospects.

PROSPECTING   The activity of seeking out and qualifying PROSPECTS. See: PREAPPROACH

PROSPERITY   See: BUSINESS CYCLE

PROXIMO TERMS   Very similar to E.O.M. terms, but specify the date in the following month by which payment must be made in order to take the CASH DISCOUNT, so there may be no question of industry custom as there may be with E.O.M. terms. Example: 3%, 15th Proximo, n/60 indicates that a discount of 3% may be taken any time through the 15th of the month following purchase, and failing that, the full amount must be paid not later than 60 days following the first of the month following purchase.

PSP   Abbreviation for: Pooled Systems Procurement. It is in essence a modification of SYSTEMS CONTRACTING to a cost-plus basis in which the DISTRIBUTORS agree to be subject to audit. The contract is usually for eighteen months and includes various provisions for equity to BUYER and seller. Its plan can encompass a number of sources at the same time, providing commonality for a multi-plant buyer. Pioneered by General Electric.

PSTC   Abbreviation for: Pressure Sensitive Tape Council, established in 1953 as an organization of American manufacturers of tape which sticks without wetting or application of heat. There are over 350 different types of such tapes. The Council is involved in the collection of statistical data, the development of technical standards and safety and testing standards, and a program directed toward expanding the MARKET awareness of pressure sensitive tapes.

PSYCHIC INCOME   A flow of satisfactions over a period of time. There is no standard unit of measurement for this. However, everyone is able to achieve for himself a measure of the satisfaction from one group of experiences relative to another group of experiences.

PSYCHOACOUSTICS   The study of what people think they hear as compared with what is actually spoken. Applies to volume level as well as content.

PSYCHOGENIC DRIVES   Same as: SOCIOLOGICAL MOTIVES

PSYCHOGRAPHIC MARKET SEGMENTATION   The STRATEGY of segmenting a MARKET by selecting people who react in the same way to a particular emotional AP-PEAL, or who share common behavioral patterns. In contrast to: DEMO-GRAPHIC MARKET SEGMENTATION

PSYCHOGRAPHICS   Psychological profiles of potential customers in a MARKET. See: AIO

PSYCHOLOGICAL DISCOUNTING   Presenting the illusion of a reduction in price by fictitious comparisons of present price with previous price. Often, the previous price never existed, or if it did, was in existence for the briefest possible time. Illegal under our present laws unless literally true for a reasonable prior period. Sometimes called: was-is-pricing.

PSYCHOLOGICAL MOMENT   That point during a sales presentation when the SALES-MAN feels he can and should attempt a TRIAL CLOSE. May occur more than once during the same presentation.

PSYCHOLOGICAL PRICING   A pricing POLICY designed to create the impression that the PRODUCT is a bargain, or, on the other hand, of high quality or status. See: ODD PRICING, PRESTIGE PRICING

PSYCHOLOGICAL RISK   See: CONSUMER-PERCEIVED RISKS

PSYCHOLOGY   The behavioral science which studies man's behavior as derived from his inner motivations. See: SOCIOLOGY

P-SYSTEM   A system of inventory control in which the reorder period is held constant and the reorder quantity is altered. See: Q-SYSTEM

PTC   Abbreviation for: Private Truck Council of America, which changed its name in 1953 from National Council of Private Motor Truck Operators, organized in 1939. It is the only independent, national organization exclusively representing the interests of firms that operate their own trucks in furtherance of a primary commercial enterprise not including for-hire trucking. Its services have been highly innovative and its activities have resulted in beneficial legislation, regular informational bulletins, a definitive Driver's Handbook, and the Federal Highway Regulations Manual. Its coverage is for about 90% of the trucks in use on the U.S. highways.

P.T. FILE   Abbreviation for: Personal Trade File, it is an index card record kept by a RETAIL SALESPERSON of significant data about CUSTOMERS who ask for that salesperson by name for service.

PUBLICATION   In ADVERTISING, any printed unit issued regularly, containing an EDITORIAL and an advertising POLICY, directed to a specific AUDIENCE, narrow or broad.

PUBLIC DOMAIN   A term used to describe the situation wherein a melody, major literary work, patent, etc., may be used by anyone because the legal protection period has expired. See: COPYRIGHT

PUBLIC HEALTH CIGARETTE SMOKING ACT   As at April 1, 1970, this law provided that: 1) Retroactive to July 1, 1969 this Act takes precedence over any state law covering its provisions; 2) After January 1, 1971 all cigarette advertising on electronic communications media is barred; 3) Effective November 1, 1970, cigarette packages must be labeled "Warning: The Surgeon General Has Determined that Cigarette Smoking is Dangerous to Your Health;" 4) The FTC may not require such disclosures in nonelectronic media until July 1, 1971, after which it must give Congress six month's notice of plans to act; 5) Various effectiveness reports are required. Cigarettes for export are exempt from the Act.

PUBLICITY   Unpaid exposure to the MARKET, by an unnamed source, of commercially significant information about a PRODUCT or company.

PUBLIC RELATIONS   A planned program of policies and conduct designed to build confidence and increase the understanding of one or more of a firm's publics. These publics may be classified as: 1) Customers, 2) Suppliers, 3) Competitors, 4) Employees, 5) Stockholders, 6) Creditors, 7) Local Community, 8) The Government. It should be noted that these are not mutually exclusive. See: EXTERNALITIES

PUBLIC RELATIONS INSTITUTIONAL ADVERTISING   The thrust of this type of INSTITUTIONAL ADVERTISING is to enhance the reputation or the image of the FIRM. See: PATRONAGE INSTITUTIONAL ADVERTISING, PUBLIC SERVICE INSTITUTIONAL ADVERTISING

PUBLICS   See: PUBLIC RELATIONS

PUBLIC SERVICE INSTITUTIONAL ADVERTISING   The thrust of this type of INSTITUTIONAL ADVERTISING is to present and champion noncontroversial causes in the interest of the general citizenry. See: ADVERTISING COUNCIL, PATRONAGE INSTITUTIONAL ADVERTISING, PUBLIC RELATIONS INSTITUTIONAL ADVERTISING

PUBLIC WAREHOUSE   An organization which offers storage space at a fee to anyone who wishes to use the service. See: BONDED WAREHOUSE

PUBLISHERS INFORMATION BUREAU   Same as: PIB

PUB SET   Type composition done by the PUBLICATION in which the advertisement is to appear. In the general activity of publication composing rooms the quality of the work is likely to be inferior to that which can be produced by an ADVERTISING TYPOGRAPHER.

PUFFING   Moderate exaggeration in a normal attempt to make a sale, whether through ADVERTISING or SALESMANSHIP. Has been considered a legal practice. However, the boundary between puffing and deception is hazy. The increasing interest in CONSUMERISM is causing government agencies such as the FTC to take a closer and harder look at this practice. With "truth in advertising" becoming interpreted more and more literally, a seller would be wise to use caution in how he exaggerates any of the benefits of his products or services.

PULL   In RETAILING, the power of an ADVERTISEMENT to produce sales. Used in such statements as: "The ad pulled well yesterday" and "A LAYOUT of that sort has never pulled well." Sometimes used in Direct Response selling activity.

PULL DISTRIBUTION STRATEGY   See: PUSH OR PULL DISTRIBUTION STRATEGY

PULLING A PROOF   The term used to indicate the action of making a PROOF.

PULSATION   The technique in ADVERTISING of having several short but intensive periods of advertising during the year, interspersed with hiatuses, periods with little or no advertising. Some firms use a large smash at a certain time of the year, followed by a spotty cadence. Others use a more regular cadence of heavy then light or none at all. Same as: WAVE SCHEDULING, WAVING

PULSE   (1) Short for: The PULSE, Incorporated, a MARKET RESEARCH company specializing in the personal-interview aided-recall technique to determine the percent of homes tuned to a given BROADCAST MEDIUM. It renders AUDIENCE reports for RADIO, CIRCULATION classification reports for NEWSPAPERS, and special reports on CONSUMER preferences for BRANDS. It does studies for clients as requested. Its work is highly regarded in the industry. (2) To practice PULSATION.

PUNCH-CARD COUPON   A COUPON pre-punched so that data processing equipment can sense and accumulate information about redemption area and other data that the seller wants to know. See: COUPONING, CROSS-COUPONING

PUNCH-CARD EQUIPMENT   All the devices which punch standard cards with specific data, or which are intermediary to the use of that data as input to other calculating or processing devices. Same as: Tab Equipment

PURCHASE   DESIRE culminated.

PURCHASE ANALYSIS   See: PURCHASE RESEARCH, VALUE ANALYSIS, VALUE CONTROL, VALUE ENGINEERING

PURCHASE AND RESALE AGREEMENT   An agreement between an oil marketer and a tire supplier to buy the latter's tires for resale to the oil marketer's affiliated RETAILERS. Used to a lesser extent in other industries. Care must be taken that no coercion exist in the resale effort, or the entire arrangement may be considered illegal as a restraint of trade.

PURCHASE DELAY   A DELAYED RESPONSE EFFECT which is the time lag between the PERCEPTION by the PROSPECT of the MARKETING stimulus, and the prospect's becoming sufficiently motivated to buy whatever the stimulus presented. In many instances, prospects take much time comparing offers, thinking over relative benefits claims, determining financial aspects, etc., before finally responding to the stimulus with a purchase.

PURCHASE ORDER   The written document issued by the purchasing department of a firm to a vendor to procure goods to fill a requirement. Upon acceptance it acquires the legal force of a binding contract. See: REQUISITION

PURCHASE-PRIVILEGE OFFER   Same as: TRADE CARDS

PURCHASE REQUISITION   A form issued by a using department to the purchasing department requesting the acquisition of material not regularly carried in normal stock. May be issued, also, by the STORES department in order to replenish stock. See: REQUISITION

PURCHASE RESEARCH   Same as: VALUE ANALYSIS

PURCHASING   Same as: PROCUREMENT

PURCHASING AGENT   (1) A FUNCTIONAL MIDDLEMAN characterized by representation of the BUYER. (2) Applied to an employee of an industrial firm who is delegated the AUTHORITY to commit the firm for acquisition of materials and equipment. (3) In a DEPARTMENT STORE, the person authorized to acquire materials needed for operation and maintenance of the premises. Distinguish from: BUYER

PURCHASING MANUAL   May be a POLICY manual with broad applications of policy statements affecting purchasing aspects of the firm, or a Procedures manual detailing how each activity is to be handled, with implications only for the internal operation of the purchasing department, or it may be a combination of the two types.

PURCHASING POWER   Same as: BUYING POWER

PURE IMPULSE BUYING   IMPULSE BUYING where the customer buys because he becomes intrigued on the spot with the novelty or the worthiness of the offering. See: PLANNED IMPULSE BUYING, REMINDER IMPULSE BUYING, SUGGESTION IMPULSE BUYING

PUSH MONEY   A cash reward offered by a manufacturer or owner to RETAIL sales personnel for selling that manufacturer's products. Has recently come under attack as an unfair practice when initiated by a manufacturer. Commonly abbreviated: PM. Same as: Premium Money

PUSH OR PULL DISTRIBUTION STRATEGY   If push, it will have been decided to attempt to convince the WHOLESALER that it will be advantageous for him to carry the item, then he in turn will attempt to convince the RETAILER, who in turn will attempt to convince the CONSUMER of the product's merit. If pull, it will have been decided to attempt to create DEMAND directly with the consumer through various forms of promotion with the expectation that the consumer will ask the retailer for the item, who in turn will ask the wholesaler who will order it from the maker. Combination is possible.

PX   Abbreviation for: Post Exchange, a COMMISSARY STORE situated on or near a military base to service the base's personnel.

QI   Abbreviation for: QUALITY INDEX

Q-SYSTEM   A system of inventory control which holds the reorder quantity constant and varies the reorder period. See: P-SYSTEM

QUAD   A blank piece of metal placed between CHARACTERS or words. It is used to spread out or JUSTIFY lines of type.

QUADRANGLE   Same as: ADVERTISING QUADRANGLE

QUALIFIED CIRCULATION   See: CONTROLLED CIRCULATION

QUALIFIED PROSPECT   A PROSPECT who has been subjected to the QUALIFYING ACTIVITY.

QUALIFYING ACTIVITY   That activity in the selling process by means of which a PROSPECT is determined to have the definitional characteristics.

QUALIFYING DIMENSIONS   (1) Those characteristics of people in a TARGET MARKET which make them eligible to buy a PRODUCT. (2) Same as: QUALIFYING DECISIONS

QUALIFYING FACTORS   Those PROSPECT characteristics which potentially place people within a MARKET in one of the areas of a MARKET GRID. Sometimes called: Qualifying Dimensions. See: DETERMINING FACTORS

QUALITATIVE MARKET ANALYSIS   Study of the MARKET with the objective of securing information which may ultimately affect the nature of the product. Also called: Product Research

QUALITY   (1) That characteristic of a product or service which makes it suitable for the purpose intended. The word "suitability" is more accurate than the word "quality." The grade of goods bought should not be better than that demanded by the need of the use to which the goods are to be put in the firm. (2) Used in a loose way to denote relative class or grade, e.g., "high", "medium", or "low" quality. See: ECONOMIC QUALITY, TECHNICAL QUALITY

QUALITY CONTROL   In PURCHASING, this is accomplished by inspection of incoming goods by one or more of these methods: visual check by markings (for standard brand packaged material with a good QUALITY record); examination in detail of part of a lot (a statistical DECISION RULE may be developed to accept or reject materials with a reasonably good quality record); examination in detail of each item in a lot (for materials with many points to be considered, or with a poor quality record); regular laboratory tests (for materials of importance whose chemical or physical properties are crucial to the firm's activities); occasional laboratory tests (for items of lesser significance such as many in the SUPPLIES category).

QUALITY-COST RATIO   See: COST-RATIO METHOD

QUALITY DESCRIPTION   In PURCHASING, the communication to the supplier of the nature and characteristics of the item wanted. The following methods of description are ordinarily used: specification of physical and/or chemical properties; specification of material and method of manufacture; specification of performance; BRAND; blueprint; SAMPLE; market grade; some combination of these.

QUALITY EFFECT   For products the relative competitive merits of which are not well known or easily discovered, price may become the indicator of usefulness or the probability of relative satisfactions. The PERCEPTION of the CONSUMER is the controlling variable here. See: LAW OF DEMAND

QUALITY INDEX   A relative measure of the per capita purchasing power of a geographical area, published annually by Sales & Marketing Management magazine. The QI for the nation = 100. Significant only if used with some measure of market size. See: INDEX OF SALES ACTIVITY

QUANTITATIVE MARKET ANALYSIS   Study of the MARKET with the objective of determining how much can be sold for what uses, when, and in what parts of the total market. The unit of measurement usually is either the use or the user.

QUANTITY DISCOUNT   (1) Same as: PATRONAGE DISCOUNT, but may apply to size of single orders only. (2) In ADVERTISING, same as: BULK DISCOUNT

QUARTER HOUR PERSONS   Same as: AVERAGE QUARTER HOUR PERSONS

QUARTER SHOWING   In TRANSIT ADVERTISING, the message of an advertiser in every fourth unit of a system. Sometimes used in OUTDOOR ADVERTSING instead of #25 showing.

QUARTILE   These divide the ARRAY into four equal parts. See: MEDIAN

QUASI-CHAIN   A group of RETAIL STORES, independently owned, but affiliated with some type of central organization. See: COOPERATIVE CHAIN, FRANCHISING, VOLUNTARY CHAIN

QUESTION   See these types: DICHOTOMOUS, DIRECTED-RESPONSE, FREE RESPONSE, OPEN-ENDED, PAIRED COMPARISON

QUESTIONNAIRE   A device which provides for the orderly gathering of responses from RESPONDENTS. It may be printed and given or sent to respondents for completion and return, or it may be administered orally by trained field representatives who themselves record the respondent's answers to the questions asked. See: FIXED-ALTERNATIVE QUESTION, OPEN-ENDED QUESTION, SCALES

QUOTA   (1) Same as: SALES QUOTA   (2) A physical limit set on the import of a PRODUCT. It may be mandatory or voluntary. A form of NTB.

QUOTA CONTROL SAMPLING   Same as: QUOTA SAMPLING

QUOTA SAMPLING   A type of JUDGMENT SAMPLING in which interviewers look for specific numbers of RESPONDENTS with known characteristics. Differs from RANDOM SAMPLING in that each unit in the UNIVERSE does not have an equal chance of selection.

RAB   Abbreviation for: Radio Advertising Bureau, an organization of stations, NETWORKS, and representatives the major ojective of which is to promote RADIO as an ADVERTISING MEDIUM.

RABBLE HYPOTHESIS   An assumption that mankind is a horde of unorganized individuals actuated by self-interest. Not much adhered to by today's managers. See: SMALL GROUP THEORY

RACK   A floor stand designed to hold merchandise on shelves, on hooks, or in pockets. The RACK JOBBER will supply these as an integral part of his service if the store does not insist on having its own matching units.

RACK JOBBER   A LIMITED-FUNCTION WHOLESALER who supplies merchandise and sets up displays, and who receives payment only for items sold.

RADIO   An audio BROADCAST ADVERTISING MEDIUM devoted largely to music and news. Coverage is geographic, but some stations in one area may appeal to specific ethnic or age groups. Reasonably flexible to the advertiser, it has two limitations: no possibility of later reference by the AUDIENCE and no graphic portrayals. An estimated 350 million sets are in use, of which about 90 million are in cars.

RADIO ADVERTISING BUREAU   Same as: RAB

RAGS   Trade colloquialism for ready-to-wear apparel. Sometimes applied exclusively to women's wear, or fashions.

RAIL-BRIDGE   In this plan, shippers can send CONTAINERS by ship across
either ocean, then across the United States by rail, then across the
second ocean to final destinations. See: MINI-BRIDGE

RAIL PASSENGER SERVICE ACT   The Federal Act which established the NATIONAL
RAILWAY PASSENGER CORPORATION. See: AMTRAK

RAILPAX   Same as: AMTRAK See: NATIONAL RAILWAY PASSENGER CORPORATION

RAILWAY PROGRESS INSTITUTE   Same as: RPI

RANDOM ACCESS   In ADP, a technique for retrieving data from a computer system in which the obtaining of new information is independent of the AD-
DRESS of the information most recently acquired. See: SEQUENTIAL ACCESS

RANDOM FLUCTUATION   See: TIME SERIES

RANDOMIZED PAIRED COMPARISON DESIGN   Same as: RPC

RANDOMNESS   See: RANDOM SAMPLING, TEST OF RANDOMNESS

RANDOM SAMPLING   A form of PROBABILITY SAMPLING in which each unit of the
UNIVERSE has an equal chance of selection. See: QUOTA SAMPLING, TEST OF
RANDOMNESS, Z

RANGE   The crudest, most easily computed measure of DISPERSION. It is the
difference between the highest and the lowest numbers in an ARRAY. Sometimes observations are grouped into quantities of observations having
values with lower and upper limits. The difference between these limits
is called a range, also.

RATE BASE   A MAGAZINE'S CIRCULATION guaranteed as the base for its rate
structure. Should the circulation fall below this number for a period
of time, the advertiser would get a refund. Should the circulation rise
above this number, after a time the magazine would probably raise its
rates.

RATE CARD   An issue piece of one unit of the ADVERTISING MEDIA giving the
space or time rates, the mechanical requirements data, and other pertinent information specified by the unit.

RATE DIFFERENTIAL   The difference between the higher rate charged by AD-
VERTISING MEDIA to national as compared to local advertisers, in some
cases as much as double. Because of the controversy which has arisen
over the ethics of this practice, many NEWSPAPERS and other local media
have adopted rate schedules that do not discriminate. See: ONE-TIME RATE

RATED POSTER   A POSTER for which there is available an appraisal as to competition, visibility, incoming or outgoing traffic, area characteristics,
and/or traffic volume.

RATE HOLDER   In ADVERTISING PRINT MEDIA, a minimum-size advertisement put
in to accomodate the lowest rate requirement where the rate is based on
the frequency of insertion.

RATE PROTECTION   The length of time an ADVERTISER is guaranteed a specific
rate schedule.

RATE STOPS   Same as: FREEZE RATE

RATING   See: RATING POINT

RATING POINT   (1) A unit of measurement equal to 1% of the TELEVISION
HOMES REACHED. If a program or commercial gets a 40 rating, through
whatever mechanism is used to make the measurement, it means that about
40% of all such homes watch it. See: GROSS RATING POINTS (2) ADVERTIS-
ING EXPOSURES equal to 1% of the population of a MARKET.

RATIONALIZATION   A defense mechanism used unconsciously in which a person
explains his behavior by substituting blameless motives for the less-

acceptable real ones. Important for a seller to understand so that he may recognize, or discover through research, how to overcome barriers to his product or service. See: COGNITIVE DISSONANCE, FRUSTRATION

RATIONALIZED RETAILING   A managerial philosophy of RETAIL program control involving centralized control at a high level.

RATIO SCALE   Considered the highest order of the various types of scales, it has an absolute zero point from which the qualities attributed by RESPONDENTS can be plotted, quantified, and the various points can be expressed as ratios of one another, giving information concerning how much more or less is perceived. See: INTERVAL SCALE, NOMINAL SCALE, ORDINAL SCALE, PERCEPTION, SCALING

RAW MATERIALS   Products of nature which enter into the physical product being made, and which have been processed only enough for convenience in their DISTRIBUTION. Distinguish from the accounting usage which includes all items entering the final product whether processed by the firm or not. See: FABRICATING MATERIALS, PARTS

RBO   Abbreviation for: RESIDENT BUYING OFFICE

REACH   The total AUDIENCE a MEDIUM actually gets to, in unduplicated individuals. See: COVERAGE, CUME, EXPOSURE, FREQUENCY

READING NOTICE   A print ADVERTISEMENT which looks like EDITORIAL MATTER. Must be clearly designated as an advertisement. In some newspapers, the small advertisements which appear on the bottom of the first page. Not accepted by all PUBLICATIONS. See: ADVERTORIAL

READ TIME   See: ACCESS TIME

REAL INCOME   The actual group of products and/or services that a person's MONEY INCOME will permit him to acquire. See: DISCRETIONARY INCOME

REAL OTHER   How an individual perceives other people really view his/her abilities, personality, other traits. Not necessarily in tune with reality. See: IDEAL OTHER, SELF-CONCEPT

REAL TIME PROCESSING   In ADP, the processing of data sufficiently rapidly that the results of the processing are available in time to influence the process being controlled. The computer's user is able to adjust or inject inputs as he gets the results of prior processing.

REAM   As to paper, now fairly well standardized at 500 sheets when packaged. When ordering paper in bulk quantities, 1,000 sheet counts are usually used as a basis.

REAR-END DISPLAY   An outside TRANSIT ADVERTISING display placed on the rear of vehicles. Same as: Tail-Light Display

REASON-WHY APPROACH   Same as: FACTUAL APPROACH

RECEIPT-OF-GOODS TERMS   Same as: ROG

RECEIVING APRON   See: APRON SYSTEM

RECIPROCITY   The "we will buy from you if you will buy from us" idea. Now generally suspect as a PROCUREMENT policy in industry. May be illegal in practice under existing ANTI-TRUST LAWS as a restraint of trade or a lessening of competition. See: TRADE RELATIONS

RECOGNIZED AGENCY   An ADVERTISING AGENCY acknowledged by the various publishers or broadcasting stations as acceptable to receive a commission for the space or time it buys for advertisers. The agency is responsible for paying the charges, less commission and CASH DISCOUNT. It bills its clients at full rate. See: 15 & 2, HOUSE SHOP

RECONSIGNMENT   The changing of the bill of lading or air bill as to CONSIGNEE or destination while shipment is in transit. See: DIVERSION IN TRANSIT

RECORD   In ADP, a group of related facts or FIELDS treated as a unit. A record usually contains an event (a transaction) or a thing (a specific product).

RECORDING DELAY   A DELAYED RESPONSE EFFECT which is the time lag between the actual purchase of an item and the producer's recognition of the purchase in his records. The speed with which this is accomplished may greatly affect the efficacy of management's decision-making.

RECORD LAYOUT   In ADP, a listing of all the FIELDS of information in a RECORD, and the way they are arranged in the record.

RECOVERY   (1) The difference between the buying price and the selling price of merchandise. Essentially the same as GROSS PROFIT. See: MARGIN, MARKUP   (2) See: BUSINESS CYCLE

REDEMPTION CENTER   A store maintained by a trading-stamp company where holders may redeem filled stamp books for merchandise.

REDEMPTION STORE   Same as: REDEMPTION CENTER

REDUNDANCY   In ADP, that part of the whole information content that can be left out without loss of essential information. In EDP systems, planned redundancy is often included as a check on the accuracy of information transmission.

REEFER   (1) Trade shortword for: refrigerated ships   (2) Any refrigerated unit of a TRANSPORTATION system.

REFERENCE GROUP   The "they" whose approval of decisions a person seeks; whose OPINIONS, ATTITUDES, and BELIEFS serve as a model to a person. "They" may consist in classmates, fellow workers, friends, even a wife or husband. It is of marketing significance that a person may have different reference groups relative to different types of purchases. See: ANTICIPATORY GROUPS, ASPIRATION GROUPS, AUTOMATIC GROUPS, MEMBERSHIP GROUPS, NEGATIVE REFERENCE GROUPS, PARTICIPATION GROUPS

REFERRAL PREMIUM   A reward offered to a satisfied CUSTOMER should any PROSPECTS suggested by the customer buy the PRODUCT.

REFRIGERATION RESEARCH FOUNDATION   Same as: TRRF

REFUSAL-TO-DEAL   Decisions by the U.S. Supreme Court indicate that presently a company can refuse to deal with a buyer only if the refusal involves no joint action between that company and other buyers so that a conspiracy to fix prices or to restrain trade may not be found in the refusal. Current legislation makes it illegal to refuse to deal with someone because of race, religion, or national origin. See: COLGATE DOCTRINE

REGIONAL ISSUE   Many large MAGAZINES provide a means for an advertiser to buy only the geographic area appropriate for his business by making available special editions for sections of the country. Some make available DEMOGRAPHIC editions as well.

REGIONAL PLAN   A LOCAL PLAN on a larger geographic scale. May include a whole state or several adjacent states. The MEDIA selected may include geographic editions of MAGAZINES, or limited NETWORKS of RADIO or TELEVISION. See: NATIONAL PLAN, SELECTIVE PLAN

REGIONAL SHOPPING CENTER   The largest of the shopping center types. One or more DEPARTMENT STORES provide the main drawing power, supplemented by many smaller stores. They are set up to serve 100,000 to 250,000 people living in a radius of 6 to 10 miles; they may draw from much farther away. They are usually located outside a business district in an area of easy access by roads.

REGIONAL STATION   A RADIO station authorized to use up to about 5,000 watts of power, giving it a range which may cover an entire state. See: CLEAR-CHANNEL STATION, LOCAL STATION

REGIONAL WHOLESALER   Same as: SECTIONAL WHOLESALER

REGISTER   Perfect correspondence in printing, as evidenced by correct super-imposition of each plate in color printing so that the colors mix properly.

REGISTER MARKS   Cross lines placed in the margin of COPY so that when plates are made for the various colors, REGISTER may be easily achieved by perfect alignment of the printing.

REGISTRATION OF MARK   See: PRINCIPAL REGISTER

REGRATING   Activity involving such acts as conspiracy and the spreading of false reports so as to increase the price of food. A criminal act in the 16th Century. Certain of these acts remain so today. See: ENGROSSING, FORESTALLING

REGRESSION   A way of coping with FRUSTRATION by reverting to a typically immature behavior. See: AGGRESSION, AUTISM, IDENTIFICATION, PROJECTION, RATIONALIZATION, REPRESSION

REGRESSION ANALYSIS   Determination of the relationship between variables. An equation can be developed from which the relationship is chartable as a line. The relationship and any associated TREND is thereby made more discernable. A tool of simple CORRELATION, it can be used, also, to guide the analyst in uncovering causal relationships between variables. PARAMETRIC.

REGULAR COMMON CARRIER CONFERENCE OF ATA   One of the more than a dozen conferences of the ATA, it acts as the voice and instrument of motor COMMON CARRIERS who operate a scheduled freight service between TERMINALS over "regular or fixed" routes. It is the catalyst for the formation of basic INDUSTRY policies and for publicizing them. Its common carrier emblem is used to identify members as lawful, regulated, highway common carriers of integrity.

REGULAR WHOLESALER   Same as: SERVICE WHOLESALER

REILLY'S LAW   Same as: LAW OF RETAIL GRAVITATION

REINFORCEMENT   See: LAW OF DISUSE, LAW OF EFFECT, LAW OF USE

RELATED-ITEM DISPLAY   The combination of several items, all related in use in some way, into a single display. Example: flour, sugar, candied fruit, nuts, and the like displayed together at holiday times.

RELATIVE ADVANTAGE   With respect to the DIFFUSION RATE, the potential MARKET'S PERCEPTION of how much more UTILITY the innovation has than those PRODUCTS which it replaces or with which it competes. See: CHARACTERISTICS OF INNOVATIONS

RELEASE   A legal document authorizing an advertiser to use a person's name or photograph.

RELIABILITY   The quality data have when repetition of the same research will produce essentially the same results.

RELIEF PRINTING   LETTERPRESS printing. Contrast with: GRAVURE, PLANOGRAPHIC, SILK-SCREEN

REMINDER ADVERTISING   Same as: NAME ADVERTISING, RETENTIVE ADVERTISING

REMINDER IMPULSE BUYING   IMPULSE BUYING where the customer is reminded in the store of the need to replenish his stock by the visual prod alone. See: PLANNED IMPULSE BUYING, PURE IMPULSE BUYING, SUGGESTION IMPULSE BUYING

RENTIER   Most commonly used now to designate a person dependent upon a fixed income derived from investments such as rent from real estate, interest from bonds, or an annuity.

REORDER SYSTEM   Same as: Q-SYSTEM

REP   Familiar short form for: MANUFACTURERS' REPRESENTATIVE

REPEATING TECHNIQUE   Same as: MIRROR RESPONSE TECHNIQUE

REPLACEMENT FERTILITY   An elegant way of expressing the concept of zero population growth. See: ZPG

REPLACEMENT MARKET   Same as: AFTER-MARKET

REPLACEMENT POTENTIAL   The total amount in dollars, or the number in units, of the sales opportunity of an item to present users who will need to replace it in a given period of time.

REPLACEMENT RATE   The frequency with which a PRODUCT is purchased by CONSUMERS.

REPLENISHMENT SYSTEM   Same as: P-SYSTEM

REPRESSION   A defense mechanism used unconsciously to reduce tensions induced by motivational conflicts, by excluding from consciousness any feelings or thoughts that cause pain or shame. May go so far as to deny by self-deception the existence of a motive or a goal. Governed in large measure by the CULTURE of one's group. See: COGNITIVE DISSONANCE, FRUSTRATION

REQUEST REPEAT SYSTEM   Same as: ARQ

REQUISITION   (1) The action taken by a using unit of a firm to make known its requirements to the proper supplying agency within the firm. (2) The form used for the above. See: BILL OF MATERIAL, PURCHASE REQUISITION, STORES REQUISITION, TRAVELING REQUISITION

RESALE PRICE MAINTENANCE   See: FAIR TRADE LAW

RESELLER   Same as: JOBBER

RESELLER SALESMAN   A description applied by some oil companies to a person employed to sell, counsel, and work with service station operators who are under commission or lease agreements. He operates within a given territory.

RESERVE STOCK   (1) Same as: BACK-UP MERCHANDISE   (2) Same as: BUFFER INVENTORY

RESIDENT BUYING OFFICE   (1) A FUNCTIONAL MIDDLEMAN representing a group of RETAILERS in the MARKET to supply them with information and buying assistance. See: SALARIED OFFICE   (2) An office established by a retailer or a group of retailers for exclusive service. Services are essentially the same as(1). Not to be confused with "central buying."

RESIDENT SALESPERSON   A supplier's SALESPERSON stationed inside the doors of one of the supplier's KEY ACCOUNTS. Giving full time attention to the one customer's problems and requirements with respect to his company's LINE, the resident salesperson is able to improve the profit realization of both companies. In one instance, a can supplier was permitted to set up a can-making operation in a brewer's plant, to the mutual advantage of both. Although costly on an absolute basis, such an arrangement may prove relatively inexpensive on the more realistic basis of a cost-effectiveness rationale. See: 80-20 PRINCIPLE

RESIDUAL   An additional fee paid to the talent used in a program or commercial each time the unit is run over a number agreed upon for the first fee. These are generally governed by union agreements. Should be anticipated in developing an ADVERTISING BUDGET because residuals may add up to significant sums.

RESIZING   The production of the means of running an advertisement in various sizes to fit different units of space.

RESOURCE   Used in PROCUREMENT to denote a chosen supplier of a given requirement.   The choice of resources may entail a complex analysis of a
number of factors.

RESPONDENT   One who answers a QUESTIONNAIRE or is interviewed in a research study.

RESPONSE FUNCTION   The effect a change in any of the FOUR P'S is expected
to produce on a FIRM'S sales or profits.   Often plotted as a curve on a
graph to reflect the effects of varying changes in the component MARKETING
MIX elements.

RESPONSE VARIABLE   Same as: DEPENDENT VARIABLE

RETAIL ADVERTISING   Same as: LOCAL ADVERTISING

RETAIL COOPERATIVE WAREHOUSING   Essentially the same as: COOPERATIVE CHAIN

RETAILER.   A business mainly concerned with selling to CONSUMERS.   See:
BOUTIQUE, CHAIN STORE, COOPERATIVE CHAIN, DEPARTMENTIZED SPECIALTY STORE,
DEPARTMENT STORE, GENERAL STORE, LIMITED-LINE STORE, RETAIL STORE COOPER-
ATIVE, SPECIALTY SHOP, SUPERETTE, SUPERMARKET, VARIETY STORE, VOLUNTARY
CHAIN

RETAILER-SPONSORED COOPERATIVE   Same as: COOPERATIVE CHAIN

RETAILING   That business activity mainly concerned with selling to
CONSUMERS.

RETAILING THE INVOICE   RETAIL prices are marked on the seller's invoice
as authorization for the markers in the receiving area.   See: PRERETAIL-
ING

RETAIL INSTALLMENT CREDIT ACCOUNT   Same as: ALL-PURPOSE REVOLVING ACCOUNT

RETAIL INSTITUTION CYCLE   A thesis that on a more or less definite cycle
innovators come along with new RETAILING ideas sufficiently appealing to
CONSUMERS as to establish a new retail form which other retailers of that
type of goods must emulate or risk becoming obsolete in the MARKET.
See: INVITATION POINT THEORY, WHEEL OF RETAILING

RETAIL METHOD OF INVENTORY VALUATION   Recordings are made for each department of costs and resale values entering the department, and of resale
values leaving the department.   At any time, the difference in resale
values will give the theoretical, or book, inventory at resale prices.
This amount may be reduced to cost, if desired, by applying the cumulative percent which cost is of all resale values charged to the department, as adjusted for changes.   Physical inventories are taken periodically and the book inventories are corrected to reflect actual counts.
The physical inventories are taken at marked selling prices, avoiding the
need for translating to costs for each item through COST CODES.   The cost
of the physical inventory so taken is then found for accounting purposes
by the technique described above.   Of major advantage where prices do not
change very frequently, where it is desired to control stock shortages,
and where control of the inventory level is generally important on a continuing basis.   See: MARKDOWN, MARKDOWN CANCELLATION, MARKUP, MARKUP
CANCELLATION

RETAIL RATE   In ADVERTISING, same as: LOCAL RATE

RETAIL STORE COOPERATIVE   A store owned and managed by a number of CON-
SUMERS who use the store as a source of supply for at least a certain
type of merchandise.   Returns to participants are frequently determined
by the proportion of business each participant accounts for out of the
total done by the store.   See: ROCHDALE PLAN

RETENTIVE STAGE   The stage a product or service has reached, proposed by a
certain classification, when its acceptance as a particular BRAND is so
wide that the advertiser need but keep reminders before his customers

with minimum effort and expense to retain patronage and loyalty. See: SPIRAL

RETURN ON ASSETS MANAGED   Same as: ROAM

RETURN ON INVESTMENT   Same as: ROI

RETURN ON TIME INVESTED   Same as: ROTI

RETURNS TO SCALE   The relationship between the profit that results and an increase in the size of the FIRM measured in output. May be: INCREASING RETURNS TO SCALE, in which profit rises in some proportion; DECREASING RETURNS TO SCALE, in which profit declines as the firm grows larger; or CONSTANT RETURNS TO SCALE, in which increase in firm size has no effect on profit.

REVERSE   (1) An engraving opposite in value to the original, such as white letters on a black background. (2) Left-to-right reversal of objects as printed.

REVERSE ELASTICITY   A Phenomenon sometimes observed on INDUSTRIAL DEMAND wherein in the short term an increase in price will trigger an increase in buying and a decrease in price a decrease in buying, apparently caused by the expectations of buyers that the initial action is but the beginning of a series of similar actions to come of which the buyers are trying to take maximum advantage.

REVERSE INTEGRATION   The purchasing from others of functions which were formerly performed by the firm.

REVERSE-ORDER PERCEPTION   An effect frequently observed in RETAIL STORES where customers are found to favor a higher price for a certain item, e.g., $1.95 rather than $1.45. What causes this is not clear, but it has been suggested that it may have something to do with what seems to be an inherent propensity toward even prices as a point of reference, so that $1.95 is perceived as basically $2.00 and therefore a bargain of a sort, while $1.45 may be perceived as basically $1.00 and therefore an overpricing. See: COST-PRICE JUDGMENT, FAIR-PRICE REFERENCE REACTION, PRICE-AURA EFFECT

REVIVAL   See: BUSINESS CYCLE

REVOLVING ACCOUNT   Same as: REVOLVING CHARGE ACCOUNT   See: ALL-PURPOSE REVOLVING ACCOUNT

REVOLVING CHARGE ACCOUNT   A CREDIT system which allows a customer to make repeated purchases on account as long as the charge balance does not exceed an established amount and the customer makes his agreed-upon payments regularly. The RETAILER using this system usually adds a given percent to the balance left due at the end of any month. See: TRUTH-IN-LENDING LAW

R-F-M BASIS   A way of maintaining the names on a MAIL ORDER list to provide maximum efficiency in PROMOTION. The divisions are: recency of last purchase, frequency of purchase, and dollar amount of purchase. The effect is to define MARKET SEGMENTS more clearly. See: LIST

RHOCHREMATICS   The science of managing the entire system of material flow, involving as an integrated system the basic functions of producing and marketing in a selection of the most efficient combination of activities to achieve the firm's goals.

RIDER   Same as: Apron in APRON SYSTEM

RIDING A SHOWING   In OUTDOOR ADVERTISING, the advertiser's riding around with the PLANT OPERATOR to inspect the sites of the specific boards to be included in the SHOWING.

RIESMAN MODEL   See: THEORY OF SOCIAL CHARACTER

RIFLE APPROACH   A way of trying to gain an objective by careful aiming of the effort to a selected target. See: SHOTGUN APPROACH

RING   Essentially the same as PIT, but the latter term is more frequently limited to grain EXCHANGES while "ring" is more frequently applied to the trading area assigned to other commodities.

RISK   See: CONSUMER-PERCEIVED RISKS, MARKETING RISKS

RISK REDUCTION   Buyers often want to buy yet hesitate because it involves the possibility of suffering some type of loss. A buyer will try to reduce the risk to a point he considers acceptable. Aware marketers try to offer methods by means of which a buyer can reduce his risk, often classified as time loss, hazard loss, ego loss, and money loss. The major risk relievers are (no order of significance intended): free sample, major brand image, private testing, money-back guaranty, endorsements, brand loyalty, government testing, store image, word of mouth, shopping, and expensive model. There is some evidence that brand reputation and brand loyalty rank high with purchasers as risk relievers.

RISK RELIEVER   See: RISK REDUCTION

RISK-TAKING   A MARKETING FUNCTION characterized by the presence of the possibility of losses inherent in the nature of economic activity. See: MARKETING RESEARCH

RIVAL GOODS   Same as: SUBSTITUTIONAL GOODS

ROADBLOCKING   A practice sometimes used in the early stages of an ADVERTISING CAMPAIGN whereby the ADVERTISER will engage the same time slot on all three major NETWORKS so that the presented ADVERTISEMENT'S message may have the maximum opportunity for contact with the intended AUDIENCE.

ROAM   Abbreviation for: Return on Assets Managed. In general similar to ROI, but based on total assets rather than investment assets.

ROB   Abbreviation for: run-of-book, a basis for setting ADVERTISING rates by MAGAZINES. The placing of the ADVERTISEMENT within that PUBLICATION will be at the publisher's convenience and discretion. See: ROP, ROS

ROBINSON-PATMAN ACT   Enacted in 1936, this revision of the CLAYTON ACT was an attempt to clarify prohibited discriminations. While still not entirely clear, it does provide additional strength for the law. Its main provisions: to prohibit fees by sellers to BROKERS acting for BUYERS, supplementary services such as advertising allowances by sellers disproportionately to buyers, price differentials to competing buyers not justified by savings to sellers, knowingly to induce or receive a prohibited discrimination in price, and pricing for the purpose of destroying competition or eliminating a competitor. See: BACK-HAUL ALLOWANCE, CELLER-KEFAUVER ANTI-MERGER ACT, FEDERAL TRADE COMMISSION ACT, SHERMAN ACT, WHEELER-LEA ACT

ROCHDALE PLAN   Developed by a group of flannel weavers in Rochdale, England, who organized as the Rochdale Society of Equitable Pioneers, this plan was the first to incorporate the principles which led to the success of cooperatives: open membership, democratic control, sale at prevailing prices, patronage dividends, limited interest on capital, sale for cash, and educational activity.

R.O.G.   Abbreviation for: receipt-of-goods terms. Under these terms the discount period does not begin until the day the customer receives the shipment. Most often used when the time in shipment may be longer than the discount period. The net period is usually computed from the invoice date, as in the instance of ordinary dating.

ROI   Abbreviation for: Return on Investment, a concept borrowed from finance. Often used as a tool for deciding among alternative marketing plans.

ROLE DEMAND See: THEORY OF ROLE ENACTMENT

ROLE EXPECTATIONS See: THEORY OF ROLE ENACTMENT

ROLE LOCATION See: THEORY OF ROLE ENACTMENT

ROLE SKILLS See: THEORY OF ROLE ENACTMENT

ROLL-ON/ROLL-OFF VESSEL A ship especially constructed to accommodate delivery of vehicular and rolling-stock CARGO without the need for cranes or other heavy lifting equipment. Same as: Ro-Ro

ROLL-OUT Gradual expansion of a new PRODUCT into new MARKETS from a local introduction.

ROP Abbreviation for: run-of-paper. Indicates that the position of the advertisement will be at the newspaper publisher's discretion. Rates are constructed to take this into account. See: PREFERRED POSITION

RO-RO Same as: ROLL-ON/ROLL-OFF VESSEL

RORSCHACH TEST A PROJECTIVE TECHNIQUE borrowed from clinical psychology, it consists of a series of non-structured inkblots. The RESPONDENT is asked to explain or interpret the "picture." Most persons project their own personalities into the responses, giving clues about their probable behavior, hopefully extrapolated into the MARKET PLACE. Requires highly skilled analysts.

ROS Abbreviation for: run-of-schedule-time. Same for BROADCAST MEDIA as ROP for newspapers. Time is allocated wherever in the schedule the station sees fit. Rates are constructed to reflect this.

ROTARY PLAN In OUTDOOR ADVERTISING, an arrangement whereby the advertiser's message is moved periodically to different preselected locations, rather than remaining on the same BULLETIN in one location for a year. Achieves exposure to a more varied AUDIENCE.

ROTATED MERCHANDISE CONTROL A system which provides for the physical count of a certain part of a RETAILER'S inventory on a rotated or staggered basis by scheduling specific counts for certain days. See: CLASSIFICATION CONTROL, DOLLAR CONTROL, OPEN-TO-BUY CONTROL, PARTIAL VISUAL MERCHANDISE CONTROL, PERPETUAL MERCHANDISE CONTROL, UNIT CONTROL, WANT-SLIP SYSTEM

ROTATION A series of advertisements repeated in sequence after the entire series has been run.

ROTI Abbreviation for: Return on Time Invested, a measure of the PRODUCTIVITY achieved by calling on accounts in a SALES TERRITORY. By calculating this for each of a SALESPERSON'S accounts, the optimum allocation of time and the optimum number of calls for each account can be determined. Comparable to ROI in finance.

ROTTEN APPLE CONCEPT A legal concept that holds that a culprit must be deprived of the fruits of his wrongdoing. Forms the basis of much governmental action regarding ANTI-TRUST and TRUTH IN ADVERTISING.

ROUGH A preliminary sketch of an advertisement submitted for approval before the COMPREHENSIVE is begun.

ROUGHLY COINCIDENT INDICATOR See: BUSINESS INDICATOR

ROUND TURN The execution at different times for the same PRINCIPAL of a purchase transaction and a sale transaction which offset each other, usually on an organized EXCHANGE facility and commonly in commodity activity. Sometimes called just: turn.

ROUTE (1) The scheduled movement of a transit vehicle as shown on a map indicating the sections covered by each vehicle. In some MARKETS, advertisers may select only those routes specifically appropriate to their products or services. See: SECTOR PLAN (2) The particular sequence of visits over a geographic territory made by a SALESMAN or a delivery man. Total sales cost can be reduced if the route is planned properly. There are mathematical techniques which can help the planning.

ROUTE PLAN Essentially the same as HUCKSTERING, but may involve a larger VARIETY of merchandise and may be on a more regular visit basis.

ROUTINE (1) A set of INSTRUCTIONS in ADP arranged in the proper sequence to direct the computer to perform a desired operation. (2) A subdivision of a PROGRAM consisting of two or more instructions that are functionally related.

ROUTING OUT Removing DEAD METAL from a printing PLATE.

RPC Abbreviation for: Randomized Paired Comparison design, an experimenter's technique in MARKETING RESEARCH in which the experimental units to be used are stratified into units of two on the basis of some factor known to produce variability in experimental results. Of two treatments to be used to discover differences in response, one of each pair will randomly receive one treatment, the other one of the pair will automatically receive the second. To the extent that pairing was properly done, this method can produce greater PRECISION than can a CRL.

RPI Abbreviation for: Railway Progress Institute, the national trade organization of the railway supply industry providing locomotives, cars, tracks, signals, etc. It acts as a clearinghouse for information both technical and of public affairs interest. It publishes a newsletter, special memoranda, and bulletins.

RPM Abbreviation for: Resale Price Maintenance. See: FAIR TRADE LAW

RTW Abbreviation for and short reference form for: ready-to-wear.

RULE OF REASON A broad rule at law in which the entire area of the conditions surrounding an action must be examined before judging the action legal or illegal. Enunciated in the landmark Standard Oil Case with reference to ANTI-TRUST provisions (221 U.S. 1, 1911), the Supreme Court said it"must ordinarily consider the facts peculiar to the business to which the restraint is applied; its condition before and after the restraint was imposed; the nature of the restraint and its effect, actual or probable. The history of the restraint, the evil believed to exist, the reason for adopting the particular remedy, the purpose or end sought to be attained, are all relevant facts." Since then the application of this rule has been eroded gradually in favor of the PER SE principle.

RULE OF THUMB See: HEURISTIC

RUN (1) The performance of one or a group of routines by a computer. The computer's beginning and completion of one PROGRAM. (2) Same as: SHOWING, i.e., full-run, etc. (3) See: TEST OF RANDOMNESS

RUNNER An item of FASHION MERCHANDISE for which a firm finds it necessary to place many repeat orders. It merits continuous promotion during the period of its popularity. See: FAD

RUN-OF-BOOK Same as: ROB

RUN-OF-PAPER Same as: ROP

RUN-THROUGH TRAIN Trains on a plan that usually involves the cooperation of two or more railroads to bypass classification yards and equipment changes, stopping only for crew changes or safety checks, to run from origin to destination directly.

RUNZHEIMER PLAN A method for compensating SALESPERSONS for the use of their automobiles on their routes, it is based on separate studies of ownership and operating expenses in about thirty United States areas. It takes into account variations in types of cars, miles driven, and geographical conditions. The plan is continually updated to reflect current data for the company's clients.

RURAL AREA An area in which the density of population is less than 150 per square mile. See: SUBURBIA

SADDLE-STITCHING Binding a PUBLICATION or BOOKLET by means of wire or plastic through the center fold so that the pages will lie flat when opened. Contrast with: SIDE-STITCHING

SAE Abbreviation for: Society of Automotive Engineers, a group which sets standards on a variety of items in the automotive and petroleum INDUSTRIES.

SAFETY NEEDS According to MASLOW'S HIERARCHY OF NEEDS, these become the motivational force in human behavior after the PHYSIOLOGICAL NEEDS have been satisfied. Safety needs include protection, physical safety, order, routine, familiarity, and certainty.

SAFETY STOCK An amount of an item carried in inventory in excess of normal requirements to reduce out-of-stock conditions caused by sales fluctuations, or by failures by suppliers to deliver as promised for whatever reason. See: CUSHION

SAG Abbreviation for: Screen Actors Guild, an association of talent that is empowered to negotiate collective bargaining agreements with motion picture and television producers.

SAI Abbreviation for: Sales Activity Index, a measure of the retail sales per capita of an area compared with that of the country, as calculated by Sales & Marketing Management magazine. A high index may indicate many nonresident shoppers and/or heavy buying by residents or business concerns.

SALARIED OFFICE See: RESIDENT BUYING OFFICE

SALARIED STATION A service station owned and operated by an oil company.

SALARY-OPERATED SERVICE STATION Same as: SALARIED STATION

SALE-BELOW-COST LAWS Same as: UNFAIR PRACTICES ACTS

SALES ACTIVITY INDEX Same as: SAI

SALES AGENT Same as: SELLING AGENT

SALES ANALYSIS See: PERFORMANCE ANALYSIS

SALES CLERK A person in a RETAIL STORE whose task it is to record the customers' purchases, who frequently is responsible for maintaining stock, and who sometimes assists the customer in making a selection. Little or no SALESMANSHIP is practiced by this employee.

SALES COORDINATION Another way of denoting RECIPROCITY activities.

SALES DEMONSTRATION Showing how the product works and what it will do. Very effective where applicable and where the PROSPECT can be made a part of the action.

SALES ENGINEER A SALESPERSON who represents a firm which produces products of a scientific or technical nature, so that skill is required to determine the exact product for a specific application. Most of these salespersons have science degrees, although this is not necessarily mandatory.

SALES FERTILITY Applied to various MARKETS so as to indicate the relative amount of effort in each which it is estimated would be required to produce a certain sales volume; or another way, how much sales volume could be expected from a given market with a specified amount of MARKETING effort. In general, the ability of a market to "grow" sales.

SALES FORCE ADMINISTRATION The activities involving recruiting, selecting, training, assigning, compensating, motivating, and controlling the sales force, whether internal or external. See: SALES FORCE STRATEGY

SALES FORCE PERFORMANCE ANALYSIS   See: PERFORMANCE ANALYSIS

SALES FORCE STRATEGY   The activities involving the designing and assigning of territories, the determination of the optimal size of the sales force, the developing of optimal calling patterns for various customers, and the setting of QUOTAS and incentives for SALESPERSONS.

SALES FORECAST   An estimate of sales for a future period assuming certain economic conditions and other pertinent forces, such as a proposed promotional program. May be in dollars or in units. May be for an individual item, a product LINE, or the firm's total sales. See: FORECASTING

SALES MANAGER   Usually the individual in a firm who makes and carries out sales POLICIES, and who is responsible for recruiting, training, and controlling an INSIDE SALESFORCE and/or a FIELD SALESFORCE.

SALESMANSHIP   The art of successfully persuading PROSPECTS or CUSTOMERS to buy PRODUCTS or services from which they can derive suitable benefits, thereby increasing their total satisfactions. It is the opposite of CONMANSHIP. If done properly, the seller will benefit as well as the buyer. See: CREATIVE SELLING, HIGH-PRESSURE SELLING, LOW-PRESSURE SELLING, SERVICE SELLING

SALES OBJECTIVE   Same as: SALES QUOTA

SALESPERSON   A person who practices SALESMANSHIP.

SALES POTENTIAL   Used in general to mean the same as: MARKET SHARE (2)

SALES PROMOTION   (1) In a general sense, all types of MARKETING activities designed to increase DEMAND. Sometimes called "demand creation" or "demand stimulation." (2) In a narrower sense, applied to all the above activities except ADVERTISING and SALESMANSHIP. The inclusiveness may vary with the user, but is generally thought to include PREMIUM PLANS, TRADE SHOWS, SAMPLING, sales meetings, sales contacts, SWEEPSTAKES, Sales Bulletins, sales training, HOUSE ORGANS, DEALER AIDS, sales films, and similar types.

SALES PROMOTION AGENCY   An organization specializing in supplying broad SALES PROMOTION services to clients. See: ADVERTISING AGENCY

SALES PROMOTION EXECUTIVES ASSOCIATION   Same as: SPEA

SALES QUOTA   A portion of a SALES FORECAST for a company as assigned to a territory, region, field representative, or branch. It is a part of the basic planning by means of which the company's goals are set. The sales quota is used primarily as a measurement and control device. It may be used effectively in an incentive program.

SALES REPRESENTATIVE   (1) Essentially the same as: SALESPERSON. This is probably the more common usage. (2) Sometimes used to mean the same as: MANUFACTURERS' REPRESENTATIVE

SALES TERMS   Same as: TERMS OF SALE

SALES TERRITORY   A segment of a FIRM'S total MARKET. May be defined by type of CUSTOMER or PROSPECT, or may be set by geographic boundaries, whichever makes for best TERRITORIAL MANAGEMENT.

SALES TO THIRDS   Same as: TRADE SALES

SALON   A shop within a store, or an independent store, where high-priced apparel and accessories are sold. Usually decorated to fit the image of high quality. See: BOUTIQUE

SALUTORY PRODUCTS   While providing high benefits over a period of time, the CONSUMER has yet to recognize such benefits and so holds them in low esteem, e.g., a food made from a plentiful but bony fish that to be usable must be ground up whole and then reconstituted.

SALVAGE   The term applied broadly to the process of turning into cash all items owned by a firm but which cannot be used by it in their present status. Such items include commodities, materials, parts, equipments, and supplies classified as EXCESS, WASTE, SCRAP, or OBSOLETE. Frequently used as a noun to mean the same as SCRAP.

SAMPLE   (1) A collection of units chosen in such a way that it represents the whole. A vast literature exists on the procedures for developing samples and on tests for judging their usefulness. (2) A unit of a product which is representative of all units of that product. See: BUYING BY SAMPLE (3) A portion of a GOOD given free to a PROSPECT.

SAMPLING   (1) In PROMOTION, the technique by means of which a MARKET is exposed to new products, PACKAGES, or package sizes through the sending or giving to PROSPECTS of a miniature or an actual unit. (2) A blanket term covering a variety of techniques in MARKETING RESEARCH all designed to provide information about a large POPULATION from data assembled about relatively few units from that population. See these types of sampling: ACCEPTANCE, AREA, CLUSTER, CONVENIENCE, DISPROPORTIONAL, DOUBLE, JUDGMENT, PROBABILITY, QUOTA, SEQUENTIAL, SIMPLE RANDOM, STRATIFIED, SYSTEMATIC See also: EXPERIMENTAL DESIGN, EXTERNAL VALIDITY, RANDOMNESS, SAMPLING PRECISION, STRUCTURED QUESTIONNAIRE

SAMPLING ACCURACY   The degree to which the PARAMETER of the POPULATION CHARACTERISTIC is correctly estimated by the SAMPLE STATISTIC. See: SAMPLING ERROR

SAMPLING ERROR   The difference between the UNIVERSE STATISTIC and the SAMPLE STATISTIC of the same measure. If the process is a form of RANDOM SAMPLING, the difference can be considered caused by chance only. See: TEST FOR RANDOMNESS

SAMPLING FRAME   A list of all the SAMPLING units in the UNIVERSE.

SAMPLING PRECISION   The degree of VARIANCE a STATISTIC would show on repeated SAMPLING. The smaller the variance, the greater the RELIABILITY of the SAMPLE statistic, and the larger the number of significant numerical places with which it may be stated. The ACCURACY of a sample statistic is determined both by its precision (reliability) and by its VALIDITY.

SAMPLING RIGHTS   In PURCHASING, the AUTHORITY granted managers to review some or all of their subordinates' performances. See: ALLOCATION RIGHTS, CRITERIA RIGHTS, EVALUATION RIGHTS, POLICY RIGHTS, STRATEGY RIGHTS

SANS SERIF   A type FACE that has no SERIFS. The vertical strokes are quite straight and plain. The type used to print the terms in this book is sans serif.

SATISFACTION   A PURCHASE enjoyed.

SATISFICING   (1) A POLICY of management which attempts to achieve results which the company's PUBLICS will accept as satisfactory, particularly the stockholders as regards profit and the government as regards market performance. Thus a price may be set which does not maximize profit but does produce a "satisfactory" one. (2) The CONSUMER satisfices when he decides on an action which will give h im acceptable although not necessarily maximum satisfaction. Usually there are many trade-off factors that he has no time to, or cannot, evaluate fully.

SATURATION   (1) A MEDIA PLAN designed to achieve maximum IMPACT, COVERAGE, or both by means of large FREQUENCY and wide coverage over a relatively concentrated period of time. (2) The stage in the market development for a product in which the majority of sales are to replace the product owned with a new one of the same kind. Characterized by high SEGMENTATION, competitive cost structure, trade-ins common, stabilized competition, and high entry barriers.

SATURATION CAMPAIGN   Same as: SATURATION (1)

SCALES   A type of FIXED-ALTERNATIVE QUESTION that requires an evaluative choice as the response. The RESPONDENT may be presented with words such as "Never, Sometimes, Frequently, Always," or a purely numerical sequence used to mark a group of items in order of importance to the respondent.

SCALING   A process that results in a separation of collected data into groups on some planned basis. See: INTERVAL SCALE, NOMINAL SCALE, ORDINAL SCALE, RATIO SCALE

SCALPER   A member of an organized EXCHANGE who trades for himself and tries to gain by taking advantage of small, though rapid, fluctuations in price, perhaps price differentials in trading among the various exchanges.

SCATTER PLAN   (1) Buying PARTICIPATIONS on a number of different NETWORK programs to REACH a greater variety of AUDIENCE. (2) Buying a number of specially selected SPOTS.

SCHLOCK MERCHANDISING   Emphasis to the extreme on special bargains or special purchase incentives. Frequently associated with the hard sell of inferior or shoddy merchandise.

SCOTCHLITE   A trade name applicable to a type of outdoor sign letters used for their unusually efficient light-reflecting capability.

SCRAMBLED MERCHANDISING   A condition in RETAILING in which a store takes on merchandise to sell that is unrelated to the regular LINES of the store, e.g., greeting cards in a hardware store.

SCRAP   Material or equipment which it is not possible, or economical, to use and which has, therefore, been discarded. Proper production processes may normally produce scrap. Often used to denote the general category of items more specifically classified as EXCESS, SCRAP, WASTE, and OBSOLETE. See: WASTE

SCRAP CONSULTANT   An expert in the kinds and grades of SCRAP, of which there are more than 500 types, who hires out his expertise to a firm with the objective of advising the best program for segregating, grading, handling, and accounting for the firm's scrap. This puts a firm which has no other expertise about such items on a par with the scrap buyers and gives greater control over this fringe but important business activity.

SCRATCHBOARD   A drawing board specially coated with India ink which the artist scratches off so that his design appears white against a black background.

SCREEN ACTORS GUILD   Same as: SAG

SCSA   Abbreviation for: Standard Consolidated Statistical Area. It contains an SMSA with a population of at least one million and one or more adjacent SMSA's that are related to it by high-density population centers and intermetropolitan commuting of workers.

SEA FOOD ACT   ESTABLISHMENTS processing sea foods may, at their request, be inspected by the Bureau of Commercial Fisheries of the Department of the Interior and may then display a shield indicating that their products have been prepared under its rules.

SEARCH   The process by means of which BUYERS collect and analyze the information that will enable them to determine the criteria on which to evaluate potential vendors and to identify alternative product offerings. Although not always put in formal reference, each buyer stops the search when he determines in his own way that the expected value of additional information is less than the cost of gathering that information. Each buyer develops his own search rules, which may be routine or highly individual. All rules involve <u>selective perception</u>, the tendency to rely on some sources of information and to ignore others. As success or failure results from the activity, the search rules are modified, resulting in continuous <u>organizational learning</u>. CONSUMERS call this: shopping.

SEARCH GOODS   Products the qualities of which can be ascertained relatively easily before purchase. See: EXPERIENCE GOODS

SEARCH RULES   See: SEARCH

SEASONAL DATING   Same as: ADVANCE DATING

SEASONAL FLUCTUATION   See: TIME SERIES

SEASONAL MERCHANDISE   Items bought to meet customer demand at specific seasons of the year, e.g., beach chairs, grass seed, winter clothing.

SEASON DATING   Same as: ADVANCE DATING

SECONDARY CENTRAL MARKET   An area in which the DISPERSION of agricultural CONSUMERS' GOODS finds its first stages of division into smaller markets closer to smaller RETAILERS. See: PRIMARY CENTRAL MARKET

SECONDARY DATA   Those data gathered by others, rather than by the research-er himself, and available for reference, e.g., Census statistics. See: PRIMARY DATA

SECONDARY GROUP   A group which an individual joins by conscious and deliberate choice. Often called "special-interest" group. See: PRIMARY GROUP

SECONDARY INDIVIDUAL   In CENSUS data, either a member of a HOUSEHOLD whose head is not a relative, or an individual who lives in group quarters. See: PRIMARY INDIVIDUAL

SECONDARY MEANING   A TRADEMARK that normally would not be protectable be-cause of its descriptive nature may acquire through long-continued, ex-clusive use by a single company a sufficient recognition as identifying the PRODUCT that it will be protected because of the additional (secondary) meaning.

SECONDARY MOTIVES   Same as: SOCIAL MOTIVES

SECONDARY NEEDS   Learned as response to the particular CULTURE or general environment in which one lives. Same as: ACQUIRED NEEDS   See: PRIMARY NEEDS

SECONDARY SHOPPING DISTRICT   A well-developed cluster of STORES outside the CENTRAL BUSINESS DISTRICT that serves a population of several thou-sand people. Found in larger cities, it has characteristics similar to those of the main shopping districts of smaller cities. While the sale of CONVENIENCE GOODS predominates, SHOPPING GOODS and SPECIALTY GOODS are of considerable significance.

SECONDARY TRADING AREA   A geographic territory beyond the PRIMARY TRADING AREA in which a particular MARKETING institution has less-than-proportion-ate buying and/or selling advantages. See: AREA STRUCTURE, ZONE OF INDIFFERENCE

SECOND COVER   See: COVER

SECTIONAL EDITION   Same as: REGIONAL ISSUE

SECTIONAL WHOLESALER   A WHOLESALER who restricts his coverage to a limited number of states or parts of states. Same as: REGIONAL WHOLESALER   See: LOCAL WHOLESALER, NATIONAL WHOLESALER

SECTOR PLAN   A geographically selective way of buying TRANSIT ADVERTISING which permits the advertiser to specify coverage only in certain areas of the MARKET. Same as: SECTOR SHOWING   See: ROUTE

SECTOR SHOWING   Same as: SECTOR PLAN

SECURED DISTRIBUTION   A FIELD WAREHOUSING method in which carload lots are shipped to a DISTRIBUTOR'S premises to be released according to a prearranged plan by the bonded warehouseman as the distributor needs the goods. Makes better credit control possible while avoiding sales lost to competitors because the distributor is out of stock.

SECURITY NEEDS   Same as: SAFETY NEEDS

SEGMENTATION   Division of a MARKET into SUBGROUPS with similar motivations. May be a TACTIC to increase PRODUCT acceptance by recognizing product APPEALS, but there is a danger of overconcentration in a particular segment to which selling effort is applied to the extent that the firm is blinded to other possibilities. The most widely used bases for segmenting a market are: DEMOGRAPHICS, geographics, personality, use of product, PSYCHOGRAPHICS, preference, ATTITUDES, values, and benefits. Usually a coarser division than FRAGMENTATION.

SEGUE   In BROADCAST MEDIA, the transition without interruption from one musical selection to another. Pronounced: segway.

SELECTED DISTRIBUTION AUDIT   See: CCAB

SELECTIVE ATTENTION   Essentially the same as: SELECTIVE PERCEPTION See: SEARCH

SELECTIVE BUYING MOTIVE   A PRODUCT MOTIVE applicable to the market situation which obtains once a product concept has been generally accepted and competition has set in. It then becomes necessary for the CONSUMER to choose among the products offered to provide that type of benefit. See: PRIMARY BUYING MOTIVE

SELECTIVE DEMAND   Refers to the DEMAND for a particular maker's type of a general class of PRODUCT. May be a preference for a certain BRAND. See: PRIMARY DEMAND

SELECTIVE DEMAND ADVERTISING   ADVERTISING which tries to establish SELECTIVE BUYING MOTIVES within the AUDIENCE. See: PRIMARY DEMAND ADVERTISING

SELECTIVE DISTORTION   The changing or misdirection of currently received information that is inconsistent with the recipient's prior beliefs or feelings. Important concept in SALESMANSHIP. See: PERCEPTION, SEARCH, SELECTIVE RETENTION

SELECTIVE DISTRIBUTION   Same as: LIMITED DISTRIBUTION

SELECTIVE HEADLINE   A HEADLINE which is directed to the interest of a particular SEGMENT of the MARKET.

SELECTIVE PERCEPTION   See: SEARCH

SELECTIVE PLAN   A STRATEGY for selecting MEDIA which is based on the common special interest of the product's users wherever they are located. Here the problem is not so much the cost, but just how to get the message to them. Specialized publications, DIRECT MAIL, and special sections of newspapers may prove effective. Sometimes combined with a geographic plan. See: LOCAL PLAN, NATIONAL PLAN, REGIONAL PLAN

SELECTIVE RETENTION   The propensity of a person to remember informative stimuli that support prior beliefs or feelings, and to forget those that are at odds. Important concept in SALESMANSHIP. See: PERCEPTION, SEARCH, SELECTIVE DISTORTION

SELECTIVE STAGE   Same as: COMPETITIVE STAGE

SELECTIVE STOCKING   Balancing the cost of service with the cost of keeping inventory to determine what items should be stocked at each distribution point. It may be found that a group of slower-moving items may profitably be stocked at only a limited number or just one of the possible ones.

SELF-ACTUALIZATION NEEDS   The highest of the five levels in MASLOW'S HIERARCHY OF NEEDS, after EGOISTIC NEEDS have been accommodated. Most people do not reach this level of self-fulfillment, to become whatever they are capable of becoming.

SELF CONCEPT   The image one has of one's self as a person with a particular set of characteristics, traits, possessions, role, behavior. Same as ACTUAL SELF-CONCEPT, SELF IMAGE See: IDEAL OTHER, REAL OTHER

SELF-IMAGE   The way an individual perceives himself/herself. See: IDEAL SELF, LOOKING-GLASS SELF, PERCEPTION Same as: Real Self

SELF-LIQUIDATING PREMIUM   An item offered as a special give-away the entire cost of which is paid by the CONSUMER. To be successful as a PROMOTION, the item must be a real value, timely, available, pretested, and offered in a way that does not include material offensive to DEALERS. See: PREMIUM

SELF-LIQUIDATOR   Same as: SELF-LIQUIDATING PREMIUM

SELF-MAILER   Any piece of DIRECT MAIL ADVERTISING which is designed to be addressed directly on the piece, which is usually folded or of several pages, and mailed without enclosure in an envelope.

SELF-ROLE CONGRUENCE   See: THEORY OF ROLE ENACTMENT

SELF-SELECTION   Merchandise is so arranged in a RETAIL STORE that the customer can make a choice without the aid of a SALES CLERK. Once the choice is made, the merchandise is handed to a nearby sales clerk who takes whatever steps are necessary to complete the sale. Differs from self-service in that under self-service the customer not only makes an unaided decision, but brings the choice to a check-out station where payment is made and the purchase wrapped. Many stores provide services such as credit, and assistance of a technical nature in departments such as cameras, although the organization is basically on a self-service pattern. See: SIMPLIFIED SELLING

SELF-SERVICE   See: SELF-SELECTION

SELLER ACTIVITY STIMULI   Those forces which shape a part of the behavior of a buying unit in the MARKET as the result of the MARKETING efforts of individuals and firms. These are difficult to measure alone because they are so interrelated with other stimuli which either reinforce or offset them. See: EXTERNAL STIMULI, INDIVIDUAL CHANGE STIMULI, INTERNAL STIMULI

SELLER'S CALL   Same as: CALL PURCHASE

SELLERS' MARKET   A condition of the MARKET in which vendors are able to prescribe the conditions of a transaction because demand exceeds supply. See: BUYERS' MARKET

SELLING   (1) A MARKETING FUNCTION phases of which are: to create DEMAND, search out buyers, carry out negotiations about terms, and transfer title. ADVERTISING, SALESMANSHIP, and PROMOTION are subactivities of this function. (2) That marketing activity which, if properly carried out, results in a maximization of customers' satisfactions. Creates POSSESSION UTILITY.

SELLING AGENT   An intermediary in the title transferring process who is characterized by the fact that he is responsible for disposing of the entire output of his PRINCIPAL, usually with considerable latitude in setting prices and TERMS OF SALE. The only FUNCTIONAL MIDDLEMAN who is frequently involved in financing his principal, whom he represents in the MARKET continuously.

SELLING CALENDAR   A plan for PROMOTIONS that gives specific dates for each intended special selling event.

SELLING COST INDEX   See: SURVEY OF SELLING COSTS

SELLING ERROR   Usually involving careless or inadequate display or selling techniques, this is one of the least excusable causes for MARKDOWNS. See: BUYING ERROR, PRICING ERROR

SELLING SHORT   Same as: SHORT SELLING

SEMANTIC DIFFERENTIAL SCALE   A widely used technique for measuring meaning
and value, it employs a series of bipolar descriptive scales to be the
base for RESPONDENTS' rating purposes. It is simple relative to some
other scaling techniques and it does no more than <u>rank</u> the communication
effect in PROMOTION. It cannot give quantitative results. Also, to the
extent that some ATTITUDES cannot be verbalized, adjectives may not reveal the important attributes of what is being judged, and the words used
have different meanings for different respondents, to that extent this
technique may not produce a true view of the study's goal.

SEMI-DIRECT CHANNEL   A CHANNEL OF DISTRIBUTION characterized by the presence of a limited number, perhaps only one, MIDDLEMAN between producer
and CONSUMER or INDUSTRIAL USER. The distinction from INDIRECT CHANNEL,
being a range, cannot be specified accurately.

SEMI-FINISHED GOODS   Essentially the same as: FABRICATING MATERIALS

SEMI-JOBBING   Descriptive of the activity which occurs when a RETAILER
makes WHOLESALE sales or when a wholesaler makes retail sales. Typical
of some types of SPLIT-FUNCTION WHOLESALERS.

SEMI-MANUFACTURED GOODS   A blanket term used to designate RAW MATERIALS
which have gone through some stages of manufacturing but require more
processing before they can be used. See: FABRICATING MATERIAL

SEMI-SPECTACULAR   Essentially the same as: EMBELLISHED BULLETIN, but may
be more elaborate, with lighting and some animation.

SEND-TRANSACTION   See: TAKE-TRANSACTION

SENSATION   The instant response of the SENSORY RECEPTORS to a simple
STIMULUS.

SENSING DEVICES   Machines in ADP systems all must have devices to read the
data being presented. These may be holes punched in cards or tapes which
can permit electrical contacts to be completed, or may be through optical
scanning mechanisms able to read a variety of written or printed forms.

SENSITIVE COMMODITIES   In general, RAW MATERIALS, such as copper, jute and
crude petroleum, where the trend of price is in some respects more important than the price at a particular moment.

SENSORY RECEPTORS   The human organs capable of seeing, hearing, smelling,
tasting, and feeling. See: PERCEPTION

SENTENCE COMPLETION   One of the PROJECTIVE TECHNIQUES. The RESPONDENT is
instructed to complete a series of sentences with the first thoughts to
enter the mind. The responses, which can usually be more directly stimulated than with WORD ASSOCIATION, are grouped and interpreted. Researchers
using this technique must be highly skilled.

SEPARATION   Same as: COMMERCIAL PROTECTION, PRODUCT PROTECTION

SEQUENCER   See: SORTER

SEQUENTIAL ACCESS   In ADP, a technique of obtaining information from a
group of storage ADDRESSES ,in which the time to get new information depends on the position of the new information's address in a system which
requires serial processing. See: RANDOM ACCESS

SEQUENTIAL SAMPLING   A method of obtaining a SAMPLE from a POPULATION by
measuring one ELEMENTARY UNIT at a time and cumulating the results until
the probable SAMPLING ERROR is determined to be such that the STANDARD
ERROR is reduced to the level acceptable to the decision-maker.

SERENDIPITY   The happy faculty of finding something worthwhile through
fortuitous events.

SERIFS The short cross strokes at the tops and bottoms of CHARACTERS of certain type FACES, especially the Roman group. This $\underline{v}$ has serifs at the tops of the vertical strokes.

SERIGRAPHY Same as: SILK SCREEN

SERPENTS IN THE GARDEN A phrase sometimes used to apply to displays and inducements placed before persons who enter a RETAIL STORE to tempt them to buy.

SERVICE In TRANSIT ADVERTISING, same as SHOWING.

SERVICE AREA Same as: ACCOMMODATION AREA

SERVICE MARK A MARK used in the sale or ADVERTISING of services to identify those of one person or firm and to distinguish them from those of others. Titles, character names, and other distinctive features of radio or television programs may be registered as service marks notwithstanding that they may advertise the products of a SPONSOR.

SERVICES (1) Work performed by individuals or firms for others where no goods or commodities are transferred. Banks and utilities are among those said to create services. (2) Privileges extended to customers of a firm beyond the merchandise itself, such as wrappings, credit, returns, ASSORT-MENT, delivery, and pleasant environment.

SERVICE SELLING Those activities by means of which a SALESPERSON fills his CUSTOMERS' requirements, retains their goodwill, and assists them to become bigger and better customers. Applicable to repeat business.

SERVICE UNIT A unit for measuring the output of an activity. It may be the invoice line, the invoice, the completed order, or any other proper measure of a definable portion of a complex activity. Unit costs for each activity are determined and used as a control and as a base for preparing expense BUDGETS. See: FUNCTIONAL COST ANALYSIS

SERVICE WHOLESALER A MERCHANT selling to RETAILERS, INDUSTRIAL USERS, and other WHOLESALERS, and performing the usual complete services of such a merchant. These services include credit, delivery, redress for faulty or damaged merchandise, significantly large VARIETY and ASSORTMENT, information and education through SALESMEN, and assistance with DEALER AIDS and displays. Same as: Regular Wholesaler

SET (1) The readiness of a subject to accept a stimulus. Enhanced or changed by recent experiences. A very useful concept in SALESMANSHIP, e.g., the roofing salesman will probably find a PROSPECT more receptive after a storm has proved that his roof leaks. (2) Equivalent to "width" when applied to TYPOGRAPHY.

SETS IN USE Larger than HUT in that this includes all sets in use. Some HOUSEHOLDS have more than one television set.

SET SOLID Lines of type set without LEADING.

SETTING DISPLAY See: ASSORTMENT DISPLAY

SGU Abbreviation for: Standard Geographical Unit, a concept often used in defining sales territories, for which Census information is regularly available. Examples: counties, ZIP code areas, etc.

SHARED MONOPOLIES An obloquy frequently directed by the Justice Department at those highly concentrated OLIGOPOLIES in the economy that seem to exhibit common prices and other non-competitive MARKETING practices of a nature to invite ANTI-TRUST investigations although no direct acts of collusion, overt or covert, have occurred.

SHARE OF AUDIENCE The percent of equipped homes attentive to a BROADCAST time period of a particular NETWORK or station.

SHARE OF MARKET The percent of the total INDUSTRY sale of a product or service in a given MARKET which is achieved by an individual firm. Same as: Market Share

SHELF EXTENDER A small display tray attached to a shelf which makes the shelf appear to extend into the store aisle at that point. Effective in drawing attention to the merchandise displayed on it, which frequently is new and needs extra introductory effort.

SHELF FACING Same as: FACING

SHELF LIFE The length of time that is generally accepted as the maximum that a certain PRODUCT may remain in stock before serious enough deterioration takes place that the product should not be sold. Shelf life varies greatly, affected by many environmental conditions, such as heat, light, dust, and handling.

SHELF MISER Same as: SPACE MISER

SHELF STOCK Merchandise accessible to store patrons who may usually remove what they want from the shelves on which the items are placed. See: FLOOR STOCK, FORWARD STOCK

SHELF STRIP A promotional device designed to fit in the molding or price rail of a shelf to call attention to the product above it.

SHELF TALKER A more elaborately made or printed SHELF STRIP.

SHERIDAN STUFFER Same as: NEWSPAPER STUFFER

SHERMAN ACT Enacted in 1890, this law is the basis for our ANTI-TRUST activity. Codifying the common law, it has two major provisions: 1) that every contract in restraint of trade is declared illegal, and 2) attempts to monopolize any part of trade among the several states shall be a misdemeanor. Its real contribution was to turn restraint of trade and monopolization into offenses against the Federal Government, to require enforcement by federal officials, to provide penalties of fine and/or imprisonment, and to provide suit for triple damages by injured parties. It has been amended a number of times. See: CELLER-KEFAUVER ANTI-MERGER ACT, CLAYTON ACT, FEDERAL TRADE COMMISSION ACT, ROBINSON-PATMAN ACT, WHEELER-LEA ACT

SHIP-A-TRAIN A service offered by some railroads whereby a shipper who can commit a specified minimum number of trailers or CONTAINERS within a 24-hour period will be given a special train at special rates.

SHIPPER COOPERATIVE Performs essentially the same services as a FREIGHT FORWARDER, but returns any profits to members. Reliable estimates place the number of such organizations at about 500.

SHIPPING PLATFORM APPROACH A way of creating CHANNELS OF DISTRIBUTION by simply concentrating on getting the goods out of the plant to somebody. It is fundamentally unsound because it makes no provision for understanding the logical potential user, and may be dangerous to the extent that wrong channel decisions are the result.

SHIP'S OPTION See: MEASUREMENT RATE

SHOOK (1) A set of parts of a box or piece of furniture, ready to be put together. (2) A set of staves and headings enough to assemble a cask.

SHOPLIFTING A major problem for RETAILERS. Recent estimates of the total loss from this form of theft amount to several billions of dollars annually and increasing rapidly. Control was complicated by the necessity to permit suspects to leave the premises before apprehending, but a number of states have modified this provision to permit in-store approach. Professionals account for the largest portion of this loss, but youg people have been known to engage in this activity as fun. Recently an increasing number of incidents have involved the elderly.

SHOPPER   (1) A publication consisting mainly of ADVERTISEMENTS by local MERCHANTS, sent free to a controlled list intended to provide saturation coverage of a relevant area. See: CONTROLLED CIRCULATION   (2) A person engaged in SEARCH activity.

SHOPPING   See: SEARCH

SHOPPING CENTER   See: MALL, PLANNED SHOPPING CENTER, REGIONAL SHOPPING CENTER, SHOPPING PLAZA, STRIP CENTER

SHOPPING CENTER PANEL   In OUTDOOR ADVERTISING, a PANEL suspended from light posts in the parking area, to which advertisers' messages may be affixed. Available in many, but not all, shopping centers.

SHOPPING GOODS   The type of item for which reasonable alternates exist and which the CONSUMER usually wishes to purchase only after comparing price, QUALITY, and STYLE in a number of sources. See: CONVENIENCE GOODS, SPECIALTY GOODS

SHOPPING GUIDE   Same as: SHOPPER

SHOPPING PLAZA   A large building erected in a shopping district to act as a vertical CONTROLLED SHOPPING CENTER. The various areas of the building are rented to different RETAILERS. See: MALL

SHOPPING RADIUS   The area around a STORE from which it normally attracts CUSTOMERS. Sometimes expressed in distance terms. See: TRADING AREA

SHORT   Usually used in reference to the individual who is engaged in SHORT SELLING.

SHORTAGE   See: BOOK INVENTORY

SHORT HEDGE   A HEDGE in which the contract to sell commodity is in the FUTURES MARKET.

SHORT-HOUR   A part-time employee, especially the ones who assist at PEAK HOURS in RETAILING.

SHORTLINER   In the farm equipment manufacturing business, a FIRM that makes complete units or whole items most of which are dependent on the tractor for power or application. The main job is joining a large number of small parts, many of which are purchased, into subassemblies.

SHORT POSITION   Making a contract to deliver in the future at a fixed price a commodity which one does not presently own. A firm or SPECULATOR may take this position when there is a strong belief that the price of the commodity will decline. A gain is anticipated through covering the contract in the then SPOT MARKET. See: LONG POSITION

SHORT RATE   The higher rate an advertiser must pay if he does not use the amount of space or time specified in his contract, which is usually an agreed probable amount at the outset and subject to this adjustment. Does not apply to FLAT RATE contracts.

SHORT RUN   (1) Technically, a period of time too brief to make any real adjustment in actual manufacturing capacity. See: LONG RUN   (2) More popularly, a period of short duration from the present into the near future.   Often called: Short term.

SHORT SELLING   Contracting for the future delivery of a commodity one does not presently own, with the idea of making a profit on a falling price situation. May occur also through the SPOT SALE of a borrowed quantity of commodity. Same as: Selling Short

SHORT-STORY COPY   Same as: NARRATIVE COPY

SHORT TERM   See: SHORT RUN

SHORT TON   2,000 pounds. See: GROSS TON

SHOTGUN APPROACH   A way of trying to accomplish an objective by spraying a
large amount of activity over a broad area, e.g., advertising aimed at
everyone can end up hitting no one. See: RIFLE APPROACH

SHOWING   A number of POSTERS displayed in OUTDOOR or TRANSIT ADVERTISING.
The number does not indicate a numerical quantity, but only a unit for
purchasing intensity of area coverage. The trend over the past few years
has been toward using the GRP unit as the basis, and offering assortments
of 100, 50, 25 GRP units. See: FULL-SHOWING, HALF-SHOWING, QUARTER-SHOWING,
#100 SHOWING, #50 SHOWING, RIDING A SHOWING

SHRINKAGE   (1) The minus difference between actual physical inventory and
the amount shown as should be on hand by the book inventory. May be
caused by recording or counting errors, but more often is the result of
thefts by customers or employees. See: SHOPLIFTING   (2) The difference
between the weight of natural grain and its weight after proper drying
to remove the moisture, which if left in could cause STORAGE problems
involving insect and disease complications. The handling for moisture
removal may also result in a dry weight loss due to removal of chaff,
pieces of kernels, and dust. (3) The weight loss of a commodity which
normally results during processing into a finished product.

SHRINK LENS   Same as: ANAMORPHIC LENS

SHRINK-WRAP   A way of covering or PACKAGING something by using a strong,
impervious material which shrinks tight around the object when heat is
applied. Devices have been developed which can accomodate large items,
such as UNIT LOADS. An item so covered avoids the need for other weather
protection. An item which does not require boxing as a protective device
may be shipped so covered, attached to a pair of blocks for fork-lift
handling purposes.

SHUT-OUT CARGO   A charge against a vessel based on the number of tons of
outbound cargo received by the vessel for loading but not actually loaded,
rather left to remain on the wharf after the vessel departs. The charge
usually starts the day after the vessel shutting out cargo departs from
the assigned berth, and ceases on the date the vessel which actually lifts
the cargo begins to receive her own cargo.

SIDE-STITCHING   A method of binding a MAGAZINE or a BOOKLET by stitching
through or stapling the pages from front to back near their edges. The
pages will not lie flat when opened. Contrast with: SADDLE-STITCHING

SIGNAL   That which is BROADCAST. When it is said of a station that its
signal is good in a given area, that means its programs can be received
clearly in that area. See: AM, FM, FREQUENCY

SIGNATURE   (1) In BROADCASTING, a sound effect or specific music which
identifies a program or commercial. (2) The advertiser's name as shown
in the advertisement. (3) A sheet of paper which will fold into four,
or multiples of four, pages of a given size.

SIGNIFICANCE   (1) In a number, the values known and assumed relevant. A
decimal point is frequently used to designate relevance. For example,
100 probably has one significant digit, but 100.00 has five significant
digits. (2) The values found in the process of CORRELATION that indicate
whether the data are useful for decision-making.

SILENT SALESMAN   (1) A coin- or bill-operated machine used in VENDING.
(2) Any POP display. (3) Sometimes applied to DIRECT MAIL items.

SILHOUETTE HALFTONE   Same as: OUTLINE HALFTONE

SILK SCREEN   A method of printing which uses a screen made of a textile
of strong fiber. The material is made impervious where ink should not
penetrate, thus forming a stencil. When ink is pressed through the
screen, the design is printed on the subject. Lends itself well to color
operations.

SIMPLE RANDOM SAMPLING   The most direct approach to selecting a PROBABIL-
ITY SAMPLE. The process provides that not only must each element of a
POPULATION, but also each possible combination of elements, have the same
chance of being included in the sample. Ensures that the personal judgment of the selector does not enter into the choices. A TABLE OF RANDOM
NUMBERS is often used as a tool in determining the elements because purely
blind choice is frequently difficult to effect. Thus, an automatic ran-
domization method is achieved. Quite generally used in shortened form
as: random sampling.

SIMPLIFICATION   The process of reducing the number of different items in
a firm's LINES. May be the result of industry STANDARDIZATION, research
of the firm's experience with customer desires, or the sale of a portion
of the firm's manufacturing facilities. See: DIVERSIFICATION

SIMPLIFIED SELLING   A term used broadly in RETAILING to include SELF-SELEC-
TION, SELF-SERVICE, better fixtures, improved LAYOUT, more effective displays, and techniques to speed up sales transactions.

SIMULATION   An analysis, usually on a computer, of how a particular system, such as the formula for a marketing model, is likely to conclude.
It may be applied to past data for the purpose of testing its VALIDITY,
assuming that future operations will continue within the framework of
known interacting forces; or to prediction of future results, given promotional and advertising expenditures, MARKET STRUCTURE, actions of competitors, and other pertinent factors. The intent is to replicate a
real-world situation. See: DYNAMIC SIMULATION, STATIC SIMULATION,
SYMBOLIC SIMULATION

SIMULATION MODEL   Same as: MATHEMATICAL MODEL

SINE QUA NON   A Latin phrase meaning: without which, nothing; in transla-
tion into modern English: an indispensable thing or condition, something
prerequisite to the existence of something else.

SINGLE ITEM PRICING   Same as: UNIT PRICING

SINGLE-PRICE POLICY   The POLICY of selling the entire ASSORTMENT of a certain category of merchandise at a single fixed price so that the buyer
can concentrate only on the merchandise offered. Example: all hats, $5.
Distinguish from: ONE-PRICE POLICY

SINGLE RATE   The charge made by a station that does not distinguish
between local and national ADVERTISERS. See: LOCAL RATE, ONE-TIME RATE

SINGLE-STAGE SAMPLING   See: CLUSTER SAMPLING

SIQUIS   Applied to the first OUTDOOR ADVERTISING efforts in England. Taken
from the Latin "Si Quis" (If Anybody) or in the modern fashion, "To Whom
It May Concern." The Romans had begun all public notices with the words
"Si Quis" and later posters exhorting people to buy a certain product
acquired this phrase as a name.

SISTER PUBLICATIONS   PERIODICALS produced by the same publisher.

SISTER-STORE CONCEPT   Same as: EQUAL-STORE CONCEPT

SITUATIONAL ANALYSIS   Joint reference to analyses of a FIRM'S external
environment and its internal situation.

SIU   Abbreviation for: sets in use, as applicable to television ADVERTISING.

SIX C'S · Factors entering into MARKETING STRATEGY decisions. They should be
analyzed carefully before any decision is made. They are: commodity,
company, competitors, channel members, consumers, community.

SKEWNESS   The amount of departure from symmetry of a FREQUENCY CURVE. It
is said to be negatively skewed when the peak is away from the y axis and
positively skewed when the peak is close to the y axis. See: KURTOSIS

SKID   Essentially the same as a PALLET but made so that the supporting cross-members will accommodate sliding across a surface.

SKIDS   Wood runners attached as protection to the exterior of a shipping case.

SKIMMING PRICE   The setting of price high initially with the objective of getting the best out of the MARKET rather than the most. The intent is to appeal to those persons in the market who are interested in new things and are little, if at all, conscious of price. Same as: SKIM-THE-CREAM PRICE

SKIM-THE-CREAM PRICE   Same as: SKIMMING PRICE

SKIP LOSS   A loss caused by the disappearance of a credit customer while still owing a balance to the creditor.

SKU   Abbreviation for: Stock-Keeping Unit, a measure of inventory size.

SKYTRAIN   A low-cost, shuttle service on the North Atlantic air transport routes. Passengers are accepted on a first-come, first-served basis, reservations not allowed. Also, any food or drink on board must be paid for separately.

SLACK FILLING   The practice of using deceptively oversized PACKAGES. Not legal under present laws. See: FTC

SLEEPER   An item of merchandise which suddenly shows increased popularity. May even develop into a RUNNER with timely PROMOTION.

SLEEPER EFFECT   The action occasioned at some time by an impression received earlier from a now-forgotten source. ADVERTISING is said to have such effects, although tracing them has proved illusive in most cases. The belief in this effect, held by some distinguished personalities in the fields of MARKETING and economics, has led to the proposal that advertising should be capitalized rather than treated as a current expense. Resolution of this accounting problem awaits more definite understanding of advertising's workings in a MARKET.

SLICE-OF-LIFE COMMERCIAL   A COMMERCIAL that shows how an individual overcomes an obstacle to a goal by using the advertised PRODUCT. See: IDENTIFICATION (2) See: NARRATIVE COPY

SLOGAN   That piece of verbal material in an ADVERTISEMENT which is designed to be repeated and remembered exactly as presented. May be print or oral. Often used in political and idealogical campaigns.

SLUG   (1) A cast line of type. (2) A temporary, identification memo put on COPY but not to be reproduced.

SLURRY   Pulverized coal or other solid, insoluble material mixed with water or other liquid for sending through a pipeline. An increasingly important technique which makes possible the use of relatively inexpensive pipeline facilities, with in some instances such as wood chips, partial processing on the way.

SMALL GROUP THEORY   A modern explanation for employee behavior which emphasizes the work group, a small, self-governing team which can work for or against some objective proposed by management.

SMORGASBORD PLAN   A compensation plan for SALESPEOPLE that permits the individual to select the mix of salary, commissions, bonuses, and fringe benefits preferred as most applicable to efficient filling of the individual's requirements.

SMSA   Abbreviation for: Standard Metropolitan Statistical Area. Revised criteria by the U.S. Office of Management and Budget provide that an SMSA must include either (1) one city with a population of at least 50,000, or (2) one city with a population of at least 25,000 which, when combined with contiguous places having a population density of at least 1,000 per square mile, will have a population of at least 50,000 (provided that the city and contiguous places are in a county or counties with a population of at least 75,000). A contiguous county is included in an SMSA if at least 75% of the resident labor force is nonagricultural, and if it meets at least two criteria of metropolitan character and one criterion of metropolitan integration. Minimum criteria of character: (1) 25% of population is urban, (2) population gain of 15% between two most recent decennial censuses, (3) density of 50 persons per square mile. Minimum criteria of integration: (1) 15% of resident employed workers work in the area, (2) 15% of the county's employed workers live in the area, (3) sum of workers commuting to and from the central county or counties equals 20% of the employed workers living in the county. SMSA's are defined along county lines except in New England where towns and cities are units of definition.

SNAPPER   An extra special incentive used to stimulate CONSUMER purchases of a product being promoted heavily.

SNIFFER   A display which uses odor to attract attention or to enhance the appeal of a product.

SNIPE   Same as: OVERLAY

SNOB EFFECT   The extent to which DEMAND for a CONSUMERS' GOOD is diminished because many others are using it. This effect is seen in the field of exclusive fashion in which the demand curve is sloped positively until the design is copied and made available at popular prices, after which the curve becomes sharply negative as the patrons of such fashion disassociate themselves from the general public. See: LAW OF DEMAND

SNOWBALLING   The phenomenon that frequently is experienced in a GROUP INTERVIEW situation when a comment by one person evokes a chain of responses from the others in the group. See: STIMULATION

SNPA   Abbreviation for: Southern Newspaper Publishers Association, a regional trade association representing about 400 daily newspapers in 14 Southeastern and Southwestern states. Its main purpose is to advance the welfare and promote the best interests of its member newspapers so that they may better serve their regions, people, and nation.

SOCIAL CLASSES   Groups of people who are more or less equal to one another in prestige and community status; they readily and regularly interact among themselves formally and informally; and they share the same goals and ways of looking at life. W. Lloyd Warner and Associates have distinguished among six social classes, now widely accepted:
   1) Upper-Upper or "Social Register" consists of locally prominent families, usually with at least second or third generation wealth. Basic values: living graciously, upholding family reputation, reflecting the excellence of one's breeding, and displaying a sense of community responsibility. About 1/2 of 1% of the population.
   2) Lower-Upper or "Nouveau Riche" consists of the more recently arrived and never-quite-accepted wealthy families. Goals: blend of Upper-Upper pursuit of gracious living and the Upper-Middle drive for success. About 1 1/2 % of the population.
   3) Upper-Middle are moderately successful professional men and women, owners of medium-sized businesses, young people in their twenties and early thirties who are expected to arrive at the managerial level by their middle or late thirties. Motivations: success at a career, cultivating charm and polish. About 10% of the population.
   4) Lower-Middle are mostly non-managerial office workers, small business owners, highly paid blue-collar families. Goals: Respectability, and Striving to live in well-maintained homes, neatly furnished in more-or-less "right" neighborhoods, and to do a good job at their work. They will save for a college education for their children. Top of the "Average Man

World." About 30%-35% of the population.

    5) Upper-Lower or "Ordinary Working Class" consists of semi-skilled workers. Although many make high pay, they are not particularly interested in respectability. Goals: enjoying life and living well from day to day, to be at least Modern, and to work hard enough to keep safely away from the slum level. About 40% of the population.

    6) Lower-Lower are unskilled workers, unassimilated ethnics, and the sporadically employed. Outlooks: apathy, fatalism, "get your kicks whenever you can." About 15% of the population, but have less than half of the purchasing power.

    Note that these classes are not entirely homogeneous. They include subgroups many of which overlap the class lines as shown due to considerable upward or downward mobility. For a discussion of the marketing significance of these classes see the still fresh: Richard P. Coleman, "The Significance of Social Stratification," in Marketing and the Behavioral Sciences, Perry Bliss, ed. (Boston: Allyn and Bacon, Inc., 1962) pp. 156-171.

SOCIAL-CULTURAL SEGMENTATION   See: CULTURE, SEGMENTATION, SOCIAL CLASSES

SOCIAL ETHIC   A moral practice that goes beyond the BUSINESS ETHIC in that it requires in addition that business be sensitive to all of society's many problems.

SOCIALIZATION   (1) The whole process by which an individual develops, through transactions with other people, his specific patterns of socially pertinent behavior. (2) The process of the individual's learning of tastes and behaviors. Refers to processes affecting present and eventual behavior. See: ANTICIPATORY SOCIALIZATION

SOCIAL MAN   The more recent concept of the buyer who is influenced in his decisions at least as much by sociological forces as by his individual preferences. For example, a purchasing agent buying office supplies must take into account the preferences of the secretaries, and may thus compromise his personal likes and dislikes with those of the ones for whom he buys. See: ECONOMIC MAN

SOCIAL MARKETING   The MARKETING activities involved in attempts to influence the acceptance of social ideas and to gain desired AUDIENCE action to implement into socially useful programs what present knowledge permits.

SOCIAL MOBILITY   The possibility of movement of individuals in a society from one SOCIAL CLASS to another. Aspirations normally would be upward, although downward movements do occur. In the United States, unlike most other countries, upward social mobility is relatively easy, especially between the several lower and middle classes.

SOCIAL MOTIVES   Those MOTIVES which are involved with man's relationships with others, according to the NORMS of that particular CULTURE. See: PHYSIOLOGICAL MOTIVES

SOCIAL NEEDS   The third level of MASLOW'S HIERARCHY OF NEEDS, after SAFETY NEEDS. Include affection, friendship, belonging, acceptance, love.

SOCIAL RISK   See: CONSUMER-PERCEIVED RISKS

SOCIAL STRATIFICATION   See: SOCIAL CLASSES

SOCIETY OF PACKAGING AND HANDLING ENGINEERS   Same as: SPHE

SOCIOGRAPHICS   An encompassing term used to denote group influences on CONSUMER behavior. See: CULTURE, DEMOGRAPHICS, PSYCHOGRAPHICS, REFERENCE GROUPS, SOCIAL CLASS

SOCIOLOGIST   A social scientist who examines man's relationships with man in group interactions.

SOCIOLOGY   The behavioral science which studies man's behavior in groups.

SOFT GOODS Generally applied to ready-to-wear items and domestics. See: HARD GOODS

SOFT MARKET Same as: BUYERS' MARKET

SOFT SELL Same as: LOW-PRESSURE SELLING

SOLID Type set with a minimum of spacing. See: SET SOLID

SOLID MATTER MATTER in which the lines of type are SET SOLID.

SORT In ADP, to arrange items of information according to rules set up to be dependent on some key or FIELD in the RECORDS. See: SORTER

SORTER In ADP, a machine capable of putting data into a particular order as directed. Without a device such as this, the arrangement of data for reports or for further processing would be very difficult. Also called: Sequencer.

SORTING See: ASSORTING

SORTING OUT The activity of separating a collection of objects into groups of like kind, grade, and quality.

SOURCE MARKETING The practice of having vendors price merchandise prior to shipment. Price tickets may be furnished by the buyer or the vendor. If the latter, the buyer supplies the necessary information. Some vendors supply already marked tickets with the invoice, so the RETAILER need merely peel and stick.

SOUTHERN NEWSPAPER PUBLISHERS ASSOCIATION Same as: SNPA

SPACE (1) Same as: QUAD (2) See: LINEAGE

SPACE CONTRACT An agreement between the advertiser and the publisher on the rate structure for the publication. After agreement on the probable amount of space to be used, billing will be made currently on the rate for that amount as though it had actually been earned, with an accurate accounting to be made at the end of the contract period. See: SHORT RATE

SPACE MISER A POINT-OF-PURCHASE display so designed that it holds for easy dispensing a considerable quantity of product, at the same time delivering a promotional message. Often intended to fit on a shelf where the product is normally stocked. Also called: Shelf Miser.

SPACE SPOTS NEWSPAPER advertisements of small size, usually 50 to 150 AGATE LINES, purchased on a volume basis by a NATIONAL ADVERTISER.

SPAN OF CONTROL The number of subordinates a supervisor may manage successfully or at least satisfactorily. Often set at six as an optimum, but the number varies considerably with circumstances. Same as: Span of Supervision

SPAN OF RECALL The number of BRANDS an individual is capable of naming when called upon to do so. Information derived from research seems to indicate that for most people the number is around seven. See: EVOKED SET

SPAN OF SUPERVISION Same as: SPAN OF CONTROL

SPEA Abbreviation for: Sales Promotion Executives Association, a non-partsan professional and educational organization which attempts to advance SALES PROMOTION to business and INDUSTRY through meetings, bulletins, and annual International Conferences. The Association grants an annual scholarship to a group or individual to assist in the study of a particular facet of sales promotion. Membership totals about 1,500.

SPECIAL FEATURES Regularly run BROADCASTS of a particular interest, such as weather reports, stock market reports, reports of ski conditions in season, news broadcasts, etc. Usually sold to advertisers at a higher rate than ROS.

SPECIAL INTEREST GROUP   See: SECONDARY GROUP

SPECIAL INTEREST PUBLISHING   A recent trend in MAGAZINE publishing which seeks to carve out distinct MARKET SEGMENTS. In general, a contrasting approach to the earlier magazine posture as serving a wide national MARKET. Probably a result of a growing realization that a magazine can serve a highly targeted AUDIENCE that television cannot reach effectively.

SPECIALIZATION Division of a total procedure into a series of individual activities each of which is then assigned to be mastered by a particular person. An assembly line is an example, as is the buying of fuel, steel, paper, and equipment each by a different person in the same FIRM.

SPECIAL-LINE RETAILER   Same as: SPECIALTY STORE

SPECIALTIES   Same as: ADVERTISING NOVELTY

SPECIALTY   Same as: ADVERTISING NOVELTY

SPECIALTY ADVERTISING FIELD   The branch of ADVERTISING that uses ADVERTISING NOVELTIES as the ADVERTISING MEDIUM to deliver the message.

SPECIALTY ADVERTISING INFORMATION BUREAU   The organization within the SPECIALTY ADVERTISING field devoted to maintaining an interest in the field by disseminating information about uses of the MEDIUM. It has numerous books dealing with the field and publishes the bi-monthly Specialty Advertising Report.

SPECIALTY DISTRIBUTOR   Actually a WHOLESALER in the SPECIALTY ADVERTISING FIELD, this FIRM handles various types of ADVERTISING NOVELTIES and provides assistance in planning the composition of an ADVERTISING CAMPAIGN using such items. Same as: ADVERTISING SPECIALTY DISTRIBUTOR, SPECIALTY ADVERTISING COUNSELLOR See: DIRECT SELLING HOUSE

SPECIALTY GOODS   The category specifying an item which has such an attraction for a CONSUMER that he will go considerably out of his way to buy it. Applies also to an item for which no reasonable substitute exists and which provides benefits which are in demand. See: CONVENIENCE GOODS, SHOPPING GOODS

SPECIALTY SALESPERSONS   See: SPECIALTY SELLING

SPECIALTY SELLING   Applied generally to the sale at the home or place of business of merchandise or services not available in stores, e.g., home improvements, insurance, and encyclopedias. The men who accomplish the selling are called specialty salespersons. Advertising is placed to get LEADS for them. Should not be considered in the same concept as SPECIALTY GOODS.

SPECIALTY SHOP   A relatively small-scale RETAIL STORE which makes its appeal on a broad selection of a restricted class of merchandise. Has no necessary relationship to SPECIALTY GOODS. See: BOUTIQUE, SPECIALTY STORE

SPECIALTY STORE   Essentially the same as: SPECIALTY SHOP, but this term is more frequently used to designate a RETAIL ESTABLISHMENT so preferred by some CUSTOMERS that they will buy there all their wants of CONVENIENCE, SHOPPING, AND SPECIALTY GOODS.

SPECIALTY SUPPLIER   A FIRM that manufactures or otherwise processes ADVERTISING NOVELTIES for sale through a variety of outlets. See: DIRECT SELLING HOUSE, SPECIALTY ADVERTISING COUNSELLOR, SPECIALTY DISTRIBUTOR

SPECIALTY WHOLESALER   A WHOLESALER who carries a limited number of items within one field. Usually a MERCHANT WHOLESALER. Has no necessary relationship to SPECIALTY GOODS.

SPECIFIC DUTY   A levy on imports made as a fixed money charge per physical unit. See: TARIFF

SPECTACULAR   A large, permanent, non-standardized sign making use of elaborate lighting and action effects. The high cost generally requires confining to the highest traffic areas of metropolitan centers. See: OUT-
DOOR ADVERTISING

SPECULATIVE BUYING   See: FORWARD ORDER

SPECULATIVE PRESENTATION   In the field of ADVERTISING, a demonstration by
an ADVERTISING AGENCY to a prospective client showing what the agency
would do if awarded the contract. Developing such a presentation, with
tentative plans for advertisements, MEDIA, etc., has proved to be very
expensive. Many agencies have terminated this competitive practice.

SPECULATOR   A more or less well-informed person who buys and sells commodities in the FUTURES MARKET with the purpose of making a profit on a price
turn favorable to his position. See: GAMBLER, LONG, SHORT

SPEED TABLE   A display table placed in the APRON of a RETAIL STORE. The
merchandise so displayed is usually of a special sale or other character
associated with quick acceptance and purchase by customers coming into
contact with the display. See: DUMP BIN, JUMBLE BASKET, MERCHANDISER

SPHE   Abbreviation for: Society of Packaging and Handling Engineers, established in 1945 to foster the advancement of scientific PACKAGING, materials handling, and shipping. Some 2,000 members representing about 800
companies belong to the Society. It has a speakers bureau, publishes
technical information, and has developed an industrial packaging course
for use in accredited colleges.

SPIFF   Same as: PUSH MONEY

SPINARAMA   The trade name for a triangular OUTDOOR ADVERTISING unit, usually mobile, which carries three POSTERS and is turned by the wind. Often
seen in shopping center parking lots, less often in other locations.

SPINDLE   Same as: J-HOOK

SPINNERS' MARKET   A MARKET in the trading in cotton which is between the
CENTRAL MARKETS and the mills. Here either those who deal in the central markets or their representatives are the sellers and the mills are
the buyers. Same as: Mill Market

SPIRAL   According to the classification held by a number of advertising
theorists, the way a product or service evolves with relation to its
acceptance by its prospective public. This is a continuous process, moving to a new beginning point in the spiral as acceptance increases; however, it is recognized that some products or services will not advance
further after some point is reached. See: PIONEERING STAGE, COMPETITIVE
STAGE, RETENTIVE STAGE

SPLC   Abbreviation for: Standard Point Location Code, a tariff-oriented
code which, while yet incomplete, has won the acceptance and active support of many carriers and shippers. It is expected that the result of
current research will permit the construction of an SPLC that will be
accepted throughout the United States. The TDCC is deeply involved in
this activity.

SPLIT FUNCTION WHOLESALER   A MERCHANT WHOLESALER who is VERTICALLY INTE-
GRATED so that he operates on two or more levels of the CHANNEL OF DIS-
TRIBUTION   See: SEMI-JOBBING

SPLIT ITEM   One which a firm both makes and buys simultaneously.

SPLIT RUN   Two or more ADVERTISEMENTS of the same size but different ver-
sions in the same position in different copies of the same issue of a
publication, used to test different appeals or LAYOUTS, or to feature
different products in the regional editions of a national MAGAZINE.

SPOILAGE   Where used in an attempt to differentiate from WASTE, spoilage consists of those produced items that are found to be defective.   Then the term "waste" is applied to materials lost in the manufacturing process or which have little recovery value.   In most instances this distinction provides small significance.

SPOILS ALLOWANCE   Same as: SWELL ALLOWANCE, but applied to perishables.

SPONSOR   The firm or individual or organization that pays for the cost of talent and/or time for a broadcast feature, or the advertisement in print MEDIA, and who is identified as such.

SPONSORED FILMS   Films sponsored by ADVERTISERS to promote a PRODUCT through an educational selling message designed to create goodwill with selected groups of persons.   Sometimes called BUSINESS FILMS, but this title more properly belongs to films designed to be shown only before business, technical, or professional groups.   See: THEATRICAL FILMS

SPONSORSHIP   The financial backing, with identification of source, of an activity such as ADVERTISING.   See: ALTERNATE SPONSORSHIP, FULL-PROGRAM SPONSOR, PARTICIPATING PROGRAM

SPOT   The time bought for a COMMERCIAL on a BROADCAST MEDIUM.   May be 10-, 20-, 30-, or 60-second spots.   Some stations offer other time units.   See: SPOT RADIO, SPOT TELEVISION

SPOT ANNOUNCEMENT   Same as: SPOT

SPOT CAMPAIGN   An ADVERTISING CAMPAIGN using SPOT RADIO or SPOT TELEVISION alone, or both together.

SPOT COMMODITY   A commodity bought or sold to arrive or be delivered at a specified "current" time.   Same as: Cash Commodity

SPOT DEAL   A transaction involving the immediate delivery of a commodity.

SPOT DISPLAY   Merchandise arranged prominently in store aisles with some attention-getting device attached.   May also be put on APRONS.

SPOT MARKET   The environment in which commodities are available for immediate delivery.   Same as: Cash Market

SPOT RADIO or SPOT TELEVISION   A program issued directly from a station on behalf of a national advertiser, in contrast to NETWORK BROADCAST or LOCAL BROADCAST.   Not to be confused with radio or television SPOT.

SPREAD   (1) The difference between the price of a commodity in the SPOT MARKET and in the FUTURES MARKET at the same time.   (2) Two facing pages in a PUBLICATION over which one advertisement is printed.   Same as: DOUBLE TRUCK

SPREADER   A trader in commodities who seeks to gain from differences in the futures prices of the same commodities on different COMMODITY EXCHANGES by buying on one and selling on another.   He can gain if eventually the prices for his contract month are the same on both exchanges. The amount of his gain is determined by the size of the difference in his contract prices, or the "spread."

SQUARE END   A premium space in TRANSIT ADVERTISING, located near doors of rail transit vehicles.

SQUARE HALFTONE   A HALFTONE which has an over-all screen and in which the corners are squared.   Usually the entire picture is shown.

SRDS   Abbreviation for: Standard Rate and Data Service, an organization accepted as the standard source of ADVERTISING MEDIA information.   Publishes current information for each unit on rates, mechanical requirements, closing dates, etc.

SRO METHOD   In SALESMANSHIP, a CLOSING technique in which the PROSPECT is told that if the sale is not concluded now, the likelihood is small that the prospect will be able to get the item later. (SRO stands for "standing room only.")

STABLE MARKET   A MARKET characterized by few short-term price fluctuations. In a stable market a BUYER can do little to influence prices. An <u>unstable</u> market shows frequent short-term price fluctuations; it is applicable mainly to certain RAW MATERIALS.

STAFF   Those persons in a FIRM who carry out the functions designed to provide services to those who are in the direct line of AUTHORITY in that activity of the firm which is concerned with the firm's output. See: LINE

STAGGERED SCHEDULE   A CAMPAIGN in TRANSIT ADVERTISING that runs in waves of two or three months over a stated period of time, each wave divided from another by a period of no advertising. See: PULSATION

STANDARD CONSOLIDATED STATISTICAL AREA   Same as: SCSA

STANDARD COSTS   (1) Those costs expected to exist at an assumed production level. (2) Unit costs at STANDARD VOLUME.

STANDARD DENSITY   Compression of a bale of cotton to about 22 1/2 pounds per cubic foot. See: HIGH DENSITY

STANDARD DEVIATION   The most important of the measures of DISPERSION, it is typically used to specify the percent of the measurements in an ARRAY that are located within a certain distance from a central point. It may be defined technically as being equal to the square root of the mean of the squared deviations (from the mean).

STANDARD ERROR   The STANDARD DEVIATION of the MEANS of the SAMPLES taken from a particular POPULATION. Also called: Standard Error of the Means

STANDARD ERROR OF ESTIMATE   A measure which provides a numerical value $\pm$ within which the actual value lies, at a 68% probability. Designated by the symbol $S(yx)$. When the number of observations is small, the $S(yx)$ may be quite large. It then depends on how nearly correct the decision-maker requires his data to be. A larger SAMPLE may be needed to provide the better data. Formulae are available to determine sample sizes necessary to achieve required PRECISION (the extent to which sample results deviate from the results that would have been secured from a complete enumeration of the population using the same data collection methods). Where errors occur that are not the result of SAMPLING, these may be added to the sampling error to get a concept called "degree of accuracy." PARAMETRIC.

STANDARD ERROR OF THE MEANS   Same as: STANDARD ERROR

STANDARD GEOGRAPHICAL UNIT   Same as: SGU

STANDARD INDUSTRIAL CLASSIFICATION SYSTEM   Each INDUSTRIAL MARKET SEGMENT is identified with a number. Statistics are collected by the government according to these numbers, thereby providing a great deal of information for the marketer. Abbreviated: SIC.

STANDARDIZATION   The establishment of criteria of limits to which grades of goods are expected to conform. May be internal for just one firm, applicable to an INDUSTRY as a whole, or apply across all activity of a certain kind in the economy. Combined with GRADING, one of the MARKETING FUNCTIONS

STANDARDIZED LEARNING APPROACH   In SALESMANSHIP, generally refers to the use of the AIDCAS PROCESS.

STANDARD METROPOLITAN STATISTICAL AREA   Same as: SMSA

STANDARD PACKAGE   The quantity of an item normally shipped in one carton.

STANDARD POINT LOCATION CODE   Same as: SPLC

STANDARD RATE AND DATA SERVICE, INC. Same as: SRDS

STANDARD SIZE PAGE A page size used by newspapers, usually 8 columns wide by 300 AGATE LINES deep, making a full page chargeable at 2,400 lines, although this may vary with the policy of the individual newspaper. Same as: Large Size Page See: TABLOID SIZE PAGE

STANDARD TRANSPORTATION COMMODITY CODE Same as: STCC

STANDARD VOLUME Anticipated sales over an estimated business cycle reduced to an annual basis.

STANDING DETAILS In ADVERTISING, the elements which are to appear in every advertisement, such as LOGO, TRADEMARK, COPYRIGHT symbol, picture of product, price, where available, SLOGAN, JINGLE, etc.

STANDING MATTER MATTER which has been assembled to be held for use in the future, usually as the result of a HOLD ORDER.

STANDING ORDER An authorization to a vendor to ship certain merchandise as available, or on a fixed-quantity basis per time interval.

STANDING ROOM ONLY A technique used in CLOSING. The SALESPERSON tells the PROSPECT that if the sale is not concluded now, the likelihood of being able to acquire the offering later may be close to zero. Also called: Last Chance Method See: TRIAL CLOSE

STAND OF PAPER In OUTDOOR ADVERTISING, the sheets of paper which make up one complete POSTER.

STAPLE ITEMS For a certain store, the types of merchandise which customers expect to find in that particular store and which is in generally continuous demand. If out of stock, the store may lose the customer for a longer period than represented by that one sale. See: BASIC STOCK

STARCH SERVICES A continuing MARKET RESEARCH service organization specializing in the measurement of readers' reactions to and readership of MAGAZINE ADVERTISEMENTS. Highly respected.

STATE-OF-BEING SEGMENTATION One of a four-way classification of the STRATEGIES of SEGMENTATION, this refers to the physical, DEMOGRAPHIC, or geographic characteristics of populations. The other three are: BENEFIT SEGMENTATION, PRODUCT USAGE SEGMENTATION, and STATE-OF-MIND SEGMENTATION

STATE-OF-MIND SEGMENTATION One of a four-way classification of the STRATEGIES of SEGMENTATION, this refers to the psychological characteristics of populations, especially with relationship between ATTITUDES and behavior. The other three are: BENEFIT SEGMENTATION, PRODUCT USAGE SEGMENTATION, and STATE-OF-BEING SEGMENTATION

STATE OF NATURE Same as: STATE OF THE UNIVERSE

STATE OF THE UNIVERSE A description of certain conditions surrounding the situation faced. Uncertainty about the accuracy of this description can rarely be dispelled entirely. Decisions must be made, nevertheless. Statistical methods have been evolved which deal with the lessening of the risk of being wrong about the TRUE STATE OF THE UNIVERSE.

STATE OF THE WORLD Same as: STATE OF THE UNIVERSE

STATIC SIMULATION A type of SIMULATION in which all components of a system which can be identified are identified and replicated. Functional relationships among the components are included. See: DYNAMIC SIMULATION, SYMBOLIC SIMULATION

STATION IDENTIFICATION Same as: I.D.

STATION POSTER Really a variety of POSTER PANEL, but confined in display to the stations of subways, rapid transit systems on the surface, and suburban railroads. See: TRANSIT ADVERTISING

STATISTIC   A numerical datum that describes something about an ELEMENTARY UNIT in the POPULATION of interest.

STATISTICAL ABSTRACT OF THE UNITED STATES   Intended to be a convenient statistical reference and a guide to the more detailed data in the original sources, this volume published annually by the Bureau of the Census reproduces more than 1,000 tables of data including the DEMOGRAPHIC, social, political, and economic structures of the United States. Its supplement volume, Historical Statistics of the United States from Colonial Times to 1957, converts each of the about 3,000 different series into data consistent with original definitions, which the Abstract has of necessity changed from time to time as required by a dynamic economy.

STATISTICS OF INCOME   Separate volumes based on federal income tax returns for individuals, partnerships, and corporations contain data by major INDUSTRY, asset size, and other important breakdowns. It is published annually by the Internal Revenue Service of the Treasury Department.

STATUS FLOAT PHENOMENON   A suggested explanation for the seeming upward flow of FASHION influence from lower- to higher-status levels. For example, college professors have been known to adopt the dress preferences of students, and the long hair of the hippy culture has found its way into otherwise conservative circles, although in modified manner. See: TRICKLE-ACROSS THEORY, TRICKLE-DOWN THEORY

STATUS QUO   A Latin phrase meaning the existing state or condition.

STAY-OUT PRICE   Same as: PREEMPTIVE PRICE

STCC   Abbreviation for: Standard Transportation Commodity Code, an attempt to establish uniformity in the actual descriptions of commodities by the various carriers. The TDCC is pressing this activity forward together with many other groups, but acceptance thus far has been limited, mainly due to the difficulty of eliminating variance between BILL OF LADING descriptions and those shown in the STCC. The future success of this project does appear likely.

STEEL CARRIERS CONFERENCE OF ATA   Affiliated with the ATA since 1965, this organization of steel haulers, steel shippers, and allied INDUSTRIES acts as an information clearing house for all sorts of data applicable to the steel and trucking interests as a whole. Safety of operations has been one of its principal objectives, and it works closely with regulatory agencies toward this goal. It conducts various meetings and issues regularly a Newsletter and a Safety Bulletin, as well as other documents as the need occurs.

STEEL SERVICE CENTER   Now changing name to METAL SERVICE CENTER because of the need to carry other metals. See: METAL WAREHOUSE

STEREO   Same as: STEREOTYPE

STEREOTYPE   A printing plate made by pouring molten metal into a device into which a MAT has been fixed and allowing it to cool and harden. Many newspapers are still printed from stereotype; many, however, are going to PHOTO-COMPOSITION.

STICKERS   Items of merchandise which have not sold after a reasonable time and are taking up space that should be devoted to better-moving items. See: DEAD STOCK

STIMULATION   The phenomenon that occurs frequently in GROUP INTERVIEWS. Individual RESPONDENTS are induced to want to express their ideas and to expose their feelings as the general level of interest in the topic heightens in the group. See: SNOWBALLING

STIMULATION MARKETING   Those activities designed to bring the affected market segment from a condition of ABSENCE OF DEMAND with regard to a PRODUCT to a recognition of product benefits and a reasonable level of positive DEMAND.

STIMULUS Any unit of input to one or more of the senses. See: ABSOLUTE THRESHOLD, DIFFERENTIAL THRESHOLD, SENSATION, SENSORY RECEPTORS, WEBER'S LAW

STOCHASTIC MODEL A model in which chance or random variables have been introduced. Statistical rules are the base, and conditions of uncertainty have been entered as observed from real events.

STOCK DEPTH The number of units of specific items determined to be required to maintain ASSORTMENTS without too many lost sales due to out-of-stock conditions.

STOCKING REPRESENTATIVE A MANUFACTURERS' REPRESENTATIVE who carries an inventory for his PRINCIPAL and who ships for his principal from that inventory.

STOCK-KEEPING UNIT Same as: SKU

STOCKLESS PURCHASING A system of buying in which the financial responsibility for inventory remains with the VENDOR. The inventory may remain at the vendor's location or may be placed at the buyer's location, in which case it is called "consignment buying." There are obvious advantages to both the buyer and the seller. Not as formal and long term as SYSTEMS CONTRACTING.

STOCKOUT The situation in which a RETAILER has not anticipated CONSUMER DEMAND for a particular item, thus not having enough on hand and thereby losing sales. See: STOCK DEPTH

STOCK PLANNING RETAILERS use one or a combination of four basic methods for dealing with the variables of the MERCHANDISE BUDGET: BASIC STOCK METHOD, PERCENTAGE VARIATION METHOD, STOCK-SALES RATIO METHOD, WEEKS' SUPPLY METHOD

STOCK-ROOM SUPERVISOR Same as: MATERIALS CONTROLLER

STOCK ROTATION Placing incoming items behind those of the same kind already on hand so that the inventory may be kept fresh. If stock is not sold from displays, a system of marking is advisable to identify the items in stock the longest.

STOCK-SALES RATIO METHOD One of the four primary methods used by RETAILERS for STOCK PLANNING. Requires determination of a suitable ratio for each month. By this method, the formula is: BOM stock level = BOM stock-sales ratio x planned sales. Planning is accomplished for specific times rather than averages.

STOCKTURN Same as: TURNOVER, but used mainly in RETAILING.

STOP-OFF PRIVILEGE A transportation rate privilege which permits a shipper to distribute goods along a carrier's route. Usually offers a saving over the cost of small-lot shipments. May also be available for pick-ups as well as shipments.

STORAGE (1) A MARKETING FUNCTION characterized by the creation of TIME UTILITY by holding and preserving goods for varying periods of time. Storage is inherent in all goods handling except in those few instances where the item is put into its next use immediately upon being produced. It should be noted that all users are involved with this to some greater or lesser extent. ·(2) Preferred as a term in ADP to "memory" it is a device in which data can be stored and from which data can be obtained on call as needed.

STORAGE IN TRANSIT Same as: INTRANSIT STORAGE

STORE A business ESTABLISHMENT into which CUSTOMERS and PROSPECTS are invited to visit and to select purchases.

STORE AUDIT A periodic check of predetermined RETAIL outlets to arrive at a very accurate estimate of the sales of each of a selected group of PRODUCTS. See: NIELSEN RETAIL INDEX

STORECASTING   BROADCASTING at the point-of-purchase, providing music and news as well as announcing special offerings.

STORE DESIGN   The architectural character or decorative STYLE of a STORE. The intended projected image of the store should play a large part in determining store design.

STORE LAYOUT   Actually part of the STORE DESIGN, it is specifically the allocation of space to each selling and nonselling department of a STORE. Part of this thinking involves aisle width and arrangement. One arrangement is known as a grid pattern, in which the aisles are placed at right angles to one another, permitting maximum standardization of fixtures. The other arrangement is known as free flow layout, in which there is usually little or no regularity of aisle pattern. Arrangements within departments often use a wandering aisle, i.e., an aisle that is formed by the placement of movable fixtures. Such an arrangement may be found quite commonly in women's wear departments' areas in DEPARTMENT STORES. See: STORE TRAFFIC

STORE LIGHTING   See: 1-3-5-10 FORMULA

STORES   (1) A stock of goods maintained in such a manner as to control and record incoming goods, and to insure that goods issued are properly authorized and charged. Applied as well to the organization devoted to this activity. (2) Plural of STORE.

STORES LEDGER   Same as: BALANCE-OF-STORES RECORD

STORES RECORD   Same as: BALANCE-OF-STORES RECORD, Stores Ledger

STORES REQUISITION   A form issued by a using department to obtain materials that are carried in normal stock. The form, properly authorized, goes directly to the stores department from which the materials are supplied. See: REQUISITION

STORE TRAFFIC   The flow of customers into and throughout a STORE. Placement of merchandise in various store areas must take into account the natural and the desired pattern of customer movement to and from these areas.

STORY BOARD   A parallel sequence of sketches and COPY of the VIDEO and the AUDIO portions of a television program or commercial. It is actually a "LAYOUT" for this MEDIUM.

STORYTELLING   One of the PROJECTIVE TECHNIQUES. Given a cartoon drawing, photograph, or description, all incomplete, the RESPONDENT is asked to explain, interpret, make up an ending, or complete the stimulus object. The responses when skillfully interpreted can provide insights into behavior patterns.

STRAIGHT BILL OF LADING   A BILL OF LADING which states a specific identity to whom the goods should be delivered. It is not negotiable.

STRAIGHT REBUY.   A routine purchase probably made many times before. New data is not sought. While a majority of a firm's purchases usually are of this type, they occupy relatively little of a BUYER'S time. See: MODIFIED REBUY, NEW-TASK BUYING

STRATEGIC PLANNING   PLANNING activity directed especially toward increasing the organization's ability to adjust to external changes and to create new alternatives. Merges into ACTION PLANNING with passage of time.

STRATEGIC PRODUCT-LINE ADJUSTMENT   Determination of the number of different types of product, or different products, to be offered. See: TACTICAL PRODUCT-LINE ADJUSTMENT

STRATEGY   The art and/or science of selecting means for achieving goals.

STRATEGY RIGHTS   In PURCHASING, the AUTHORITY granted managers to develop STRATEGIES for the attainment of the OBJECTIVES they have set. See: ALLOCATION RIGHTS, CRITERIA RIGHTS, EVALUATION RIGHTS, POLICY RIGHTS, SAMPLING RIGHTS

STRATIFIED SAMPLING   A method of producing a PROBABILITY SAMPLE by selecting those elements of a POPULATION which are relevant to the HYPOTHESIS and making sure that the samples of these elements are representative. Each such population group is called a stratum. For example, it may be desirable to determine the attitude toward a college held by Freshmen and by Seniors. Studying the other classes would be irrelevant. Advantages of this type where it can be used are: appropriate representation and smaller required size of sample.

STRATIFYING THE MARKET   Estimating the number of CUSTOMERS who may be expected to buy the PRODUCT at various price levels.

STRATUM   See: STRATIFIED SAMPLING

STRICT LIABILITY   In general, under this legal concept, a person suing for recovery as the result of damage suffered through the use of an article must show that there was a defect in the article and that he was damaged as a result of that defect. See: PRIVITY OF CONTRACT, PRODUCT LIABILITY

STRIKE-ON COMPOSITION   Same as: IMPACT COMPOSITION

STRING-STREET LOCATION   A major thoroughfare on which different types of STORES are strung out for a number of consecutive blocks. Most of the trade is drawn from people using the street rather than from people living in the immediate vicinity. Many different types of stores, both RETAIL and WHOLESALE, may be found in such an area. A special kind of string-street may be found today along some major highways outside the areas of high population density.

STRIP CENTER   An open SHOPPING CENTER as opposed to an enclosed MALL.

STRIP STORE   A STORE in a STRING-STREET location.

STRUCTURAL DIRECTION   Same as: GAZE MOTION

STRUCTURE   See: STRUCTURED QUESTIONNAIRE

STRUCTURED QUESTIONNAIRE   May be disguised, in which the objective of the study is not revealed to the RESPONDENTS, or undisguised, in which the objective is revealed to the respondents. Structure refers to the degree of standardization: a QUESTIONNAIRE in which the questions to be asked and the choice of responses permitted to the respondents are completely predetermined is said to be "highly structured." See: UNSTRUCTURED-DISGUISED QUESTIONNAIRE, UNSTRUCTURED-UNDISGUISED QUESTIONNAIRE

STUFFER   Same as: NEWSPAPER STUFFER

STYLE   A characteristic or distinctive mode or method of expression, presentation, or conception in the field of some art.

STYLE-OUT   An attempt to determine precisely what features of certain goods are attracting customer buying attention by separating the fast-moving items from the slow-moving items and then examining the fast-moving items carefully to try to discover the common features which may be the reason for the greater sales. Frequently used in ready-to-wear dress departments where some items may be popular while others of the same general type, color, and material will be slow-moving. The answer might be found in belt or collar treatment, pleats, etc.

SUBCAPTION   Same as: SUBHEADLINE

SUBFAMILY   The Department of Commerce defines this as a married couple with or without children, or one parent with at least one child living in a HOUSING UNIT and related to the HEAD of the HOUSEHOLD. See: FAMILY

SUBHEADLINE   A restatement of the idea of interest to the reader in a different and more specific way than appears in the HEADLINE. Generally placed in the COPY immediately following the headline. Same as: Subcaption

SUBLIMATION   A defense mechanism used unconsciously to reduce tensions by substituting one type of response for another. Important to sellers where it is possible to propose the use of the product or service as the way to reach a goal rather than some socially less-acceptable means. See: COGNITIVE DISSONANCE

SUBLIMINAL ADVERTISING   See: SUBLIMINAL AWARENESS

SUBLIMINAL AWARENESS   Detection of STIMULI above the j.n.d. but below the conscious threshold (limen). There is no scientific evidence to indicate that such stimuli are causative of action. So-called "subliminal advertising" has in controlled experiments not been able to get an audience to carry out its suggestions. See: SUPRALIMINAL AWARENESS

SUBMARKET   A portion of a MARKET divided on the basis of common motivations. See: SEGMENTATION

SUBORDINATE PRODUCT ADVERTISING   The ADVERTISING done to develop user DEMAND for the producer of a PRODUCT that has usefulness mainly or entirely as a component of another product, e.g., glass as a PACKAGING material, a zipper as a garment closure. The thrust of such advertising is to encourage the user of the final product to purchase only those final products that incorporate the subordinate product. Same as: end-product advertising.

SUBSTITUTIONAL GOODS   GOODS or SERVICES related in use so that an increase in the price of one relative to a second results in an increase in the quantity demanded by the MARKET of the second. The CROSS-ELASTICITY value, if algebraically positive, is usually considered evidence that the two goods or services are substitutional, provided no change in the REAL INCOME of the buyer has occurred.

SUBURBIA   An area contiguous to a CENTRAL CITY, integrated with it socially and economically, and in which the population density is at least 150 persons per square mile. See: RURAL AREA, SMSA

SUGGESTED RETAIL PRICE   The LIST PRICE of an item announced by a producer as the reasonable price to be charged by a RETAILER. Care must be exercised that the making of such a suggestion does not violate our ANTITRUST LAWS.

SUGGESTION IMPULSE BUYING   IMPULSE BUYING where the IMPACT is so strong on the CONSUMER that on seeing the item for the first time he recognizes the benefits to be had from it and immediately acquires it. See: PLANNED IMPULSE BUYING, PURE IMPULSE BUYING, REMINDER IMPULSE BUYING

SUITABILITY   See: QUALITY

SUNK COSTS   This term represents an investment committed to a particular purpose the nature of which cannot be changed. In reality, they are FIXED COSTS generated by real assets which cannot be turned to other activities. In times of stress, the advice of many financial experts would be to ignore these amounts in pricing product.

SUPER   Same as: SUPERIMPOSURE

SUPEREGO   Tells the EGO what to do so that it will be within the system of manners, ideals, social morals, and religious precepts. An experienced SALESMAN will make his APPEAL directly to the superego by showing how it is fulfilled by his offering, or by neutralizing its effect through the involvement of emotion. Same as: Ego-Ideal

SUPERETTE   Same as: BANTAM STORE

SUPERGRAPHICS   A method of identifying a building by using stripes and rolling balls to move the eye toward wall-size letters on the building's exterior.

SUPERIMPOSURE   An effect used in television commercials which allows lettering to appear over the scene. The letters may be still or moving. Very effective in presenting the TRADEMARK and the SLOGAN of the product while the scene is still on. See: OPTICALS

SUPERMARKET   The RETAIL institution of the present which is most similar to the small GENERAL STORE, but in magnified dimensions. From its start in the 1930's it was the factor which united the automobile, the mechanical refrigerator, and good roads into a system of food use and shopping, which voided the corner grocery store and changed American habits of buying and eating foods, with marked effects on the food INDUSTRY. To be officially classified a supermarket, a food store must have eight or more employees. The typical supermarket sells a large number of non-food items.

SUPPLEMENT   An addition to an existing issue. Thus, a special feature section, often in the form of a MAGAZINE, distributed with a NEWSPAPER.

SUPPLEMENTAL REGISTER   All MARKS capable of distinguishing applicant's goods and used in commerce for at least one year, but otherwise not registerable on the PRINCIPAL REGISTER may be registered on this. Here a mark may consist of any TRADEMARK, SYMBOL, LABEL, PACKAGE, configuration of goods, name, word, SLOGAN, phrase, surname, geographical name, numeral, device, or any combination of these. Registration here does not constitute constructive notice or prima facie evidence and does not give the right to prevent importation of goods bearing an infringing mark, but it does give the right to sue in the United States courts.

SUPPLIES   Same as: OPERATING SUPPLIES

SUPPLY COOPERATIVE   An AGRICULTURAL COOPERATIVE mainly concerned with buying member needs and then reselling these to members. Many have become VERTICALLY INTEGRATED. There are presently a number of tax benefits available to such a cooperative in addition to the general cost advantage usually present when buying in large quantities.

SUPPLY CURVE   The plot of the schedule which shows for all possible prices the quantities of a good which will be offered for sale to the MARKET, considering the factors prevailing at any one time.

SUPRALIMINAL AWARENESS   Detection of STIMULI by an individual on the conscious level. See: SUBLIMINAL AWARENESS

SURFACING APPROACH   A MOTIVATION RESEARCH technique in which the surface of awareness is gradually worked toward by building up information from subjective tests to objective ones, starting at the subconscious level.

SURPLUS MATERIAL   Same as: EXCESS MATERIAL

SURPRINT   Same as: OVERPRINT

SURVEY   A unique investigation using a SAMPLE as a data base for each new study.

SURVEY OF BUYING POWER   A detailed DEMOGRAPHIC, geographic, and socioeconomic statistical report of CONSUMER power to buy goods of various types. A basic MARKET reference. Published annually by Sales & Marketing Management magazine, it includes merchandise line sales by city, county, and state, and five-year projections for METROPOLITAN MARKETS. See: BUYING POWER INDEX, CONSOLIDATED METROPOLITAN AREA, SMSA

SURVEY OF CURRENT BUSINESS   About 2,600 different statistical series are reported monthly in this publication by the Office of Business Economics in the Department of Commerce. They cover BUSINESS INDICATORS, construction activity, foreign transactions, commodity prices, transportation activity, and many more to constitute a summary of the economic accounts of the United States.

SURVEY OF INDUSTRIAL PURCHASING POWER   An annual special issue of <u>Sales & Marketing Management Magazine</u> designed to give very recent county data about industrial activity. The data include only plants with 20 or more employees (these do 95% of the industrial buying although they represent only one-third of all plants) and are divided in 4-digit SIC totals.

SURVEY OF SELLING COSTS   An annual compilation by <u>Sales & Marketing Management Magazine</u> for 80 important MARKETS showing the basic selling costs of food, lodging, and auto rentals, as well as compensation rates and methods, cost of meetings and sales training devices, and a "selling cost index" for a typical weekly cost per SALESPERSON, using 1971 as the base year.

SURVEY RESEARCH DESIGN   A design in MARKETING RESEARCH such that evidence is collected through various techniques of questioning that produce data indirectly inferring the PAYOFF. Typically a QUESTIONNAIRE-associated activity. See: EXPERIMENT, HISTORICAL DESIGN

SWEEPSTAKES   A type of promotion which awards substantial prizes on the basis of a chance drawing. No element of skill is involved, nor is an order or a purchase necessary. See: CONTEST

SWELL ALLOWANCE   A reduction from invoice cost to provide for the loss of merchandise value due to damage in transit. See: SPOILS ALLOWANCE

SWITCHING CUSTOMER   Same as: T.O. PROCEDURE

SWITCH PITCH   An attempt made by a SALESPERSON for a BROADCAST MEDIUM to get the buyer of a time schedule to accept another arrangement after the buy has been made. The alternative arrangement may or may not be to the ADVERTISER'S advantage, and may be presented immediately after the buy or at some later time. Usually applies to the effort of a representative to obtain business placed on a competitive station in a MARKET.

SWITCH TRADER   In the process of international COUNTERTRADE, an individual who has the information and expertise to move the goods involved in a BARTER transaction to a third country where a MARKET exists.

SYMBIOTIC MARKETING   An arrangement whereby one firm sells and promotes a product made or controlled by another FIRM. For example, a toothpaste company selling razor blades made by another, independent, company.

SYMBOL   An instance in which the experience of an object, action, or picture brings an understanding not only of itself, but also of some other ideas and feelings. See: PERCEPTION

SYMBOLIC SIMULATION   A type of SIMULATION that uses flow charts to trace the component flows in a defined system. The FIRM'S anticipated MARKETING MIX could be diagrammed. A new symbolization must be prepared for each alternative. See: DYNAMIC SIMULATION, STATIC SIMULATION

SYMMETRICAL BALANCE   Same as: FORMAL BALANCE

SYMPTOM   A condition which indicates the existence of a PROBLEM. Care must be exercised not to confuse the symptom with the problem. The root cause or base of the problem must be searched out before the problem can be solved. It is not always easy to formulate the right questions to which answers should be sought. See: PRELIMINARY RESEARCH

SYNDICALISM   An economic system in which the workers of each INDUSTRY exercise control over that industry.

SYNDICATED SUPPLEMENT   A SUPPLEMENT edited and printed by a publishing company which provides it to non-competing newspapers.

SYNDICATOR   A FIRM engaged in supplying merchandise and associated BROCHURES, CATALOGS, envelopes and advice to mass mailers, such as the issuers of the various bank credit cards, who wish to enter the field of selling merchandise by mail. See: BANGTAIL

SYNECTICS   A form of brainstorming, in which the problem is defined so broadly, rather than specifically, that the participants have no inkling at first of what the basic problem is, but just the essence of it.

SYNERGISTIC EFFECT   The enhancement of the IMPACT of each MEDIUM when secondary media are used to supplement the primary media (the most important for the particular goal). When this occurs, the whole may be greater than the sum of the parts.

SYSTEMATIC FREIGHT EQUALIZATION   Same as: FREIGHT EQUALIZATION

SYSTEMATIC SAMPLING   A method of developing a PROBABILITY SAMPLE by selecting elements from a POPULATION at a uniform interval of a specified order, or space, or time. It differs from SIMPLE RANDOM SAMPLING in that each combination of elements does not have an equal chance of being selected. There is also the possibility of introducing a recurring BIAS of unpredictable significance if the element at the interval chosen is of a type more, or less, favorable to the HYPOTHESIS. For example, if one wished to find out what users think about the ease of parking in a certain SHOPPING CENTER lot and the lot is marked so that every twentieth space is a corner space, using a pattern which would ask the occupant of each twentieth space for an opinion would not produce a sample that would have VALIDITY. Another interval would have to be chosen.

SYSTEMS APPROACH   A way of studying MARKETING which examines and analyzes the behavioral interrelationships among the various elements of the marketing structure, including the power structure and the communications network.

SYSTEMS-COMPLETING PRODUCT   A PRODUCT which makes widely available an already accepted technology.

SYSTEMS CONTRACTING   A form of purchasing which allows for little or no stock to be carried by the buyer. The purchase agreement is based on a catalog furnished by the supplier for the items agreed upon, usually a large group of repetitive materials. The supplier agrees to carry sufficient quantities of all items in the catalog and to respect the prices listed in it for a specified period of time. Requisitioners in the buyer firm's departments order directly, in approved quantities. When established carefully, numerous benefits accrue to both the buyer and the supplier. See: BLANKET ORDER, STOCKLESS PURCHASING

SYSTEMS SELLING   Same as: SYSTEMS CONTRACTING, but limited to the vendor's point of view.

t   (1) A statistical measure similar to Z, but applicable to those instances in which the STANDARD DEVIATION of the POPULATION is not known and the SAMPLE size on which the standard deviation of the sample is based is less than 30 (some statisticians hold this number to be 50). Tables are available, just as for Z. See: DEGREES OF FREEDOM   (2) Abbreviation for: time or times. Used to show the FREQUENCY with which an advertisement is to appear, as in 5-t, 10-t, etc.

TAA   (1) Abbreviation for: Transit Advertising Association, the national association of the TRANSIT ADVERTISING MEDIUM. Organized in 1942, it serves as a central source of information, supports research, established standards, and offers a variety of creative and educational services to further the effectiveness of the medium wherever used. Distinguish from ATA, with which TAA cooperates. (2) Abbreviation for: Transportation Association of America, the only national organization devoted exclusively to resolving national transport issues. It has the support of a number of national trade associations. Incorporated in 1935, its membership consists of users, investors, and carriers, with users in the major-

ity. It publishes special reports as circumstances dictate and under-
takes a variety of technical and educational projects, particularly with
efforts to preserve the private character of the transportation INDUSTRY.

TAB   Abbreviation for: Traffic Audit Bureau, an organization which inves-
tigates how many people may see a given outdoor sign within a certain
time.

TAB EQUIPMENT   See: PCM

TABLE OF RANDOM NUMBERS   A statistical tool used to help determine the elements of a SIMPLE RANDOM SAMPLE or a SYSTEMATIC RANDOM SAMPLE. The table
is so constructed that the numbers have no repetitive order or pattern,
and are quite often listed in rows and columns of five digit units. One
needs but to number all the elements of a POPULATION, then start at any
point in the table, taking from there the total number of numbers which
thus correspond to the elements to make up the SAMPLE.

TABLOID INSERTS   Separate, pre-printed sections of ADVERTISEMENTS inside
NEWSPAPERS.

TABLOID SIZE PAGE   A page size used by some newspapers, which is usually
5 or 6 columns wide by 200 AGATE LINES deep, making the full page 1,000
or 1,200 lines. See: STANDARD SIZE PAGE

TABULATION   The process of separating and counting the number of data
responses that fall into the various classes established by CODING and
EDITING. Simple tabulation involves the number for a single variable.
Cross tabulation involves the number of cases that have aspects of two
or more variables the relationships among which are considered simultaneously.

TABULATOR   The basic device in the punched card section of an ADP system.
It summarizes the punched card data and prints the transcribed information on the desired form. This machine is frequently referred to as an
accounting machine. See: TAB EQUIPMENT

TACIT COLLUSION   See: CONSCIOUS PARALLELISM

TACTICAL PRODUCT-LINE ADJUSTMENT   Determination of the number of variations
of any given product to be offered. See: STRATEGIC PRODUCT-LINE ADJUST-
MENT

TACTICS   The means by which a firm's goals may be reached. See: STRATEGY

TACV   Abbreviation for: tracked air-cushion vehicle, a wheel-less vehicle
supported on a surface by a thin cushion of air while moving in or on a
guide track. The DOT is engaged in stimulating research to produce a
satisfactory operating system. Speeds up to 300 miles per hour are
theoretically possible with a high degree of safety.

TAG   The short message presented by a local announcer at the end of a commercial that was recorded. It usually includes the address of the local
RETAILER and other pertinent information.

TAIL-LIGHT DISPLAY   Same as: REAR-END DISPLAY

TAKE-ONES   Coupons, post-cards, brochures, and the like, attached to, or
placed in pockets attached to, inside TRANSIT ADVERTISING pieces. The
passenger who is so inspired by the advertisement tears off or takes out
a take-one to request more information or receive a benefit connected
with the product or service advertised.

TAKE OVER PROCEDURE   Same as: T.O. PROCEDURE

TAKE-TRANSACTION   The CUSTOMER carries the purchase away. Contrast with
the SEND-TRANSACTION in which the purchase is delivered to the customer.
May involve a cash sale or a charge sale of some type.

TAKE-WITH   Same as: TAKE-TRANSACTION

TAMB   Abbreviation for: Transit Advertising Measurement Bureau, an organization which collects information about advertiser expenditure data on the TRANSIT ADVERTISING MEDIUM and disseminates this data broken into three categories of total dollar volume: national and local, inside and outside, product and service.

TAME CAT DISTRIBUTOR   A WHOLESALER owned and controlled by a manufacturer.

TAPE PLAN   A promotion often used by SUPERMARKETS over a period of time offering a variety of PREMIUMS in return for cash register tapes totaling certain amounts. In some instances cash enough may be required in addition to the tapes to make the promotion SELF-LIQUIDATING. Same as: Cash-Register-Tape Redemption Plan

TAP LINE   A relatively short railroad usually operated by the INDUSTRY it serves and connecting with a TRUNK LINE. May be owned or controlled.

TARGET   (1) The one to whom a selling message is addressed. (2) A MARKET in which a selling effort is made. (3) The MARKETING objective toward which organization resources are directed.

TARGET MARKET   Same as: TARGET (2)

TARGET POPULATION   The specifically defined POPULATION from which a SAMPLE is to be drawn.

TARGET PRICING   An approach to pricing in which the firm attempts to determine that price which will give it the wanted rate of return on its total costs at a STANDARD VOLUME. Because sales volume is a base for the price decision, and because price is a determinant of sales volume, attention to DEMAND CURVE estimates, rather than operating percent of capacity estimates, is more likely to provide valid information.

TARIFF   (1) A duty or tax on imports levied by a country. (2) A schedule of rates charged for the transportation of goods and/or people, together with governing rules and regulations. CARRIERS must have their tariffs approved by a governmental supervising agency. For interstate shipments the agency is the ICC.

TARIFF HARMONIZATION   A reduction in TARIFFS (1) that narrows the disparity among levies on the same item. See: TARIFF PREFERENCE

TARIFF PREFERENCE   A system of TARIFF treatment favoring certain PRODUCTS of a country or group of countries. See: GSP

TARNISHED HALO EFFECT   The extension by one person into unrelated areas of an unfavorable attitude based on an unfortunate experience with another person in one specific situation. See: HALO EFFECT

TASK METHOD   A method of arriving at an advertising BUDGET by determining a sales goal and then deciding the cost of attaining that goal through advertising. The only one of the methods which is based on careful planning and evaluation. May be applied as well to the development of the total MARKETING MIX budget.   See: ASSESSMENT METHOD, PERCENTAGE OF LAST YEAR'S SALES METHOD, PERCENTAGE OF NEXT YEAR'S SALES METHOD, PLUNGE METHOD

TAT   Abbreviation for: Thematic Apperception Test, one of the STORYTELLING techniques, a copyrighted series of pictures about which the RESPONDENT is to tell stories. Some pictures are clearly defined, others ambiguous or obscure. From the responses it is possible to delineate a person's personality traits. Requires highly skilled interpreters.

TBA   Abbreviation for: Tires, Batteries, and Accessories.

TBEA   Abbreviation for: Truck Body and Equipment Association, an organization of over 500 manufacturers of a very large VARIETY of items related to this INDUSTRY. Since its founding in 1947 it has kept its members informed through frequent letters of pertinent data about legislation, labor, engineering research, vehicle safety, and accounting and statistics. It runs an annual convention and exposition attended by thousands of persons representing firms and public bodies interested in new developments in truck and accessories design.

TDCC   Abbreviation for: Transportation Data Coordinating Committee, organized in 1968 with membership from leading shippers, carriers, and banks. Its goals of code standardization, coordination of data exchange, and the development of a computerized system for exchanging transportation data among all modes and all types and sizes of shippers have been endorsed by such organizations as the NITL, TAA, ATA, AMA, ICC, CAB, and others of similar representation and prestige. Its members need not reveal any confidential data; they supply what they choose. The hope is that this effort will result in the near future in a transportation network that will be a system of intermodal services with uniform administrative procedures that are computerized to the maximum degree.

t DISTRIBUTION   Used in considering the difference between the MEANS of two small SAMPLES to discover whether the values indicate a significant difference. An essential assumption is that the samples come from normal UNIVERSES with the same VARIANCES. (See U TEST.) Based on the required level of significance and other numerical criteria derived from observed data, tables showing the "critical value of t" will provide a range within which if the calculated value of t falls, the NULL HYPOTHESIS should be accepted. If outside this range, the alternate HYPOTHESIS is significant. PARAMETRIC. See: t (1)

TEAM TRACK   A spur track for public use where products can be shipped by rail for transfer to trucks and delivery to final destination.

TEAR SHEETS   Copies of advertisements torn from publications, sent to advertisers for checking and as proof that the advertisements were run.

TEASER CAMPAIGN   See: CAMPAIGN PLAN

TECHNICAL EFFICIENCY   One aspect of the concept of marketing efficiency, it is the accomplishment of a particular task with the least input of resources in relation to the output of product or service. Competitive pressure toward increasing technical efficiency leads to the performing by individual firms of MARKETING FUNCTIONS in lowest cost combinations, and the presence in the economy of lowest cost combinations of type and number of firms. See: EXCHANGE EFFICIENCY, INNOVATIVE EFFICIENCY

TECHNICAL QUALITY   This is concerned purely with design and other physical properties. See: QUALITY

TECHNICAL SALESMAN   Same as: SALES ENGINEER

TELEPHONE COINCIDENTAL METHOD   An AUDIENCE RESEARCH method whereby a pre-selected SAMPLE of persons is called during a program time and asked: "Do you have a television set? How many are watching it? What program?" While this method measures the size of the audience quickly and directly, it has the disadvantages that questions must be brief, and calls cannot be made very early in the morning or very late at night. Because of its immediacy, it is the most widely used method of audience research. See: DIARY METHOD, MECHANICAL RECORDER METHOD, PERSONAL INTERVIEW METHOD

TELERAIL AUTOMATED INFORMATION NETWORK   Same as: TRAIN

TELEVISION   A broadcast MEDIUM providing both visual and aural communication possibilities, as well as motion. Perhaps the most expensive, considered absolutely, of the ADVERTISING MEDIA, it provides relatively more AUDIENCE per dollar than NEWSPAPERS, although it is quite poor as regards selectivity. Same problems as RADIO, and in addition the increasing tendency of viewers to block out commercials mentally.

TELEVISION BUREAU OF ADVERTISING   Same as: TvB

TELEVISION HOME   A home containing one or more television sets. See: HUT

TENSION   A state of being in which an individual is aware of a need and is prompted to behavior intended to produce SATISFACTION of the need.   See: EQUILIBRIUM, MOTIVE

TENSION THEORY   A body of thought about CONSUMER behavior in the MARKET, based on the explanation that when a need is not satisfied, a state of stress occurs that activates an individual to seek equilibrium, i.e., a state in which stress has been reduced through attainment of the appropriate satisfactions. See: THEORY

TERMINAL   (1) In the petroleum INDUSTRY, a primary bulk facility which receives products from a refinery, usually by vessel or pipeline, and transships to secondary bulk storage as well as delivers to CUSTOMERS in its own general area. (2) In general, any facility designed to receive, transfer, and/or dispatch quantities of materials or numbers of persons, e.g., railroad, airline, truck, bus terminals.

TERMINAL OPERATOR   A marketer of gasoline and/or heating oils who buys, assembles, stores, sells and transports these. He engages mainly in WHOLESALE activities. Same as: Cargo Distributor

TERMINAL PERFORMANCE CONTROL   Same as: TPC

TERMS OF SALE   This phrase refers in general to invoice dating and to discounts. See: ADVANCE DATING, ANTICIPATION DISCOUNT, CHAIN DISCOUNT, C.O.D., CONCEALED DISCOUNT, CONSIGNMENT TERMS, CUMULATIVE DISCOUNT, C.W.O., EXTRA DATING, FUNCTIONAL DISCOUNT, MEMORANDUM TERMS, M.O.M., PATRONAGE DISCOUNT, PROXIMO TERMS, QUANTITY DISCOUNT, ROG, SEASON DATING, TRADE DISCOUNT, VOLUME DISCOUNT

TERRITORIAL MANAGEMENT   The activities involved in planning, effecting, and controlling the operations within SALES TERRITORIES so as to achieve the sales and profit objectives of that group of MARKETING opportunities.

TERRITORY   Same as: SALES TERRITORY

TEST GROUP   The group of individuals who are exposed to the objects, procedures, displays, prices, ADVERTISING, or some other variable about which a particular MARKETING RESEARCH activity is studying the effectiveness. See: CONTROL GROUP

TESTIMONIAL   An opinion given by the endorser of a product, directed toward inducing others to use the product. Really effective only when the endorser is actually an expert or someone with whom the AUDIENCE can IDENTIFY. The use of testimonials in advertising continues to come under attack by all groups concerned with eliminating misleading advertising.

TEST-MAILING PLAN   A method of testing the applicability of a LIST and/or the efficacy of a mailing piece. By sending different mailings to different parts of a list to see which secures the best response, the particular mailing piece may be judged. By sending the same, known effective, mailing piece to parts of different lists, the lists may be judged. Because the art of compiling lists of various sorts has been developed to a fine point by specialist firms, it is seldom desirable to go through the expense of testing a list. When the results of the trial-size mailings are known, it is then possible to decide whether larger mailings, perhaps to a list of millions of addresses, is warranted. See: COST PER INQUIRY, COST PER SALE, DIRECT MAIL ADVERTISING

TEST MARKETING   The new product and its marketing program are tried out in a small number or representative customer environments. VALIDITY is subject to various problems, such as competition's activities, total cost of testing, and representativeness of the locale to the rest of the MARKET.

TEST OF RANDOMNESS   This test, used to see if a sequence is RANDOM, is called a "one-sample runs test." The basis is the order in which the specific SAMPLE observations were obtained. "Run" is defined as a series of identical occurrances that are preceded and followed by different occurrances or by none at all. If the computed value of Z is less than the table value of Z, the sample can be considered random. The importance of this concept stems from the fact that any time a researcher uses a sample STATISTIC to make an estimate about a PARAMETER, he can make probability statements about the ACCURACY of his estimate only if he is dealing with a RANDOM SAMPLE. The concept is simple. Achieving random- ness is not simple. PARAMETRIC. See: NORMAL PROBABILITY CURVE

TEST PROGRAM   In ADP, a set of data with a known answer put through the system before processing real data to be sure everything is in order for the RUN.

TEXTILE PRODUCTS IDENTIFICATION ACT   A Federal law which requires that sellers of yarns and fabrics and household articles made of these, which are made from natural or synthetic fibers other than wool, to affix LABELS showing the percent by weight of each fiber they contain and to identify the fibers by generic name determined by the FTC in consultation with the trade.

T.F.   (1) Abbreviation for: TILL-FORBID. An order to continue placing an advertisement in each issue of a publication until the order is cancelled. (2) Also used for: copy is to follow.

THEATRICAL FILMS   Films sponsored by ADVERTISERS showing the role of the advertiser's PRODUCT in a sufficiently entertaining way to be used in theaters as short subjects between features. See: BUSINESS FILMS, SPONSORED FILMS

THEMATIC APPERCEPTION TEST   Same as: TAT

THE OPERATING COUNCIL OF AMERICAN TRUCKING ASSOCIATIONS   Same as: TOC

THEORY   A related group of FACTS, PRINCIPLES, and HYPOTHESES.

THEORY OF ACHIEVEMENT MOTIVATION   A sociopsychological explanation of human behavior as dependent for its motivational strength on the expectation that the activity will produce a particular consequence of recognized benefit to the individual while at the same time avoiding negative con- sequences. Applies only to achievement-oriented activity. Proposed by David C. McClelland. See: BEHAVIOR THEORIES

THEORY OF COGNITIVE DISSONANCE   See: COGNITIVE DISSONANCE

THEORY OF COMPARATIVE ADVANTAGE   This THEORY makes the explanation that international trade happens as a result of specialization of some sort which makes it advantageous for a country to produce and sell certain goods because they can be produced competitively, and to purchase goods of which the reverse is true. Does not completely explain modern internation- al goods movements and production.

THEORY OF ROLE ENACTMENT   A sociopsychological explanation of human behavior as the resultant of role expectations, which define the range of tolerated behavior; role location, which locates an individual in the social struc- ture; role demand, which imposes constraints on the choice of role; role skills, which define one's level of task competence; self-role congruence, which holds that role enactment will be effective to the extent that self characteristics are consistent with role expectations; and audience, which refers to the desired impression to be made on the observers present during the role enactment. Proposed by Erving Goffman. See: BEHAVIOR THEORIES

THEORY OF SOCIAL CHARACTER   A sociopsychological explanation of human be- havior as determined by the way society enforces conformity and molds social character. Proposed by David Riesman et al. See: BEHAVIOR THEORIES, INNER-DIRECTEDNESS, OTHER-DIRECTEDNESS, TRADITION-DIRECTEDNESS

THE PULSE, INCORPORATED   Same as: PULSE

THEYISM   A term sometimes applied to the habit of blaming someone else for one's weakness or shortcomings. For example, "They ought to clean up the environment" says the car passenger as he casually drops his hamburger wrapper from the car window.

THIRD COVER   See: COVER

THOMAS REGISTER OF AMERICAN MANUFACTURERS   This multi-volume publication, issued annually by the Thomas Publishing Company, lists the manufacturers of specific products and tells their addresses, branch offices, and subsidiaries.

THREE B'S   See: BETTER BUSINESS BUREAU

THREE C'S OF CREDIT   The three factors commonly considered in deciding whether an individual's CREDIT should be accepted (usually stated as "extending credit"). These are: Character, the indication of determination to pay; Capacity, a measure of ability to pay (liquidity); and Capital, financial resources or net worth.

THRESHOLD   See: ABSOLUTE THRESHOLD

THRESHOLD LEVEL   See: DIFFERENTIAL THRESHOLD

THRESHOLD LEVEL OF EXPENDITURES   The minimum amount a FIRM must expend just to function in a MARKET and get any sales at all.

THROUGHPUT   The movement of merchandise through DEALERS and on to the CONSUMER. The benefit derived in selling through the dealer and not to the dealer.

THUMBNAIL   A ROUGH in small, crude sketch. Just the notion of how a LAYOUT is to appear.

TICKLER FILE   A device in which memoranda or other documents are arranged according to the date on which actions regarding them are to be initiated. Opening this type of file to a given date will reveal all the actions required to be taken on that date. Useful as a reminder for a wide spectrum of activities.

TICKY-TACK   A very rough permanent model constructed just to provide a basis for judging size and general appearance. Frequently used in the POINT-OF-PURCHASE DISPLAY industry.

TIE-IN SALE   An additional sale made to a customer who has already been sold another product or service. Usually an item related in use in some way to the other. See: ADDED SELLING

TIGHT MARKET   Same as: SELLERS' MARKET

TILL-FORBID   Same as: T.F.

TIME-BUDGETING OF PURCHASES   An attempt to even out changes in the prices of items used by buying small quantities at short intervals. This practice assures that the firm's average price for an item will closely approximate the true average for the period. Likely to increase the total cost of purchasing. See: EOQ

TIME CLEARANCE   The process of making available on certain stations, as in a NETWORK, a specific program time period.

TIME LOSS RISK   See: RISK REDUCTION

TIME RATE OF DEMAND   The quantity of a product which the MARKET will absorb at a particular price per period of time.

TIME SERIES   A set of ordered observations of a quantitative variable taken at successive points in time. Must test for RANDOMNESS; unless this can be rejected, no trend equation will have meaning. A time series has four components, each of which is a type of fluctuation that must be considered.

1) Trend, long-term growth or decay. May be linear or non-linear;
2) Seasonal, regularly recurring fluctuation of a periodic character;
3) Cyclical, a wavelike fluctuation about Trend. Varies from one cycle to another; 4) Erratic or Random, completely unsystematic. A recently introduced method of time series analysis is "exponential smoothing." This method has many advantages over older "moving average" methods in ease of calculation and use in FORECASTING. It is adjustable for each component.

TIME SLICE   In ADP, the unit of time devoted by a time-shared computer system to performing the task required by a specific user. See: ANSWERING TIME, CONNECT TIME

TIME UTILITY   The characteristic of a GOOD which makes it possible to satisfy a human WANT based on time preference. STORAGE creates time utility. See: UTILITY

TIP-IN   (1) To mount a HALFTONE on a page. (2) The process of fastening a sheet onto another page, such as in binding an INSERT into a MAGAZINE. (3) To place a color portion on an otherwise black-and-white page.

TIPRCC   Abbreviation for: Trucking Industry Public Relations Coordinating Committee, authorized as a unit of the American Trucking Associations to provide an organization through which trucking industry public relations specialists can work to improve company, supply, state association, and total trucking industry public relations efforts. The Committee holds an annual meeting and provides current information. Any person who is involved in public relations and employee communications in a trucking firm, association, or supply industry may join merely by applying. There are no dues.

TIR   Abbreviation for: Transport International Routier See: CARNET

TIRE AND RIM ASSOCIATION   Same as: TRA

TITLE   Legal evidence of ownership.

T.M.C. Abbreviation for: Total Manufacturing Cost

TO ARRIVE   A sale practice used by COUNTRY ELEVATORS in which a definite price for the grain has been agreed upon between elevator and buyer, but the elevator retains responsibility in all other regards until the grain arrives at destination. Eliminates the risk of price change during the transportation period. See: ON TRACK

TOC   Abbreviation for: The Operations Council of American Trucking Associations, consisting of a membership of about 600 motor carriers and allied industries. It is primarily involved in managerial applications of new developments in trucking, and in fostering instructional workshops and courses of study. It works closely with those colleges and universities that offer transportation courses.

TOEHOLD DOCTRINE   A way of interpreting our ANTI-TRUST LAWS, currently in vogue, which holds that a large company may legally acquire a small firm in another, concentrated industry, but may not acquire a leading firm in that industry. See: POTENTIAL COMPETITION DOCTRINE

TOFC   Abbreviation for: Trailer On Flatcar Service. See: PIGGYBACK

TOKEN ORDER   (1) A small order placed usually with a view to testing the acceptability of the item. (2) A small order placed as the simplest way of getting rid of an overly persistent SALESPERSON.

TOMBSTONE ADVERTISEMENT   An advertisement in solemn style, spare in LAYOUT, usually a simple listing of an item with accompanying names of sources of supply. Often applied to advertisements announcing major securities offerings.

TONNAGE   An advertising term used to denote the amount of money spent. CETERIS PARIBUS, memory of the advertising will be longer and truer after a larger campaign.

TOOL-CRIB SUPERVISOR   Essentially the same as: MATERIALS CONTROLLER

TOP-DOWN APPROACH   Same as: OPEN-TO-BUY CONTROL

TOP DOWN TECHNIQUE   A budgeting technique in RETAILING in which the budgeter
starts with a gross amount and then allocates specific amounts to designated
CLASSIFICATIONS of merchandise. See: BOTTOM OF TECHNIQUE

TOP-END DISPLAY   A premium space in TRANSIT ADVERTISING. Classified an
inside display, it is usually located over inter-vehicle doors. Same as:
Over-Door Display

TOP-LIGHTING   See: BUSORAMA

TOP MANAGEMENT   The highest decision-making ECHELON in a FIRM'S organization, usually where overall firm POLICIES are set. Generally composed
of the firm's president and his immediate associates and subordinates.
See: BOTTOM MANAGEMENT, MIDDLE MANAGEMENT

T.O. PROCEDURE   A sales technique in which one SALESPERSON transfers his
PROSPECT to another salesperson to close the sale. Often the transfer
is to someone of higher authority in the firm. Comes about as an effort
to overcome sales resistance stemming from an undetermined OBJECTION.

TOTAL AUDIENCE   In RADIO ADVERTISING, usually defined as males and females
12 years of age or older within a given area. Most frequently the base
for the RATE CARD. See: TARGET

TOTAL BUS   The contract arrangement in which an ADVERTISER using TRANSIT
ADVERTISING employs all the advertising space available on the vehicle.
See: BASIC BUS

TOTAL COST APPROACH   An analytical approach to profit decisions which
recognizes that distribution decisions have a critical impact on total
business costs and that, therefore, analysis of various alternate distribution plans involving CHANNELS OF DISTRIBUTION, WAREHOUSES, rail vs
air vs truck vs water shipping systems, is crucial to the maximizing of
profit within each firm's internal and external constraints.

TOTAL FERTILITY RATE   The number of children that a representative SAMPLE
of 1,000 women would bear in their lifetimes if, at every age level from
15 to 44, they bore children at BIRTH RATES registered for the age level
in the year under consideration. See: GENERAL FERTILITY RATE

TOTAL MARKET APPROACH   The use of a MARKETING MIX for the entire MARKET for
a particular PRODUCT. SEGMENTATION is presumed undesirable.

TOTAL-MARKETING INFORMATION SYSTEM   Same as: MIS

TOTAL PRODUCT   Essentially the same as the MARKETING MIX of a firm, it
applies equally to services. The broad approach to the firm's offerings,
including all aspects of customer getting, keeping, and satisfying.

TPC   Abbreviation for: Terminal Performance Control, initiated on the
Burlington Northern Railroad. It is a day-to-day report designed to
alert terminal management to situations causing cars to be delayed or
mishandled. See: ACT, COMPASS, TRAIN, UMLER

TRA   Abbreviation for: Tire and Rim Association, the organization which
sets industry standards for tire, rim, tube, etc., sizes.

TRADE ADVERTISING   ADVERTISING directed at RETAILERS and WHOLESALERS.

TRADE CARDS   A plan in which a RETAILER punches into a card the amount a
customer purchases until a total is reached which qualifies the customer
to buy a PREMIUM at a SELF-LIQUIDATING price. Sometimes the premium is
given with no additional cash required. Same as: Purchase-Privilege Offer

TRADE CHANNEL   Same as: CHANNEL OF DISTRIBUTION

TRADE CHARACTER   An animated object, an animal, or an invented person designed to personify and identify a product or an advertiser.

TRADE DEAL   Same as: DEAL

TRADE DISCOUNT   Same as: FUNCTIONAL DISCOUNT

TRADEMARK   Any word, name, symbol, device, or any combination of these adopted and used by a manufacturer or MERCHANT to identify his goods and distinguish them from those of others. It is a BRAND NAME used on goods moving in the channels of trade. Rights in a trademark are acquired only by use, and the use ordinarily must continue if the rights are to be preserved. That provision is made to register a trademark in the Patent Office does not imply that such registration in itself creates or establishes any exclusive rights. However, registration is recognition by the government of the right of the owner to use the mark in commerce to distinguish his goods from those of others. BRAND is the everyday term; TRADEMARK is the legal counterpart. Trademarks are registered for twenty years and may be renewed every twenty years thereafter if not abandoned, cancelled, or surrendered. See: PRINCIPAL REGISTER, SUPPLEMENTAL REGISTER, SECONDARY MEANING, CERTIFICATION MARK, COLLECTIVE MARK, SERVICE MARK, ARBITRARY MARK, COINED WORD

TRADE NAME   A name that applies to a business as a whole. The same name may be used to identify a product, when it will be a TRADEMARK, too.

TRADE PAPER   A PUBLICATION addressed to those who buy for resale, featuring information on how they can do business more effectively in certain LINES, thereby increasing profit. ADVERTISING in a trade paper almost invariably is devoted to assuring DEALERS how profit can be enhanced by handling the advertised products. See: TRADE ADVERTISING

TRADE PRICE   The producer's price to a MIDDLEMAN.

TRADE PUFFING   Same as: PUFFING

TRADE REFERENCE   A credit evaluation given by one firm regarding another firm with which it has been doing business. It is usually limited to what is derived from actual experience with the object firm's history of payment and complaint.

TRADE REGULATION RULE   Same as: TRR

TRADE RELATIONS   A more sophisticated term for RECIPROCITY.

TRADE SALES   Used to distinguish sales to non-controlled parties from sales made among the divisions or subsidiaries of one corporation. Same as: SALES TO THIRDS

TRADE SERVICE DEPARTMENT   A department within a firm as organized, which is given the responsibility of handling customer orders prior to shipment. Occurs mainly where the product is complex or produced in a number of seemingly similar, but significantly different, forms.

TRADE SHOW   An event organized in some large, central place which allows a large number of suppliers to convene at one time to show their wares to CUSTOMERS and PROSPECTS.

TRADE SHOW AUDIT   See: CCAB

TRADE SPECIALTY HOUSE   An INDUSTRIAL DISTRIBUTOR which serves a particular kind of customer, carrying a full line of the items required by him, e.g., hotel and restaurant supplies, shoe repair supplies, etc.

TRADE STYLE   Sometimes used as a reference to the distinctive way a firm displays its name in print in advertising and on its stationery. See: LOGOTYPE

TRADE ZONE   Same as: FOREIGN TRADE ZONE

TRADING AREA   A region around a firm or a shopping district whose limits are set by the costs of selling or delivering goods.

TRADING CENTER   In most cases corresponds to a STANDARD METROPOLITAN AREA.

TRADING STAMP EXCHANGE   A business that will exchange for a generally small
fee the stamps issued by one company for those issued by another.   Some
will sell stamps to anyone who does not have enough to redeem exactly what
is wanted.   In 1972 the Supreme Court blocked further suits by the Sperry
& Hutchinson Co. (S & H Green Stamps) against trading stamp exchanges on
the grounds proposed by the FTC, which brought the action, that S&H was
"unfair" to consumers.   Previously, S&H had brought and won 43 lawsuits
against the exchanges during the years 1904 to 1966.   The suits were in
19 different states and 8 different Federal districts.

TRADING UNIT   As part of its activity to regularize trading, each COMMODITY
EXCHANGE establishes a specific quantity of a commodity which constitutes
the standard quantity of a futures contract.   Such a quantity is the
trading unit.   See: FUTURES MARKET

TRADING UP   A legitimate business activity in which a SALESMAN tries to
interest PROSPECTS or CUSTOMERS in goods of higher price which the salesman feels can be proved to provide superior benefits.

TRAFFIC   (1) People and property carried by transportation facilities.
(2) The activity within a FIRM designed to determine the proper routing for
incoming shipments.   Sometimes includes outgoing shipments as well.   (3)
The number of individuals who enter a STORE or department.   (4) The
directional flow of people into and out of a store or a store area.

TRAFFIC APPLIANCES   A blanket term which usually includes all portable
electric housewares such as toasters, mixers, blenders, irons, etc.
See: MAJOR APPLIANCES

TRAFFIC AUDIT BUREAU   Same as: TAB

TRAFFIC BUILDER   (1) A relatively low-cost PREMIUM offered as an inducement to visit a STORE for a DEMONSTRATION.   (2) An item of popular demand
reduced in price dramatically to get people in where they can be exposed
to other, profitable items.

TRAFFIC ITEMS   CONSUMER products of sufficiently high frequency of replacement that they can be used to bring CUSTOMERS to a STORE or department.

TRAFFIC MANAGEMENT   Usually divided into: traffic planning concerned with
the use of transportation systems; and traffic analysis, concerned with
the evaluation of these services in terms of the efficiency of the LOGIS-
TICS SYSTEM.   It is essentially a balancing of the total cost of transport against the speed and certainty benefits of delivery by setting up
and operating a proper system of communications.

TRAFFIC TIME   Same as: DRIVE TIME

TRAILERSHIP SERVICE   Same as: FISHYBACK SERVICE

TRAIN   Acronym for: TeleRail Automated Information Network.   Operational
since 1970, it is a computer-communication system linking over 66 major
United States and Canadian railroads with summary and detail reports of
the inter-road movements of the more than 180,000 cars interchanged each
average day, thus providing a perpetual inventory system.   Has the
capacity to provide quickly a history file giving all movements of cars
for a given month and for the period to date.   About 83% of actual inter-
changes are reported within four days.   See: ACI, COMPASS, TPC, TRAIN II,
UMLER

TRAIN II   An expansion of the TRAIN system into a quicker and more sophisticated recording and reporting capability.   TRAIN II will update the master
freight car file hourly instead of daily, and will have short-range loadings forecasting ability.   Long-range FORECASTING will be attempted.

TRANSFER EFFECT   An attribute possessed by an offering which makes it possible for that product or service to force a transfer of a CONSUMER'S
purchase allegiance to the source making it available.   See: BUDGET EFFECT

TRANSIENT RATE   Same as: ONE-TIME RATE

TRANSIT ADVERTISING   An ADVERTISING MEDIUM designed primarily to present
the advertiser's message to an AUDIENCE which is enroute from one point
to another in a vehicle of public transportation, or which is exposed to
vehicles carrying passengers from one point to another. The top SMSA
MARKETS account for over 600 million monthly rides. An advertisement
in this medium is often designed much like a full page in a MAGAZINE
because the average ride is relatively long, 22.5 minutes.
See: BASIC BUS, CAR CARD, FRONT END DISPLAY, HEADLIGHT DISPLAY, RUN, SERVICE,
SHOWING, STATION POSTER, TOTAL BUS TRAVELING DISPLAY

TRANSIT ADVERTISING ASSOCIATION   Same as: TAA

TRANSIT ADVERTISING COMPANY   A management firm that represents local
transit systems for the sale of advertising space on and in their
vehicles or station facilities.

TRANSIT ADVERTISING MEASUREMENT BUREAU   Same as: TAMB

TRANSITION TIME   Same as: FRINGE TIME

TRANSIT WAREHOUSE   Same as: DISTRIBUTION WAREHOUSE

TRANSLATOR STATION   A station that rebroadcasts programs from another station on another channel but is not permitted to originate programs or
commercials locally. It has no local studio.

TRANSLOADING   Similar to INTRANSIT STORAGE, but the destination is not a
centralized facility, merely a central location, and the merchandise does
not await CUSTOMER orders but is reshipped in groups to different customers. The merchandise may be stored and then mixed with other groups for
the small added Intransit Charge. The effect is still to receive less-
than-carload service and pay the cheaper carload rate.

TRANSPORTATION   (1) A MARKETING FUNCTION characterized by the physical
movement of goods. Creates PLACE UTILITY. (2) Applied broadly to the
types of services provided and performed by the different kinds of
carriers.

TRANSPORTATION ADVERTISING   Same as: TRANSIT ADVERTISING

TRANSPORTATION ASSOCIATION OF AMERICA   Same as: TAA

TRANSPORTATION DATA COORDINATING COMMITTEE   Same as: TDCC

TRANSPORT INTERNATIONALE ROUTIER   Same as: TIR

TRANS-SHIPPING   Selling by a DEALER OR DISTRIBUTOR to a dealer or distributor in another territory who either cannot or does not wish to buy from
the regular sources available. Frequently, the trans-shipper, because of
volume or special buying, can sell for less, making it attractive for
others to buy from him. He usually sells for cash only, sometimes thereby trading on the credit terms of his sources. A highly controversial
practice, especially in the major appliance and television businesses.

TRAVELING DISPLAY   A POSTER PANEL appearing on the outside of a bus,
usually below the windows on the bus' side. See: TRANSIT ADVERTISING

TRAVELING REQUISITION   A form used to acquire items used and ordered re-
peatedly. Durable enough to withstand handling many times, it is at home
in the requisitioning department, from which it passes to the supplying
department and then back after action has been taken. See: REQUISITION

TREND   The tendency of a time-series over a long term. It usually involves EXTRAPOLATION of past data into the near future.

TRIALABILITY   With respect to the DIFFUSION RATE, how easy it is to try the
innovation on a limited commitment. If it cannot be SAMPLED, the risk may
be perceived as very high, slowing the ADOPTION PROCESS. See: CHARACTERIS-
TICS OF INNOVATION

TRIAL CLOSE   In SALESMANSHIP, any attempt based on some FEEDBACK to induce action to buy at any time during the sales presentation before completing the planned, full presentation. If not successful, may be tried again during the remainder of the presentation, but not so often as to create an adverse reaction in the PROSPECT. See: PSYCHOLOGICAL MOMENT

TRICKLE-ACROSS THEORY   An explanation of the FASHION CYCLE which involves the action of personal influence within social strata. Empirical evidence has shown that for some types of goods the social classes accept innovations more readily to the extent that the features of the innovations and the characteristics of the class culture are compatible. See: TRICKLE-DOWN THEORY

TRICKLE-DOWN THEORY   Now considered mainly invalid, this theory holds that FASHION changes start at the highest social levels and gradually filter down to the lowest. There is considerable empirical evidence that the SOCIAL CLASSES are not that dependent for behavior approval on their classes farther up in the class hierarchy. See: TRICKLE-ACROSS THEORY

TRIO OF NEEDS   See: MASLOW'S HIERARCHY OF NEEDS

TRIOSK   A relatively new ADVERTISING MEDIUM consisting of three-sided kiosks placed in selected positions in major SHOPPING CENTERS. The triosk displays advertising on one side, art on the other two. The art draws the traffic, which is then exposed to the advertising. The success of this concept is not yet established.

TRIPLE SPOTTING   Three commercials run in succession without intervening news or entertainment. See: BACK-TO-BACK, CLUTTER

TRI-VISION SIGN   Same as: MULTI-VISION SIGN

TROUGH   See: BUSINESS CYCLE

TRR   Abbreviation for: Trade Regulation Rule, an industry-wide guideline for action issued by the FTC after investigation of practices and most often, open hearings. They have covered a wide spectrum of merchandise and practices, and have become more forceful as CONSUMERISM has become more prominent. It is possible that a recent Supreme Court ruling may have voided them by finding a lack of congressional authority for their establishment. Whether Congress will resolve the uncertainty by enacting legislation specifically granting this power is not possible to forecast.

TRRF   Abbreviation for: The Refrigeration Research Foundation. See: NARW

TRUCK BODY AND EQUIPMENT ASSOCIATION   Same as: TBEA

TRUCK DISTRIBUTOR   Same as: TRUCK JOBBER

TRUCKING INDUSTRY PUBLIC RELATIONS COORDINATING COMMITTEE   Same as: TIPRCC

TRUCK JOBBER   A type of MERCHANT WHOLESALER who combines the activities of SALESMAN with those of deliveryman, who usually sells for cash, and whose stock is usually limited to nationally advertised specialties and fast-moving items of a perishable or semi-perishable nature. Also occurs in a few areas of the INDUSTRIAL MARKET. Same as: Truck Distributor, Wagon Distributor, Wagon Jobber

TRUCKLOAD   (1) The quantity or weight of freight required to qualify for the truckload rate. (2) A truck loaded to its carrying capacity. See: CARLOAD

TRUCKTAINER   A system developed by Stedman Industries Limited of Canada that provides for transporting three 15-foot CONTAINERS on a 45-foot frame drawn by a truck power unit. The containers can be left standing on their own legs at destination for the handling of contents while the power unit moves off to haul other loads.

TRUCK TRAILER MANUFACTURERS ASSOCIATION   Same as: TTMA

TRUE PANEL   A PANEL in which the RESPONDENTS are measured again and again with respect to the same group of variables. See: OMNIBUS PANEL

TRUE STATE OF THE UNIVERSE   A complete and accurate description of the environment of a given PROBLEM. Usually not possible to determine exactly, but only within acceptable limits of the risk of error. See: STATE OF THE UNIVERSE

TRUNK LINE   The main line of a major transportation system, operating over a large area and connecting with TAP LINES.

TRUTH-IN-ADVERTISING ACT   Essentially the WHEELER-LEA ACT together with associated judicial decisions giving the FTC expanded powers.

TRUTH-IN-LENDING ACT   An Act of Congress requiring that every borrower be informed clearly of the total charges or interest he is to pay on his loan or instalment plan, and the EQUIVALENT RATE OF SIMPLE INTEREST applicable thereto. Same as: Consumer Credit Protection Act

TRUTH-IN-PACKAGING ACT   Same as: FAIR PACKAGING AND LABELING ACT

TSO   Abbreviation for: Time Sharing Option, as applied to data processing equipment.

TTMA   Abbreviation for: Truck Trailer Manufacturers Association, organized in 1943, having about 200 firm and several thousand individual members making trailers and essential components. It cooperates with many other organizations to provide current technical and informational support to its members, e.g., it is a leading contributor to the CONTAINER STANDARDIZATION program of the ASA. The TTMA publishes an annual detailed directory of its membership as well as numerous manuals and bulletins.

TURBULENCE   A stage in the development of the MARKET for a product which represents the critical survival period for marginal producers. Characterized by the leveling of market growth, changes in CHANNELS OF DISTRIBUTION, reduction in numer of competitors, frequent model changes and product line SIMPLIFICATION by DEALERS. See: SATURATION

TURN   Same as: ROUND TURN

TURN AND EARN THEORY   Denotes an attempt to explain profit level in terms of inventory TURNOVER as the central factor. Probably an oversimplification of a usually complex relationship among many factors contributing to profit.

TURNKEY OPERATION   A business unit designed, constructed, equipped, and stocked by someone other than the final operator or tenant. It is so complete that all the operator need do is turn the key in the door to begin operating.

TURNOVER   (1) In manufacturing, mainly cost of goods sold divided by average inventory priced at cost. (2) In RETAILING, mainly total sales divided by average inventory at selling prices.

TURN OVER PROCEDURE   Same as: T.O. PROCEDURE

t VALUE   See: t DISTRIBUTION

TvB   Abbreviation for: Television Bureau of Advertising, an organization of stations, NETWORKS, and representatives the major purpose of which is to promote and improve the use of television as an ADVERTISING MEDIUM.

TvQ   An AUDIENCE appeal rating made available to its subscribers by Marketing Evaluations, Inc., successor to the service offered by Home Testing Institute. The scores are determined by dividing the number of people saying they are familiar with a program into the number calling it "one of my favorites." DEMOGRAPHIC divisions are available.

TWIG   A very small BRANCH located in a NEIGHBORHOOD SHOPPING CENTER, that usually carries only a part of the RETAILER'S offerings, e.g., only women's ready-to-wear.

TWO-LIFETIME GUARANTEE   A promise by the maker of a PRODUCT used in conjunction with another product to repair or replace the product should it prove defective in a defined way for the period of use with the original adjunct product and an additional period of use with the original adjunct product's replacement.   See: LIFETIME GUARANTEE

TYING CONTRACT   An agreement that as a condition of being allowed to buy or lease a product, associated products will be bought only from the vendor or lessor of the contract product.   Certain practices of this type have been declared illegal under our ANTI-TRUST LAWS.

TYPE FACE   Same as: FACE

TYPE FONT   Same as: FONT

TYPE HIGH   0.918 inch, the height of all LETTERPRESS plates and type must be to print properly.

TYPE I ERROR   Occurs when the NULL HYPOTHESIS is rejected but should not be because it is true.   Also called: alpha error.   See: TYPE II ERROR

TYPE PAGE   That area of a page that type can use.   It is the total area of a page less the required margins as planned.

TYPE II ERROR   Occurs when the NULL HYPOTHESIS is not rejected but should be because it is false.   Also called: beta error.   See: TYPE I ERROR

TYPOGRAPHY   The art of selecting and arranging type in order to deliver the printed message most effectively.   See: ADVERTISING TYPOGRAPHER

u.c.   Abbreviation for: upper case.   Capital letters.

UCC   Abbreviation for: UNIFORM COMMERCIAL CODE

ULTERIOR MOTIVE   What the source of a communication hopes to achieve as the end result of his message.   Receivers are often influenced by their own ulterior motives which a marketer must understand in order to be clear in his communications.   See: IMMEDIATE PURPOSE

ULTIMATE CONSUMER   Same as: CONSUMER.   Although frequently used to make a distinction between the "final user" and intermediate "consumers" who do something that provides the "final user" with a product or service, the term is really redundant.   When one reflects that the consumer is always the "final user," there is no point to designating him "ultimate."   See: INDUSTRIAL USER

UMBRELLA BRAND   Same as: FAMILY BRAND

UMLER   Acronym for: Universal Machine Language Equipment Register. This computerized system permits 154 applications.   It makes possible a complete analysis of the entire United States freight car fleet by any one or a combination of attributes, so that dispatching, tracing, planning, and the like, may be made more efficient.   Over 30 participating railroads use this system.   The magnetic tape file is maintained in the Washington, DC, headquarters of the AAR.   Forms the data base for TRAIN. See: ACI

UNCONTROLLABLE VARIABLES   The various environments in which a FIRM exists that affect the degree of freedom of decision-making possible within the firm.   From the MICROMARKETING view, little if anything can be done by a firm to influence these environments, among which are usually thought to be the legal, social, political, economic, cultural, and resources environments (sometimes called "climates").

UNDERRUN   To produce fewer of a publication or advertising piece than was contracted for.   The opposite of: OVERRUN

UNDISGUISED-UNSTRUCTURED QUESTIONNAIRE   Same as: UNSTRUCTURED-UNDISGUISED QUESTIONNAIRE

UNDUPLICATED AUDIENCE   Same as: CUME

UNEARNED DISCOUNT   A cash discount taken by a customer who has not really met the terms stipulated to qualify for the discount. Custom among firms varies greatly as to whether the deduction will finally be permitted.

UNFAIR PRACTICES ACTS   State laws which establish a floor below which the prices of any items may not legally be set. The floor is either invoice cost, or invoice cost plus a modest percent. Designed to keep a well-financed seller from putting his competition out of business by selling below cost for a while.   Same as: Unfair Sales Acts

UNFAIR SALES ACTS   Same as: UNFAIR PRACTICES ACTS

UNFAIR TRADE PRACTICES ACTS   Same as: UNFAIR PRACTICES ACTS.

UNIFORM COMMERCIAL CODE   A law now adopted by virtually every state, that covers most of the possible transactions involving the purchase and sale of products and services.

UNIFORM DELIVERED PRICING   The POLICY of selling to all purchasers of the same type at the same transportation-included price, wherever their location within the country. See: POSTAGE STAMP PRICING

UNIMODAL   See: MODE

UNIQUE USER   By changing the specifications of a material or other merchandise in some way, a firm may be the only one to use it that way, thus effecting a method of avoiding the problems posed by the ROBINSON-PATMAN ACT regarding "like kind."

UNITARY DEMAND   See: ELASTICITY OF DEMAND

UNIT AUDIT   See: CCAB

UNIT CONTROL   That type of BUYING control which uses unit detail to determine the buying activity. No consideration is given to total dollars of purchases.

UNITED STATES INDUSTRIAL OUTLOOK   Published annually by the Department of Commerce, its data include recent trends and a FORECAST for over 100 INDUSTRIES, each over the signature of a Department expert.

UNITED STATES TRADEMARK ASSOCIATION   Same as: USTA

UNITIZATION   Designing and arranging the letters, numerals, punctuation marks and signs of a FONT according to aesthetically pleasing width groups. Width units can be based on an EM or the SET SIZE of the font, and are the basis for the counting mechanisms of PHOTOCOMPOSITION equipment.

UNITIZED TRAIN   A train of perhaps 100 cars made up to shuttle between mine and user, carrying a material such as coal on a continuous basis. The cars remain a unit of the number originally established until the activity is terminated or a major change is found necessary. Modifications of this concept have been instituted using some fewer number of cars, or on a cooperative arrangement among railroads running a unit train coast to coast.

UNIT LOAD   Any material in cartons, bales, bags, barrels or other kind of packaging which is made into a module that can be moved by a fork-lift truck. Unit loads may be strapped to a PALLET or a SKID, or affixed to either with a SHRINK-WRAP which has the additional advantage of being weather-proof.

UNIT PRICING   (1) The practice of pricing all items per one - no 3/47¢, 5/89¢, etc. In the grocery business some firms have had success with this, others have not. (2) The practice of pricing each item so that the price tag shows the price per unit of weight or volume in the package. · There is an increasing tendency for those government agencies that have the decision power to require this type of pricing. It is born of CONSUMERISM. The prestigious American Marketing Association endorsed this practice in principle in the early part of 1972.

UNIT STORE   The ESTABLISHMENT of a mercantile firm which has but one place of business. Sometimes applied to a single store of a CHAIN.

UNIT TRAIN   Same as: UNITIZED TRAIN

UNITY   A principle in advertising that dictates that all of the elements used in an advertisement must form in combination a single impression that supports the one basic idea presented by the advertisement.

UNITY OF COMMAND   A PRINCIPLE of management that dictates that any one employee should have but one boss, and should know to whom to report and to be responsible. See: SPAN OF CONTROL

UNIVERSAL FUNCTIONS OF MARKETING   See: MARKETING FUNCTION

UNIVERSAL MACHINE LANGUAGE EQUIPMENT REGISTER   Same as: UMLER

UNIVERSAL PRODUCT CODE   Same as: UPC

UNIVERSE   In statistics, the totality of units under consideration or study. Same as: POPULATION See: SAMPLING

UNIVERSE MEAN   The arithmetic MEAN found by using all the quantitative values of the units in a UNIVERSE.

UNSELFISH DISPLAY   Differs from ALTRUISTIC DISPLAY in that this display or program uses merchandise not sold by the STORE.

UNSOUGHT GOODS   Sometimes applied to those items of which the MARKET has not as yet recognized the benefits, or indeed the very existence. Essentially the same as: NEED

UNSTABLE MARKET   See: STABLE MARKET

UNSTRUCTURED-DISGUISED QUESTIONNAIRE   An instrument of data gathering in which the objective of the study is not made known, and the questions elicit open-ended responses from RESPONDENTS. Used in MOTIVATION RESEARCH. Constructed mainly of PROJECTIVE TECHNIQUES. See: STRUCTURED QUESTIONNAIRE, UNSTRUCTURED-UNDISGUISED QUESTIONNAIRE

UNSTRUCTURED-UNDISGUISED QUESTIONNAIRE   A QUESTIONNAIRE distinguished by the characteristic that the purpose of the study is clear to the RESPONDENTS but the questions elicit open-ended responses. See: STRUCTURED QUESTIONNAIRE, UNSTRUCTURED-DISGUISED QUESTIONNAIRE

UNSYSTEMATIC FREIGHT EQUALIZATION   The practice of meeting competitors' locational discounts and delivered prices in order to maintain MARKET SHARE. An unfair pricing practice if used with predatory intent. A firm with high FIXED COSTS and large capacity may have no other price-setting choices. See: FREIGHT EQUALIZATION

UPC   Abbreviation for: Universal Product Code, an arrangement of light and dark bars which can be read by an OPTICAL SCANNER. The pattern combinations are unique for certain products and makers, so that identification is unambiguous. The UPC is by deliberate design entirely compatible with the DC.

UPPER CASE   Same as: u.c.

UPPER-LOWER CLASS   See: SOCIAL CLASSES

UPPER-MIDDLE CLASS   See: SOCIAL CLASSES

UPPER-UPPER CLASS   See: SOCIAL CLASSES

UPTURN   See: BUSINESS CYCLE

URGE LINE   In ADVERTISING, same as: CLOSE

USER BEHAVIOR SEGMENTATION   See: BRAND LOYALTY, SEGMENTATION

USE-SYSTEM   A set of habitual procedures which produce the satisfactions one seeks. Important in that products have VALUE only as a means of facilitating a use-system. These systems usually involve a highly complex group of satisfactions.

USE VALUE   The specific characteristics of something which enable it to accomplish a particular function and thereby make it desirable from the viewpoint of VALUE ANALYSIS.

USTA   Abbreviation for: The United States Trademark Association. Established in 1878 to "protect the interests of the public in the use of trademarks and trade names and to promote the interests of the Members of the Association and of trademark owners generally in the use of their trademarks and trade names and to collect and disseminate information concerning the use, registration, and protection of trademarks and trade names in the United States and its territories and in foreign countries." Its membership includes: companies owning TRADEMARKS, attorneys specializing in trademark matters, ADVERTISING AGENCIES, PUBLIC RELATIONS counselors, business associations, PACKAGE designers, and other interested parties.

U TEST   Used to test whether two independent SAMPLES are drawn from the same UNIVERSE or two universes having the same MEAN. Can be used when it is desirable to avoid the assumptions that must be made in a PARAMETRIC test. It is also shorter. The method provides for an ARRAY of values which is used to rank one sample's values. The computation results in a Z value. If this value is within the range specified by the F Distribution Table, the NULL HYPOTHESIS is not rejected. Always a two-tail test. Can be applied without making the assumption that the samples come from NORMAL UNIVERSES with the same VARIANCES, required if the t distribution were used to test for significant differences in two sample means. NONPARAMETRIC.

UTILITY   The capacity of a GOOD or SERVICE to satisfy a human WANT. In plural form refers to the Basic Economic Utilities. See: FORM UTILITY, PLACE UTILITY, TIME UTILITY

VAC   Abbreviation for: Verified Audit Circulation Corporation, a private, CIRCULATION audit service verifying paid, free, CONTROLLED, franchise, bulk, or any other form of circulation. It physically counts every name on the publisher's circulation list and verifies this by a direct mail SAMPLING technique. Its audit can prove the currency, classification, and actual receiving of the circulation list.

VAGUELY RIGHT APPROACH   The philosophy that it is better to be just vaguely right than to be precisely wrong.

VALANCE   A roll-on strip of identification or advertising material designed to be secured along the upper edge of a window, wall, counter, or shelf.

VALIDITY   The characteristic data have when they measure what they purport to measure. The answers to questions asked of RESPONDENTS often seem, if taken at face value, to give usable information when in fact virtually each respondent has interpreted the questions differently, in effect has answered a different set of questions. Any conclusions drawn from such a study can be correct only by accident.

VALUE   (1) The characteristic of a service or a GOOD which induces people to sacrifice some portion of their purchasing power, past, present, or future, in order to obtain it. (2) The UTILITY of a product measured in money terms. (3) In COLOR, the degree of lightness or darkness. Sometimes called: depth.

VALUE ADDED   The concept in MARKETING that indicates that the process of exchange adds to the individual UTILITY available to the participants and to the total utility available to the whole exchange system.

VALUE ANALYSIS   By investigating the performance of a material or a PART in terms of its function and its unit price, this activity attempts to develop the most effective specifications at the lowest ultimate product cost. It will consider the effects of various substitutes, different manufacturing methods, real labor cost, source factors, etc.

VALUE CONTROL   Same as: VALUE ANALYSIS

VALUE ENGINEERING   Same as: VALUE ANALYSIS, but often applied at a products design stage.

VALUE JUDGMENT   As applied to a buyer of goods or services, the result of his comparison of the desirability of two or more alternatives. This involves intangible qualities as well as price in terms of money. See: COGNITIVE JUDGMENT, CONATIVE JUDGMENT, NORMATIVE JUDGMENT

VALUE MARKETING   A concept of a MARKETING system which integrates marketing, design, and communications into a mix made specifically for a particular business situation. By methodical research and observation of the flow of goods and services in a MARKET, factors not pertinent can be eliminated while PACKAGING, product and corporate image activities, and TRADEMARK and environment design may be given the required emphasis.

VALUE OF A CUSTOMER   The total revenue expected to come from a CUSTOMER in all future periods together, less all expenditures associated with securing that total revenue except the cost of the advertising which is credited with acquiring the customer. Useful in determining rather quickly the profitability position of a given advertisement. Only as good as the estimate of the total revenue.

VALU-PRICING   Essentially the same as UNIT PRICING (2) but sometimes the cost per unit of measure is displayed on a sign next to the item on its display rack.

VAMPIRE VIDEO   Sometimes applied to those attention-getting devices in a television COMMERCIAL that are much more memorable than the SPONSOR'S story about the PRODUCT.

VARIABLE COSTS   Those costs which depend on and change with the production level. When the plant is not operating, these costs are zero. See: FIXED COSTS

VARIABLE LEVY   Used in the EC on agricultural imports. As international commodity prices drop, the levy rises.

VARIABLE PRESENTATION   A sales presentation adaptable by a SALESPERSON to the particular situation, personality, and/or needs of an individual PROSPECT. Unstructured in any formal way, but the important appeals have all been predetermined. See: CANNED PRESENTATION

VARIABLE PRICE POLICY   A pricing POLICY in which the price finally is reached by negotiation between the seller and the BUYER. It allows for bargaining, which a ONE-PRICE POLICY does not. See: VARIABLE PRICING Same as: Flexible Price Policy

VARIABLE PRICING   A system of pricing in RETAILING which requires an examination of each item to blend such factors as customer services, SALES CLERK'S product knowledge, store image, competition, ASSORTMENT and VARIETY, and customer satisfaction so as to arrive at that perfect blend which will give the price the customer expects and is thus willing to pay. In this system all items have prices unrelated to cost or list price with a standard discount, or with the intent to undersell the competition. This system dictates, among other things, the taking of a small MARKDOWN on seasonal merchandise just prior to the peak of DEMAND, so that sales may be stimulated while demand is still growing. See: AT-THE-MARKET PRICES, BLIND ITEMS, MARKET-MINUS PRICES, MARKET-PLUS PRICES, MERCHANDISING, VARIABLE PRICE POLICY

VARIABLE SALES PRESENTATION Same as: VARIABLE PRESENTATION

VARIABLE SLOT LOCATION SYSTEM A way of placing goods in a WAREHOUSE by assigning incoming items to whatever locations happen to be vacant at that time. The use of a computer within the total warehousing activity can help ORDER-PICKING by keeping continuous track of where any item is. See: FIXED SLOT LOCATION SYSTEM

VARIANCE See: VARIANCE ANALYSIS

VARIANCE ANALYSIS The difference between actual and standard costs is the variance. This difference must be studied so that the unexpected changes in prices of direct labor and materials may be separated from the effects of changes in PRODUCTIVITY. The process tends to be a complex accounting activity.

VARIETY Indicates different general types of products. See: ASSORTMENT

VARIETY STORE A RETAIL STORE offering a wide ASSORTMENT and VARIETY of articles mainly of relatively low price. It is usually departmentized as to merchandise, but not necessarily as to accounting unless of large size. The purchase of the typical customer is small.

VDT Abbreviation for: Video Display Terminal, a typewriter with a TV tube attached that displays what has been typed on the typewriter or fed into the VDT from a wire service or a computer. Retyping of COPY is eliminated and copy can be corrected easily. Display art is a capability. When what is displayed is as it should be to go, the machine can be instructed to print it. NEWSPAPERS and other PRINT MEDIA are finding such applications usually reduce overall costs. See: OCR

VEBLEN EFFECT A higher price may increase the DEMAND for goods which, because of CONSPICUOUS CONSUMPTION, have status attached to the higher price. See: LAW OF DEMAND

VEHICLE A particular NEWSPAPER, TELEVISION program, MAGAZINE or other specific alternative for delivering an advertising message. See: ADVERTISING MEDIUM

VELOX Trade name for a photographic print incorporating halftone screen dots, and from which a line engraving can be made. Costs less than the regular HALFTONE process, but for some applications may be less sharp.

VENDING A system of selling merchandise through coin-operated devices.

VENDOR The source of supply for an item or service.

VENDOR ANALYSIS. An investigation of a potential vendor's expectation of performance as to capacity, quality, delivery, service. A number of rating systems have been developed. Among the characteristics usually considered are: financial and production capacities, customer orientation, integrity, stability of labor relations, technical competence, and proximity.

VENTURE MANAGEMENT An effort by an ENTREPRENEUR and a venture investor to establish a new, profitable business by making use of the expertise of and the CAPITAL in money of each of the owners in their joint effort, as the particular contribution of each may be required.

VENTURE TEAM A group of specialists drawn from all areas of a company to work together under the leadership of an appointed manager to develop a new PRODUCT by working outside divisional lines in an effort to find an inventive approach to an opportunity in a new, and probably, highly SEGMENTED MARKET.

VENTURE TEAM APPROACH   In its broad form it can embrace the entire new PRODUCT development process from concept creation through commercialization, although it has narrow applications. It is a way of organization within a FIRM so that expertise available in many departments are concentrated on a single, complex development task.

VERIFIED AUDIT CIRCULATION CORPORATION   Same as: VAC

VERTICAL CHANNEL SYSTEM   Any CHANNEL OF DISTRIBUTION which has some type of centralization in management which coordinates activities at all levels according to common basic purposes and features. See: CHAIN STORE, COOPERATIVE CHAIN, VOLUNTARY CHAIN

VERTICAL CONCURRENCE   See: CONCURRENCE

VERTICAL CONFLICT   The competitive struggle among the different levels of TRADE CHANNEL members, e.g., manufacturers and retailers, retailers and wholesalers. See: COUNTERVAILING POWER, HORIZONTAL COMPETITION, INTER-TYPE COMPETITION

VERTICAL COOPERATIVE ADVERTISING   Same as: COOPERATIVE ADVERTISING

VERTICAL INTEGRATION   Acquisition of a company operating at a different level in the CHANNEL OF DISTRIBUTION than the acquiring company, the CONSUMER considered as the base. It is backward if the acquired company is farther away from the consumer, forward if nearer to the consumer. See: HORIZONTAL INTEGRATION

VERTICAL MARKET   A condition of a MARKET in which a manufacturer's PRODUCT can be sold to BUYERS in but one or a few INDUSTRIES. See: HORIZONTAL MARKET

VERTICAL MARKETING SYSTEM   A set of ESTABLISHMENTS that are concerned with the production and DISTRIBUTION of a specific PRODUCT or related group of products. May encourage and lead to VERTICAL INTEGRATION.

VERTICAL PUBLICATION   In INDUSTRIAL ADVERTISING, that type of PUBLICATION which reaches people in one INDUSTRY only. See: HORIZONTAL PUBLICATION

VERTICAL SATURATION   Many commercials placed by a single SPONSOR during a day's programming on a BROADCAST MEDIUM, such as might be done by a RETAILER who wishes to reach many people to build traffic for a sale to be held the next day. See: HORIZONTAL SATURATION

VERY PROMOTABLE ITEMS   Same as VPI

VEST POCKET SUPERMARKET   Same as: BANTAM STORE

VIDEO   The picture portion of a television broadcast. Sometimes popularly used as a synonym for television. See: AUDIO

VIDEO DISPLAY TERMINAL   Same as: VDT

VIGNETTE HALFTONE   A HALFTONE in which the background is made to fade away at the edges. Often oval in shape.

VISIBLE SUPPLY   Generally refers to STOCKS in recognized distribution centers which have been moved there from production areas. May include AFLOATS and other stocks with imminent availability. See: INVISIBLE SUPPLY

VISITING THE MARKET   Making a trip to a center for the type of goods a BUYER needs to acquire. The buyer may choose to visit sources of supply unaided, but more frequently will enlist the help of a RESIDENT BUYING OFFICE.

VISUALIZING   Especially as used in ADVERTISING, it is to interpret and then present an idea in pictorial form. If reinforced by a HEADLINE that relates well to the illustration, communication of the idea of interest to the reader will be effected as easily as possible. When combined in a LAYOUT that invites the reader to pause and look, maximum IMPACT will result.

VITAL STATISTICS   The data compiled from local records on the number of births, marriages, divorces, and deaths of all persons in the population.   See: DEMOGRAPHICS

VO   Abbreviation for: VOICE OVER

VOCATIONAL ADVERTISING   An umbrella term used to include farm, TRADE, INDUSTRIAL, and PROFESSIONAL ADVERTISING.

VOICE OVER   In TELEVISION, an element of narration with the speaker not visible to the AUDIENCE.

VOLUME BONUS   A purchase incentive given to customers in the form of a discount for large purchases.   May be at odds with the ROBINSON-PATMAN ACT provisions prohibiting discriminatory pricing.

VOLUME DISCOUNT   (1) Same as: PATRONAGE DISCOUNT, but may apply to single orders only.   (2) In ADVERTISING, same as: BULK DISCOUNT

VOLUME OF TRADE TRANSACTED   The sum total of the sales of all businesses in the economy.   Estimated to be about three times the GNP, due to multiple counting of the sale of an item through several resellers.

VOLUNTARY CHAIN   A group of STORES organized by a WHOLESALER around a common interest in the goods or services the wholesaler can provide.   The wholesaler usually owns the common name under which the stores operate, and the relative responsibilities of the stores and the wholesaler are delineated in a written contract.   The wholesaler most often provides PRIVATE LABEL merchandise.   Such organizations have been quite effective in a number of lines of goods in permitting small, independent RETAILERS to compete with the large retail CHAINS.   See: COOPERATIVE CHAIN

VOLUNTARY GROUP   If intended as a permanent arrangement, essentially the same as either: COOPERATIVE CHAIN or VOLUNTARY CHAIN.   Otherwise the same as: INFORMAL BUYING GROUP

VOLUNTARY WHOLESALER   A WHOLESALER who is the sponsor of a VOLUNTARY CHAIN. Such wholesalers exist in many INDUSTRIES, and frequently are involved in supplying large numbers of members, such as the over 1,100 of Super Value or the over 4,000 of Western Auto.

VPI   Abbreviation for: Very Promotable Items, those which a RETAILER sees as relatively easy to induce CONSUMERS to buy from it as the preferred source of supply.

VTA   Abbreviation for: VENTURE TEAM APPROACH

WAGON DISTRIBUTOR   Same as: TRUCK JOBBER

WAGON JOBBER   Same as: TRUCK JOBBER

WAGON RETAILER   A MERCHANT MIDDLEMAN engaged in HUCKSTERING.

WAIT ORDER   An instruction to a MEDIUM to hold an advertisement for release at a date to be determined.

WALK-OUT   An individual who enters a STORE intending to purchase something, but who leaves empty-handed.   The reasons for the non-purchase may be many; one of the most common, is non-availability of the items sought.

WANDERING AISLE   See: STORE LAYOUT

WANT   A NEED recognized.

WANT AD   An advertisement to attract job applicants.   Usually in the CLASSIFIED ADVERTISING section of a newspaper or magazine, and in the pattern of such sections.   When a greater effort is warranted, CLASSIFIED DISPLAY style is generally used.   See: BLIND AD, OPEN AD

WANT-SLIP SYSTEM   The organized recording by SALES CLERKS of merchandise asked for by customers but not in stock.   Careful attention to this activity is important because it helps to determine the VARIETY and ASSORTMENT of merchandise offered by providing FEEDBACK to the BUYERS in the firm, and it helps avoid loss of sales due to insufficient stock in the selling areas. Store buyers should be required to analyze the want-slips of their departments at regular intervals so that they will be aware of trends. Some firms require that this be done daily.

WAREHOUSE   An ESTABLISHMENT built especially for the STORAGE of goods. See: BONDED WAREHOUSE, COLD STORAGE WAREHOUSE, ELEVATOR, PUBLIC WAREHOUSE

WAREHOUSEMAN   Usually denotes the operator of a PUBLIC WAREHOUSE.

WAREHOUSE RECEIPT   A receipt given by a WAREHOUSEMAN to the owner of goods deposited in the warehouse. Because the goods may not be withdrawn without surrendering the receipt, this document can be useful as collateral for loans from financial institutions.

WAREHOUSE REPLENISHMENT TIME   The rapidity with which items sold from a WAREHOUSE can be replaced from the factory. In general, the more rapidly the system can respond to requirements, the lower the total costs of the marketing system of the firm.

WAREHOUSE STORE   A stripped-down RETAIL food operation offering a limited ASSORTMENT at discount prices mainly of foods obtained from producers on special DEALS. Items are often stacked on the floor in original cut-open boxes. Generally carries between 1,500 and 2,000 items compared to the conventional SUPERMARKET'S 10,000. Sometimes called: box store

WARRANTY   For all practical purposes the same as: GUARANTY

WASH DRAWING   A picture made by brush work using diluted India ink or water color. See: ARTIST'S MEDIUM

WAS-IS PRICING   See: PSYCHOLOGICAL DISCOUNTING

WASTE   Material or supplies which for a reason such as faulty machinery, unforeseen chemical reactions, poor handling, or carelessness in operations, the production process has in some way rendered unfit for the use intended. From a theoretical viewpoint waste should not occur; reality indicates that this condition seldom can be attained. See: SCRAP

WASTE CIRCULATION   (1) The number of persons in an AUDIENCE who are not PROSPECTS for a product or service advertised. (2) CIRCULATION in an area in which the advertiser's offering is not carried.

WATERWAYS OPERATIONS CONFERENCE   Same as: WOC

WAVE POSTING   In OUTDOOR ADVERTISING, scheduling POSTER SHOWINGS in concentrations in various areas within a MARKET so that one succeeds another.

WAVE SCHEDULING   Same as: PULSATION

WAVING   Same as: PULSATION

WAYBILL   A document made by the carrier at the point of origin of a shipment which shows the point of origin, destination, route, consignor, consignee, description of shipment, and freight charges. Distinguish from BILL OF LADING, which is a document of title.

WB   Abbreviation used as a LOGO for: WIREBOUND BOX MANUFACTURERS ASSOCIATION

WEALTH   A stock of goods owned by humans. (1) As to the nation (national wealth), the total resources of a country. (2) As to the individual, usually a total which includes claims on wealth which could be exercised. See: LIQUID WEALTH

WEBER'S LAW   Applicable to the j.n.d., it states that the stronger the initial STIMULUS, the greater the additional intensity required for the second stimulus to be detected as different. For example, an increase of $5 in a mink coat would likely not be noticed, whereas an increase of 25¢

in a package of cereal would likely get immediate awareness. See: DIFFERENTIAL THRESHOLD

WEEK'S SUPPLY METHOD One of the four primary methods used by RETAILERS for STOCK PLANNING. In situations where sales fluctuate much, this method may prove weak, because it provides for the stock level to vary directly and proportionately with sales, a condition not necessarily ectual in many instances. The STOCKTURN period is divided by the number of stockturns desired to yield the number of weeks' supply BOM.

WEIGHTED EXPOSURE VALUE A concept of use to a MEDIA planner which is calculated by multiplying the number of persons exposed to a particular advertisement in a particular medium by the value of the exposure to the various persons. Exposure to a person in the best MARKET SEGMENT is assigned the value 1.

WEIGHTED-POINT METHOD A procedure for evaluating sources of supply by establishing evaluation factors to which numerical values can be assigned as relative weights. The major advantages are that any number of factors can be included, objective considerations are likely to be forced to the fore, and the relative weights of the factors can be adjusted to meet the firm's requirements. Its disadvantage is that certain intangible factors such as service are difficult to quantify. This advantage can be overcome to a large degree by combining this method with the CATEGORICAL METHOD. See: COST-RATIO METHOD

WEIGHT OF TYPE The relative blackness, or boldness, of a type FACE.

WELFARE ECONOMICS A system of economic policies and practices instituted by a government agency to achieve the goal of the improvement of social conditions on a broad scope.

WESTERN STATES ADVERTISING AGENCIES ASSOCIATION Same as: WSAAA

WESTERN WOODEN BOX ASSOCIATION Same as: WWBA

WHARFAGE A charge made for all CARGO, except that specifically exempted, which passes over or under wharves to or from vessels, or delivered or received from vessels by other watercraft when the vessels occupy wharf berths. See: DOCKAGE

WHEELER-LEA ACT An amendment to the FEDERAL TRADE COMMISSION ACT, passed in 1938, which provided authority to the FTC to act to protect CONSUMERS in cases where injury to competitors could not be shown. Outlaws not only "unfair methods of competition" but "unfair and deceptive acts or practices" as well.

WHEEL OF RETAILING An explanation of the evolution of RETAIL institutions. The basic premise is that new retail forms first appear as low-MARGIN, low-price ESTABLISHMENTS. These upgrade their facilities and services as time passes, requiring higher margins. Eventually they become high-cost, high-price RETAILERS vulnerable to the next innovator. See: INVITATION-POINT THEORY

WHIPLASH EFFECT Changes in the DEMAND for goods which cause excessive or inadequate inventories to occur at various points in the CHANNEL OF DISTRIBUTION due to the lack of proper information and controls. They force abrupt changes in the production schedule to correct the problem. See: DERIVED DEMAND.

WHIP SHOT Same as: ZIP PAN

WHITE GOODS Large, durable CONSUMER'S GOODS usually finished in white, e.g., refrigerators, clothes washers, dryers, etc. Fashion decrees other colors from time to time.

WHITE TAILS A term used in the airplane INDUSTRY to designate planes coming down the final assembly line but which no airline has ordered as yet.

WHIZ   Same as: ZIP PAN

WHOLESALE PRICE INDEX   Same as: WPI

WHOLESALER   A business mainly concerned with selling to those who buy for resale or industrial use; in other words, for purposes other than for personal or household use. See: CAR-LOT WHOLESALER, CASH-AND-CARRY WHOLE-SALER, DESK JOBBER, DISTRIBUTOR, ELEVATOR, FULL-FUNCTION WHOLESALER, FUNCTIONAL MIDDLEMAN, GENERAL-LINE WHOLESALER, GENERAL MERCHANDISE WHOLE-SALER, INDUSTRIAL DISTRIBUTOR, LOCAL WHOLESALER, MERCHANT WHOLESALER, NATIONAL WHOLESALER, RACK JOBBER, REGIONAL WHOLESALER, REGULAR WHOLESALER, SPECIALTY WHOLESALER, TRUCK JOBBER, VOLUNTARY CHAIN

WHOLESALE-SPONSORED VOLUNTARY CHAIN   Same as: VOLUNTARY CHAIN

WHOLESALING   The activity mainly involved with selling to those who are not CONSUMERS. Although some wholesalers engage in giving form-change services, as do METALS WAREHOUSES, most of this activity involves moving items in the same form as received.

WIDOW   (1) A single word, syllable, or letter left on a line by itself. (2) A short line of type at the end of a paragraph, especially if it appears at the top of a page or column.

WIDTH OF ASSORTMENT   Refers to the number of different items of a similar nature offered by a seller, e.g., how many BRANDS of toasters, how many different styles of nurses' uniforms. See: DEPTH OF ASSORTMENT

WILL-CALL SALE   Same as: LAY-AWAY SALE

WIN-WIN SITUATION   Typical of the basic philosophy of modern SALESMANSHIP, both buyer and seller achieve SATISFACTION from a completed transaction.

WIPE   A device used in television commercials which allows one scene to appear to be pushing another scene off the screen. May be done vertical-ly, horizontally, or with a variety of geometric patterns. See: OPTICALS

WIREBOUND BOX MANUFACTURERS ASSOCIATION   The organization through which manu-facturers of wirebound PACKAGES disseminate information of new developments in the field, promote this mode of packaging over other modes, and make engineers available for free consultation on special problems.

WITHDRAWAL   A means of coping with FRUSTRATION which results in stopping the activity producing the feeling. See: AGGRESSION, AUTISM, IDENTIFICA-TION, PROJECTION, REGRESSION, RATIONALIZATION, REPRESSION

WITHDRAWALS   The items sold or purchased out of a consignment. In some industries where this practice is used, the consignee reports on and pays for these items on a periodic basis. In other industries a representative of the consignor visits the consignee to take inventory, present a bill, and if indicated, arrange for the return of unused merchandise.

W/M   Abbreviation for: weight or measurement. Used in calculating freight charges. See: CARGO TONNAGE

WOBBLER   A light-weight POINT-OF-PURCHASE piece that hangs over a point and turns with the air currents generated by the area. Sometimes hung from a steel spring to achieve more interesting action.

WOC   Abbreviation for: Waterways Operations Conference, a national organ-ization of BARGE lines started in 1972 to engage in research and other activities designed to solve operational difficulties and to develop policy statements.

WOODEN INDIAN   Used as the statuette presented to winners in POPAI'S an-nual merchandising awards contest, this image of a standing American Indian brave, used in by-gone days as advertising before a tobacco shop, is said to be the first POINT-OF-PURCHASE ADVERTISEMENT used in the United States. See: OMA

WOOL PRODUCTS LABELING ACT A Federal law which requires that products containing wool, with certain exceptions such as carpets and upholstery, must have LABELS affixed showing the percents of new wool, reused or re-processed wool, and other fibers or fillers that are used.

WORD In ADP, a set of CHARACTERS which occupies one storage location and is treated as a unit by the computer circuits. A "word" is treated as an instruction or as a quantity, depending on the prearrangement of the system. Word lengths may be fixed or variable, depending on the particular kind of computer.

WORD ASSOCIATION One of the PROJECTIVE TECHNIQUES. The RESPONDENT is asked to read a list of words and to tell the first word which comes to mind for each. Neutral words are interspersed in the list. Responses are classified, grouped, and interpreted. Considerable skill is needed by the researcher to use this technique.

WORKABLE COMPETITION A view of the MARKET held by many economists that even though competition among sellers may be imperfect, it may be regarded as effective if it offers buyers real alternatives which result in influencing price and quality by permitting them to shift their buying from one seller to another.

WORK LOAD ANALYSIS An estimate of the sales effort required to realize the potential of a SALES TERRITORY.

WPI Abbreviation for: Wholesale Price Index, a relative measure of average price changes in commodities sold in PRIMARY MARKETS in the United States, no longer compiled. It included farm products, basic materials, machinery, and equipment. Had circumscribed usefulness as a measure of the general level of prices. Actually measured prices paid to producers by WHOLE-SALERS and others. See: FINISHED GOODS INDEX, PRODUCER PRICE INDEX

WRITE-PROTECTION A means of preventing the accidental erasure of data on a reel of magnetic tape in an ADP system.

WRITE TIME See: ACCESS TIME

WSAAA Abbreviation for: Western States Advertising Agencies Association, an organization which provides members with much information of a legal, technical, and educational nature. It is the PUBLIC RELATIONS spokesman for the industry in the West.

WWBA Abbreviation for: Western Wooden Box Association, an organization of interests in the sawn wooden box industry. Its primary purpose is to promote the use of sawn wooden containers for picking, packing, and shipping of fruits and vegetables, including the fostering of STANDARD methods of manufacture and inspection of boxes and SHOOK. The Association advertises in TRADE JOURNALS and provides field service to many interests, including the California State Department of Agriculture and the Agricultural Schools.

X A symbol used in EXPERIMENTAL DESIGN to denote the exposure of the DEPENDENT VARIABLE to the treatment for which the test was designed. See: O

X-HEIGHT The height of the letter "x" in a specific FONT of type. Different type styles have different x-heights. Thus, despite their being of the same POINT size, more or less of the face of the type block will be used by the letters. Because other CHARACTERS in the font will be proportioned to the "x" the appearance of COPY in a particular type style will have a characteristic appearance. Before specifying what type style is to be used, it would be wise to refer to a type specimen sheet.

XOGRAPH The picture produced by the XOGRAPHY process.

XOGRAPHY   A way of printing which produces pictures which appear to be three-dimensional to the unaided eye. Xographs have been used to good effect in advertisements, and as cover pictures for some magazines.

YANKEE PEDDLER   An itinerant MERCHANT, the forerunner of the modern traveling SALESPERSON, prominent in the United States from the late seventeenth century through the post-Civil War period. Originally based in New England, hence the name. Same as: Pack Peddler See: DRUMMER

YARDSTICK   Some criterion of price, cost, quantity, achievement, or the like, against which is compared the record of an individual or a FIRM. It is one factor in the "control" aspect of management. Correct interpretation of the relationship between the yardstick and the actual record is basic to any decision-making affecting future efforts.

YEARLY ORDER   Same as: BLANKET ORDER

YES, BUT TECHNIQUE   A SALESMANSHIP technique used in dealing with OBJECTIONS. The SALESPERSON first exhibits sympathy for the PROSPECT'S point of view, but then proceeds to show how that point of view is unfounded or does not recognize some significant consideration. Also called: Agreeing and Neutralizing Technique, or Agree and Counterattack Technique.

"YOU" ATTITUDE   In ADVERTISING, keeping always in mind that the message must be directed as to but one person. Each one who is exposed to the message should feel that it is directed to him alone. While millions may be exposed to the same message, every individual who receives it is a single PROSPECT. For maximum effectiveness, the message should make him feel that the advertiser has singled him out to be addressed.

Z   See: NORMAL PROBABILITY CURVE

ZBB   Abbreviation for: ZERO-BASED BUDGETING

ZERO-BASED BUDGETING   A procedure for developing an expenditure-revenue plan for a given period of time. The procedure requires total rejustification for all aspects of the plan starting from zero for each new period. New considerations must be assessed and compared to traditional approaches.

ZERO-BASED MEDIA PLANNING   The PRINCIPLE of ZERO-BASED BUDGETING applied to the selection of MEDIA for an ADVERTISING CAMPAIGN. Involves the same principles of trading off alternatives to get the best possible effectiveness from the expenditures.

ZERO DEFECTS   An INSPECTION technique which precludes acceptance of any inferior parts. Used where defects can result in huge losses and high human risk. Its success depends on convincing all personnel of its great importance.

ZERO POPULATION GROWTH   Same as: ZPG

ZIP AD   A miniature, sealed BOOKLET applied to PACKAGES as they are produced, thus carrying the message to the CONSUMER right at the point of action. Can be applied manually or by machine. ·Same as: Outsert

ZIP PAN   In television, the very rapid movement of the camera across a message or a scene. Often a series of such shots are combined in sequence to create a mood or impression. Care must be exercised in using this technique to avoid more than a few seconds duration. Many viewers find it annoying, some even painful. Same as: Blur, Whip Shot, Whiz

ZONE DELIVERED PRICING   Same as: ZONE PRICING

ZONE OF INDIFFERENCE   A geographic territory beyond the SECONDARY TRADING AREA, in which a particular MARKETING institution has no advantage over competing institutions in other locational centers. See: AREA STRUCTURE, PRIMARY TRADING AREA, SECONDARY TRADING CENTER

ZONE PRICING   Similar to POSTAGE STAMP PRICING, but divides the territory into several areas in each of which the delivered price is the same to all customers, although different among the several areas. Has not been questioned legally where the zones conform to transportation-rate zones. See: BASING-POINT PRICING

ZOOMING   A device used in television commercials whereby a picture is made to appear ever larger, as though one were approaching, until the detail is as large as wished. May be done slowly or very quickly. See: OPTICALS

ZPG   Abbreviation for: Zero Population Growth, the situation in which a human population adds to itself only sufficient numbers to replace the losses from various causes. Many who work with this type of FORECASTING estimate this condition in the United States around the year 2050. This would, of course, change depending upon medical discoveries, the wanted size of families, and the ability of the economy to sustain a certain number of people at a desired standard of living, among other factors. Much attention is being given to the impact on the marketer of population changes and shifts.